ANDROID™ FOR PROGRAMMERS
AN APP-DRIVEN APPROACH
SECOND EDITION, VOLUME 1
DEITEL® DEVELOPER SERIES

Library of Congress Cataloging-in-Publication Data

On file

ISBN-13: 978-0-13357092-2
ISBN-10: 0-13-357092-4

Text printed in the United States on recycled paper at RR Donnelley in Crawfordsville, Indiana.
First printing, December 2013

ANDROID™ FOR PROGRAMMERS
AN APP-DRIVEN APPROACH
SECOND EDITION, VOLUME 1
DEITEL® DEVELOPER SERIES

Paul Deitel • Harvey Deitel • Abbey Deitel
Deitel & Associates, Inc.

PRENTICE
HALL

Upper Saddle River, NJ • Boston • Indianapolis • San Francisco
New York • Toronto • Montreal • London • Munich • Paris • Madrid
Capetown • Sydney • Tokyo • Singapore • Mexico City

Trademarks

DEITEL, the double-thumbs-up bug and DIVE-INTO are registered trademarks of Deitel & Associates, Inc.

Java is a registered trademark of Oracle and/or its affiliates. Other names may be trademarks of their respective owners.

Google, Android, Google Play, Google Maps, Google Wallet, Nexus, YouTube, AdSense and AdMob are trademarks of Google, Inc.

Microsoft and/or its respective suppliers make no representations about the suitability of the information contained in the documents and related graphics published as part of the services for any purpose. All such documents and related graphics are provided "as is" without warranty of any kind. Microsoft and/or its respective suppliers hereby disclaim all warranties and conditions with regard to this information, including all warranties and conditions of merchantability, whether express, implied or statutory, fitness for a particular purpose, title and non-infringement. In no event shall Microsoft and/or its respective suppliers be liable for any special, indirect or consequential damages or any damages whatsoever resulting from loss of use, data or profits, whether in an action of contract, negligence or other tortious action, arising out of or in connection with the use or performance of information available from the services.

The documents and related graphics contained herein could include technical inaccuracies or typographical errors. Changes are periodically added to the information herein. Microsoft and/or its respective suppliers may make improvements and/or changes in the product(s) and/or the program(s) described herein at any time. Partial screen shots may be viewed in full within the software version specified.

Microsoft® and Windows® are registered trademarks of the Microsoft Corporation in the U.S.A. and other countries. Screen shots and icons reprinted with permission from the Microsoft Corporation. This book is not sponsored or endorsed by or affiliated with the Microsoft Corporation.

Throughout this book, trademarks are used. Rather than put a trademark symbol in every occurrence of a trademarked name, we state that we are using the names in an editorial fashion only and to the benefit of the trademark owner, with no intention of infringement of the trademark.

In Memory of Amar G. Bose, MIT Professor and Founder and Chairman of the Bose Corporation:

It was a privilege being your student—and members of the next generation of Deitels, who heard our dad say how your classes inspired him to do his best work.

You taught us that if we go after the really hard problems, then great things can happen.

Harvey Deitel
Paul and Abbey Deitel

Contents

4 Twitter® Searches App 89

SharedPreferences, *Collections*, **ImageButton**, **ListView**, **ListActivity**, **ArrayAdapter**, *Implicit* **Intents** *and* **AlertDialogs**

5   Flag Quiz App   125

Fragments, Menus, Preferences, AssetManager, Tweened Animations, Handler, Toasts, Explicit Intents, Layouts for Multiple Device Orientations

6 Cannon Game App 168

Listening for Touches, Manual Frame-By-Frame Animation, Graphics, Sound, Threading, SurfaceView and SurfaceHolder

7   Doodlz App   198

Two-Dimensional Graphics, Canvas, Bitmap, Accelerometer, SensorManager, Multitouch Events, MediaStore, Printing, Immersive Mode

8   Address Book App   241

ListFragment, FragmentTransactions and the Fragment Back Stack,
Threading and AsyncTasks, CursorAdapter, SQLite and GUI Styles

Preface

Welcome to the dynamic world of Android smartphone and tablet app development with the Android Software Development Kit (SDK), the Java™ programming language, the Eclipse-based Android Development Tools IDE, and the new and rapidly evolving Android Studio IDE.

Android for Programmers: An App-Driven Approach, 2/e, Volume 1 presents leading-edge mobile computing technologies for professional software developers. At the heart of the book is our *app-driven approach*—we present concepts in the context of *seven complete working Android apps* rather than using code snippets. Chapters 2–8 each present one app. We begin each of these chapters with an introduction to the app, an app test-drive showing one or more sample executions and a technologies overview. Then we proceed with a detailed code walkthrough of the app's source code. All of the source code is available at www.deitel.com/books/AndroidFP2. We recommend that you have the source code open in the IDE as you read the book.

Sales of Android devices and app downloads have been growing exponentially. The first-generation Android phones were released in October 2008. A study by Strategy Analytics showed that by October 2013, Android had 81.3% of the global smartphone market share, compared to 13.4% for Apple, 4.1% for Microsoft and 1% for Blackberry.[1] According to an IDC report, by the end of the first quarter of 2013 Android had 56.5% of the global tablet market share, compared to 39.6% for Apple's iPad and 3.7% for Microsoft Windows tablets.[2]

There are now over one billion Android smartphones and tablets in use,[3] and more than 1.5 million Android devices are being activated daily.[4] According to IDC, Samsung is the leading Android manufacturer, accounting for nearly 40% of Android device shipments in the third quarter of 2013.

Billions of apps have been downloaded from Google Play™—Google's marketplace for Android apps. The opportunities for Android app developers are enormous.

Fierce competition among popular mobile platforms and carriers is leading to rapid innovation and falling prices. Competition among the dozens of Android device manufacturers is driving hardware and software innovation within the Android community.

Copyright Notice and Code License

All of the Android code and Android apps in the book are copyrighted by Deitel & Associates, Inc. The sample Android apps in the book are licensed under a Creative Commons Attribution

---

1. http://blogs.strategyanalytics.com/WSS/post/2013/10/31/Android-Captures-Record-81-Percent-Share-of-Global-Smartphone-Shipments-in-Q3-2013.aspx.
2. http://www.idc.com/getdoc.jsp?containerId=prUS24093213.
3. http://www.android.com/kitkat.
4. http://www.technobuffalo.com/2013/04/16/google-daily-android-activations-1-5-million.

3.0 Unported License (http://creativecommons.org/licenses/by/3.0), *with the exception that they may not be reused in any way in educational tutorials and textbooks, whether in print or digital format. Additionally, the authors and publisher make no warranty of any kind, expressed or implied, with regard to these programs or to the documentation contained in this book. The authors and publisher shall not be liable in any event for incidental or consequential damages in connection with, or arising out of, the furnishing, performance, or use of these programs. You're welcome to use the apps in the book as shells for your own apps, building on their existing functionality. If you have any questions, contact us at* deitel@deitel.com.

Intended Audience

We assume that you're a Java programmer with object-oriented programming experience. Because of the improved Android development tools, we were able to eliminate almost all XML markup in this edition. There are still two small, easy-to-understand XML files you'll need to manipulate. We use only complete, working apps, so if you don't know Java but have object-oriented programming experience in languages like C#/.NET, Objective-C/Cocoa or C++ (with class libraries), you should be able to master the material quickly, learning a good amount of Java and Java-style object-oriented programming along the way.

This book is *not* a Java tutorial, but it presents a significant amount of Java in the context of Android app development. If you're interested in learning Java, check out our publications:

- *Java for Programmers, 2/e* (www.deitel.com/books/javafp2)
- *Java Fundamentals: Parts I and II* LiveLessons videos (www.deitel.com/books/LiveLessons).
- *Java How to Program, 10/e* (www.deitel.com/books/jhtp10)

If you're not familiar with XML, see these online tutorials:

- http://www.ibm.com/developerworks/xml/newto
- http://www.w3schools.com/xml/xml_whatis.asp
- http://www.deitel.com/articles/xml_tutorials/20060401/XMLBasics
- http://www.deitel.com/articles/xml_tutorials/20060401/XMLStructuringData

Key Features

Here are some of this book's key features:

App-Driven Approach. Chapters 2–8 each present one completely coded app—we discuss what the app does, show screen shots of the app in action, test-drive it and overview the technologies and architecture we'll use to build it. Then we build the app's GUI and resource files, present the complete code and do a detailed code walkthrough. We discuss the programming concepts and demonstrate the functionality of the Android APIs used in the app.

Android SDK 4.3 and 4.4. We cover various new Android Software Development Kit (SDK) 4.3 and 4.4 features.

Fragments. Starting with Chapter 5, we use Fragments to create and manage portions of each app's GUI. You can combine several fragments to create user interfaces that take advantage of tablet screen sizes. You also can easily interchange fragments to make your GUIs more dynamic, as you'll do in Chapter 8.

Support for multiple screen sizes and resolutions. Throughout the app chapters we demonstrate how to use Android's mechanisms for automatically choosing resources (layouts, images, etc.) based on a device's size and orientation.

Eclipse-Based Android Development Tools (ADT) IDE coverage in the print book. The free Android Development Tools (ADT) integrated development environment (IDE)—which includes Eclipse and the ADT plugin—combined with the free Java Development Kit (JDK) provide all the software you'll need to create, run and debug Android apps, export them for distribution (e.g., upload them to Google Play™) and more.

Android Studio IDE. This is the preferred IDE for the future of Android app development. Because it's new and evolving rapidly, we put our discussions of it online at:

```
http://www.deitel.com/books/AndroidFP2
```

We'll show how to import existing projects so you can test-drive our apps. We'll also demonstrate how to create new apps, build GUIs, modify resource files and test your apps. If you have any questions, contact us at deitel@deitel.com.

Immersive Mode. The status bar at the top of the screen and the menu buttons at the bottom can be hidden, allowing your apps to fill more of the screen. Users can access the status bar by swiping down from the top of the screen, and the system bar (with the back button, home button and recent apps button) by swiping up from the bottom.

Printing Framework. Android 4.4 KitKat allows you to add printing functionality to your apps, such as locating available printers over Wi-Fi or the cloud, selecting the paper size and specifying which pages to print.

Testing on Android Smartphones, Tablets and the Android Emulator. For the best app-development experience, you should test your apps on actual Android smartphones and tablets. You can still have a meaningful experience using just the Android emulator (see the Before You Begin section), however it's processor-intensive and can be slow, particularly with games that have a lot of moving parts. In Chapter 1, we mention some Android features that are not supported on the emulator.

Multimedia. The apps use a broad range of Android multimedia capabilities, including graphics, images, frame-by-frame animation and audio.

Uploading Apps to Google Play. Chapter 9, Google Play and App Business Issues, walks you through the registration process for Google Play and setting up a merchant account so you can sell your apps. You'll learn how to prepare apps for submission to Google Play, find tips for pricing your apps, and resources for monetizing them with in-app advertising and in-app sales of virtual goods. You'll also find resources for marketing your apps. Chapter 9 can be read after Chapter 1.

Features

Syntax Coloring. For readability, we syntax color the code, similar to Eclipse's and Android Studio's use of syntax coloring. Our syntax-coloring conventions are as follows:

```
comments appear in green
keywords appear in dark blue
constants and literal values appear in light blue
all other code appears in non-bold black
```

Code Highlighting. We emphasize the key code segments in each program by enclosing them in yellow rectangles.

Using Fonts for Emphasis. We use various font conventions:

- The defining occurrences of key terms appear in **bold maroon** for easy reference.
- On-screen IDE components appear in **bold Helvetica** (e.g., the **File** menu).
- Program source code appears in Lucida (e.g., int x = 5;).

In this book you'll create GUIs using a combination of visual programming (point and click, drag and drop) and writing code.

We use different fonts when we refer to GUI elements in program code versus GUI elements displayed in the IDE:

- When we refer to a GUI component that we create in a program, we place its class name and object name in a Lucida font—e.g., "Button saveContactButton."
- When we refer to a GUI component that's part of the IDE, we place the component's text in a **bold Helvetica** font and use a plain text font for the component's type—e.g., "the **File** menu" or "the **Run** button."

Using the > Character. We use the > character to indicate selecting a menu item from a menu. For example, we use the notation **File > New** to indicate that you should select the **New** menu item from the **File** menu.

Source Code. All of the book's source code is available for download from:

```
www.deitel.com/books/AndroidFP2
www.informit.com/title/0133570924
```

Documentation. All the Android and Java documentation you'll need to develop Android apps is available free at http://developer.android.com and http://www.oracle.com/technetwork/java/javase/downloads/index.html. The documentation for Eclipse is available at www.eclipse.org/documentation. The documentation for Android Studio is available at http://developer.android.com/sdk/installing/studio.html.

Chapter Objectives. Each chapter begins with a list of learning objectives.

Figures. Hundreds of tables, source code listings and Android screen shots are included.

Software Engineering. We stress program clarity and performance, and concentrate on building well-engineered, object-oriented software.

Index. We include an extensive index for reference. The page number of the defining occurrence of each key term in the book is highlighted in the index in **bold maroon**.

Working with Open-Source Apps

There are numerous free, open-source Android apps available online which are excellent resources for learning Android app development. We encourage you to download open-source apps and read their source code to understand how they work. **Caution: The terms of open-source licenses vary considerably.** Some allow you to use the app's source code freely for any purpose, while others stipulate that the code is available for personal use only—not for creating for-sale or publicly available apps. **Be sure to read the licensing agreements carefully. If you wish to create a commercial app based on an open-source app, you should consider having an intellectual property attorney read the license; be aware that these attorneys charge significant fees.**

Android for Programmers: An App-Driven Approach, Second Edition, Volume 2

Volume 2, which will be published in 2014, contains additional app-development chapters that introduce property animation, Google Play game services, video, speech synthesis and recognition, GPS, the Maps API, the compass, object serialization, web services, audio recording and playback, Bluetooth®, HTML5 mobile apps and more. **For the status of Volume 2 and for continuing book updates, visit**

```
http://www.deitel.com/books/AndroidFP2
```

Android Fundamentals, Second Edition LiveLessons Video Training Products

Our *Android Fundamentals, Second Edition* LiveLessons videos show you what you need to know to start building robust, powerful Android apps with the Android Software Development Kit (SDK) 4.3 and 4.4, the Java™ programming language and the Eclipse™ and Android Studio integrated development environments (IDEs). It will include approximately 20 hours of expert training synchronized with *Android for Programmers, Second Edition* (Volumes 1 and 2). The videos for Volume 1 will be available spring 2014. For additional information about Deitel LiveLessons video products, visit

```
www.deitel.com/livelessons
```

or contact us at deitel@deitel.com. You can also access our LiveLessons videos if you have a subscription to Safari Books Online (www.safaribooksonline.com).

Join the Deitel & Associates, Inc. Social Networking Communities

To receive updates on this and our other publications, new and updated apps, online Resource Centers, instructor-led onsite training courses, partner offers and more, join the Deitel social networking communities on Facebook® (http://www.deitel.com/deitelfan), Twitter® (@deitel), LinkedIn® (http://bit.ly/DeitelLinkedIn) Google+™ (http://google.com/+DeitelFan), and YouTube® (http://youtube.com/user/DeitelTV) and subscribe to the *Deitel® Buzz Online* newsletter (http://www.deitel.com/newsletter/subscribe.html).

Contacting the Authors

We'd sincerely appreciate your comments, criticisms, corrections and suggestions for improvement. Please address all questions and other correspondence to:

```
deitel@deitel.com
```

We'll respond promptly, and post corrections and clarifications on:

www.deitel.com/books/AndroidFP2

and on Facebook, Twitter, Google+, LinkedIn and the *Deitel® Buzz Online*.

Visit www.deitel.com to:

- Download code examples
- Check out the growing list of programming Resource Centers
- Receive updates for this e-book, subscribe to the free *Deitel® Buzz Online* e-mail newsletter at www.deitel.com/newsletter/subscribe.html
- Receive information on our *Dive Into® Series* instructor-led programming language training courses offered at customer sites worldwide

Acknowledgments

Thanks to Barbara Deitel for long hours devoted to this project—she created all of our Android Resource Centers, and patiently researched hundreds of technical details.

This book was a cooperative effort between professional and academic divisions of Pearson. We appreciate the efforts and 18-year mentorship of our friend and professional colleague Mark L. Taub, Editor-in-Chief of the Pearson Technology Group. Mark and his team handle all of our professional books and LiveLessons video products. Kim Boedigheimer recruited distinguished members of the Android community and managed the review team for the Android content. We selected the cover art and Chuti Prasertsith and Sandra Schroeder designed the cover. John Fuller manages the production of all of our Deitel Developer Series books.

We also appreciate the guidance, wisdom and energy of Tracy Johnson, Executive Editor, Computer Science. Tracy and her team handle all of our academic textbooks. Carole Snyder recruited the book's academic reviewers and managed the review process. Bob Engelhardt manages the production of our academic publications.

We'd like to thank Michael Morgano, a former colleague of ours at Deitel & Associates, Inc., now an Android developer at Imerj™, who co-authored the first editions of this book and our book, *iPhone for Programmers: An App-Driven Approach*. Michael is an extraordinarily talented software developer.

Reviewers of the Content from **Android for Programmers: An App-Driven Approach** *and* **Android How to Program** *Recent Editions*

We wish to acknowledge the efforts of our first and second edition reviewers. They scrutinized the text and the code and provided countless suggestions for improving the presentation: Paul Beusterien (Principal, Mobile Developer Solutions), Eric J. Bowden, COO (Safe Driving Systems, LLC), Tony Cantrell (Georgia Northwestern Technical College), Ian G. Clifton (Independent Contractor and Android App Developer, Daniel Galpin (Android Advocate and author of *Intro to Android Application Development*), Jim Hathaway (Application Developer, Kellogg Company), Douglas Jones (Senior Software Engineer, Fullpower Technologies), Charles Lasky (Nagautuck Community College), Enrique Lopez-Manas (Lead Android Architect, Sixt, and Computer Science Teacher at the University of Alcalá in Madrid), Sebastian Nykopp (Chief Architect, Reaktor), Michael Pardo (Android Developer, Mobiata), Ronan "Zero" Schwarz (CIO, OpenIntents), Arijit Sengupta (Wright State University), Donald Smith (Columbia College), Jesus Ubaldo Quevedo-Torrero (University of Wisconsin, Parkside), Dawn Wick (Southwestern Community College) and Frank Xu (Gannon University).

Well, there you have it! *Android for Programmers: An App-Driven Approach, Second Edition, Volume 1* will quickly get you developing Android apps. We hope you enjoy reading the book as much as we enjoyed writing it!

Paul Deitel
Harvey Deitel
Abbey Deitel

About the Authors

Paul Deitel, CEO and Chief Technical Officer of Deitel & Associates, Inc., is a graduate of MIT, where he studied Information Technology. He holds the Java Certified Programmer and Java Certified Developer certifications, and is an Oracle Java Champion. Through Deitel & Associates, Inc., he has delivered hundreds of programming courses worldwide to clients, including Cisco, IBM, Siemens, Sun Microsystems, Dell, Fidelity, NASA at the Kennedy Space Center, the National Severe Storm Laboratory, White Sands Missile Range, Rogue Wave Software, Boeing, SunGard Higher Education, Nortel Networks, Puma, iRobot, Invensys and many more. He and his co-author, Dr. Harvey M. Deitel, are the world's best-selling programming-language textbook/professional book/video authors.

Dr. Harvey Deitel, Chairman and Chief Strategy Officer of Deitel & Associates, Inc., has more than 50 years of experience in computing. Dr. Deitel earned B.S. and M.S. degrees in Electrical Engineering from MIT and a Ph.D. in Mathematics from Boston University. In the 1960s, through Advanced Computer Techniques and Computer Usage Corporation, he worked on the teams building various IBM operating systems. In the 1970s, he built commercial software systems. He has extensive college teaching experience, including earning tenure and serving as the Chairman of the Computer Science Department at Boston College before founding Deitel & Associates, Inc., in 1991 with his son, Paul Deitel. The Deitels' publications have earned international recognition, with translations published in Simplified Chinese, Traditional Chinese, Korean, Japanese, German, Russian, Spanish, French, Polish, Italian, Portuguese, Greek, Urdu and Turkish. Dr. Deitel has delivered hundreds of programming courses to corporate, academic, government and military clients.

Abbey Deitel, President of Deitel & Associates, Inc., is a graduate of Carnegie Mellon University's Tepper School of Management where she received a B.S. in Industrial Management. Abbey has been managing the business operations of Deitel & Associates, Inc. for 16 years. She has contributed to numerous Deitel & Associates publications and, together with Paul and Harvey, is the co-author of *Android for Programmers: An App-Driven Approach, 2/e, iPhone for Programmers: An App-Driven Approach, Internet & World Wide Web How to Program, 5/e, Visual Basic 2012 How to Program, 6/e* and *Simply Visual Basic 2010, 5/e.*

Deitel® Dive-Into® Series Corporate Training

Deitel & Associates, Inc., founded by Paul Deitel and Harvey Deitel, is an internationally recognized authoring and corporate training organization, specializing in Android and iOS app development, computer programming languages, object technology and Internet and web software technology. The company's clients include many of the world's largest corporations, government agencies, branches of the military, and academic institutions. The company offers instructor-led training courses delivered at client sites worldwide on major programming languages and platforms, including Android app development, Objective-C and iOS app development, Java™, C++, Visual C++®, C, Visual C#®, Visual Basic®, XML®, Python®, object technology, Internet and web programming and a growing list of additional programming and software development courses.

Through its 37-year publishing partnership with Prentice Hall/Pearson, Deitel & Associates, Inc., publishes leading-edge programming professional books, college textbooks and *LiveLessons* video courses. Deitel & Associates, Inc. and the authors can be reached at:

```
deitel@deitel.com
```

To learn more about Deitel's *Dive-Into® Series* Corporate Training curriculum, visit:

```
www.deitel.com/training
```

To request a proposal for worldwide on-site, instructor-led training at your organization, e-mail deitel@deitel.com.

Individuals wishing to purchase Deitel books and *LiveLessons* video training can do so through www.deitel.com. Bulk orders by corporations, the government, the military and academic institutions should be placed directly with Pearson. For more information, visit

```
www.informit.com/store/sales.aspx
```

Before You Begin

In this section, you'll set up your computer for use with this book. The Android development tools are frequently updated. Before reading this section, check the book's website

```
http://www.deitel.com/books/AndroidFP2/
```

to see if we've posted an updated version.

Font and Naming Conventions

We use fonts to distinguish between on-screen components (such as menu names and menu items) and Java code or commands. Our convention is to show on-screen components in a sans-serif bold **Helvetica** font (for example, **Project** menu) and to show file names, Java code and commands in a sans-serif Lucida font (for example, the keyword public or class Activity). When specifying commands to select in menus, we use the **>** notation to indicate a menu item to select. For example, **Window > Preferences** indicates that you should select the **Preferences** menu item from the **Window** menu.

Software and Hardware System Requirements

To develop Android apps you need a Windows®, Linux or Mac OS X system. To view the latest operating-system requirements visit:

```
http://developer.android.com/sdk/index.html
```

and scroll down to the **SYSTEM REQUIREMENTS** heading. We developed the apps in this book using the following software:

- Java SE 7 Software Development Kit
- Android SDK/ADT Bundle based on the Eclipse IDE
- Android SDK versions 4.3 and 4.4

You'll see how to obtain each of these in the next sections.

Installing the Java Development Kit (JDK)

Android requires the *Java Development Kit (JDK)* version 7 (JDK 7) or 6 (JDK 6). *We used JDK 7.* To download the JDK for Windows, OS X or Linux, go to

```
http://www.oracle.com/technetwork/java/javase/downloads/index.html
```

You need only the JDK. Choose the 32-bit or 64-bit version based on your computer hardware and operating system. Most recent computers have 64-bit hardware—check your system's specifications. If you have a 32-bit operating system, you must use the 32-bit JDK. Be sure to follow the installation instructions at

```
http://docs.oracle.com/javase/7/docs/webnotes/install/index.html
```

Android Integrated Development Environment (IDE) Options

Google now provides two Android IDE options:

- Android SDK/ADT bundle—a version of the *Eclipse IDE* that comes preconfigured with the latest Android Software Development Kit (SDK) and the latest Android Development Tools (ADT) plugin. At the time of this writing, these were Android SDK version 4.4 and ADT version 22.3.

- Android Studio—Google's new Android IDE based on IntelliJ® IDEA and their preferred future IDE.

The Android SDK/ADT bundle has been widely used in Android app development for several years. Android Studio, introduced in May 2013, is an *early access version* and will be evolving rapidly. For this reason, we'll stay with the widely used Android SDK/ADT bundle in the book, and as online supplements at

```
http://www.deitel.com/books/AndroidFP2
```

we'll provide Android Studio versions of the Chapter 1 Test-Drive section and the Building the GUI section for each app, as appropriate.

Installing the Android SDK/ADT Bundle

To download the Android SDK/ADT bundle, go to

```
http://developer.android.com/sdk/index.html
```

and click the **Download the SDK ADT Bundle** button. When the download completes, extract the ZIP file's contents to your system. The resulting folder has an `eclipse` subfolder containing the Eclipse IDE and an `sdk` subfolder containing the Android SDK. As with the JDK, you can choose a 32-bit or 64-bit version. The Android SDK/ADT bundle 32-bit version should be used with the 32-bit JDK, and the 64-bit version with the 64-bit JDK.

Installing Android Studio

The IDE instructions in the printed book use the Android SDK/ADT bundle. You can also optionally install and use Android Studio. To download Android Studio, go to

```
http://developer.android.com/sdk/installing/studio.html
```

and click the **Download Android Studio** button. When the download completes, run the installer and follow the on-screen instructions to complete the installation. [*Note:* For Android 4.4 development in Android Studio, Android now supports Java SE 7 language features, including the diamond operator, multi-catch, `Strings` in `switch` and try-with-resources.]

Set the Java Compiler Compliance Level and Show Line Numbers

Android does not fully support Java SE 7. To ensure that the book's examples compile correctly, configure Eclipse to produce files that are compatible with Java SE 6 by performing the following steps:

1. Open Eclipse (⬡ or ⬤), which is located in the `eclipse` subfolder of the Android SDK/ADT bundle's installation folder.

2. When the **Workspace Launcher** window appears, click **OK**.

3. Select **Window > Preferences** to display the **Preferences** window. On Mac OS X, select **ADT > Preferences**….

4. Expand the **Java** node and select the **Compiler** node. Under **JDK Compliance**, set the **Compiler compliance level** to 1.6 (to indicate that Eclipse should produce compiled code that's compatible with Java SE 6).

5. Expand the **General > Editors** node and select **TextEditors**, then ensure that **Show line numbers** is selected and click **OK**.

6. Close Eclipse.

Android 4.3 SDK

This book's examples were written using the Android 4.3 and 4.4 SDKs. At the time of this writing, 4.4 was the version included with the Android SDK/ADT bundle and Android Studio. You should also install Android 4.3 (and any other versions you might want to support in your apps). To install other Android platform versions, perform the following steps (skipping Steps 1 and 2 if Eclipse is already open):

1. Open Eclipse. Depending on your platform, the icon will appear as ⟨⟩ or ⬤.

2. When the **Workspace Launcher** window appears, click **OK**.

3. On Mac OS X, if you see a window indicating "**Could not find SDK folder '/Users/** *YourAccount***/android-sdk-macosx/',**" click **Open Preferences** then **Browse…** and select the sdk folder located where you extracted the Android SDK/ADT bundle.

4. Select **Window > Android SDK Manager** to display the **Android SDK Manager** (Fig. 1).

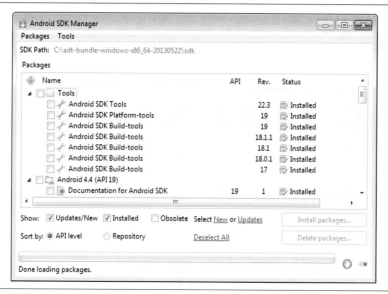

Fig. 1 | Android SDK Manager window.

5. The **Android SDK Manager**'s **Name** column shows all of the tools, platform versions and extras (such as APIs for interacting with Google services, like Maps) that you

can install. Uncheck the **Installed** checkbox. Then, if any of **Tools**, **Android 4.4 (API19)**, **Android 4.3 (API18)** and **Extras** appear in the **Packages** list, ensure that they're checked and click **Install # packages...** (# is the number of items to be installed) to display the **Choose Packages to Install** window. Most items in the **Extras** node are optional. For this book, you'll need the **Android Support Library** and **Google Play services**. The **Google USB Driver** is necessary for Windows users who wish to test apps on Android devices.]

6. In the **Choose Packages to Install** window, read the license agreements for each item. When you're done, click the **Accept License** radio button, then click the **Install** button. The status of the installation process will be displayed in the **Android SDK Manager** window.

Creating Android Virtual Devices (AVDs)

The **Android emulator**, included in the Android SDK, allows you to test apps on your computer rather than on an actual Android device. This is useful if you're learning Android and don't have access to Android devices, but can be *very* slow, so a real device is preferred if you have one. There are some hardware acceleration features that can improve emulator performance (`developer.android.com/tools/devices/emulator.html#acceleration`). Before running an app in the emulator, you must create an **Android Virtual Device** (AVD) which defines the characteristics of the device you want to test on, including the screen size in pixels, the pixel density, the physical size of the screen, size of the SD card for data storage and more. To test your apps for multiple Android devices, you can create AVDs that emulate each unique device. For this book, we use AVDs for Google's Android reference devices—the Nexus 4 phone, the Nexus 7 small tablet and Nexus 10 large tablet—which run unmodified versions of Android. To do so, perform the following steps:

1. Open Eclipse.

2. Select **Window > Android Virtual Device Manager** to display the **Android Virtual Device Manager** window, then select the **Device Definitions** tab (Fig. 2).

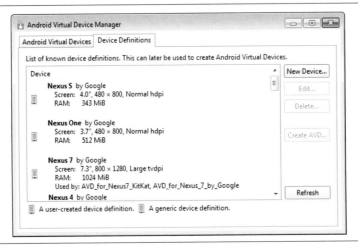

Fig. 2 | Android Virtual Device Manager window.

3. Google provides preconfigured devices that you can use to create AVDs. Select **Nexus 4 by Google**, then click **Create AVD...** to display the **Create new Android Virtual Device (AVD)** window (Fig. 3), then configure the options as shown and click **OK** to create the AVD. If you check **Hardware keyboard present**, you'll be able to use your computer's keyboard to type data into apps that are running in the AVD, but this may prevent the soft keyboard from displaying on the screen. If your computer does not have a camera, you can select **Emulated** for the **Front Camera** and **Back Camera** options. Each AVD you create has many other options specified in its config.ini. You can modify this file as described at

http://developer.android.com/tools/devices/managing-avds.html

to more precisely match the hardware configuration of your device.

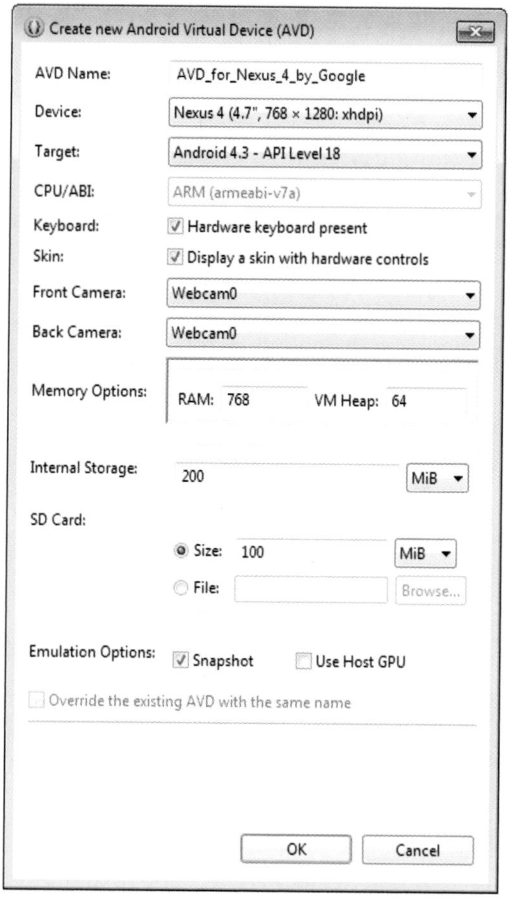

Fig. 3 | Configuring a Nexus 4 smartphone AVD for Android 4.3.

4. We also configured Android 4.3 AVDs that represent Nexus 7 by Google and Nexus 10 by Google for testing our tablet apps. Their settings are shown in Fig. 4. In

addition, we configured Android 4.4 AVDs for the Nexus 4, Nexus 7 and Nexus 10 with the names: AVD_for_Nexus_4_KitKat, AVD_for_Nexus_7_KitKat, and AVD_for_Nexus_10_KitKat,

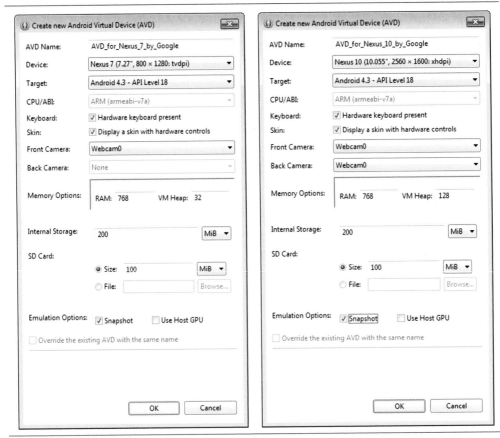

Fig. 4 | Configuring Nexus 7 and Nexus 10 tablet AVDs.

(Optional) Setting Up an Android Device for Development

As we mentioned, testing apps on AVDs can be slow due to AVD performance. If you have an Android device available to you, you should test the apps on that device. In addition, there are some features that you can test only on actual devices. To execute your apps on Android devices, follow the instructions at

    http://developer.android.com/tools/device.html

If you're developing on Microsoft Windows, you'll also need the Windows USB driver for Android devices. In some cases on Windows, you may also need device-specific USB drivers. For a list of USB driver sites for various device brands, visit:

    http://developer.android.com/tools/extras/oem-usb.html

Obtaining the Book's Code Examples

The examples for *Android for Programmers, 2/e, Volume 1* are available for download at

```
http://www.deitel.com/books/AndroidFP2/
```

If you're not already registered at our website, go to www.deitel.com and click the **Register** link. Fill in your information. Registration is free, and we do not share your information with anyone. Please verify that you entered your registration e-mail address correctly— you'll receive a confirmation e-mail with your verification code. *You must click the verification link in the e-mail before you can sign in at* www.deitel.com *for the first time.* Configure your e-mail client to allow e-mails from deitel.com to ensure that the verification e-mail is not filtered as junk mail. We send only occasional account-management e-mails unless you register separately for our free *Deitel® Buzz Online* e-mail newsletter at

```
http://www.deitel.com/newsletter/subscribe.html
```

Next, visit www.deitel.com and sign in using the **Login** link below our logo in the upper-left corner of the page. Go to http://www.deitel.com/books/AndroidFP2/. Click the **Examples** link to download a ZIP archive file containing the examples to your computer. Double click the ZIP file to unzip the archive, and make note of where you extract the file's contents on your system.

A Note Regarding the Android Development Tools

Google *frequently* updates the Android development tools. This often leads to problems compiling our apps when, in fact, the apps do not contain any errors. If you import one of our apps into Eclipse or Android Studio and it does not compile, there is probably a minor configuration issue. Please contact us by e-mail at deitel@deitel.com or by posting a question to:

- Facebook®—facebook.com/DeitelFan
- Google+™—google.com/+DeitelFan

and we'll help you resolve the issue.

You've now installed all the software and downloaded the code examples you'll need to study Android app development with *Android for Programmers, 2/e, Volume 1* and to begin developing your own apps. Enjoy!

Introduction to Android

Objectives

In this chapter you'll be introduced to:

- The history of Android and the Android SDK.
- Google Play Store for downloading apps.
- The Android packages used in this book to help you create Android apps.
- Basic object-technology concepts.
- Key software for Android app development, including the Android SDK, the Java SDK, the Eclipse integrated development environment (IDE) and Android Studio.
- Important Android documentation.
- Test-driving an Android drawing app in Eclipse (in the print book) and in Android Studio (online).
- Characteristics of great Android apps.

1.1 Introduction

Welcome to Android app development! We hope that working with *Android for Programmers: An App-Driven Approach, 2/e* will be an informative, challenging, entertaining and rewarding experience for you.

This book is geared toward *Java programmers*. We use only complete working apps, so if you don't know Java but have object-oriented programming experience in another language, such as C#, Objective-C/Cocoa or C++ (with class libraries), you should be able to master the material quickly, learning Java and Java-style object-oriented programming as you learn Android app development.

App-Driven Approach

We use an **app-driven approach**—new features are discussed in the context of complete working Android apps, with one app per chapter. For each app, we first describe it, then have you *test-drive* it. Next, we briefly overview the key **Eclipse IDE** (integrated development environment), Java and **Android SDK** (Software Development Kit) technologies we use to implement the app. For apps that require it, we walk through designing the GUI *visually* using Eclipse. Then we provide the complete source-code listing, using line numbers, *syntax coloring* and *code highlighting* to emphasize the key portions of the code. We also show one or more screen shots of the running app. Then we do a detailed code walkthrough, emphasizing the new programming concepts introduced in the app. You can download the source code for all of the book's apps from http://www.deitel.com/books/androidFP2/.

For each chapter, we also provide **Android Studio** IDE versions of any Eclipse-specific instructions. Because Android Studio is an early access version and will be evolving rapidly, we provide the Android Studio instructions on the book's website

```
http://www.deitel.com/books/AndroidFP2
```

This will enable us to keep the instructions up to date.

1.2 Android—The World's Leading Mobile Operating System

Android device sales are growing quickly, creating enormous opportunities for Android app developers.

- The first-generation Android phones were released in October 2008. By October 2013, a Strategy Analytics report showed that Android had 81.3% of the global *smartphone* market share, compared to 13.4% for Apple, 4.1% for Microsoft and 1% for Blackberry.[1]

- According to an IDC report, by the end of the first quarter of 2013 Android had 56.5% of the global *tablet* market share, compared to 39.6% for Apple's iPad and 3.7% for Microsoft Windows tablets.[2]

- As of April 2013, more than 1.5 million Android devices (including smartphones, tablets, etc.) were being activated daily.[3]

- At the time of this writing, there were over *one billion* activated Android devices.[4]

- Android devices now include smartphones, tablets, e-readers, robots, jet engines, NASA satellites, game consoles, refrigerators, televisions, cameras, health-care devices, smartwatches, automobile in-vehicle "infotainment" systems (for controlling the radio, GPS, phone calls, thermostat, etc.) and more.[5]

1.3 Android Features

Openness and Open Source

One benefit of developing Android apps is the openness of the platform. The operating system is *open source* and free. This allows you to view Android's source code and see how its features are implemented. You can also contribute to Android by reporting bugs (see `http://source.android.com/source/report-bugs.html`) or by participating in the Open Source Project discussion groups (`http://source.android.com/community/index.html`). Numerous open-source Android apps from Google and others are available on the Internet

---

1. `http://blogs.strategyanalytics.com/WSS/post/2013/10/31/Android-Captures-Record-81-Percent-Share-of-Global-Smartphone-Shipments-in-Q3-2013.aspx`.
2. `http://www.idc.com/getdoc.jsp?containerId=prUS24093213`.
3. `http://www.technobuffalo.com/2013/04/16/google-daily-android-activations-1-5-million`.
4. `http://venturebeat.com/2013/09/03/android-hits-1b-activations-and-will-be-called-kitkat-in-next-version`.
5. `http://www.businessweek.com/articles/2013-05-29/behind-the-internet-of-things-is-android-and-its-everywhere`.

(Fig. 1.1). Figure 1.2 shows you where you can get the Android source code, learn about the philosophy behind the open-source operating system and get licensing information.

URL	Description
http://en.wikipedia.org/wiki/ List_of_open_source_Android _applications	Extensive list of open-source apps, organized by category (e.g., games, communication, emulators, multimedia, security).
http://developer.android.com/ tools/samples/index.html	Google's sample apps for the Android platform; includes over 60 apps and games such as Lunar Lander, Snake and Tic Tac Toe.
http://github.com/	GitHub allows you to share your apps and source code and contribute to others' open-source projects.
http://sourceforge.net	SourceForge also allows you to share apps and source code and contribute to others' open-source projects.
http://f-droid.org/	Hundreds of free and open-source Android apps including the Adblock Plus advertisement blocker, aMetro public transportation navigation, AnySoftKeyboard (available in several languages), Apollo music player, Chinese Checkers game, DroidWeight weight tracker, Earth Live Wallpaper and more.
http://blog.interstellr.com/ post/39321551640/14-great- android-apps-that-are-also- open-source	Lists 14 open-source Android apps with links to the code.
http://www.openintents.org/ en/libraries	Provides nearly 100 open-source libraries that can be used to enhance app capabilities.
http://www.androidviews.net	Customized GUI controls for enhancing your app's appearance.
http://www.stackoverflow.com	Stack Overflow is a question-and-answer website for programmers. Users can vote on each answer, and the best responses rise to the top.

Fig. 1.1 | Open-source Android app and library resource sites.

Title	URL
Get Android Source Code	http://source.android.com/source/downloading.html
Governance Philosophy	http://source.android.com/about/philosophy.html
Licenses	http://source.android.com/source/licenses.html
FAQs	http://source.android.com/source/faqs.html

Fig. 1.2 | Resources and source code for the open-source Android operating system.

The openness of the platform spurs rapid innovation. Unlike Apple's *proprietary* iOS, which is available only on Apple devices, Android is available on devices from dozens of original equipment manufacturers (OEMs) and through numerous telecommunications carriers worldwide. The intense competition among OEMs and carriers benefits customers.

Java

Android apps are developed with Java—one of the world's most widely used programming languages. Java was a logical choice for the Android platform, because it's powerful, free, open source and millions of developers already know it. Experienced Java programmers can quickly dive into Android development, using Google's Android APIs (Application Programming Interfaces) and others available from third parties.

Java is object oriented and has access to extensive class libraries that help you develop powerful apps quickly. GUI programming in Java is *event driven*—in this book, you'll write apps that respond to various user-initiated *events* such as *screen touches*. In addition to directly programming portions of your apps, you'll also use the Eclipse and Android Studio IDEs to conveniently drag and drop predefined objects such as buttons and textboxes into place on your screen, and label and resize them. Using these IDEs, you can create, run, test and debug Android apps quickly and conveniently.

Multitouch Screen

Android smartphones wrap the functionality of a mobile phone, Internet client, MP3 player, gaming console, digital camera and more into a handheld device with full-color *multitouch screens*. With the touch of your fingers, you can navigate easily between using your phone, running apps, playing music, web browsing and more. The screen can display a keyboard for typing e-mails and text messages and entering data in apps (some Android devices also have physical keyboards).

Gestures

The multi-touch screens allow you to control the device with *gestures* involving one touch or multiple simultaneous touches (Fig. 1.3).

Gesture name	Physical action	Used to
Touch	Tap the screen once.	Open an app, "press" a button or a menu item.
Double touch	Tap the screen twice.	Zoom in on pictures, Google Maps and web pages. Tap the screen twice again to zoom back out.
Long press	Touch the screen and hold your finger in position.	Select items in a view—for example, checking an item in a list.
Swipe	Touch the screen, then move your finger in the swipe direction and release.	Flip item-by-item through a series, such as photos. A swipe automatically stops at the next item.
Drag	Touch and drag your finger across the screen.	Move objects or icons, or scroll through a web page or list.
Pinch zoom	Pinch two fingers together, or spread them apart.	Zoom in and out on the screen (e.g., resizing text and pictures).

Fig. 1.3 | Some common android gestures.

Built-in Apps

Android devices come with several default apps, which may vary, depending on the device, the manufacturer or the mobile service carrier. These typically include **Phone**, **People**, **Email**, **Browser**, **Camera**, **Photos**, **Messaging**, **Calendar**, **Play Store**, **Calculator** and more.

Web Services

Web services are software components stored on one computer that can be accessed by an app (or other software component) on another computer over the Internet. With web services, you can create **mashups**, which enable you to rapidly develop apps by quickly *combining* complementary web services, often from different organizations and possibly other forms of information feeds. For example, 100 Destinations (`www.100destinations.co.uk`) combines the photos and tweets from Twitter with the mapping capabilities of Google Maps to allow you to explore countries around the world through the photos of others.

Programmableweb (`http://www.programmableweb.com/`) provides a directory of over 9,400 APIs and 7,000 mashups, plus how-to guides and sample code for creating your own mashups. Figure 1.4 lists some popular web services. According to Programmableweb, the three most widely used APIs for mashups are Google Maps, Twitter and YouTube. We use Twitter web services in Chapter 4.

Web services source	How it's used
Google Maps	Mapping services
Twitter	Microblogging
YouTube	Video search
Facebook	Social networking
Instagram	Photo sharing
Foursquare	Mobile check-in
LinkedIn	Social networking for business
Groupon	Social commerce
Netflix	Movie rentals
eBay	Internet auctions
Wikipedia	Collaborative encyclopedia
PayPal	Payments
Last.fm	Internet radio
Amazon eCommerce	Shopping for books and lots of other products
Salesforce.com	Customer Relationship Management (CRM)
Skype	Internet telephony
Microsoft Bing	Search
Flickr	Photo sharing
Zillow	Real-estate pricing
Yahoo Search	Search
WeatherBug	Weather

Fig. 1.4 | Some popular web services (`http://www.programmableweb.com/apis/directory/1?sort=mashups`).

1.4 Android Operating System

The Android operating system was developed by Android, Inc., which was acquired by Google in 2005. In 2007, the Open Handset Alliance™—which now has 84 company members (http://www.openhandsetalliance.com/oha_members.html)—was formed to develop, maintain and evolve Android, driving innovation in mobile technology and improving the user experience while reducing costs.

Android Version Naming Convention

Each new version of Android is named after a dessert, going in alphabetical order (Fig. 1.5).

Android version	Name
Android 1.5	Cupcake
Android 1.6	Donut
Android 2.0–2.1	Eclair
Android 2.2	Froyo
Android 2.3	Gingerbread
Android 3.0–3.2	Honeycomb
Android 4.0	Ice Cream Sandwich
Android 4.1–4.3	Jelly Bean
Android 4.4	KitKat

Fig. 1.5 | Android version numbers and the corresponding names.

1.4.1 Android 2.2 (Froyo)

Android 2.2 (also called **Froyo**, released in May 2010) introduced external storage, allowing you to store apps on an external memory device rather than just in the Android device's internal memory. It also introduced the **Android Cloud to Device Messaging (C2DM)** service. **Cloud computing** allows you to use software and data stored in the "cloud"—i.e., accessed on remote computers (or servers) via the Internet and available on demand—rather than having it stored on your desktop, notebook computer or mobile device. Cloud computing gives you the flexibility to increase or decrease computing resources to meet your resource needs at any given time, making it more cost effective than purchasing expensive hardware to ensure that you have enough storage and processing power for occasional peak levels. Android C2DM allows app developers to send data from their servers to their apps installed on Android devices, even when the apps are *not* currently running. The server notifies the apps to contact it directly to receive updated app or user data.[6] C2DM is now deprecated in favor of Google Cloud Messaging.

For information about additional Android 2.2 features—OpenGL ES 2.0 graphics capabilities, the media framework and more—visit http://developer.android.com/about/versions/android-2.2-highlights.html.

---

6. http://code.google.com/android/c2dm/.

1.4.2 Android 2.3 (Gingerbread)

Android 2.3 (Gingerbread), released later in 2010, added more user refinements, such as a redesigned keyboard, improved navigation capabilities, increased power efficiency and more. It also added several developer features for communications (e.g., technologies that make it easier to make and receive calls from within an app), multimedia (e.g., new audio and graphics APIs) and gaming (e.g., improved performance and new sensors, such as a gyroscope for better motion processing).

One of the most significant new features in Android 2.3 was support for **near-field communication (NFC)**—a short-range wireless connectivity standard that enables communication between two devices within a few centimeters. NFC support and features vary by Android device. NFC can be used for payments (for example, touching your NFC-enabled Android device to a payment device on a soda machine), exchanging data such as contacts and pictures, pairing devices and accessories and more.

For a more Android 2.3 developer features, see `http://developer.android.com/about/versions/android-2.3-highlights.html`.

1.4.3 Android 3.0 through 3.2 (Honeycomb)

Android 3.0 (Honeycomb) included user-interface improvements specifically for large-screen devices (e.g., tablets), such as a redesigned keyboard for more efficient typing, a visually appealing 3D user interface, easier navigation between screens within an app and more. New Android 3.0 developer features included:

- fragments, which describe portions of an app's user interface and can be combined into one screen or used across multiple screens
- a persistent Action Bar at the top of the screen providing users with options for interacting with apps
- the ability to add large-screen layouts to existing apps designed for small screens to optimize your app for use on different screen sizes
- a visually attractive and more functional user interface, known as "Holo" for its holographic look and feel
- a new animation framework
- improved graphics and multimedia capabilities
- ability to use multicore processor architectures for enhanced performance
- increased Bluetooth support (e.g., enabling an app to determine if there are any connected devices such as headphones or a keyboard)
- and an animation framework for animating user-interface or graphics objects.

For a list of Android 3.0 user and developer features and platform technologies, go to `http://developer.android.com/about/versions/android-3.0-highlights.html`.

1.4.4 Android 4.0 through 4.0.4 (Ice Cream Sandwich)

Android 4.0 (Ice Cream Sandwich), released in 2011, merged Android 2.3 (Gingerbread) and Android 3.0 (Honeycomb) into one operating system for use on all Android devices. This allowed you to incorporate into your smartphone apps Honeycomb's features that previously were available only on tablets—the "Holo" user interface, a new launcher (used to customize the device's home screen and launch apps) and more—and easily scale your apps to work on different devices. Ice Cream Sandwich also added several APIs for improved communication between devices, accessibility for users with disabilities (e.g., vision impairments), social networking and more (Fig. 1.6). For a complete list of Android 4.0 APIs, see `http://developer.android.com/about/versions/android-4.0.html`.

Feature	Description
Face detection	Using the camera, compatible devices can determine the positioning of the user's eyes, nose and mouth. The camera can also track the user's eye movement, allowing you to create apps that change perspective, based on where the user is looking.
Virtual camera operator	When filming video of multiple people, the camera will automatically focus on the person who is speaking.
Android Beam	Using NFC, **Android Beam** allows you to touch two Android devices to share content (e.g., contacts, pictures, videos).
Wi-Fi Direct	Wi-Fi P2P (peer-to-peer) APIs allow you to connect multiple Android devices using Wi-Fi. The devices can communicate wirelessly at a greater distance than when using Bluetooth.
Social API	Access and share contact information across social networks and apps (with the user's permission).
Calendar API	Add and share events across multiple apps, manage alerts and attendees and more.
Accessibility APIs	Use the new Accessibility Text-to-Speech APIs to enhance the user experience of your apps for people with disabilities such as vision impairments and more. The explore-by-touch mode allows users with vision impairments to touch anywhere on the screen and hear a voice description of the touched content.
Android@Home framework	Use the **Android@Home framework** to create apps that control appliances in users' homes, such as, thermostats, irrigation systems, networked light bulbs and more.
Bluetooth Health Devices	Create apps that communicate with Bluetooth health devices such as scales, heart-rate monitors and more.

Fig. 1.6 | Some Android Ice Cream Sandwich developer features (`http://developer.android.com/about/versions/android-4.0.html`).

1.4.5 Android 4.1–4.3 (Jelly Bean)

Android Jelly Bean, released in 2012, includes support for external displays, improved security, appearance enhancements (e.g., resizable app widgets and larger app notifications) and performance improvements that make switching between apps and screens more seamless (Fig. 1.7). For the Jelly Bean features list, see `http://developer.android.com/about/versions/jelly-bean.html`.

Feature	Description
Android Beam	You can use Android Beam to easily pair your smartphone or tablet with wireless Bluetooth® speakers or special headphones.
Lock screen widgets	Create widgets that appear on the user's screen when the device is locked, or modify your existing home-screen widgets so that they're also visible when the device is locked.
Photo Sphere	APIs for working with the new panoramic photo features that enable users to take 360-degree photos, similar to those used for Google Maps Street View.
Daydreams	Daydreams are interactive screensavers that are activated when a device is docked or charging. Daydreams can play audio and video and respond to user interactions.
Language support	New features help your apps reach international users, such as bidirectional text (left-to-right or right-to-left), international keyboards, additional keyboard layouts and more.
Developer options	Several new tracking and debugging features help you improve your apps, such as bug reports that include a screen shot and device state information.

Fig. 1.7 | Some Android Jelly Bean features (`http://developer.android.com/about/versions/jelly-bean.html`).

1.4.6 Android 4.4 (KitKat)

Android 4.4 KitKat, released in October 2013, includes several performance improvements that make it possible to run the operating system on all Android devices, including older, memory-constrained devices, which are particularly popular in developing countries.[7]

Enabling more users to update to KitKat will reduce the "fragmentation" of Android versions in the market, which has been a challenge for developers who previously had to design apps to run across multiple versions of the operating system, or limit their potential market by targeting their apps to a specific version of the operating system.

Android KitKat also includes security and accessibility enhancements, improved graphics and multimedia capabilities, memory-use analysis tools and more. Figure 1.8 lists some of the key new KitKat features. For a complete list, see

```
http://developer.android.com/about/versions/kitkat.html
```

Feature	Description
Immersive mode	The status bar at the top of the screen and the menu buttons at the bottom can be hidden, allowing your apps to fill more of the screen. Users can access the status bar by swiping down from the top of the screen, and the system bar (with the back button, home button and recent apps button) by swiping up from the bottom.

Fig. 1.8 | Some Android KitKat features (`http://developer.android.com/about/versions/kitkat.html`). (Part 1 of 2.)

---

7. `http://techcrunch.com/2013/10/31/android-4-4-kitkat-google/`.

Feature	Description
Printing framework	Build printing functionality into your apps, including locating available printers over Wi-Fi or the cloud, selecting the paper size and specifying which pages to print.
Storage access framework	Create document storage providers that allow users to browse, create and edit files (e.g., documents and images) across multiple apps.
SMS provider	Create SMS (Short Message Service) or MMS (Multimedia Messaging Service) apps using the new SMS provider and APIs. Users can now select their default messaging app.
Transitions framework	The new framework makes it easier to create transition animations.
Screen recording	Record video of your app in action to create tutorials and marketing materials.
Enhanced accessibility	The captioning manager API allows apps to check the user's captioning preferences (e.g., language, text styles and more).
Chromium WebView	Supports the latest standards for displaying web content including HTML5, CSS3 and a faster version of JavaScript.
Step detector and step counter	Create apps that detect whether the user is running, walking or climbing stairs and count the number of steps.
Host Card Emulator (HCE)	HCE enables any app to perform secure NFC transactions (e.g., mobile payments) without the need for a secure element on the SIM card controlled by the wireless carrier.

Fig. 1.8 | Some Android KitKat features (`http://developer.android.com/about/versions/kitkat.html`). (Part 2 of 2.)

1.5 Downloading Apps from Google Play

At the time of this writing, there were over one million apps in **Google Play**, and the number is growing quickly.[8] Figure 1.9 lists some popular free and fee-based apps. You can download apps through the **Play Store** app installed on the device. You can also log into your Google Play account at `http://play.google.com` through your web browser, then specify the Android device on which to install the app. It will then download via the device's WiFi or 3G/4G connection. In Chapter 9, Google Play and App Business Issues, we discuss additional app stores, offering your apps for free or charging a fee, app pricing and more.

Google Play category	Some popular apps in the category
Books and Reference	Kindle, Wikipedia, Audible for Android, Google Play Books
Business	Office Suite Pro 7, Job Search, Square Register, GoToMeeting
Comics	ComicRack, Memedroid Pro, Marvel Comics, Comic Strips

Fig. 1.9 | Some popular Android apps in Google Play. (Part 1 of 2.)

---

8. `en.wikipedia.org/wiki/Google_Play`.

Google Play category	Some popular apps in the category
Communication	Facebook Messenger, Skype™, GrooVe IP
Education	Duolingo: Learn Languages Free, TED, Mobile Observatory
Entertainment	SketchBook Mobile, Netflix, Fandango® Movies, iFunny :)
Finance	Mint.com Personal Finance, Google Wallet, PayPal
Games: Arcade & Action	Minecraft—Pocket Edition, Fruit Ninja, Angry Birds
Games: Brain & Puzzle	Where's My Water?, Draw Something, Can You Escape
Games: Cards & Casino	Solitaire, Slots Delux, UNO™ & Friends, DH Texas Poker
Games: Casual	Candy Crush Saga, Hardest Game Ever 2, Game Dev Story
Health & Fitness	RunKeeper, Calorie Counter, Workout Trainer, WebMD®
Lifestyle	Zillow Real Estate, Epicurious Recipe App, Family Locator
Live Wallpaper	PicsArt, GO Launcher EX, Beautiful Widgets Pro
Media & Video	MX Player, YouTube, KeepSafe Vault, RealPlayer®
Medical	Epocrates, ICE: In Case of Emergency, Medscape®
Music & Audio	Pandora®, Shazam, Spotify, Ultimate Guitar Tabs & Chords
News & Magazines	Flipboard, Pulse News, CNN, Engadget, Drippler
Personalization	Beautiful Widgets Pro, Zedge™, GO Launcher EX
Photography	Camera ZOOM FX, Photo Grid, InstaPicFrame for Instagram
Productivity	Adobe® Reader®, Dropbox, Google Keep, SwiftKey Keyboard
Shopping	eBay, Amazon Mobile, Groupon, The Coupons App
Social	Facebook®, Instagram, Vine, Twitter, Snapchat, Pinterest
Sports	SportsCenter for Android, NFL '13, Team Stream™
Tools	Titanium Backup PRO, Google Translate, Tiny Flashlight®
Transportation	Uber, Trapster, Lyft, Hailo™, Ulysse Speedometer
Travel & Local	Waze, GasBuddy, KAYAK, TripAdvisor, OpenTable®
Weather	WeatherBug, AccuWeather, The Weather Channel
Widgets	Zillow, DailyHoroscope, Starbucks, Family Locator

Fig. 1.9 | Some popular Android apps in Google Play. (Part 2 of 2.)

1.6 Packages

Android uses a collection of *packages*, which are named groups of related, predefined classes. Some of the packages are Android specific, some are Java specific and some are Google specific. These packages allow you to conveniently access Android OS features and incorporate them into your apps. The Android packages help you create apps that adhere to Android's unique look-and-feel conventions and style guidelines (http://developer.android.com/design/index.html). Figure 1.10 lists the packages we discuss in this book. For a complete list of Android packages, see developer.android.com/reference/packages.html.

Package	Description
`android.app`	Includes high-level classes in the Android app model. (Chapter 3's **Tip Calculator** app.)
`android.content`	Access and publish data on a device. (Chapter 6's **Cannon Game** app.)
`android.content.res`	Classes for accessing app resources (e.g., media, colors, drawables, etc.), and device-configuration information affecting app behavior. (Chapter 5's **Flag Quiz** app.)
`android.database`	Handling data returned by the content provider. (Chapter 8's **Address Book** app.)
`android.database.sqlite`	SQLite database management for private databases. (Chapter 8's **Address Book** app.)
`android.graphics`	Graphics tools used for drawing to the screen. (Chapter 5's **Flag Quiz** app and Chapter 7's **Doodlz** app.)
`android.hardware`	Device hardware support. (Chapter 7's **Doodlz** app.)
`android.media`	Classes for handling audio and video media interfaces. (Chapter 6's **Cannon Game** app.)
`android.net`	Network access classes. (Chapter 4's **Twitter® Searches** app.)
`android.os`	Operating-systems services. (Chapter 3's **Tip Calculator** app.)
`android.preference`	Working with an app's user preferences. (Chapter 5's **Flag Quiz** app.)
`android.provider`	Access to Android content providers. (Chapter 7's **Doodlz** app.)
`android.support.` `  v4.print`	Android Support Library features for using the Android 4.4 printing framework. (Chapter 7's **Doodlz** app.)
`android.text`	Rendering and tracking text on a device. (Chapter 3's **Tip Calculator** app.)
`android.util`	Utility methods and XML utilities. (Chapter 6's **Cannon Game** app.)
`android.widget`	User-interface classes for widgets. (Chapter 3's **Tip Calculator** app.)
`android.view`	User interface classes for layout and user interactions. (Chapter 4's **Twitter® Searches** app.)
`java.io`	Streaming, serialization and file-system access of input and output facilities. (Chapter 5's **Flag Quiz** app.)
`java.text`	Text formatting classes. (Chapter 4's **Twitter® Searches** app.)
`java.util`	Utility classes. (Chapter 4's **Twitter® Searches** app.)
`android.graphics.` `  drawable`	Classes for display-only elements (e.g., gradients, etc.). (Chapter 5's **Flag Quiz** app.)

Fig. 1.10 | Android and Java packages used in this book, listed with the chapter in which they *first* appear. We discuss additional packages in Volume 2.

1.7 Android Software Development Kit (SDK)

The Android SDK provides the tools you'll need to build Android apps. It's available at no charge through the Android Developers' site. See the Before You Begin section for details on downloading the Android app-development tools you'll need to develop Android apps, including the Java SE, the Android SDK/ADT Bundle (which includes the Eclipse IDE) and the Android Studio IDE.

Android SDK/ADT Bundle

The Android SDK/ADT Bundle—which includes the Eclipse IDE—is the most widely integrated development environment for Android development. Some developers use only a text editor and command-line tools to create Android apps. The Eclipse IDE includes:

- Code editor with support for syntax coloring and line numbering
- Auto-indenting and auto-complete (i.e., type hinting)
- Debugger
- Version control system
- Refactoring support

You'll use Eclipse in Section 1.9 to test-drive the **Doodlz** app. Starting in Chapter 2, **Welcome** App, you'll use Eclipse to build apps.

Android Studio

Android Studio, a new Android IDE based on the JetBrains IntelliJ IDEA Java IDE (`http://www.jetbrains.com/idea/`), was announced in 2013 and is Google's preferred Android IDE of the future. At the time of this writing, Android Studio was available only as an *early access preview*—many of its features were still under development. For each chapter, we also provide Android Studio versions of any Eclipse-specific instructions on the book's website

```
http://www.deitel.com/books/AndroidFP2
```

To learn more about Android Studio, installing it and migrating from Eclipse, visit `http://developer.android.com/sdk/installing/studio.html`.

Android Development Tools (ADT) Plugin for Eclipse

The **Android Development Tools (ADT) Plugin for Eclipse** (part of the Android SDK/ADT Bundle) allows you to create, run and debug Android apps, export them for distribution (e.g., upload them to Google Play), and more. ADT also includes a visual GUI design tool. GUI components can be dragged and dropped into place to form GUIs without any coding. You'll learn more about ADT in Chapter 2.

The Android Emulator

The **Android emulator**, included in the Android SDK, allows you to run Android apps in a simulated environment within Windows, Mac OS X or Linux, without using an actual Android device. The emulator displays a realistic Android user-interface window. It's particularly useful if you do not have access to Android devices for testing. You should certainly test your apps on a variety of Android devices before uploading them to Google Play.

Before running an app in the emulator, you'll need to create an **Android Virtual Device (AVD)**, which defines the characteristics of the device on which you want to test, including the hardware, system image, screen size, data storage and more. If you want to test your apps for multiple Android devices, you'll need to create separate AVDs to emulate each unique device, or use a service (like `testdroid.com` or `appthwack.com`) that enables you to test on many different devices.

We used the emulator (not an actual Android device) to take most but not all of the Android screen shots for this book. You can reproduce on the emulator most of the

Android gestures (Fig. 1.11) and controls (Fig. 1.12) using your computer's keyboard and mouse. The gestures on the emulator are a bit limited, since your computer probably cannot simulate all the Android hardware features. For example, to test GPS apps in the emulator, you'll need to create files that simulate GPS readings. Also, although you can simulate orientation changes (to *portrait* or *landscape* mode), simulating particular **accelerometer** readings (the accelerometer allows the device to respond to up/down, left/right and forward/backward acceleration) requires features that are not built into the emulator. There is a *Sensor Simulator* available at

```
https://code.google.com/p/openintents/wiki/SensorSimulator
```

that you can use to send simulated sensor information into an AVD to test other sensor features in your apps. Figure 1.13 lists Android functionality that's *not* available on the emulator. You can, however, upload your app to an Android device to test these features. You'll start creating AVDs and using the emulator to develop Android apps in Chapter 2's **Welcome** app.

Gesture	Emulator action
Touch	Click the mouse once. Introduced in Chapter 3's **Tip Calculator** app.
Double touch	Double click the mouse. Introduced in Chapter 6's **Cannon Game** app.
Long press	Click and hold the mouse.
Drag	Click, hold and drag the mouse. Introduced in Chapter 6's **Cannon Game** app.
Swipe	Click and hold the mouse, move the pointer in the swipe direction and release the mouse. Introduced in Chapter 8's **Address Book** app.
Pinch zoom	Press and hold the *Ctrl* (*Control*) key. Two circles that simulate the two touches will appear. Move the circles to the start position, click and hold the mouse and drag the circles to the end position.

Fig. 1.11 | Android gestures on the emulator.

Control	Emulator action
Back	*Esc*
Call/dial button	*F3*
Camera	*Ctrl-KEYPAD_5*, *Ctrl-F3*
End call button	*F4*
Home	*Home* button
Menu (left softkey)	*F2* or *Page Up* button
Power button	*F7*

Fig. 1.12 | Android hardware controls on the emulator (for additional controls, go to `http://developer.android.com/tools/help/emulator.html`). (Part 1 of 2.)

Control	Emulator action
Search	*F5*
* (right softkey)	*Shift-F2* or *Page Down* button
Rotate to previous orientation	*KEYPAD_7, Ctrl-F11*
Rotate to next orientation	*KEYPAD_9, Ctrl-F12*
Toggle cell networking on/off	*F8*
Volume up button	*KEYPAD_PLUS, Ctrl-F5*
Volume down button	*KEYPAD_MINUS, Ctrl-F6*

Fig. 1.12 | Android hardware controls on the emulator (for additional controls, go to `http://developer.android.com/tools/help/emulator.html`). (Part 2 of 2.)

Android functionality not available on the emulator

- Making or receiving real phone calls (the emulator allows simulated calls only)
- Bluetooth
- USB connections
- Device-attached headphones
- Determining connected state of the phone
- Determining battery charge or power charging state
- Determining SD card insert/eject
- Sensors (accelerometer, barometer, compass, light sensor, proximity sensor)

Fig. 1.13 | Android functionality not available on the emulator (`http://developer.android.com/tools/devices/emulator.html`).

1.8 Object-Oriented Programming: A Quick Refresher

Android uses object-oriented programming techniques, so in this section we review the basics of object technology. We use all of these concepts in this book.

Building software quickly, correctly and economically remains an elusive goal at a time when demands for new and more powerful software are soaring. *Objects*, or more precisely—as we'll see in Chapter 3—the *classes* objects come from, are essentially *reusable* software components. There are date objects, time objects, audio objects, video objects, automobile objects, people objects, etc. Almost any *noun* can be reasonably represented as a software object in terms of *attributes* (e.g., name, color and size) and *behaviors* (e.g., calculating, moving and communicating). Software developers are discovering that using a modular, object-oriented design-and-implementation approach can make software development groups much more productive than they could be with earlier popular techniques like "structured programming"—object-oriented programs are often easier to understand, correct and modify.

1.8.1 The Automobile as an Object

To help you understand objects and their contents, let's begin with a simple analogy. Suppose you want to *drive a car and make it go faster by pressing its accelerator pedal*. What must happen before you can do this? Well, before you can drive a car, someone has to *design* it. A car typically begins as engineering drawings, similar to the *blueprints* that describe the design of a house. These drawings include the design for an accelerator pedal. The pedal *hides* from the driver the complex mechanisms that actually make the car go faster, just as the brake pedal *hides* the mechanisms that slow the car, and the steering wheel *hides* the mechanisms that turn the car. This enables people with little or no knowledge of how engines, braking and steering mechanisms work to drive a car easily.

Just as you cannot cook meals in the kitchen of a blueprint, you cannot drive a car's engineering drawings. Before you can drive a car, it must be *built* from the engineering drawings that describe it. A completed car has an *actual* accelerator pedal to make it go faster, but even that's not enough—the car won't accelerate on its own (hopefully!), so the driver must *press* the pedal to accelerate the car.

1.8.2 Methods and Classes

Let's use our car example to introduce some key object-oriented programming concepts. Performing a task in a program requires a **method**. The method houses the program statements that actually perform its tasks. The method hides these statements from its user, just as the accelerator pedal of a car hides from the driver the mechanisms of making the car go faster. A program unit called a **class** houses the methods that perform the class's tasks. For example, a class that represents a bank account might contain one method to *deposit* money to an account, another to *withdraw* money from an account and a third to *inquire* what the account's current balance is. A class is similar in concept to a car's engineering drawings, which house the design of an accelerator pedal, steering wheel, and so on.

1.8.3 Instantiation

Just as someone has to *build a car* from its engineering drawings before you can actually drive a car, you must *build an object* of a class before a program can perform the tasks that the class's methods define. The process of doing this is called *instantiation*. An object is then referred to as an **instance** of its class.

1.8.4 Reuse

Just as a car's engineering drawings can be *reused* many times to build many cars, you can *reuse* a class many times to build many objects. **Reuse** of existing classes when building new classes and programs saves time and effort. Reuse also helps you build more reliable and effective systems, because existing classes and components often have gone through extensive *testing*, *debugging* and *performance* tuning. Just as the notion of *interchangeable parts* was crucial to the Industrial Revolution, reusable classes are crucial to the software revolution that has been spurred by object technology.

1.8.5 Messages and Method Calls

When you drive a car, pressing its gas pedal sends a *message* to the car to perform a task— that is, to go faster. Similarly, you *send messages to an object*. Each message is a **method call** that tells a method of the object to perform its task. For example, a program might call a particular bank-account object's *deposit* method to increase the account's balance.

1.8.6 Attributes and Instance Variables

A car, besides having capabilities to accomplish tasks, also has *attributes*, such as its color, its number of doors, the amount of gas in its tank, its current speed and its record of total miles driven (i.e., its odometer reading). Like its capabilities, the car's attributes are represented as part of its design in its engineering diagrams (which, for example, include an odometer and a fuel gauge). As you drive an actual car, these attributes are carried along with the car. Every car maintains its *own* attributes. For example, each car knows how much gas is in its own gas tank, but *not* how much is in the tanks of *other* cars.

An object, similarly, has attributes that it carries along as it's used in a program. These attributes are specified as part of the object's class. For example, a bank-account object has a *balance attribute* that represents the amount of money in the account. Each bank-account object knows the balance in the account it represents, but *not* the balances of the *other* accounts in the bank. Attributes are specified by the class's **instance variables**.

1.8.7 Encapsulation

Classes **encapsulate** (i.e., wrap) attributes and methods into objects—an object's attributes and methods are intimately related. Objects may communicate with one another, but they're normally not allowed to know how other objects are implemented—implementation details are *hidden* within the objects themselves. This **information hiding** is crucial to good software engineering.

1.8.8 Inheritance

A new class of objects can be created quickly and conveniently by **inheritance**—the new class absorbs the characteristics of an existing one, possibly customizing them and adding unique characteristics of its own. In our car analogy, a "convertible" certainly *is an* object of the more *general* class "automobile," but more *specifically*, the roof can be raised or lowered.

1.8.9 Object-Oriented Analysis and Design (OOAD)

How will you create the code for your programs? Perhaps, like many programmers, you'll simply turn on your computer and start typing. This approach may work for small programs, but what if you were asked to create a software system to control thousands of automated teller machines for a major bank? Or suppose you were asked to work on a team of 1,000 software developers building the next U.S. air traffic control system? For projects so large and complex, you should not simply sit down and start writing programs.

To create the best solutions, you should follow a detailed **analysis** process for determining your project's **requirements** (i.e., defining *what* the system is supposed to do) and developing a **design** that satisfies them (i.e., deciding *how* the system should do it). Ideally, you'd go through this process and carefully review the design (and have your design reviewed by other software professionals) before writing any code. If this process involves analyzing and designing your system from an object-oriented point of view, it's called an **object-oriented analysis and design (OOAD) process**. Languages like Java are object oriented. Programming in such a language, called **object-oriented programming (OOP)**, allows you to implement an object-oriented design as a working system.

1.9 Test-Driving the Doodlz App in an Android Virtual Device (AVD)

In this section, you'll run and interact with your first Android app. The **Doodlz** app allows you to drag your fingers on the screen to "paint." You can control the brush sizes and colors using options provided in the app's *options menu*. There is no need to look at the app's code—you'll build the app and study its code in Chapter 7.

The following steps show how to import the app's project into Eclipse and how to test-drive the app in the Nexus 4 Android Virtual Device (AVD) that you set up in the Before You Begin section following the Preface. Later in this section, we'll also discuss how to run the app on a tablet AVD and on an Android device. When the app is running in an AVD, you can create a new painting by "dragging your finger" anywhere on the canvas. You "touch" the screen by using the mouse.

Android SDK/ADT Bundle and Android Studio IDEs

The IDE screen captures in the following steps (and throughout this book) were taken on a computer running Windows 7, the Java SE 7 JDK and the Android SDK/ADT Bundle that you installed in the Before You Begin section. Because Android Studio is an early access version and will be evolving rapidly, we provide the Android Studio instructions for this test-drive on the book's website

```
www.deitel.com/books/AndroidFP2
```

This will enable us to update the instructions in response to Google's changes. Both the Android SDK/ADT Bundle and Android Studio use the *same* Android emulator, so once an app is running in an AVD, the steps are identical.

1.9.1 Running the Doodlz App in the Nexus 4 Smartphone AVD

To test-drive the **Doodlz** app, perform the following steps:

1. *Checking your setup.* If you have not done so already, perform the steps specified in the Before You Begin section located after the Preface.

2. *Opening Eclipse.* Open the `eclipse` subfolder of the Android SDK/ADT bundle's installation folder, then double click the Eclipse icon (or , depending on your platform).

3. *Specifying your workspace location.* When the **Workspace Launcher** window appears, specify where you'd like the apps that you create to be stored, then click **OK**. We used the default location—a folder named `workspace` in your user directory. A **workspace** is a collection of projects, and each project is typically an app or a library that can be shared among apps. Each workspace also has its own settings, such as where various Eclipse subwindows are displayed. You can have many workspaces and switch between them for different development tasks—for example, you could have separate workspaces for Android app development, Java app development and web app development, each with its own custom settings. If this is your first time opening Eclipse, the **Welcome** page (Fig. 1.14) is displayed.

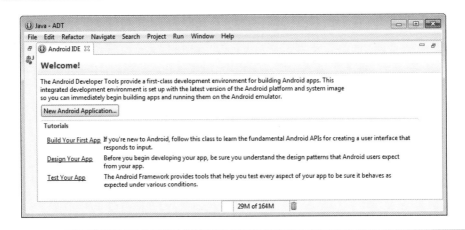

Fig. 1.14 | **Welcome** page in Eclipse.

4. *Launching the Nexus 4 AVD.* For this test-drive, we'll use the Nexus 4 smart-phone AVD that you configured for Android 4.4 (KitKat) in the Before You Be-gin section—in Section 1.9.2, we'll show the app running in a tablet AVD. An AVD can take several minutes to load, so you should launch it in advance of when you intend to use it and keep it running in the background while you're building and testing your apps. To launch the Nexus 4 AVD, select **Window > Android Virtual Device Manager** to display the **Android Virtual Device Manager** dialog (Fig. 1.15). Select the Nexus 4 AVD for Android KitKat and click **Start...**, then click the **Launch** button in the **Launch Options** dialog that appears. You should not attempt to execute the app until the AVD finishes loading. Once the AVD appears as shown in Fig. 1.16, unlock the AVD by dragging the mouse pointer from the lock icon to the edge of the screen.

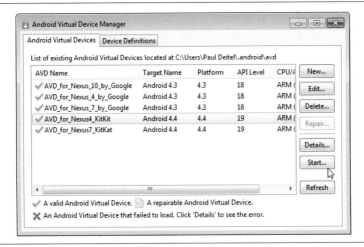

Fig. 1.15 | **Android Virtual Device Manager** dialog.

Drag the mouse pointer from the lock icon to the edge of the screen to unlock the AVD

Fig. 1.16 | Nexus 4 AVD home screen (for Android 4.4) when the AVD finishes loading.

5. *Importing the Doodlz app's project.* Select **File > Import...** to open the **Import** dialog (Fig. 1.17(a)). Expand the **General** node and select **Existing Projects into Workspace**, then click **Next >** to proceed to the **Import Projects** step (Fig. 1.17(b)). Click the **Browse...** button to the right of the **Select root directory** textbox. In the **Browse**

a) **Import** dialog

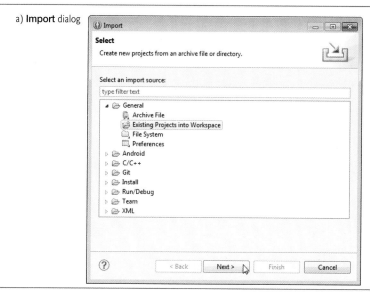

Fig. 1.17 | Importing an existing project. (Part 1 of 2.)

b) **Import** dialog's **Import Projects** step

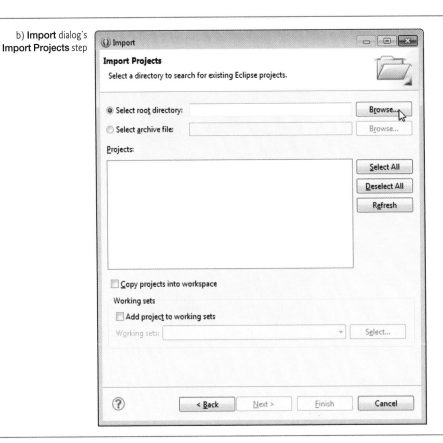

Fig. 1.17 | Importing an existing project. (Part 2 of 2.)

For **Folder** dialog, locate the **Doodlz** folder in the book's examples folder, select it and click **Open**. Click **Finish** to import the project into Eclipse. The project now appears in the **Package Explorer** window (Fig. 1.18) at the left side of Eclipse. If the **Package Explorer** window is not visible, you can view it by selecting **Window > Show View > Package Explorer**.

Fig. 1.18 | **Package Explorer** window.

6. *Launching the Doodlz app.* In Eclipse, right click the **Doodlz** project in the **Package Explorer** window, then select **Run As > Android Application** (Fig. 1.19). This will execute **Doodlz** in the AVD that you launched in Step 4 (Fig. 1.20).

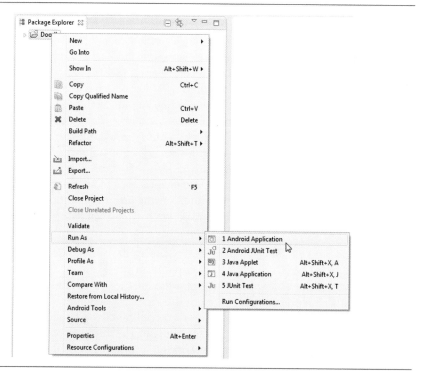

Fig. 1.19 | Launching the **Doodlz** app.

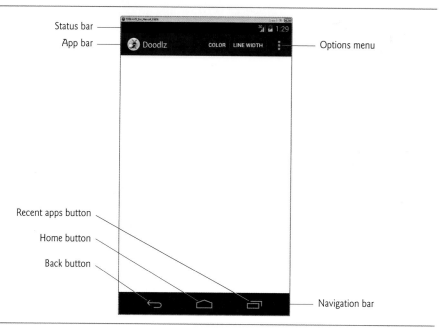

Fig. 1.20 | **Doodlz** app running in the Android Virtual Device (AVD).

7. *Exploring the AVD and immersive mode.* At the AVD screen's bottom are various **soft buttons** that appear on the device's touch screen. You touch these (by using the mouse in an AVD) to interact with apps and the Android OS. The *back button* goes back to the app's prior screen, or back to a prior app if you're in the current app's initial screen. The *home button* returns you to the device's home screen. The *recent apps button* allows you to view the recently used apps list, so that you can switch back to them quickly. At the screen's top is the app's *app bar*, which displays the app's icon and name and may contain other app-specific soft buttons—some appear on the app bar (**COLOR** and **LINE WIDTH** in Fig. 1.20) and the rest appear in the app's *options menu* (⋮). The number of options on the app bar depends on the size of the device—we discuss this in Chapter 7. Android 4.4 supports a new *immersive mode* that enables apps to use the entire screen. In this app, you can tap once in the white drawing area to hide the device's status and navigation bars as well as the app's action bar. You can redisplay these by tapping the drawing area again or by swiping from the top edge of the screen.

8. *Understanding the app's options.* To display the options that do not appear on the app bar, touch (i.e., click) the options menu (⋮) icon. Figure 1.21(a) shows the action bar and options menu on the Nexus 4 AVD and Fig. 1.21(b) shows them on a Nexus 7 AVD—options shown on the action bar appear in small capital letters. Touching **COLOR** displays a GUI for changing the line color. Touching **LINE WIDTH** displays a GUI for changing the thickness of the line that will be drawn. Touching **Eraser** sets the drawing color to white so that as you draw over colored areas, the color is erased. Touching **Clear** first confirms whether you wish to erase the entire image, then clears the drawing area if you do not cancel the action. Touching **Save Image** saves the image into the device's **Gallery** of images. On Android 4.4, touching **Print** displays a GUI for selecting an available printer so can print your image or save it as a PDF document (the default). You'll explore each of these options momentarily.

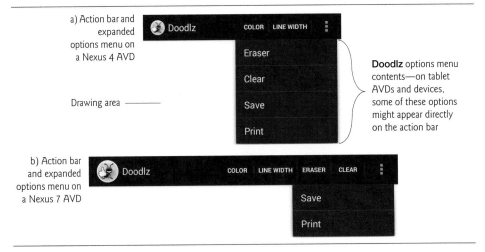

a) Action bar and expanded options menu on a Nexus 4 AVD

Drawing area

Doodlz options menu contents—on tablet AVDs and devices, some of these options might appear directly on the action bar

b) Action bar and expanded options menu on a Nexus 7 AVD

Fig. 1.21 | **Doodlz** options menu expanded.

9. *Changing the brush color to red.* To change the brush color, first touch **COLOR** on the action bar to display the **Choose Color** dialog (Fig. 1.22). Colors are defined using the *ARGB color scheme* in which the *alpha* (i.e., *transparency*), red, green and blue components are specified by integers in the range 0–255. For alpha, 0 means *completely transparent* and 255 means *completely opaque*. For red, green and blue, 0 means *none* of that color and 255 means the *maximum amount* of that color. The GUI consists of **Alpha**, **Red**, **Green** and **Blue** SeekBars that allow you to select the amount of alpha, red, green and blue in the drawing color. You drag the SeekBars to change the color. As you do, the app displays the new color below the SeekBars. Select a red color now by dragging the **Red** SeekBar to the right as in Fig. 1.22. Touch the **Set Color** button to return to the drawing area.

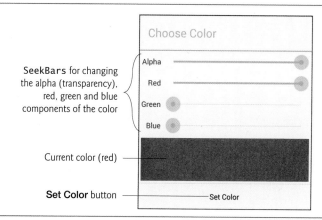

SeekBars for changing the alpha (transparency), red, green and blue components of the color

Current color (red)

Set Color button

Fig. 1.22 | Changing the drawing color to red.

10. *Changing the line width.* To change the line width, touch **LINE WIDTH** on the action bar to display the **Choose Line Width** dialog. Drag the SeekBar for the line width to the right to thicken the line (Fig. 1.23). Touch the **Set Line Width** button to return to the drawing area.

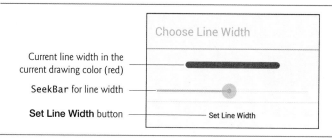

Current line width in the current drawing color (red)

SeekBar for line width

Set Line Width button

Fig. 1.23 | Changing the line thickness.

11. *Drawing the flower petals.* Tap the screen to enter immersive mode, then drag your "finger"—the mouse when using the emulator—on the drawing area to draw flower petals (Fig. 1.24).

Fig. 1.24 | Drawing flower petals.

12. ***Changing the brush color to dark green.*** Tap the screen to leave immersive mode then touch **COLOR** to display the **Choose Color** dialog. Select a dark green color by dragging the **Green** SeekBar to the right and ensuring that the **Red** and **Blue** SeekBars are at the far left (Fig. 1.25(a)).

a) Selecting dark green as the drawing color

b) Selecting a thicker line

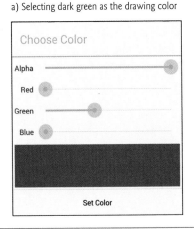

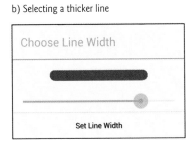

Fig. 1.25 | Changing the color to dark green and making the line thicker.

13. ***Changing the line width and drawing the stem and leaves.*** Touch **LINE WIDTH** to display the **Choose Line Width** dialog. Drag the SeekBar for the line width to the right to thicken the line (Fig. 1.25(b)). Tap the screen to re-enter immersive

mode, then draw the flower stem and leaves. Repeat Steps 12 and 13 for a lighter green color and thinner line, then draw the grass (Fig. 1.26).

Fig. 1.26 │ Drawing the stem and grass.

14. ***Finishing the drawing.*** Tap the screen to exit immersive mode. Next, change the drawing color to blue (Fig. 1.27(a)) and select a narrower line (Fig. 1.27(b)). Then tap the screen to enter immersive mode and draw the raindrops (Fig. 1.28).

a) Selecting blue as the drawing color

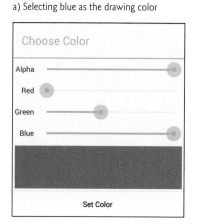

b) Selecting a thinner line

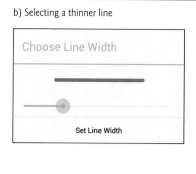

Fig. 1.27 │ Changing the line color to blue and narrowing the line.

Fig. 1.28 | Drawing the rain in the new line color and line width.

15. *Saving the image.* You can save your image to the device's **Gallery** app by selecting **Save** from the options menu ⋮. You can then view this image and others stored on the device by opening the **Gallery** app.

16. *Printing the image.* To print the image, select **Print** from the options menu. This displays the print dialog, which allows you to save the image as a PDF document by default. To select a printer, tap **Save as PDF** and select from the available printers. If no printers appear in the list, you may need to configure Google Cloud Print for your printer. For information on this, visit

```
http://www.google.com/cloudprint/learn/
```

17. *Returning to the home screen.* You can return to the AVD's home screen by tapping the home (⬛) button on the AVD. To view the drawing in the **Gallery** app touch ⊞ to display the list of apps installed on the AVD. You can then open the **Gallery** app to view the drawing.

1.9.2 Running the Doodlz App in a Tablet AVD

To test the app in a tablet AVD, first launch the AVD by performing Step 4 in Section 1.9.1, but select the Nexus 7 AVD rather than the Nexus 4 AVD. Next, right click the **Doodlz** project in Eclipse's **Package Explorer** window and select **Run As > Android Application**. If multiple AVDs are running when you launch an app, the **Android Device Chooser** dialog (Fig. 1.29) appears so that you can choose the AVD on which to install and execute the app. In this case, both the Nexus 4 and Nexus 7 AVDs were running on our system, so there were two Android virtual devices on which we could possibly run the app. Select the Nexus 7 AVD and click **OK**. This app runs in portrait orientation (the width is less than the height) on phone and small tablet devices. If you run the app on a large tablet AVD (or large tablet device) the app runs in landscape orientation (the width is greater than the height). Figure 1.30 shows the app running in the Nexus 7 AVD. If the AVD is too tall to display on your screen, you can change the AVD's orientation by typing *Ctrl + F12* (on a Mac use *fn + control + F12*). On some keyboards the *Ctrl* key is labeled *Control*.

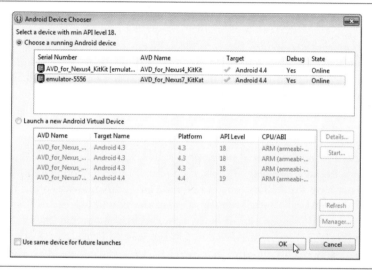

Fig. 1.29 | Android **Device Chooser** dialog.

Fig. 1.30 | Drawing in the Nexus 7 AVD.

1.9.3 Running the Doodlz App on an Android Device

If you have an Android device, you can easily execute an app on it for testing purposes.

1. *Enabling the developer options on the device.* First, you must enable debugging on the device. To do so, go to the device's **Settings** app, then select **About phone**, (or **About tablet**) locate the **Build number** (at the bottom of the list) and tap it repeatedly until you see the message **You are now a developer** on the screen. This will enable an entry named **Developer options** to the **Settings** app.

2. *Enabling debugging on the device.* Return to the **Settings** app, select **Developer options** and ensure that **USB debugging** is checked—this is the default when you first enable the developer options on the device.

3. *Connecting your device.* Next, connect the device to your computer via the USB cable that came with your device. If you're a Windows user, recall from the Before You Begin section that you might need to install a USB driver for your device. See the following two web pages for details:

```
developer.android.com/tools/device.html
developer.android.com/tools/extras/oem-usb.html
```

4. *Running Doodlz on the Android device.* In Eclipse, right click the **Doodlz** project in the **Package Explorer** window, then select **Run As > Android Application**. If you do not have any AVDs open, but do have an Android device connected, the IDE will automatically install the app on your device and execute it. If you have one or more AVDs open and/or devices connected, the **Android Device Chooser** dialog (Fig. 1.29) is displayed so that you can select the device or AVD on which to install and execute the app.

Preparing to Distribute Apps

When you build apps for distribution via app stores like Google Play, you should test the apps on as many actual devices as you can. Remember that some features can be tested *only* on actual devices. If you don't have many devices available to you, create AVDs that simulate the various devices on which you'd like your app to execute. When you configure each AVD to simulate a particular device, look up the device's specifications online and configure the AVD accordingly. In addition, you can modify the AVD's config.ini file as described in the section **Setting hardware emulation options** at

```
developer.android.com/tools/devices/
    managing-avds-cmdline.html#hardwareopts
```

This file contains options that are not configurable via the **Android Virtual Device Manager**. Modifying these options allows you to more precisely match the hardware configuration of an actual device.

1.10 Building Great Android Apps

With over 800,000 apps in Google Play,[9] how do you create an Android app that people will find, download, use and recommend to others? Consider what makes an app fun, useful, in-

---

9. http://www.pureoxygenmobile.com/how-many-apps-in-each-app-store/.

teresting, appealing and enduring. A clever app name, an attractive icon and an engaging description might lure people to your app on Google Play or one of the many other Android app marketplaces. But once users download the app, what will make them use it regularly and recommend it to others? Figure 1.31 shows some characteristics of great apps.

Characteristics of great apps

Great Games
- Entertaining and fun.
- Challenging.
- Progressive levels of difficulty.
- Show your scores and use leaderboards to record high scores.
- Provide audio and visual feedback.
- Offer single-player, multiplayer and networked versions.
- Have high-quality animations.
- Offloading input/output and compute-intensive code to separate threads of execution to improve interface responsiveness and app performance.
- Innovate with augmented reality technology—enhancing a real-world environment with virtual components; this is particularly popular with video-based apps.

Useful Utilities
- Provide useful functionality and accurate information.
- Increase personal and business productivity.
- Make tasks more convenient (e.g., maintaining a to-do list, managing expenses).
- Make the user better informed.
- Provide topical information (e.g., the latest stock prices, news, severe storm warnings, traffic updates).
- Use location-based services to provide local services (e.g., coupons for local businesses, best gas prices, food delivery).

General Characteristics
- Up-to-date with the latest Android features, but compatible with multiple Android versions to support the widest possible audience.
- Work properly.
- Bugs are fixed promptly.
- Follow standard Android app GUI conventions.
- Launch quickly.
- Are responsive.
- Don't require too much memory, bandwidth or battery power.
- Are novel and creative.
- Enduring—something that your users will use regularly.
- Use professional-quality icons that will appear in Google Play and on the user's device.

Fig. 1.31 | Characteristics of great apps. (Part 1 of 2.)

Characteristics of great apps

General Characteristics (cont.)

- Use quality graphics, images, animations, audio and video.
- Are intuitive and easy to use (don't require extensive help documentation).
- Accessible to people with disabilities (http://developer.android.com/guide/topics/ui/accessibility/index.html).
- Give users reasons and a means to tell others about your app (e.g., you can give users the option to post their game scores to Facebook or Twitter).
- Provide additional content for content-driven apps (e.g., game levels, articles, puzzles).
- Localized (Chapter 2) for each country in which the app is offered (e.g., translate the app's text and audio files, use different graphics based on the locale, etc.).
- Offer better performance, capabilities and ease-of-use than competitive apps.
- Take advantage of the device's built-in capabilities.
- Do not request excessive permissions.
- Are designed to run optimally across a broad variety of Android devices.
- Future-proofed for new hardware devices—specify the exact hardware features your app uses so Google Play can filter and display it in the store for only compatible devices (http://android-developers.blogspot.com/2010/06/future-proofing-your-app.html).

Fig. 1.31 | Characteristics of great apps. (Part 2 of 2.)

1.11 Android Development Resources

Figure 1.32 lists some of the key documentation from the Android Developer site. As you dive into Android app development, you may have questions about the tools, design issues, security and more. There are several Android developer newsgroups and forums where you can get the latest announcements or ask questions (Fig. 1.33). Figure 1.34 lists several websites where you'll find Android development tips, videos and resources.

Title	URL
App Components	http://developer.android.com/guide/components/index.html
Using the Android Emulator	http://developer.android.com/tools/devices/emulator.html
Package Index	http://developer.android.com/reference/packages.html
Class Index	http://developer.android.com/reference/classes.html
Android Design	http://developer.android.com/design/index.html
Data Backup	http://developer.android.com/guide/topics/data/backup.html
Security Tips	http://developer.android.com/training/articles/security-tips.html

Fig. 1.32 | Key online documentation for Android developers. (Part 1 of 2.)

Title	URL
Managing Projects from Eclipse with ADT	`http://developer.android.com/guide/developing/ projects/projects-eclipse.html`
Getting Started with Android Studio	`http://developer.android.com/sdk/installing/ studio.html`
Debugging	`http://developer.android.com/tools/debugging/index.html`
Tools Help	`http://developer.android.com/tools/help/index.html`
Performance Tips	`http://developer.android.com/training/articles/perf- tips.html`
Keeping Your App Responsive	`http://developer.android.com/training/ articles/perf-anr.html`
Launch Checklist (for Google Play)	`http://developer.android.com/distribute/googleplay/publish/ preparing.html`
Get Started with Publishing	`http://developer.android.com/distribute/googleplay/publish/ register.html`
Managing Your App's Memory	`http://developer.android.com/training/articles/memory.html`
Google Play Developer Distribution Agreement	`http://play.google.com/about/ developer-distribution-agreement.html`

Fig. 1.32 | Key online documentation for Android developers. (Part 2 of 2.)

Title	Subscribe	Description
Android Discuss	*Subscribe using Google Groups:* `android-discuss` *Subscribe via e-mail:* `android-discuss- subscribe@googlegroups.com`	A general Android discussion group where you can get answers to your app-development questions.
Stack Overflow	`http://stackoverflow.com/ questions/tagged/android`	Use this list for beginner-level Android app-development questions, including getting started with Java and Eclipse, and questions about best practices.
Android Developers	`http://groups.google.com/ forum/?fromgroups#!forum/ android-developers`	Experienced Android developers use this list for troubleshooting apps, GUI design issues, performance issues and more.
Android Forums	`http://www.androidforums.com`	Ask questions, share tips with other developers and find forums targeting specific Android devices.

Fig. 1.33 | Android newsgroups and forums.

Android development tips, videos and resources	URL
Sample Android apps from Google	http://code.google.com/p/apps-for-android/
O'Reilly article, "Ten Tips for Android Application Development"	http://answers.oreilly.com/topic/862-ten-tips-for-android-application-development/
Bright Hub™ website for Android programming tips and how-to guides	http://www.brighthub.com/mobile/google-android.aspx
The Android Developers Blog	http://android-developers.blogspot.com/
The Sprint® Application Developers Program	http://developer.sprint.com/site/global/develop/mobile_platforms/android/android.jsp
HTC's Developer Center for Android	http://www.htcdev.com/
The Motorola Android development site	http://developer.motorola.com/
Top Android Users on Stack Overflow	http://stackoverflow.com/tags/android/topusers
AndroidDev Weekly Newsletter	http://androiddevweekly.com/
Chet Haase's Codependent blog	http://graphics-geek.blogspot.com/
Cyril Mottier's Android blog	http://cyrilmottier.com/
Romain Guy's Android blog	http://www.curious-creature.org/category/android/
Android Developers Channel on YouTube®	http://www.youtube.com/user/androiddevelopers
Android Video Playlists	http://developer.android.com/develop/index.html
What's New in Android Developer Tools	http://www.youtube.com/watch?v=lmv1dTnhLH4
Google I/O 2013 Developer Conference session videos	http://developers.google.com/events/io/sessions

Fig. 1.34 | Android development tips, videos and resources.

1.12 Wrap-Up

This chapter presented a brief history of Android and discussed its functionality. We provided links to some of the key online documentation and to the newsgroups and forums you can use to connect with the developer community. We discussed features of the Android operating system and provided links to some popular free and fee-based apps on Google Play. We introduced the Java, Android and Google packages that enable you to use the hardware and software functionality you'll need to build a variety of Android apps. You'll use many of these packages in this book. We also discussed Java programming and the Android SDK. You learned the Android gestures and how to perform each on an Android device and on the emulator. We provided a quick refresher on basic object-technology concepts, including classes, objects, attributes and behaviors. You test-drove the **Doodlz** app on the Android emulator for both smartphone and tablet AVDs. In the next chapter, you'll build your first Android app using only visual programming techniques. The app will display text and two images. You'll also learn about Android accessibility and internationalization.

Welcome App

Dive-Into® the Android Developer Tools: Introducing Visual GUI Design, Layouts, Accessibility and Internationalization

Objectives

In this chapter you'll:

- Learn the basics of the Android Developer Tools (the Eclipse IDE and the ADT Plugin), which you'll use to write, test and debug your Android apps.

- Use the IDE to create a new app project.

- Design a graphical user interface (GUI) visually (without programming) using the IDE's **Graphical Layout** editor.

- Display text and two images in a GUI.

- Edit the properties of GUI components.

- Build and launch an app in the Android emulator.

- Make the app more accessible to visually impaired people by specifying strings for use with Android's TalkBack and Explore-by-Touch features.

- Support internationalization so your app can display strings localized in different languages.

Outline

2.1 Introduction

In this chapter, *without writing any code* you'll build the **Welcome** app that displays a welcome message and two images. You'll use the *Android Developer Tools IDE* to create an app that runs on Android phones. You'll see in later chapters that you can also create apps that run on tablets or on both phones and tablets. You'll create a simple Android app (Fig. 2.1) using the IDE's **Graphical Layout editor**, which allows you to build GUIs using *drag-and-*

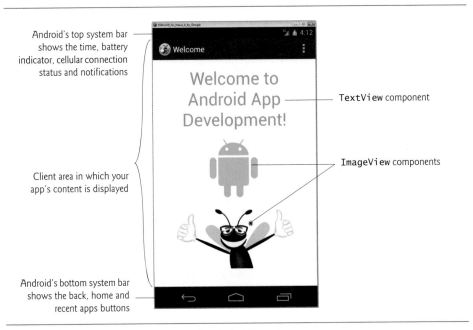

Android's top system bar shows the time, battery indicator, cellular connection status and notifications

TextView component

ImageView components

Client area in which your app's content is displayed

Android's bottom system bar shows the back, home and recent apps buttons

Fig. 2.1 | **Welcome** app running in the Android emulator.

drop techniques. You'll execute your app in the Android *emulator* (and on an Android phone, if you have one available). Finally, you'll learn how to make the app more *accessible* for people with disabilities and how to *internationalize* it to display strings *localized* in different languages. On the book's website—http://www.deitel.com/books/AndroidFP2—we provide an *Android Studio IDE* version of this chapter. This chapter assumes that you've read the Preface, Before You Begin and Section 1.9.

2.2 Technologies Overview

This section introduces the technologies you'll learn in this chapter.

2.2.1 Android Developer Tools IDE

This chapter introduces the *Android Developer Tools IDE*. You'll use it to create a new project (Section 2.3). As you'll see, the IDE creates a default GUI that contains the text "Hello world!" You'll then use the IDE's **Graphical Layout** editor and **Properties** window to visually build a simple graphical user interface (GUI) consisting of text and two images (Section 2.5).

2.2.2 TextViews and ImageViews

This app's text is displayed in a **TextView** and its pictures are displayed in **ImageViews**. The default GUI created for this app contains a TextView, which you'll modify by using the IDE's **Properties** window to configure various options, such as the TextView's text, font size and font color (Section 2.5.3). Next, you'll use the **Graphical Layout** editor's **Palette** of GUI controls to drag and drop ImageViews onto the GUI (Section 2.5.4).

2.2.3 App Resources

It's considered good practice to define all strings and numeric values in resource files that are placed in the subfolders of a project's res folder. You'll learn in Section 2.5.3 how to create resources for strings (such as the text on a TextView) and measurements (such as a font's size). You'll also learn how to use a built-in Android color resource to specify the TextView's font color.

2.2.4 Accessibility

Android contains many *accessibility* features to help people with various disabilities use their devices. For example, people with visual and physical disabilities can use Android's **TalkBack** to allow a device to speak screen text or text that you provide to help them understand the purpose and contents of a GUI component. Android's **Explore by Touch** enables the user to touch the screen to hear TalkBack speak what's on the screen near the touch. Section 2.7 shows how to enable these features and how to configure your app's GUI components for accessibility.

2.2.5 Internationalization

Android devices are used worldwide. To reach the largest possible audience with your apps, you should consider customizing them for various *locales* and spoken languages—this is known as **internationalization**. Section 2.8 shows how to provide Spanish text for the **Welcome** app's TextView and the ImageViews' accessibility strings, then shows how to test the app on an AVD configured for Spanish.

2.3 Creating an App

This book's examples were developed using the versions of the Android Developer Tools (version 22.x) and the Android SDK (versions 4.3 and 4.4) that were current at the time of this writing. We assume that you've read the Before You Begin section, and set up the Java SE Development Kit (JDK) and the Android Developer Tools IDE that you used in the test-drive in Section 1.9. This section shows you how to use the IDE to create a new project. We'll introduce additional features of the IDE throughout the book.

2.3.1 Launching the Android Developer Tools IDE

To launch the IDE, open the *Android SDK/ADT bundle* installation folder's `eclipse` sub-folder, then double click the Eclipse icon ({} or ●), depending on your platform). When you start the IDE for the first time, the **Welcome** page (shown originally in Fig. 1.13) is displayed. If it is not displayed, select **Help > Android IDE** to display it.

2.3.2 Creating a New Project

A **project** is a group of related files, such as code files and images that make up an app. To create an app, you must first create its project. To do so, click the **New Android Application...** button on the **Welcome** page to display the **New Android Application dialog** (Fig. 2.2). You can also do this by selecting **File > New > Android Application Project** or by clicking the **New** (□ ▼) toolbar button's drop-down list and selecting **Android Application Project**.

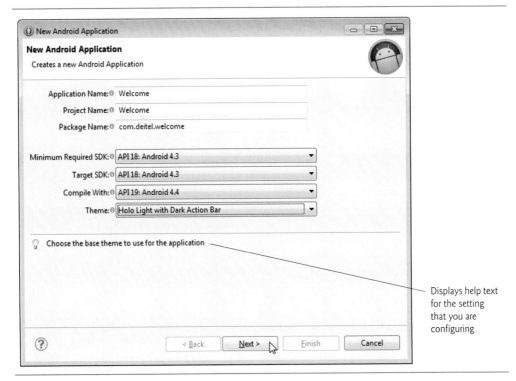

Fig. 2.2 | **New Android Application** dialog.

2.3.3 New Android Application Dialog

In the **New Android Application** dialog's first step (Fig. 2.2), specify the following information, then click **Next >**:

1. **Application Name:** field—Your app's name. Enter `Welcome` in this field.

2. **Project Name:** field—The project's name, which is displayed in the project's *root node* in the IDE's **Package Explorer** tab. By default, the IDE sets this to the app name *without spaces* and with each word capitalized—for an app named `Address Book`, the project name would be `AddressBook`. If you prefer to use a different name, enter it in the **Project name:** field.

3. **Package Name:** field—The Java package name for your app's source code. Android and the Google Play store use this as the app's *unique identifier*, which must remain the same through *all* versions of your app. The package name normally begins with your company's or institution's domain name *in reverse*—ours is `deitel.com`, so we begin our package names with `com.deitel`. Typically, this is followed by the app's name. By convention, package names use only lowercase letters. The IDE specifies a package name that begins with `com.example` by default—this is for learning purposes *only* and must be changed if you intend to distribute your app.

4. **Minimum Required SDK:** field—The *minimum Android API level* that's required to run your app. This allows your app to execute on devices at that API level and *higher*. We use the API level 18, which corresponds to Android 4.3—the lower of the two versions we use in this book. Figure 2.3 shows the Android SDK versions and API levels. Other versions of the SDK are now *deprecated* and should *not* be used. The percentage of Android devices running each platform version is shown at:

`http://developer.android.com/about/dashboards/index.html`

SDK version	API level	SDK version	API level	SDK version	API level
4.4	19	4.0.3–4.0.4	15	2.2	8
4.3	18	4.0.1	14	2.1	7
4.2.x	17	3.2	13	1.6	4
4.1.x	16	2.3.3–2.3.7	10		

Fig. 2.3 | Android SDK versions and API levels. (`http://developer.android.com/about/dashboards/index.html`)

5. **Target SDK:** field—The *preferred* API level. We use level 19 (Android 4.4) for this book's apps. At the time of this writing, 26% of Android devices still used level 10. When developing apps for distribution, you often want to target as many devices as possible. For example, to target devices with Android 2.3.3 and higher (98% of all Android devices), you'd set the **Minimum Required SDK** to 10. If it's set to an earlier API level than the **Target SDK**, *you must ensure either that your app does not use features from API levels above the **Minimum Required SDK** or that it can detect the API level on the device and adjust its functionality accordingly.* The *Android Lint* tool that the IDE runs in the background points out unsupported features that you use.

6. **Compile With:** field—The version of the API used when compiling your app. Normally this is the same as the **Target SDK**, but it could be an earlier version that supports all the APIs used in your app.

7. **Theme:** field—Your app's default Android *theme*, which gives the app a look-and-feel that's consistent with Android. There are three themes you can choose from— *Holo Light, Holo Dark* and *Holo Light with Dark Action Bars* (the default specified by the IDE). When designing a GUI, you can choose from many variations of the Holo Light and Holo Dark themes. For this chapter we'll use the default theme, and we'll discuss themes in more detail in subsequent chapters. For more information about each theme and to see sample screen captures, visit

```
http://developer.android.com/design/style/themes.html
```

2.3.4 Configure Project Step

In the **New Android Application** dialog's **Configure Project** step (Fig. 2.4), leave the default settings as shown and click **Next >**. These settings allow you in subsequent steps to specify your app's icon and configure your app's `Activity`—a class that controls the app's execution.

Fig. 2.4 | **New Android Application** dialog—**New Android Application** step 2.

2.3.5 Configure Launcher Icon Step

When your app is installed on a device, its icon and name appear with all other installed apps in the *launcher*, which you can access via the ⊞ icon on your device's home screen. Android runs on a wide variety of devices that have different screen sizes and resolutions.

To ensure that your images look good on all devices, you should provide several versions of each image your app uses. Android can automatically choose the correct image based on various specifications, such as the screen's resolution (width and height in pixels) or DPI (dots per inch). We discuss these mechanisms starting in Chapter 3. You can find more information about designing for varying screen sizes and resolutions at

> http://developer.android.com/training/multiscreen/index.html

and about icons in general at

> http://developer.android.com/design/style/iconography.html

The **Configure Launcher Icon** step (Fig. 2.5) enables you to configure the app's icon from an existing image, a piece of clip art or text. It takes what you specify and creates versions scaled to 48-by-48, 72-by-72, 96-by-96 and 144-by-144 to support various screen resolutions. For this app, we used an image named `DeitelOrange.png`. To use it, click **Browse...** to the right of the **Image File:** field, navigate to the `images` folder in the book's examples folder, select `DeitelOrange.png` and click **Open**. Previews of the scaled images are shown in the dialog's **Preview** area. These images will be placed into appropriate folders in the app's project. Images do not always scale well. For apps that you intend to place in the Google Play store, you might want to have an artist design icons for the appropriate resolutions. In Chapter 9, we discuss submitting apps to the Google Play store and list several companies that offer free and fee-based icon design services. Click **Next >** to continue to the **Create Activity** step.

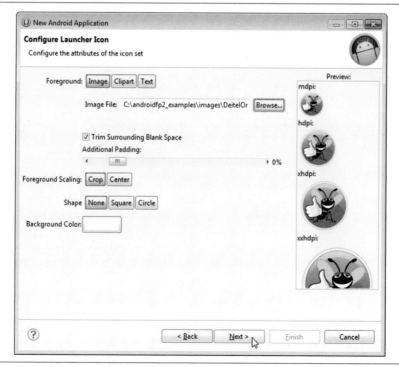

Fig. 2.5 | **New Android Application** dialog—**Configure Launcher Icon** step.

2.3.6 Create Activity Step

In the **Create Activity** step (Fig. 2.6), you select the template for your app's Activity. **Templates** save you time by providing preconfigured starting points for commonly used app designs. Figure 2.7 briefly describes the three templates shown in Fig. 2.6. For this app, select **Blank Activity**, then click **Next >**. We'll use the other templates in later chapters.

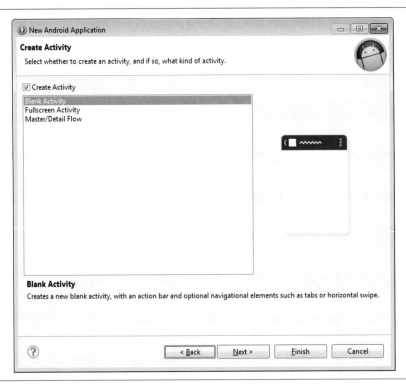

Fig. 2.6 | New Android Application dialog—**Create Activity** step.

Template	Description
Blank Activity	Used for a *single-screen app* in which you build most of the GUI yourself. Provides an *action bar* at the top of the app that displays the app's name and can display controls that enable a user to interact with the app.
Fullscreen Activity	Used for a *single-screen app* (similar to **Blank Activity**) that occupies the entire screen, but can toggle visibility of the device's status bar and the app's action bar.
Master/Detail Flow	Used for an app that displays a *master list* of items from which a user can choose one item to see its *details*—similar to the built-in **Email** and **People** apps. For tablets, the master list and details are shown side-by-side on the same screen. For phones, the master list is shown on one screen, and selecting an item displays the item's details in a separate screen.

Fig. 2.7 | Activity templates.

2.3.7 Blank Activity Step

This step depends on the template selected in the previous step. For the **Blank Activity** template, this step allows you to specify:

- **Activity Name**—MainActivity is the default name provided by the IDE. This is the name of a subclass of Activity that controls the app's execution. Starting in Chapter 3, we'll modify this class to implement an app's functionality.

- **Layout Name**—activity_main.xml is the default file name provided by the IDE. This file stores an XML representation of the app's GUI. In this chapter, you'll build the GUI (Section 2.5) using visual techniques.

- **Navigation Type**—None is the default specified by the IDE. The **Welcome** app does not provide any functionality. In an app that supports user interactions, you can select an appropriate **Navigation Type** to enable the user to browse through your app's content. We'll discuss navigation options in more detail in later apps.

Click **Finish** to create the project.

Fig. 2.8 | **New Android Application** dialog—**Blank Activity** step.

2.4 Android Developer Tools Window

When you finish creating the project, the IDE opens both `MainActivity.java` and `activity_main.xml`. Close `MainActivity.java` so that the IDE appears as shown in Fig. 2.9. The IDE shows the **Graphical Layout** editor so you can begin designing your app's GUI. In this chapter, we discuss only the IDE features we need to build the **Welcome** app. We'll introduce many more IDE features throughout the book.

Editor windows—like the **Graphical Layout**
editor for `activity_main.xml`—appear here

Package Explorer

Outline with the currently
selected item's **Properties**

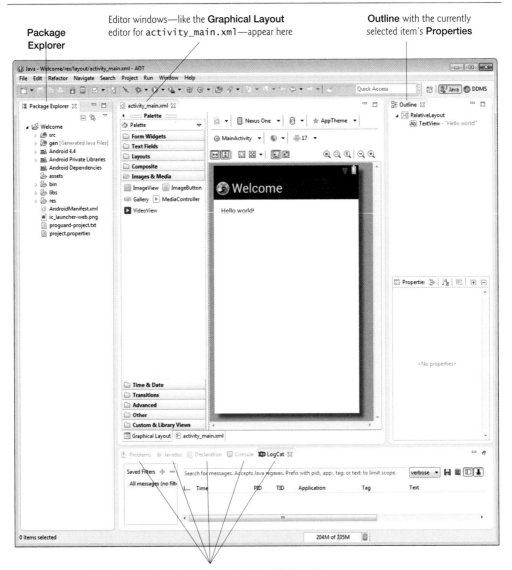

Tabbed interface to the **Problems**, **Javadoc**, **Declaration**,
Console and **LogCat** windows occupies the center column

Fig. 2.9 | `Welcome` project open in the Android Developer Tools.

2.4.1 Package Explorer Window

The **Package Explorer** window provides access to all of the project's files. Figure 2.10 shows the **Welcome** app project in the **Package Explorer** window. The **Welcome** node represents the project. You can have many projects open in the IDE at once—each will have its own *top-level node*. Within a project's node, the contents are organized into folders and files. In this chapter, you'll use only files located in the res folder, which we discuss in Section 2.4.4—we'll discuss the other folders as we use them in later chapters.

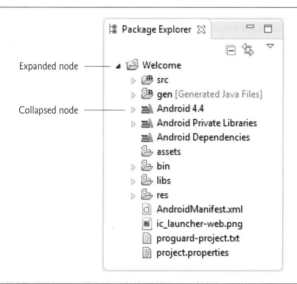

Fig. 2.10 | **Package Explorer** window.

2.4.2 Editor Windows

To the right of the **Package Explorer** in Fig. 2.9 is the **Graphical Layout** editor window. When you double click a file in the **Package Explorer**, its contents are displayed in an appropriate editor window, depending on the file's type. For a Java file, the Java source-code editor is displayed. For an XML file that represents a GUI (such as activity_main.xml), the **Graphical Layout** editor is displayed.

2.4.3 Outline Window

The **Outline** is displayed at the right side of the IDE (Fig. 2.9). This window shows information related to the file that's currently being edited. For a GUI, this window shows all the elements that compose the GUI. For a Java class, it shows the class's name and its methods and fields.

2.4.4 App Resource Files

Layout files like activity_main.xml (in the project's res/layout folder) are considered app *resources* and are stored in the project's **res** folder. Within that folder are subfolders for different resource types. The ones we use in this app are shown in Fig. 2.11, and the others (`menu`, `animator`, `anim`, `color`, `raw` and `xml`) are discussed as we need them through the book.

Resource subfolder	Description
`drawable`	Folder names that begin with `drawable` typically contain images. These folders may also contain XML files representing shapes and other types of drawables (such as the images that represent a button's *unpressed* and *pressed* states).
`layout`	Folder names that begin with `layout` contain XML files that describe GUIs, such as the `activity_main.xml` file.
`values`	Folder names that begin with `values` contain XML files that specify values for *arrays* (`arrays.xml`), *colors* (`colors.xml`), *dimensions* (`dimen.xml`; values such as widths, heights and font sizes), *strings* (`strings.xml`) and *styles* (`styles.xml`). These file names are used by convention but are *not* required—actually, you can place all resources of these types in *one* file. It's considered best practice to define the data from hard-coded arrays, colors, sizes, strings and styles as *resources* so they can be modified easily without changing the app's Java code. For example, if a *dimension resource* is referenced from many locations in your code, you can change the resource file once, rather than locating all occurrences of a hard-coded dimension value in your app's Java source files.

Fig. 2.11 | Subfolders of the project's `res` folder that are used in this chapter.

2.4.5 Graphical Layout Editor

When you first create a project, the IDE opens the app's `activity_main.xml` file in the **Graphical Layout** editor (Fig. 2.12). You can also double click the `activity_main.xml` file in your app's `res/layout` folder to open the **Graphical Layout** editor.

Selecting the Screen Type for GUI Design

Android devices can run on many types of devices. In this chapter, you'll design an Android phone GUI. As we mentioned in the Before You Begin section, we use an AVD that emulates the Google Nexus 4 phone for this purpose. The **Graphical Layout** editor comes with many device configurations that represent various screen sizes and resolutions that you can use to design your GUI. For this chapter, we use the predefined **Nexus 4**, which we selected in the screen-type drop-down list in Fig. 2.12. This does not mean that the app can execute only on a Nexus 4 device—it simply means that the design is for devices similar in screen size and resolution to the Nexus 4. In later chapters, you'll learn how to design your GUIs to scale appropriately for a wide range of devices.

2.4.6 The Default GUI

The default GUI (Fig. 2.12) for a **Blank Page** app consists of a `RelativeLayout` with a light-gray background (specified by the theme we chose when creating the project) and a `TextView` containing `"Hello world!"`. A **RelativeLayout** arranges GUI components *rel-*

The **Palette** contains **Widgets** (GUI components), **Layouts** and other items that can be dragged and dropped on the canvas

Screen-type drop-down list specifies devices to which you can target your GUI's design—select **Nexus 4** for this chapter

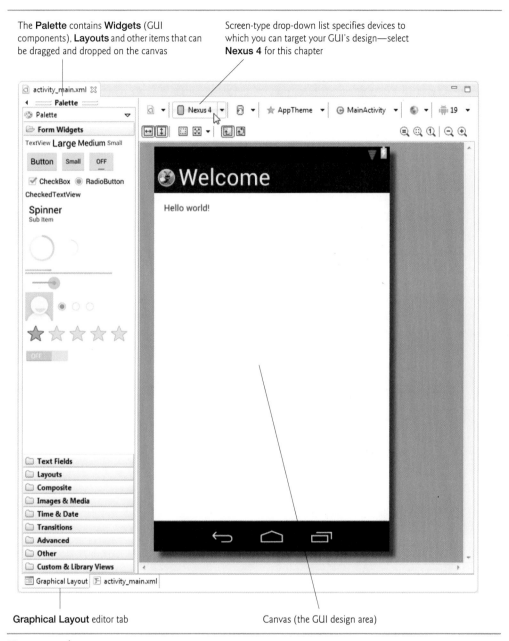

Graphical Layout editor tab

Canvas (the GUI design area)

Fig. 2.12 | **Graphical Layout** editor view of the app's default GUI.

ative to one another or *relative to the layout itself*—for example, you can specify that a GUI component should appear *below* another GUI component and *centered horizontally* within the RelativeLayout. A **TextView** displays text. We'll say more about each of these in Section 2.5.

2.5 Building the App's GUI with the Graphical Layout Editor

You'll now create the **Welcome** app's GUI. The IDE's **Graphical Layout** editor allows you to build your GUI by dragging and dropping GUI components—such as TextViews, ImageViews and Buttons—onto an app. By default, the GUI layout for a **Blank App** is stored in an XML file called **activity_main.xml**, located in the project's res folder in the layout subfolder. In this chapter, we'll use the **Graphical Layout** editor and the **Outline** window to build the app and will *not* study the generated XML. The Android development tools have improved to the point that, in most cases, you do not need to manipulate the XML markup directly.

2.5.1 Adding Images to the Project

For this app, you'll need to add the Deitel bug image (bug.png) and the Android logo image (android.png) to the project. These are located with the book's examples in the images folder's Welcome subfolder. *File names for image resources—and all the other resources you'll learn about in later chapters—must be in all lowercase letters.*

Because Android devices have various *screen sizes*, *resolutions* and *pixel densities* (that is, dots per inch or DPI), you typically provide images in varying resolutions that the operating system chooses based on a device's pixel density. For this reason your project's res folder contains several subfolders that begin with the name drawable. These folders store images with different pixel densities (Fig. 2.13).

Density	Description
drawable-ldpi	*Low density*—approximately 120 dots-per-inch.
drawable-mdpi	*Medium density*—approximately 160 dots-per-inch.
drawable-hdpi	*High density*—approximately 240 dots-per-inch.
drawable-xhdpi	*Extra high density*—approximately 320 dots-per-inch.
drawable-xxhdpi	*Extra Extra high density*—approximately 480 dots-per-inch.
drawable-xxxhdpi	*Extra Extra Extra high density*—approximately 640 dots-per-inch.

Fig. 2.13 | Android pixel densities.

Images for devices that are similar in pixel density to the Google Nexus 4 phone we use in our phone AVD are placed in the folder drawable-hdpi. Images for devices with higher pixel densities (such as those on some phones and tablets) are placed in the drawable-xhdpi or drawable-xxhdpi folders. Images for the medium- and low-density screens of older Android devices are placed in the folders drawable-mdpi and drawable-ldpi, respectively.

For this app, we're providing only one version of each image. If Android cannot find an image in the appropriate drawable folder, it will scale the version from another drawable folder up or down to different densities as necessary.

Look-and-Feel Observation 2.1

Low-resolution images do not scale well. For images to render nicely, a high-pixel-density device needs higher resolution images than a low-pixel-density device.

Look-and-Feel Observation 2.2

For detailed information on supporting multiple screens and screen sizes in Android, visit `http://developer.android.com/guide/practices/screens_support.html`.

Perform the following steps to add the images to this project:

1. In the **Package Explorer** window, expand the project's res folder.

2. Locate and open images folder's Welcome subfolder on your file system, then drag the images onto the res folder's drawable-hdpi subfolder. In the **File Operation** dialog that appears, ensure that **Copy Files** is selected, then click **OK**. In general, you should use PNG images, but JPG and GIF images are also supported.

These images can now be used in the app.

2.5.2 Changing the Id Property of the RelativeLayout and the TextView

When a GUI is displayed in the **Graphical Layout** editor, you can use the **Properties** window at the bottom of the **Outline** window to configure the selected layout's or component's properties without editing the XML directly. To select a layout or component, either click it in the **Graphical Layout** editor or select its node in the **Outline** window (Fig. 2.14).

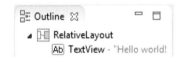

Fig. 2.14 | Hierarchical GUI view in the **Outline** window.

You should rename each layout and component with a relevant name, especially if the layout or component will be manipulated programmatically (as we'll do in later apps). Each object's name is specified via its **Id** property. You can use the **Id** to access and modify a component without knowing its exact location in the XML. As you'll see shortly, the **Id** can also be used to specify the *relative positioning* of components in a RelativeLayout.

Select the RelativeLayout, then at the top of the **Properties** window set its value to

```
@+id/welcomeRelativeLayout
```

The + in the syntax @+id indicates that a *new id* (that is, a variable name) should be created with the identifier to the right of the forward slash (/). Next, select the TextView and set its **Id** property to

```
@+id/welcomeTextView
```

The **Properties** window should now appear as in Fig. 2.15.

Fig. 2.15 | **Properties** window after changing the **Id** properties of the `RelativeLayout` and `TextView` in the app's default GUI.

2.5.3 Configuring the `TextView`

The **Welcome** app's default GUI already contains a `TextView`, so we'll simply modify its properties.

*Configuring the **TextView**'s Text Property Using a String Resource*
According to the Android documentation for application resources

```
http://developer.android.com/guide/topics/resources/index.html
```

it's considered a good practice to place strings, string arrays, images, colors, font sizes, dimensions and other app resources in XML file within the subfolders of the project's `res` folder, so that the resources can be managed separately from your app's Java code. This is known as *externalizing* the resources. For example, if you externalize color values, all components that use the same color can be updated to a new color simply by changing the color value in a central resource file.

If you wish to *localize* your app in several languages, storing the strings *separately* from the app's code allows you to change them easily. In your project's `res` folder, the subfolder `values` contains a `strings.xml` file that's used to store the app's default language strings—English for our apps. To provide localized strings for other languages, you can create separate `values` folders for each language, as we'll demonstrate in Section 2.8.

To set the `TextView`'s **Text property**, create a new string resource in the `strings.xml` file as follows:

1. Ensure that the `welcomeTextView` is selected.

2. Locate its **Text** property in the **Properties** window, then click the ellipsis button to the right of the property's value to display the **Resource Chooser** dialog.

3. In the **Resource Chooser** dialog, click the **New String...** button to display the **Create New Android String** dialog (Fig. 2.16).

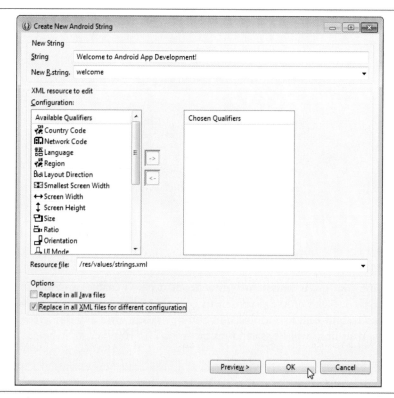

Fig. 2.16 | **Create New Android String** dialog.

4. Fill the **String** and **New R.string** fields as shown in Fig. 2.16, check the **Replace in all XML file for different configurations** checkbox then click **OK** to dismiss the dialog and return to the **Resource Chooser** dialog. The **String** field specifies the text that will be displayed in the TextView, and the **R.string** field specifies the string resource's name so that we can reference it in the TextView's **Text** property.

5. The new string resource named welcome is automatically selected. Click **OK** in the **Resource Chooser** dialog to use this resource.

In the **Properties** window, the **Text** property should now appear as in Fig. 2.17. The syntax @string indicates that a string resource will be selected from the strings.xml file (located in the project's res/values folder) and welcome indicates which string resource to select.

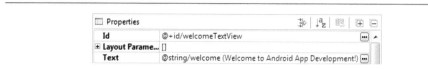

Fig. 2.17 | **Properties** window after changing the TextView's Text property.

Configuring the TextView's *Text Size Property—Scaled Pixels and Density-Independent Pixels*

The sizes of GUI components and text can be specified in various measurement units (Fig. 2.18). The documentation for supporting multiple screen sizes

```
http://developer.android.com/guide/practices/screens_support.html
```

recommends that you use *density-independent pixels* for the dimensions of GUI components and other screen elements, and *scale-independent pixels* for font sizes.

Unit	Description
px	pixel
dp or dip	density-independent pixel
sp	scale-independent pixel
in	inches
mm	millimeters

Fig. 2.18 | Measurement units.

Defining your GUIs with **density-independent pixels** enables the Android platform to *scale* the GUI, based on the pixel density of a given device's screen. One *density-independent pixel* is equivalent to one pixel on a 160-dpi screen. On a 240-dpi screen, each density-independent pixel will be scaled by a factor of 240/160 (i.e., 1.5). So, a component that's 100 *density-independent pixels* wide will be scaled to 150 *actual pixels* wide. On a screen with 120 dpi, each density-independent pixel is scaled by a factor of 120/160 (i.e., 0.75). So, the same component that's 100 density-independent pixels wide will be 75 actual pixels wide. *Scale-independent pixels* are scaled like density-independent pixels, and they're also scaled by the user's *preferred font size* (as specified in the device's settings).

You'll now increase the TextView's font size and add some padding above the Text-View to separate the text from the edge of the device's screen. To change the font size:

1. Ensure that the welcomeTextView is selected.

2. Locate its **Text Size property** in the **Properties** window, then click the ellipsis button to the right of the property's value to display the **Resource Chooser** dialog.

3. In the **Resource Chooser** dialog, click the **New Dimension...** button.

4. In the dialog that appears, specify welcome_textsize for the **Name** and 40sp for the **Value**, then click **OK** to dismiss the dialog and return to the **Resource Chooser** dialog. The letters sp in the value 40sp indicate that this is a *scale-independent pixel* measurement. The letters dp in a dimension value (e.g., 10dp) indicate a *density-independent pixel* measurement.

5. The new dimension resource named welcome_textsize is automatically selected. Click **OK** to use this resource.

Configuring Additional TextView *Properties*
Use the **Properties** window to specify the following additional TextView properties:

- Set its **Text Color property** to @android:color/holo_blue_dark. Android has various predefined color resources. When you type @android:color/ in the **Text Color** property's value field, a drop-down list of color resources appears (Fig. 2.19). Select @android:color/holo_blue_dark from that list to make the text bright blue.

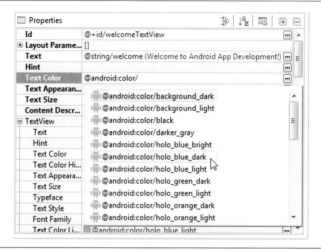

Fig. 2.19 | Setting a TextView's **Text Color** property to @android:color/holo_blue_dark.

- To center the text in the TextView if it wraps to multiple lines, set its **Gravity** property to center. To do so, click the **Value** field for this property, then click the ellipsis button to display the **Select Flag Values** dialog with the **Gravity** property's options (Fig. 2.20). Click the **center** checkbox, then click **OK** to set the value.

The **Graphical Layout** editor window should now appear as shown in Fig. 2.21.

Fig. 2.20 | Options for the **Gravity** property of an object.

Fig. 2.21 | GUI after completing the `TextView`'s configuration.

2.5.4 Adding `ImageViews` to Display the Images

Next, you'll add two `ImageViews` to the GUI to display the images you added to the project in Section 2.5.1. You'll do this by dragging the `ImageViews` from the **Palette**'s **Images & Media** section onto the GUI below the `TextView`. To do so, perform the following steps:

1. Expand the **Palette**'s **Images & Media** category, then drag an `ImageView` onto the canvas as shown in Fig. 2.22. The new `ImageView` appears below the `welcome-TextView` node. When you drag a component onto the canvas area, the **Graphical Layout** editor displays *green rule markers* and a tooltip appears. The rule markers help you position components in the GUI. The tooltip displays how the GUI component will be configured if you drop it at the current mouse position. The tooltip in Fig. 2.22 indicates that the `ImageView` will be *centered horizontally* in the parent layout (also indicated by the dashed rule marker that extends from the top to the bottom of the GUI) and will be placed below the `welcomeTextView` component (also indicated by the dashed rule marker with an arrowhead).

2. When you drop the `ImageView`, the **Resource Chooser** dialog (Fig. 2.23) appears so that you can choose the image resource to display. For every image you place in a `drawable` folder, the IDE generates a resource ID (i.e., a resource name) that you can use to reference that image in your GUI design and in code. The resource ID is the image's file name without the extension—for `android.png`, the resource ID is `android`. Select `android` and click **OK** to display the droid image. When you add a new component to the GUI, it's automatically selected and its properties are displayed in the **Properties** window.

Fig. 2.22 | Dragging and dropping an `ImageView` onto the GUI.

Fig. 2.23 | Selecting the `android` image resource from the **Resource Chooser** dialog.

3. The IDE sets the new ImageView's **Id** property to @+id/imageView1 by default. Change this to @+id/droidImageView. An **Update References?** dialog appears to confirm the *renaming* operation. Click **Yes**. Next, a **Rename Resource** dialog appears to show you all the changes that will be made. Click **OK** to complete the renaming operation.

4. Repeat Steps 1–3 above to create the bugImageView. For this component, drag the ImageView below the droidImageView, select the bug image resource from the **Resource Chooser** dialog and set the **Id** property to @+id/bugImageView in the **Properties** window, then save the file.

The GUI should now appear as shown in Fig. 2.24.

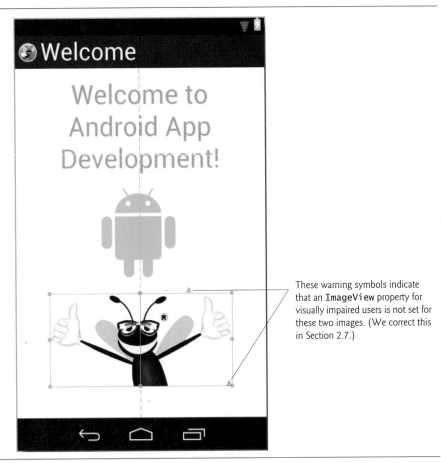

These warning symbols indicate that an ImageView property for visually impaired users is not set for these two images. (We correct this in Section 2.7.)

Fig. 2.24 | Completed GUI design.

2.6 Running the Welcome App

To run the app in an *Android Virtual Device (AVD)* for a phone, perform the steps shown in Section 1.9.1. Figure 2.25 shows the running app in the Nexus 4 AVD that you configured in the Before You Begin section. The app is shown in *portrait* orientation, where the device's height is greater than its width. Though you can rotate your device or AVD to *landscape orientation* (where the width is greater than the height), this app's GUI was not designed for that orientation. In the next chapter, you'll learn how to restrict an app's orientation and in subsequent chapters, you'll learn how to create more dynamic GUIs that can handle both orientations.

If you'd like, you can follow the steps in Section 1.9.3 to run the app on an Android device. Though this app will run on an Android tablet AVD or a tablet device, the app's GUI will occupy only a small part of a tablet's screen. Typically, for apps that run on both phones and tablets, you'll also provide a tablet layout that makes better use of the screen's available space, as we'll demonstrate in later chapters.

Fig. 2.25 | **Welcome** app running in an AVD.

2.7 Making Your App Accessible

Android contains *accessibility* features to help people with various disabilities use their devices. For people with visual disabilities, Android's **TalkBack** can speak screen text or text that you provide (when designing your GUI or programmatically) to help the user understand the purpose of a GUI component. Android also provides **Explore by Touch**, which enables the user to hear TalkBack speak what's on the screen where the user touches.

When TalkBack is enabled and the user touches an accessible GUI component, TalkBack speaks the component's accessibility text and vibrates the device to provide feedback to users who have trouble hearing. All standard Android GUI components support accessibility. For those that display text, TalkBack speaks that text by default—e.g., when the user touches a TextView, TalkBack speaks the TextView's text. You enable TalkBack in the **Settings** app under **Accessibility**. From that page, you can also enable other Android accessibility features such as a *larger default text size* and the ability to use *gestures that magnify areas of the screen*. Unfortunately, TalkBack is *not* currently supported in AVDs, so you must run this app on a device to hear TalkBack speak the text. When you enable TalkBack, Android gives you the option to step through a tutorial of how to use TalkBack with Explore by Touch.

Enabling TalkBack for the ImageViews
In the **Welcome** app, we don't need more descriptive text for the TextView, because TalkBack will read the TextView's content. For an ImageView, however, there is no text for TalkBack to speak unless you provide it. It's considered a best practice in Android to ensure that *every* GUI component can be used with TalkBack by providing text for the **Content Description property** of any component that does not display text. For that reason, the IDE actually warned us that something was wrong with our GUI by displaying small warning (⚠) icons in the **Graphical Layout** editor next to each ImageView. These warnings—which are generated by a tool in the IDE known as *Android Lint*—indicate that we did not set the **Content Description** property of each image. The text that you provide should help the user understand the purpose of the component. For an ImageView, the text should describe the image.

To add a **Content Description** for each ImageView (and eliminate the Android Lint warnings), perform the following steps:

1. Select the droidImageView in the **Graphical Layout** editor.
2. In the **Properties** window, click the ellipsis button to the right of the **Content Description** property to open the **Resource Chooser** dialog.
3. Click the **New String...** button to display the **Create New Android String** dialog.
4. In the **String** field specify "Android logo" and in the **R.string** field specify android_logo, then press **OK**.
5. The new android_logo string resource is selected in the **Resource Chooser** dialog, so click **OK** to specify that resource as the value for the droidImageView's **Content Description** property.
6. Repeat the preceding steps for the bugImageView, but in the **Create New Android String** dialog, specify "Deitel double-thumbs-up bug logo" for the **String** field and "deitel_logo" for the **R.string** field. Save the file.

As you set each ImageView's **Content Description**, the warning icon (⚠) for that ImageView in the **Graphical Layout** editor is removed.

Testing the App with TalkBack Enabled
Run this app on a device with TalkBack enabled, then touch the TextView and each ImageView to hear TalkBack speak the corresponding text.

Learning More About Accessibility
Some apps dynamically generate GUI components in response to user interactions. For such GUI components, you can programmatically set the accessibility text. The following

Android developer documentation pages provide more information about Android's accessibility features and a checklist to follow when developing accessible apps:

```
http://developer.android.com/design/patterns/accessibility.html
http://developer.android.com/guide/topics/ui/accessibility/index.html
http://developer.android.com/guide/topics/ui/accessibility/
   checklist.html
```

2.8 Internationalizing Your App

As you know, Android devices are used worldwide. To reach the largest possible audience, you should consider customizing your apps for various locales and spoken languages—this is known as **internationalization**. For example, if you intend to offer your app in France, you should translate its resources (e.g., text, audio files) into French. You might also choose to use different colors, graphics and sounds based on the *locale*. For each locale, you'll have a separate, customized set of resources. When the user launches the app, Android automatically finds and loads the resources that match the device's locale settings.

Localization

A key benefit of defining your string values as string resources (as we did in this app) is that you can easily *localize* your app by creating additional XML resource files for those string resources in other languages. In each file, you use the same string-resource names, but provide the *translated* string. Android can then choose the appropriate resource file based on the device user's preferred language.

Naming the Folders for Localized Resources

The XML resource files containing localized strings are placed in subfolders of the project's res folder. Android uses a special folder-naming scheme to automatically choose the correct localized resources—for example, the folder values-fr would contain a strings.xml file for French and the folder values-es would contain a strings.xml file for Spanish. You can also name these folders with region information—values-en-rUS would contain a strings.xml file for United States English and values-en-rGB would contain a strings.xml file for United Kingdom English. If localized resources are not provided for a given locale, Android uses the app's *default* resources—that is, those in the res folder's values subfolder. We discuss these *alternative-resource naming conventions* in more detail in later chapters.

Adding a Localization Folder to the App's Project

Before you can add a localized version of the **Welcome** app's strings.xml file that contains Spanish strings, you must add the values-es folder to the project. To do so:

1. In the IDE's **Package Explorer** window, right click the project's res folder and select **New > Folder** to display the **New Folder** dialog.

2. In the dialog's **Folder name:** field, enter values-es, then click **Finish**.

You'd repeat these steps with an appropriately named values-*locale* folder for each language you wish to support.

Copying the `strings.xml` File into the `values-es` Folder

Next, you'll copy the strings.xml file from the values folder into the values-es folder. To do so:

1. In the IDE's **Package Explorer** window, open the res folder's values subfolder, then right click the strings.xml file and select **Copy** to copy the file.

2. Next, right click the values-es folder, then select **Paste** to place the copy of strings.xml in the folder.

Localizing the Strings

In this app, the GUI contains one TextView that displays a string and two content-description strings for the ImageViews. All of these strings were defined as string resources in the strings.xml file. You can now translate the strings in the new version of the strings.xml file. App-development companies often have translators on staff or hire other companies to perform translations. In fact, in the Google Play Developer Console—which you use to publish your apps in the Google Play store—you can find translation-services companies. For more information on the Google Play Developer Console, see Chapter 9 and

```
developer.android.com/distribute/googleplay/publish/index.html
```

For this app, you'll replace the strings

```
"Welcome to Android App Development!"
"Android logo"
"Deitel double-thumbs-up bug logo"
```

with the Spanish strings

```
"¡Bienvenido al Desarrollo de App Android!"
"Logo de Android"
"El logo de Deitel que tiene el insecto con dedos pulgares
  hacia arriba"
```

To do so:

1. In the IDE's **Package Explorer** window, double click the strings.xml file in the values-es folder to display the **Android Resources** editor, then select the welcome string resource (Fig. 2.26).

2. In the **Value** field, replace the English string "Welcome to Android App Development!" with the Spanish string "¡Bienvenido al Desarrollo de App Android!". If you cannot type special Spanish characters and symbols on your keyboard, you can copy the Spanish strings from our res/values-es/strings.xml file in the final version of the **Welcome** app (located in the WelcomeInternationalized folder with the chapter's examples). To paste the Spanish string into the **Value** field, select the English string, then right click it and select **Paste**.

3. Next, select the android_logo resource and change its **Value** to "Logo de Android".

4. Finally, select the deitel_logo resource and change its **Value** to "El logo de Deitel que tiene el insecto con dedos pulgares hacia arriba".

5. Delete the app_name, action_settings and hello_world string resources by selecting one at a time and clicking the **Remove...** button. You'll be asked to confirm each delete operation. These three resources were placed in the default strings.xml file when you created the app's project. Only the app_name string resource is used in this project. We'll explain why we deleted it momentarily.

6. Save the strings.xml file by selecting **File > Save** or clicking the 🖫 toolbar icon.

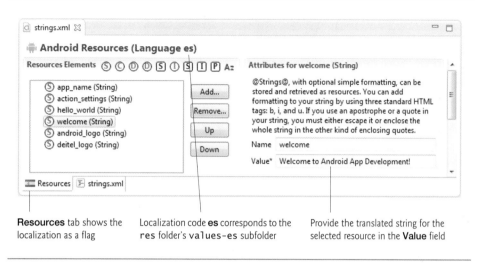

Resources tab shows the   Localization code **es** corresponds to the   Provide the translated string for the
localization as a flag   **res** folder's **values-es** subfolder   selected resource in the **Value** field

Fig. 2.26 | **Android Resources** editor with the welcome string resource selected.

Testing the App in Spanish
To test the app in Spanish, you must change the language settings in the Android emulator (or on your device). To do so:

1. Touch the home (⬛) icon on the emulator or on your device.

2. Touch the launcher (⬤) icon, then locate and touch the **Settings** app (⬛) icon.

3. In the **Settings** app, scroll to the **PERSONAL** section, then touch **Language & input**.

4. Touch **Language** (the first item in the list), then select **Español** (**España**) from the list of languages.

The emulator or device changes its language setting to Spanish and returns to the **Language & input** settings, which are now displayed in Spanish.

Next, run the **Welcome** app from the IDE, which installs and runs the internationalized version. Figure 2.27 shows the app running in Spanish. When the app begins executing, Android checks the AVD's (or device's) language settings, determines that the AVD (or device) is set to Spanish and uses the welcome, android_logo and deitel_logo string resources defined in res/values-es/strings.xml in the running app. Notice, however, that the app's name still appears in *English* in the action bar at the top of the app. This is because we did *not* provide a localized version of the app_name string resource in the res/values-es/strings.xml file. Recall that when Android cannot find a localized version of a string resource, it uses the default version in the res/values/strings.xml file.

   Common Programming Error 2.1
Modifying the names of resources can lead to runtime errors. Android uses the default resource names when loading localized resources. When you create a localized resource file, be sure to modify only the values of the resources, not their names.

Fig. 2.27 | **Welcome** app running in Spanish in the Nexus 4 AVD.

Returning the AVD (or Device) to English
To return your AVD (or Device) to English:

1. Touch the home (⬒) icon on the emulator or on your device.

2. Touch the launcher (⬤) icon, then locate and touch the **Settings** app (⬚) icon—the app is now called **Ajustes** in Spanish.

3. Touch the item **Idioma y entrada de texto** to access the language settings.

4. Touch the item **Idioma**, then in the list of languages select **English (United States)**.

TalkBack and Localization
TalkBack currently supports English, Spanish, Italian, French and German. If you run the **Welcome** app on a device with Spanish specified as the device's language and TalkBack enabled, TalkBack will speak the app's Spanish strings as you touch each GUI component.

When you first switch your device to Spanish and enable TalkBack, Android will automatically download the Spanish text-to-speech engine. If TalkBack does *not* speak the Spanish strings, then the Spanish text-to-speech engine has not finished downloading and installing yet. In this case, you should try executing the app again later.

Localization Checklist
For more information on localizing your app's resources, be sure to check out the Android *Localization Checklist* at:

```
developer.android.com/distribute/googleplay/publish/localizing.html
```

2.9 Wrap-Up

In this chapter, you used the Android Developer Tools IDE to build the **Welcome** app that displayed a welcome message and two images without writing any code. You created a simple GUI using the IDE's **Graphical Layout** editor and configured properties of GUI components using the **Properties** window.

The app displayed text in a TextView and pictures in ImageViews. You modified the TextView from the default GUI to display the app's text centered in the GUI, with a larger font size and in one of the standard theme colors. You also used the **Graphical Layout** editor's **Palette** of GUI controls to drag and drop ImageViews onto the GUI. Following best practices, you defined all strings and numeric values in resource files in the project's res folder.

You learned that Android has accessibility features to help people with various disabilities use their devices. We showed how to enable Android's TalkBack to allow a device to speak screen text or speak text that you provide to help the user understand the purpose and contents of a GUI component. We discussed Android's Explore by Touch feature, which enables the user to touch the screen to hear TalkBack speak what's on the screen near the touch. For the app's ImageViews, you provided content descriptions that could be used with TalkBack and Explore by Touch.

Finally, you learned how to use Android's internationalization features to reach the largest possible audience for your apps. You localized the **Welcome** app with Spanish strings for the TextView's text and the ImageViews' accessibility strings, then tested the app on an AVD configured for Spanish.

Android development is a combination of GUI design and Java coding. In the next chapter, you'll develop a simple **Tip Calculator** app by using the **Graphical Layout** editor to develop the GUI visually and Java programming to specify the app's behavior.

3

Tip Calculator App

Introducing GridLayout, LinearLayout, EditText, SeekBar, Event Handling, NumberFormat and Defining App Functionality with Java

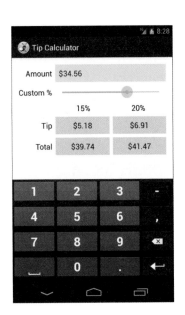

Objectives

In this chapter you'll:

- Design a GUI using LinearLayouts and a GridLayout.
- Use the IDE's **Outline** window to add GUI components to LinearLayouts and a GridLayout.
- Use TextView, EditText and SeekBar GUI components.
- Use Java object-oriented programming capabilities, including classes, objects, interfaces, anonymous inner classes and inheritance to add functionality to an Android app.
- Programmatically interact with GUI components to change the text that they display.
- Use event handling to respond to user interactions with an EditText and a SeekBar.
- Specify that the keypad should always be displayed when an app is executing.
- Specify that an app supports only portrait orientation.

3.1 Introduction

The **Tip Calculator** app (Fig. 3.1(a)) calculates and displays possible tips for a restaurant bill. As you enter each digit of a bill amount by touching the *numeric keypad*, the app calculates and displays the tip amount and total bill (bill amount + tip) for a 15% tip and a custom

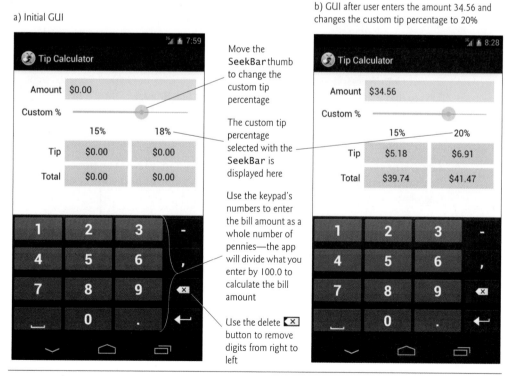

Fig. 3.1 | Entering the bill total and calculating the tip.

tip percentage (18% by default). You can specify a custom tip percentage from 0% to 30% by moving the SeekBar *thumb*—this updates the custom percentage shown and displays the custom tip and total (Fig. 3.1(b)). We chose 18% as the default custom percentage, because many restaurants in the United States add this tip percentage for parties of six people or more. The keypad in Fig. 3.1 may differ based on your AVD's or device's Android version, or based on whether you've installed and selected a custom keyboard on your device.

You'll begin by test-driving the app—you'll use it to calculate 15% and custom tips. Then we'll overview the technologies you'll use to create the app. You'll build the app's GUI using the Android Developer Tools IDE's **Graphical Layout** editor and the **Outline** window. Finally, we'll present the complete Java code for the app and do a detailed code walkthrough. We provide online an Android Studio version of Sections 3.2 and 3.4 at `http://www.deitel.com/books/AndroidFP2`.

3.2 Test-Driving the Tip Calculator App

Opening and Running the App
Open the Android Developer Tools IDE and import the **Tip Calculator** app project. Perform the following steps:

1. *Launching the Nexus 4 AVD.* For this test-drive, we'll use the Nexus 4 smartphone AVD that you configured in the Before You Begin section. To launch the Nexus 4 AVD, select **Window > Android Virtual Device Manager** to display the **Android Virtual Device Manager** dialog. Select the Nexus 4 AVD and click **Start...**, then click the **Launch** button in the **Launch Options** dialog that appears.

2. *Opening the Import Dialog.* Select **File > Import...** to open the **Import** dialog.

3. *Importing the Tip Calculator app's project.* Expand the **General** node, select **Existing Projects into Workspace**, then click **Next >** to proceed to the **Import Projects** step. Ensure that **Select root directory** is selected, then click **Browse....** In the **Browse For Folder** dialog, locate the `TipCalculator` folder in the book's examples folder, select it and click **OK**. Ensure that **Copy projects into workspace** is *not* selected. Click **Finish** to import the project. It now appears in the **Package Explorer** window.

4. *Launching the Tip Calculator app.* Right click the `TipCalculator` project in the **Package Explorer** window, then select **Run As > Android Application** to execute **Tip Calculator** in the AVD.

Entering a Bill Total
Using the numeric keypad, enter 34.56. Just type 3456—the app will position the cents to the right of the decimal point. If you make a mistake, press the delete ([✗]) button to erase one rightmost digit at a time. The TextViews under the **15%** and the custom tip percentage (**18%** by default) labels show the tip amount and the total bill for these tip percentages. All the **Tip** and **Total** TextViews update each time you enter or delete a digit.

Selecting a Custom Tip Percentage
Use the Seekbar to specify a *custom* tip percentage. Drag the Seekbar's *thumb* until the custom percentage reads **20%** (Fig. 3.1(b)). As you drag the thumb, the tip and total for this custom tip percentage update continuously. By default, the Seekbar allows you to select values from 0 to 100, but we specified a maximum value of 30 for this app.

3.3 Technologies Overview

This section introduces the IDE features and Android technologies you'll use to build the **Tip Calculator** app. We assume that you're *already* familiar with Java object-oriented programming. You'll:

- use various Android classes to create objects

- call methods on Android classes and objects

- define and call your own methods

- use inheritance to create a subclass of Android's Activity class that defines the **Tip Calculator**'s functionality

- use event handling, anonymous inner classes and interfaces to process the user's GUI interactions

3.3.1 Class Activity

Unlike many Java apps, Android apps *don't have a main method*. Instead, they have four types of executable components—*activities, services, content providers* and *broadcast receivers*. In this chapter, we'll discuss activities, which are defined as subclasses of **Activity** (package android.app). Users interact with an Activity through *views*—that is, GUI components. Before Android 3.0, a separate Activity was typically associated with each screen of an app. As you'll see, starting in Chapter 5, an Activity can manage multiple Fragments. On a phone, each Fragment typically occupies the entire screen and the Activity switches between the Fragments based on user interactions. On a tablet, activities often display multiple Fragments per screen to take better advantage of the larger screen size.

3.3.2 Activity Lifecycle Methods

Throughout its life, an Activity can be in one of several *states—active* (i.e., *running*), *paused* or *stopped*. The Activity transitions between these states in response to various *events*:

- An *active* Activity is *visible* on the screen and "has the focus"—that is, it's in the *foreground*. This is the Activity the user is interacting with.

- A *paused* Activity is *visible* on the screen but *does not* have the focus—such as when an alert dialog is displayed.

- A *stopped* activity is *not visible* on the screen and is likely to be killed by the system when its memory is needed. An Activity is *stopped* when another Activity becomes *active*.

As an Activity transitions among these states, the Android runtime calls various Activity *lifecycle methods*—all of which are defined in the Activity class

```
http://developer.android.com/reference/android/app/Activity.html
```

You'll override the **onCreate** method in *every* activity. This method is called by the Android runtime when an Activity is *starting*—that is, when its GUI is about to be displayed so that the user can interact with the Activity. Other lifecycle methods include onStart, onPause, onRestart, onResume, onStop and onDestroy. We'll discuss *most* of these in later chapters. Each activity lifecycle method you override *must* call the superclass's version; otherwise, an *exception* will occur. This is required because each lifecycle method in superclass `Activity` contains code that must execute in addition to the code you define in your overridden lifecycle methods.

3.3.3 Arranging Views with `LinearLayout` and `GridLayout`

Recall that layouts arrange views in a GUI. A **`LinearLayout`** (package **android.widget**) arranges views either *horizontally* (the default) or *vertically* and can size its views proportionally. We'll use this to arrange two `TextView`s horizontally and ensure that each uses half of the available horizontal space.

`GridLayout` (package android.widget) was introduced in Android 4.0 as a new layout for arranging views into cells in a rectangular grid. Cells can occupy *multiple* rows and columns, allowing for complex layouts. In many cases, `GridLayout` can be used to replace the older, and sometimes less efficient `TableLayout`, which arranges views into rows and columns where each row is typically defined as a `TableRow` and the number of columns is defined by the `TableRow` containing the most cells. Normally, `GridLayout` requires API level 14 or higher. However, the *Android Support Library* provides alternate versions of `GridLayout` and many other GUI features so that you can use them in older Android versions. For more information on this library and how to use it in your apps, visit:

```
http://developer.android.com/tools/support-library/index.html
```

A `GridLayout` *cannot* specify within a given row that the horizontal space should be allocated *proportionally* between multiple views. For this reason, several rows in this app's GUI will place two `TextView`s in a horizontal `LinearLayout`. This will enable you to place two `TextView`s in the same `GridLayout` cell and divide the cell's space evenly between them. We'll cover more layouts and views in later chapters—for a complete list, visit:

```
http://developer.android.com/reference/android/widget/
    package-summary.html
```

3.3.4 Creating and Customizing the GUI with the Graphical Layout Editor and the Outline and Properties Windows

You'll create `TextView`s, an `EditText` and a `SeekBar` using the IDE's **Graphical Layout** editor (that you used in Chapter 2) and **Outline** window, then customize them with the IDE's **Properties** window—which is displayed at the bottom of the **Outline** window when you're editing a GUI in the **Graphical Layout** editor. You'll do this *without* directly manipulating the XML stored in the files of the project's res folder.

An **`EditText`**—often called a *text box* or *text field* in other GUI technologies—is a *subclass* of `TextView` (presented in Chapter 2) that can display text *and* accept text input from the user. You'll specify an `EditText` for *numeric* input, allow users to enter only digits and restrict the *maximum* number of digits that can be entered.

A **`SeekBar`**—often called a *slider* in other GUI technologies—represents an integer in the range 0–100 by default and allows the user to select a number in that range by moving the `SeekBar`'s thumb. You'll customize the `SeekBar` so the user can choose a custom tip percentage *only* from the more limited range 0 to 30.

In the **Properties** window, a view's most commonly customized properties typically appear at the top with their names displayed in bold (Fig. 3.2). All of a view's properties are also organized into categories within the **Properties** window. For example, class Text-View inherits many properties from class View, so the **Properties** window displays a **Text-View** category with TextView-specific properties, followed by a **View** category with properties that are inherited from class View.

Fig. 3.2 | **Properties** window showing a TextView's most commonly customized properties.

3.3.5 Formatting Numbers as Locale-Specific Currency and Percentage Strings

You'll use class **NumberFormat** (package **java.text**) to create *locale-specific* currency and percentage strings—an important part of *internationalization*. You could also add *accessibility* strings and internationalize the app using the techniques you learned in Sections 2.7–2.8, though we did not do so in this app.

3.3.6 Implementing Interface TextWatcher for Handling EditText Text Changes

You'll use an *anonymous inner class* to implement the **TextWatcher** *interface* (from package **android.text**) to respond to *events when the user changes the text* in this app's EditText. In particular, you'll use method onTextChanged to display the currency-formatted bill amount and to calculate the tip and total as the user enters each digit.

3.3.7 Implementing Interface OnSeekBarChangeListener for Handling SeekBar Thumb Position Changes

You'll implement the SeekBar.OnSeekBarChangeListener interface (from package android.widget) to respond to the user moving the SeekBar's *thumb*. In particular, you'll use method `onProgressChanged` to display the custom tip percentage and to calculate the custom tip and total as the user moves the `SeekBar`'s thumb.

3.3.8 AndroidManifest.xml

The **AndroidManifest.xml** file is created by the IDE when you create a new app project. This file contains many of the settings that you specify in the **New Android Application** dialog, such as the app's name, package name, target and minimum SDKs, `Activity` name(s), theme and more. You'll use the IDE's **Android Manifest** editor to add a new setting to the manifest that forces the *soft keyboard* to remain on the screen. You'll also specify that the app supports only *portrait orientation*—that is, the device's longer side is vertical.

3.4 Building the App's GUI

In this section, we'll show the precise steps for building the **Tip Calculator**'s GUI. The GUI will not look like the one shown in Fig. 3.1 until you've completed the steps. As you procede through this section, the number of details presented may seem large, but they're repetitive and you'll get used to them as you use the IDE.

3.4.1 GridLayout Introduction

This app uses a **GridLayout** (Fig. 3.3) to arrange views into five *rows* and two *columns*. Each cell in a GridLayout can be *empty* or can hold one or more *views*, including layouts that *contain* other views. Views can span *multiple* rows or columns, though we did not use that capability in this GUI. You can specify a GridLayout's number of rows and columns in the **Properties** window.

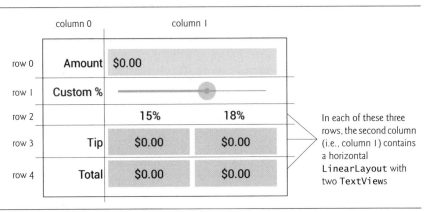

Fig. 3.3 | **Tip Calculator** GUI's GridLayout labeled by its rows and columns.

Each row's *height* is determined by the *tallest* view in that row. Similarly, the *width* of a column is defined by the *widest* view in that column. By default, views are added to a row from left to right. As you'll see, you can specify the exact row and column in which a view is to be placed. We'll discuss other GridLayout features as we present the GUI-building steps. To learn more about class GridLayout, visit:

`http://developer.android.com/reference/android/widget/GridLayout.html`

Id Property Values for This App's Views

Figure 3.4 shows the views' **Id** property values. For clarity, our naming convention is to use the view's class name in the view's **Id** property and Java variable name.

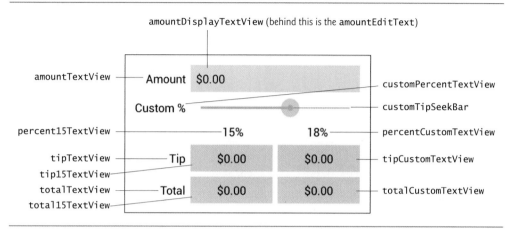

Fig. 3.4 | **Tip Calculator** GUI's components labeled with their **Id** property values.

In the right column of the first row, there are actually *two* components in the *same* grid cell—the amountDisplayTextView is *hiding* the amountEditText that receives the user input. As you'll soon see, we restrict the user's input to integer digits so that the user cannot enter invalid input. However, we want the user to see the bill amount as a *currency* value. As the user enters each digit, we divide the amount by 100.0 and display the currency-formatted result in the amountDisplayTextView. In the *U.S. locale*, if the user enters 3456, as each digit is entered the amountDisplayTextView will show the values $0.03, $0.34, $3.45 and $34.56, respectively.

LinearLayout Id Property Values

Figure 3.5 shows the **Id**s of the three horizontal LinearLayouts in the GridLayout's right column.

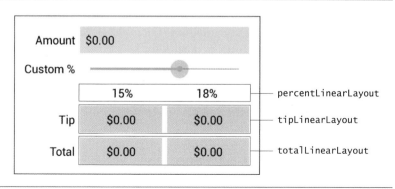

Fig. 3.5 | **Tip Calculator** GUI's LinearLayouts with their **Id** property values.

3.4.2 Creating the TipCalculator Project

The Android Developer Tools IDE allows only *one* project with a given name per workspace, so before you create the new project, delete the TipCalculator project that you testdrove in Section 3.2. To do so, right click it and select **Delete**. In the dialog that appears, ensure that **Delete project contents on disk** is *not* selected, then click **OK**. This removes the project from the workspace, but leaves the project's folder and files on disk in case you'd like to look at our original app again later.

Creating a New Blank App Project
Next, create a new **Android Application Project**. Specify the following values in the **New Android Project** dialog's first **New Android Application** step, then press **Next >**:

- **Application Name:** Tip Calculator

- **Project Name:** TipCalculator

- **Package Name:** com.deitel.tipcalculator

- **Minimum Required SDK:** API18: Android 4.3

- **Target SDK:** API19: Android 4.4

- **Compile With:** API19: Android 4.4

- **Theme:** Holo Light with Dark Action Bar

- **Create Activity:** TipCalculator

- **Build Target:** Ensure that **Android 4.3** is checked

In the **New Android Project** dialog's second **New Android Application** step, leave the default settings, then press **Next >**. In the **Configure Launcher Icon** step, click the **Browse...** button, select the DeitelGreen.png app icon image (provided in the images folder with the book's examples) and click the **Open** button, then press **Next >**. In the **Create Activity** step, select **Blank Activity** (keep the default activity name), then press **Next >**. In the **Blank Activity** step, leave the default settings, then press **Finish** to create the project. In the **Graphical Layout** editor, select **Nexus 4** from the screen-type drop-down list (as in Fig. 2.12). Once again, we'll use this device as the basis for our design.

3.4.3 Changing to a GridLayout

The default layout in a **Blank App**'s GUI is a RelativeLayout. Here, you'll change that to a GridLayout. First, right click the TextView in the **Outline** window, then select **Delete** to remove it from the GUI. Next, right click the RelativeLayout in the **Outline** window and select **Change Layout....** In the **Change Layout** dialog, select GridLayout and click **OK**. The IDE changes the layout and sets its **Id** to GridLayout1. We changed this to gridLayout using the **Id** field in the **Properties** window. By default, the GridLayout's **Orientation** property is set to horizontal, indicating that its contents will be laid out row-by-row.

Specifying Two Columns and Default Margins for the GridLayout
Recall that the GUI in Fig. 3.3 consists of two columns. To specify this, select gridLayout in the **Outline** window, then change its **Column Count** property to 2 (in the **Properties** window's **GridLayout** group). By default, there are *no margins*—spaces that separate views—

around a `GridLayout`'s cells. Set the `GridLayout`'s **Use Default Margins** property to `true` to indicate that the `GridLayout` should place margins around its cells. By default, the `Grid-Layout` uses the recommended gap between views (8dp), as specified at

```
http://developer.android.com/design/style/metrics-grids.html
```

3.4.4 Adding the `TextViews`, `EditText`, `SeekBar` and `LinearLayouts`

You'll now build the GUI in Fig. 3.3. You'll start with the basic layout and views in this section. In Section 3.4.5, you'll customize the views' properties to complete the design. As you add each view to the GUI, immediately set its **Id** property using the names in Figs. 3.4–3.5. You can change the selected view's **Id** via the **Properties** window or by right clicking the view (in the **Graphical Layout** editor or **Outline** window), selecting **Edit ID...** and changing the **Id** in the **Rename Resource** dialog that appears.

In the following steps, you'll use the **Outline** window to add views to the `GridLayout`. When working with layouts, it can be difficult to see the layout's *nested structure* and to place views in the correct locations by dragging them onto the **Graphical Layout** editor window. The **Outline** window makes these tasks easier because it shows the GUI's nested structure. Perform the following steps in the exact order specified—otherwise, the views will *not* appear in the correct order in each row. If this happens, you can reorder views by dragging them in the **Outline** window.

Step 1: Adding Views to the First Row

The first row consists of the `amountTextView` in the first column and the `amountEditText` behind the `amountDisplayTextView` in the second column. Each time you drop a view or layout onto the `gridLayout` in the **Outline** window, the view is placed in the layout's *next open cell*, unless you specify otherwise by setting the view's **Row** and **Column** properties. You'll do that in this step so that the `amountEditText` and `amountDisplayTextView` are placed in the same cell.

All of the `TextViews` in this app use the *medium*-sized font from the app's theme. The **Graphical Layout** editor's **Palette** provides *preconfigured* `TextViews` named **Large**, **Medium** and **Small** (in the **Form Widgets** section) to represent the theme's corresponding text sizes. In each case, the IDE configures the `TextView`'s **Text Appearance** property accordingly. Perform the following tasks to add the two `TextViews` and the `EditText`:

1. Drag a **Medium** `TextView` from the **Palette**'s **Form Widgets** section and drop it on the `gridLayout` in the **Outline** window. The IDE creates a new `TextView` named `textView1` and nests it in the `gridLayout` node. The default text `"Medium Text"` appears in the **Graphical Layout** editor. Change the `TextView`'s **Id** to `amountText-View`. You'll change its text in Step 6 (Section 3.4.5).

2. This app allows you to enter only *non-negative integers*, which the app divides by 100.0 to display the bill amount. The **Palette**'s **Text Fields** section provides many *preconfigured* `EditTexts` for various forms of input (e.g., numbers, times, dates, addresses and phone numbers). When the user interacts with an `EditText`, an appropriate keyboard is displayed based on the `EditText`'s *input type*. When you hover over an `EditText` in the **Palette**, a *tooltip* indicates the input type. From the **Palette**'s **Text Fields** section, drag a **Number** `EditText` (displayed with the number **42** on it) and drop it on the `gridLayout` node in the **Outline** window. Change the

EditText's **Id** to amountEditText. The EditText is placed in the *second* column of the GridLayout's *first* row.

3. Drag another **Medium** TextView onto the gridLayout node in the **Outline** window and change the **Id** to amountDisplayTextView. The new TextView is initially placed in the *first* column of the GridLayout's *second* row. To place it in the *second* column of the GridLayout's *first* row, set this TextView's **Row** and **Column** properties (located in the **Properties** window's **Layout Parameters** section) to the values 0 and 1, respectively.

Step 2: Adding Views to the Second Row

Next, you'll add a TextView and SeekBar to the GridLayout. To do so:

1. Drag a **Medium** TextView (customPercentTextView) from the **Palette**'s **Form Widgets** section onto the gridLayout node in the **Outline** window.

2. Drag a SeekBar (customTipSeekBar) from the **Palette**'s **Form Widgets** section onto the gridLayout node in the **Outline** window.

Step 3: Adding Views to the Third Row

Next, you'll add a LinearLayout containing two TextViews to the GridLayout. To do so:

1. From the **Palette**'s **Layouts** section, drag a **Linear Layout (Horizontal)** (percentLinearLayout) onto the gridLayout node in the **Outline** window.

2. Drag a **Medium** TextView (percent15TextView) onto the percentLinearLayout node in the **Outline** window. This nests the new TextView in the LinearLayout.

3. Drag another **Medium** TextView (percentCustomTextView) onto the percentLinearLayout node in the **Outline** window.

4. The percentLinearLayout and its two nested TextViews should be placed in the second column of the GridLayout. To do so, select the percentLinearLayout in the **Outline** window, then set its **Column** property to 1.

Step 4: Adding Views to the Fourth Row

Next, you'll add a TextView and a LinearLayout containing two more TextViews to the GridLayout. To do so:

1. Drag a **Medium** TextView (tipTextView) onto the gridLayout node.

2. Drag a **Linear Layout (Horizontal)** (tipLinearLayout) onto the gridLayout node.

3. Drag two **Medium** TextViews (tip15TextView and tipCustomTextView) onto the tipLinearLayout node.

Step 5: Adding Views to the Fifth Row

To create the last row of the GUI, repeat Step 4, using the **Id**s totalTextView, totalLinearLayout, total15TextView and totalCustomTextView.

Reviewing the Layout So Far

The GUI and **Outline** window should now appear as shown in Fig. 3.6. The warning symbols shown in the **Graphical Layout** editor and the **Outline** window will go away as you complete the GUI design in Section 3.4.5.

a) GUI design so far

b) Outline window showing **Tip Calculator** components

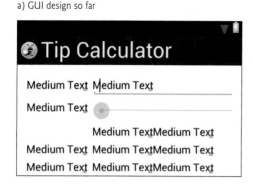

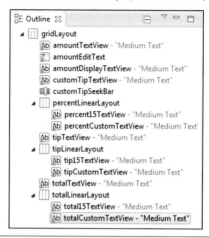

Fig. 3.6 | The GUI and the IDE's **Outline** window after adding all the views to the GridLayout.

3.4.5 Customizing the Views to Complete the Design

You'll now complete the app's design by customizing the views' properties and creating several string and dimension resources. As you learned in Section 2.5, literal string values should be placed in the strings.xml resource file. Similarly, literal numeric values that specify view dimensions (e.g., widths, heights and spacing) should be placed in the dimens.xml resource file.

Step 6: Specifying Literal Text
Specify the literal text for the amountTextView, customPercentTextView, percent-15TextView, percentCustomTextView, tipTextView and totalTextView:

1. Select the amountTextView in the **Outline** window.

2. In the **Properties** window, click the ellipsis button next to the **Text** property.

3. In the **Resource Chooser Dialog**, click **New String...**.

4. In the **Create New Android String** dialog, specify Amount in the **String** field and amount in the **New R.string** field, then click **OK**.

5. In the **Resource Chooser** dialog, click **OK** to set the amountTextView's **Text** property to the string resource identified as amount.

Repeat the preceding tasks for the other TextViews using the values shown in Fig. 3.7.

View	String	New R.string
customPercentTextView	Custom %	custom_tip_percentage
percent15TextView	15%	fifteen_percent

Fig. 3.7 | String resource values and resource IDs. (Part 1 of 2.)

View	String	New R.string
percentCustomTextView	18%	eighteen_percent
tipTextView	Tip	tip
totalTextView	Total	total

Fig. 3.7 | String resource values and resource IDs. (Part 2 of 2.)

Step 7: Right Aligning the TextViews in the Left Column

In Fig. 3.3, each of the left column's TextViews is right aligned. For the amountTextView, customPercentTextView, tipTextView and totalTextView, set the layout **Gravity** property to right—located in the **Layout Parameters** section in the **Properties** window.

Step 8: Configuring the amountTextView's Label For Property

Generally, each EditText should have a descriptive TextView that helps the user understand the EditText's purpose (also helpful for accessibility)—otherwise, *Android Lint* issues a warning. To fix this, you set the TextView's **Label For** property to the **Id** of the associated EditText. Select the amountTextView and set its **Label For** property (in the **Properties** window's **View** section) to

```
@+id/amountEditText
```

The + is required because the TextView is defined *before* the EditText in the GUI, so the EditText does not yet exist when Android converts the layout's XML into the GUI.

Step 9: Configuring the amountEditText

In the final app, the amountEditText is *hidden* behind the amountDisplayTextView and is configured to allow only *digits* to be entered by the user. Select the amountEditText and set the following properties:

1. In the **Properties** window's **Layout Parameters** section, set the **Width** and **Height** to wrap_content. This indicates that the EditText should be just large enough to fit its content, including any padding.

2. Remove the layout **Gravity** value fill_horizontal, leaving the property's value blank. We'll discuss fill_horizontal in the next step.

3. Remove the **Ems** property's value, which indicates the EditText's width, measured in uppercase M characters of the view's font. In our GridLayout, this causes the second column to be too narrow, so we removed this default setting.

4. In the **Properties** window's **TextView** section, set **Digits** to 0123456789—this allows *only* digits to be entered, even though the numeric keypad contains minus (-), comma (,), period (.) and space buttons. By default, the **Digits** property is *not* displayed in the **Properties** window, because it's considered to be an advanced property. To display it, click the **Show Advanced Properties** (🔲) toggle button at the top of the **Properties** window.

5. We restricted the bill amount to a maximum of *six* digits—so the largest supported bill amount is 9999.99. In the **Properties** window's **TextView** section, set the **Max Length** property to 6.

Step 10: Configuring the `amountDisplayTextView`

To complete the formatting of the `amountDisplayTextView`, select it and set the following properties:

1. In the **Properties** window's **Layout Parameters** section, set the **Width** and **Height** to `wrap_content` to indicate that the `TextView` should be large enough to fit its content.

2. Remove the **Text** property's value—we'll programmatically display text here.

3. In the **Properties** window's **Layout Parameters** section, set the layout **Gravity** to `fill_horizontal`. This indicates that the `TextView` should occupy all remaining horizontal space in this `GridLayout` row.

4. In the **View** section, set the **Background** to `@android:color/holo_blue_bright`. This is one of several *predefined colors* (each starts with `@android:color`) in Android's *Holo* theme. As you start typing the **Background** property's value, a dropdown list of the theme's available colors is displayed. You can also use any *custom color* created from a combination of red, green and blue components called **RGB values**—each is an integer in the range 0–255 that defines the amount of red, green and blue in the color, respectively. Custom colors are defined in *hexadecimal (base 16) format*, so the RGB components are values in the range 00–FF. Android also supports *alpha (transparency)* values in the range 0 (*completely transparent*) to 255 (*completely opaque*). To use alpha, you specify the color in the format `#AARRGGBB`, where the first two hexadecimal digits represent the alpha value. If both digits of each color component are the same, you can use the abbreviated formats `#RGB` or `#ARGB`. For example, `#9AC` is treated as `#99AACC` and `#F9AC` is treated as `#FF99AACC`.

5. Finally, you'll add some padding around the `TextView`. To do so, you'll create a new *dimension resource* named `textview_padding`, which you'll use several times in the GUI. A view's **Padding** property specifies space on all sides of the views's content. In the **Properties** window's **View** section, click the **Padding** property's ellipsis button. Click **New Dimension...** to create a new *dimension resource*. Specify `textview_padding` for the **Name** and `8dp` for the **Value** and click **OK**, then select your new *dimension resource* and click **OK**.

Step 11: Configuring the `customPercentTextView`

Notice that the `customPercentTextView` is aligned with the top of the `customTipSeekBar`'s thumb. This looks better if it's *vertically centered*. To do this, in the **Properties** window's **Layout Parameters** section, modify the **Gravity** value from `right` to

```
right|center_vertical
```

The *vertical bar* (`|`) character is used to separate *multiple* **Gravity** values—in this case indicating that the `TextView` should be *right aligned* and *centered vertically* within the grid cell. Also set the `customPercentTextView`'s **Width** and **Height** properties to `wrap_content`.

Step 12: Configuring the `customTipSeekBar`

By default, a `SeekBar`'s range is 0 to 100 and its current value is indicated by its **Progress** property. This app allows custom tip percentages from 0 to 30 and specifies a default of 18. Set the `SeekBar`'s **Max** property to 30 and the **Progress** property to 18. Also, set the **Width** and **Height** to `wrap_content`.

*Step 13: Configuring the **percent15TextView** and **percentCustomTextView***
Recall that GridLayout does *not* allow you to specify how a view should be sized relative to other views in a given row. This is why we placed the percent15TextView and percent-CustomTextView in a LinearLayout, which *does* allow *proportional sizing*. A view's layout **Weight** (in certain layouts, such as LinearLayout) specifies the view's relative importance with respect to other views in the layout. By default, all views have a **Weight** of 0.

In this layout, we set **Weight** to 1 for percent15TextView and percentCustomText-View—this indicates that they have equal importance, so they should be sized equally. By default, when we added the percentLinearLayout to the GridLayout, its layout **Gravity** property was set to fill_horizontal, so the layout occupies the remaining space in the third row. When the LinearLayout is stretched to fill the rest of the row, the TextViews each occupy *half* of the LinearLayout's width.

We also wanted each TextView to center its text. To do this, in the **Properties** window's **TextView** section, set the **Gravity** property to center. This specifies the Text-View's text alignment, whereas the *layout* **Gravity** property specifies how a view aligns with respect to the layout.

*Step 14: Configuring the **tip15TextView**, **tipCustomTextView**, **total15TextView** and **totalCustomTextView***
To finalize these four TextViews, perform the following tasks on each:

1. Select the TextView.
2. Delete its **Text** value—we'll set this programmatically.
3. Set the **Background** to @android:color/holo_orange_light.
4. Set the layout **Gravity** to center.
5. Set the layout **Weight** to 1.
6. Set the layout **Width** to 0dp—this allows the layout to use the **Weight** to determine the view's width.
7. Set the TextView **Gravity** to center.
8. Set the TextView **Padding** to @dimen/textview_padding (the *dimension resource* you created in a previous step).

Notice that there's *no horizontal space* between the TextViews in the tipLinearLayout and totalLinearLayout. To fix this, you'll specify an 8dp right margin for the tip15TextView and total15TextView. In the **Properties** window's **Layout Parameters** section, expand the **Margin** section, then set the **Right** margin to 8dp by creating a new *dimension resource* named textview_margin. Next, use this resource to set the total15TextView's **Right** margin.

*Step 15: Vertically Centering the **tipTextView** and **totalTextView***
To vertically center the tipTextView and totalTextView with the other views in their respective rows, modify their layout **Gravity** properties from right to

```
    right|center_vertical
```

When you do this for the totalTextView, the GridLayout centers this component vertically in the *remaining space from the fifth row to the bottom of the screen*. To fix this problem, drag a **Space** view (in the **Palette**'s **Layout** section) onto the gridLayout node in the **Outline** window. This creates a sixth row that occupies the rest of the screen. As its name implies, a **Space** view occupies space in a GUI. The GUI should now appear as in Fig. 3.8.

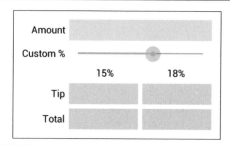

Fig. 3.8 | Final GUI design.

3.5 Adding Functionality to the App

Class MainActivity (Figs. 3.9–3.16) implements the **Tip Calculator** app's functionality. It calculates the 15% and custom percentage tips and total bill amounts, and displays them in locale-specific currency format. To view the file, open src/com.deitel/tipcalculator and double clck MainActivity.java. You'll need to enter most of the code in Figs. 3.9–3.16.

The package and import Statements
Figure 3.9 shows the package statement and import statements in MainActivity.java. The package statement in line 3 was inserted when you created the project. When you open a Java file in the IDE, the import statements are collapsed—one is displayed with a ⊕ to its left. You can click the ⊕ to see the complete list of import statements.

```
1   // MainActivity.java
2   // Calculates bills using 15% and custom percentage tips.
3   package com.deitel.tipcalculator;
4
5   import java.text.NumberFormat; // for currency formatting
6
7   import android.app.Activity; // base class for activities
8   import android.os.Bundle; // for saving state information
9   import android.text.Editable; // for EditText event handling
10  import android.text.TextWatcher; // EditText listener
11  import android.widget.EditText; // for bill amount input
12  import android.widget.SeekBar; // for changing custom tip percentage
13  import android.widget.SeekBar.OnSeekBarChangeListener; // SeekBar listener
14  import android.widget.TextView; // for displaying text
15
```

Fig. 3.9 | MainActivity's package and import statements.

Lines 5–14 import the classes and interfaces the app uses:

- Class NumberFormat of package java.text (line 5) provides numeric formatting capabilities, such as *locale-specific* currency and percentage formats.

- Class `Activity` of package `android.app` (line 7) provides the basic *lifecycle methods* of an app—we'll discuss these shortly.

- Class `Bundle` of package `android.os` (line 8) represents an app's *state information.* Android gives an app the opportunity to *save its state* before another app appears on the screen. This might occur, for example, when the user *launches another app* or *receives a phone call.* The app that's currently on the screen at a given time is in the *foreground* (the user can interact with it, and the app consumes the CPU) and all other apps are in the *background* (the user cannot interact with them, and they're typically not consuming the CPU). When another app comes into the foreground, the app that was previously in the foreground is given the opportunity to *save its state* as it's sent to the background.

- Interface `Editable` of package `android.text` (line 9) allows you to modify the content and markup of text in a GUI.

- You implement interface `TextWatcher` of package `android.text` (line 10) to respond to events when the user changes the text in an `EditText`.

- Package `android.widget` (lines 11–14) contains the *widgets* (i.e., views) and layouts that are used in Android GUIs. This app uses `EditText` (line 11), `SeekBar` (line 12) and `TextView` (line 14) widgets.

- You implement interface `SeekBar.OnSeekBarChangeListener` of package `android.widget` (line 13) to respond to the user moving the `SeekBar`'s *thumb.*

As you write code with various classes and interfaces, you can use the IDE's **Source > Organize Imports** command to let the IDE insert the `import` statements for you. For cases in which the same class or interface name appears in more than one package, the IDE will let you select the appropriate `import` statement.

Tip Calculator App `Activity` and the Activity Lifecycle

Class `MainActivity` (Figs. 3.10–3.16) is the **Tip Calculator** app's `Activity` subclass. When you created the `TipCalculator` project, the IDE generated this class as a subclass of `Activity` and provided an override of class `Activity`'s inherited `onCreate` method (Fig. 3.11). Every `Activity` subclass *must* override this method. The default code for class `MainActivity` also included an `onCreateOptionsMenu` method, which we removed because it's not used in this app. We'll discuss `onCreate` shortly.

```
16   // MainActivity class for the Tip Calculator app
17   public class MainActivity extends Activity
18   {
```

Fig. 3.10 | Class `MainActivity` is a subclass of `Activity`.

Class Variables and Instance Variables

Lines 20–32 of Fig. 3.11 declare class `MainActivity`'s variables. The `NumberFormat` objects (lines 20–23) are used to format currency values and percentages, respectively. `NumberFormat` static method `getCurrencyInstance` returns a `NumberFormat` object that formats values as currency using the device's *default locale.* Similarly, `static` method `getPercentInstance` formats values as percentages using the device's *default locale.*

```
19    // currency and percent formatters
20    private static final NumberFormat currencyFormat =
21       NumberFormat.getCurrencyInstance();
22    private static final NumberFormat percentFormat =
23       NumberFormat.getPercentInstance();
24
25    private double billAmount = 0.0; // bill amount entered by the user
26    private double customPercent = 0.18; // initial custom tip percentage
27    private TextView amountDisplayTextView; // shows formatted bill amount
28    private TextView percentCustomTextView; // shows custom tip percentage
29    private TextView tip15TextView; // shows 15% tip
30    private TextView total15TextView; // shows total with 15% tip
31    private TextView tipCustomTextView; // shows custom tip amount
32    private TextView totalCustomTextView; // shows total with custom tip
33
```

Fig. 3.11 | MainActivity class's instance variables.

The bill amount entered by the user into amountEditText will be read and stored as a double in billAmount (line 25). The custom tip percentage (an integer in the range 0–30) that the user sets by moving the Seekbar *thumb* will be multiplied by 0.01 to create a double for use in calculations, then stored in customPercent (line 26). For example, if you select 25 with the SeekBar, customPercent will store 0.25, so the app will multiply the bill amount by 0.25 to calculate the 25% tip.

Line 27 declares the TextView that displays the currency-formatted bill amount. Line 28 declares the TextView that displays the custom tip percentage based on the SeekBar *thumb's* position (see the **18%** in Fig. 3.1(a)). The variables in line 29–32 will refer to the TextViews in which the app displays the calculated tips and totals.

Overriding Method onCreate of Class Activity
The onCreate method (Fig. 3.12)—which is *auto-generated* with lines 38–39 when you create the app's project—is called by the system when an Activity is *started*. Method on-Create typically initializes the Activity's instance variables and views. This method should be as simple as possible so that the app *loads quickly*. In fact, if the app takes longer than *five seconds* to load, the operating system will display an **ANR (Application Not Responding) dialog**—giving the user the option to *forcibly terminate the app*. You'll learn how to prevent this problem in Chapter 8.

```
34    // called when the activity is first created
35    @Override
36    protected void onCreate(Bundle savedInstanceState)
37    {
38       super.onCreate(savedInstanceState); // call superclass's version
39       setContentView(R.layout.activity_main); // inflate the GUI
40
```

Fig. 3.12 | Overriding Activity method onCreate. (Part 1 of 2.)

```
41          // get references to the TextViews
42          // that MainActivity interacts with programmatically
43          amountDisplayTextView =
44             (TextView) findViewById(R.id.amountDisplayTextView);
45          percentCustomTextView =
46             (TextView) findViewById(R.id.percentCustomTextView);
47          tip15TextView = (TextView) findViewById(R.id.tip15TextView);
48          total15TextView = (TextView) findViewById(R.id.total15TextView);
49          tipCustomTextView = (TextView) findViewById(R.id.tipCustomTextView);
50          totalCustomTextView =
51             (TextView) findViewById(R.id.totalCustomTextView);
52
53          // update GUI based on billAmount and customPercent
54          amountDisplayTextView.setText(
55             currencyFormat.format(billAmount));
56          updateStandard(); // update the 15% tip TextViews
57          updateCustom(); // update the custom tip TextViews
58
59          // set amountEditText's TextWatcher
60          EditText amountEditText =
61             (EditText) findViewById(R.id.amountEditText);
62          amountEditText.addTextChangedListener(amountEditTextWatcher);
63
64          // set customTipSeekBar's OnSeekBarChangeListener
65          SeekBar customTipSeekBar =
66             (SeekBar) findViewById(R.id.customTipSeekBar);
67          customTipSeekBar.setOnSeekBarChangeListener(customSeekBarListener);
68       } // end method onCreate
69
```

Fig. 3.12 | Overriding `Activity` method `onCreate`. (Part 2 of 2.)

onCreate's Bundle *Parameter*

During the app's execution, the user could change the device's configuration by *rotating the device* or *sliding out a hard keyboard*. For a good experience, the app should continue operating smoothly through such configuration changes. When the system calls onCreate, it passes a **Bundle** argument containing the Activity's saved state, if any. Typically, you save state in Activity methods onPause or onSaveInstanceState (demonstrated in later apps). Line 38 calls the superclass's onCreate method, which is *required* when overriding onCreate.

Generated R Class Contains Resource IDs

As you build your app's GUI and add *resources* (such as strings in the strings.xml file or views in the activity_main.xml file) to your app, the IDE generates a class named **R** that contains *nested classes* representing each type of resource in your project's res folder. You can find this class in your project's **gen folder**, which contains generated source-code files. The nested classes are declared static, so that you can access them in your code with R.*ClassName*. Within class R's nested classes, the IDE creates static final int constants that enable you to refer to your app's resources programmatically from your code (as we'll discuss momentarily). Some of the nested classes in class R include:

- class **drawable**—contains constants for any drawable items, such as *images*, that you put in the various drawable folders in your app's res folder

- class **id**—contains constants for the *views* in your *XML layout files*
- class **layout**—contains constants that represent each *layout file* in your project (such as, `activity_main.xml`)
- class **string**—contains constants for each `String` in the `strings.xml` file.

Inflating the GUI

The call to **setContentView** (line 39) receives the constant **R.layout.activity_main** to indicate which XML file represents `MainActivity`'s GUI—in this case, the constant represents the `main.xml` file. Method `setContentView` uses this constant to load the corresponding XML document, which is then parsed and converted into the app's GUI. This process is known as **inflating** the GUI.

Getting References to the Widgets

Once the layout is *inflated*, you can *get references to the individual widgets* so that you can interact with them programmatically. To do so, you use class `Activity`'s `findViewById` method. This method takes an `int` constant representing a specific view's **Id** and returns a reference to the view. The name of each view's **R.id** constant is determined by the component's **Id** property that you specified when designing the GUI. For example, `amount-EditText`'s constant is `R.id.amountEditText`.

Lines 43–51 obtain references to the `TextView`s that are changed by the app. Lines 43–44 obtain a reference to the `amountDisplayTextView` that's updated when the user enters the bill amount. Lines 45–46 obtain a reference to the `percentCustomTextView` that's updated when the user changes the custom tip percentage. Lines 47–51 obtain references to the `TextView`s where the calculated tips and totals are displayed.

Displaying Initial Values in the **TextView**s

Lines 54–55 set `amountDisplayTextView`'s text to the initial `billAmount` (0.00) in a *locale-specific* currency format by calling the `currencyFormat` object's **format** method. Next, lines 56–57 call methods `updateStandard` (Fig. 3.13) and `updateCustom` (Fig. 3.14) to display initial values in the tip and total `TextView`s.

Registering the Event Listeners

Lines 60–61 get a reference to the `amountEditText`, and line 62 calls its `addTextChanged-Listener` method to register the `TextChangedListener` that will respond to *events* generated when the *user changes the text* in the `EditText`. We define this listener (Fig. 3.16) as an *anonymous-inner-class object* that's assigned to the instance variable `amountEditTextWatcher`.

Lines 65–66 get a reference to the `customTipSeekBar` and line 67 calls its `setOnSeek-BarChangeListener` method to register the `OnSeekBarChangeListener` that will respond to *events* generated when the user moves the `customTipSeekBar`'s *thumb* to change the custom tip percentage. We define this listener (Fig. 3.15) as an *anonymous-inner-class object* that's assigned to the instance variable `customSeekBarListener`.

Method **updateStandard** *of Class* **MainActivity**

Method **updateStandard** (Fig. 3.13) updates the 15% tip and total `TextView`s each time the user *changes* the bill amount. The method uses the `billAmount` value to calculate the tip amount and the total of the bill amount and tip. Lines 78–79 display the amounts in currency format.

```
70      // updates 15% tip TextViews
71      private void updateStandard()
72      {
73         // calculate 15% tip and total
74         double fifteenPercentTip = billAmount * 0.15;
75         double fifteenPercentTotal = billAmount + fifteenPercentTip;
76
77         // display 15% tip and total formatted as currency
78         tip15TextView.setText(currencyFormat.format(fifteenPercentTip));
79         total15TextView.setText(currencyFormat.format(fifteenPercentTotal));
80      } // end method updateStandard
81
```

Fig. 3.13 | Method `updateStandard` calculates and displays the 15% tip and total.

Method *updateCustom* of Class `MainActivity`

Method `updateCustom` (Fig. 3.14) updates the custom tip and total `TextViews` based on the tip percentage the user selected with the `customTipSeekBar`. Line 86 sets the `percentCustomTextView`'s text to the `customPercent` value formatted as a percentage. Lines 89–90 calculate the `customTip` and `customTotal`. Then, lines 93–94 display the amounts in currency format.

```
82      // updates the custom tip and total TextViews
83      private void updateCustom()
84      {
85         // show customPercent in percentCustomTextView formatted as %
86         percentCustomTextView.setText(percentFormat.format(customPercent));
87
88         // calculate the custom tip and total
89         double customTip = billAmount * customPercent;
90         double customTotal = billAmount + customTip;
91
92         // display custom tip and total formatted as currency
93         tipCustomTextView.setText(currencyFormat.format(customTip));
94         totalCustomTextView.setText(currencyFormat.format(customTotal));
95      } // end method updateCustom
96
```

Fig. 3.14 | Method `updateCustom` calculates and displays the custom tip and total.

Anonymous Inner Class That Implements Interface `OnSeekBarChangeListener`

Lines 98–120 of Fig. 3.15 create the *anonymous-inner-class* object named `customSeekBarListener` that responds to `customTipSeekBar`'s *events*. If you're not familiar with *anonymous inner classes*, visit the following page:

```
http://bit.ly/AnonymousInnerClasses
```

Line 67 (Fig. 3.12) registered `customSeekBarListener` as `customTipSeekBar`'s `OnSeekBarChangeListener` *event-handling* object. For clarity, we define all but the simplest event-handling objects in this manner so that we do not clutter the `onCreate` method with this code.

```
97        // called when the user changes the position of SeekBar
98        private OnSeekBarChangeListener customSeekBarListener =
99           new OnSeekBarChangeListener()
100          {
101             // update customPercent, then call updateCustom
102             @Override
103             public void onProgressChanged(SeekBar seekBar, int progress,
104                boolean fromUser)
105             {
106                // sets customPercent to position of the SeekBar's thumb
107                customPercent = progress / 100.0;
108                updateCustom(); // update the custom tip TextViews
109             } // end method onProgressChanged
110
111             @Override
112             public void onStartTrackingTouch(SeekBar seekBar)
113             {
114             } // end method onStartTrackingTouch
115
116             @Override
117             public void onStopTrackingTouch(SeekBar seekBar)
118             {
119             } // end method onStopTrackingTouch
120          }; // end OnSeekBarChangeListener
121
```

Fig. 3.15 | Anonymous inner class that implements interface OnSeekBarChangeListener to respond to the events of the customSeekBar.

Overriding Method onProgressChanged of Interface OnSeekBarChangeListener
Lines 102–119 implement interface OnSeekBarChangeListener's methods. Method onProgressChanged is called whenever the SeekBar's *thumb* position *changes*. Line 107 calculates customPercent using the method's progress parameter—an int representing the SeekBar's *thumb* position. We divide this by 100.0 to get the custom percentage. Line 108 calls method updateCustom to recalculate and display the custom tip and total.

Overriding Methods onStartTrackingTouch and onStopTrackingTouch of Interface OnSeekBarChangeListener
Java requires that you override *every* method in an *interface* that you *implement*. This app does *not* need to know when the user *starts* moving the slider's thumb (onStartTrackingTouch) or *stops* moving it (onStopTrackingTouch), so we simply provide an *empty* body for each (lines 111–119) to *fulfill* the *interface contract*.

Anonymous Inner Class That Implements Interface TextWatcher
Lines 123–156 of Fig. 3.16 create the *anonymous-inner-class* object amountEditTextWatcher that responds to amountEditText's *events*. Line 62 registered this object to *listen* for amountEditText's events that occur when the text changes.

Overriding Method onTextChanged of Interface TextWatcher
The onTextChanged method (lines 126–144) is called whenever the text in the amountEditText is *modified*. The method receives four parameters. In this example, we use only

```
122        // event-handling object that responds to amountEditText's events
123        private TextWatcher amountEditTextWatcher = new TextWatcher()
124        {
125           // called when the user enters a number
126           @Override
127           public void onTextChanged(CharSequence s, int start,
128              int before, int count)
129           {
130              // convert amountEditText's text to a double
131              try
132              {
133                 billAmount = Double.parseDouble(s.toString()) / 100.0;
134              } // end try
135              catch (NumberFormatException e)
136              {
137                 billAmount = 0.0; // default if an exception occurs
138              } // end catch
139
140              // display currency formatted bill amount
141              amountDisplayTextView.setText(currencyFormat.format(billAmount));
142              updateStandard(); // update the 15% tip TextViews
143              updateCustom(); // update the custom tip TextViews
144           } // end method onTextChanged
145
146           @Override
147           public void afterTextChanged(Editable s)
148           {
149           } // end method afterTextChanged
150
151           @Override
152           public void beforeTextChanged(CharSequence s, int start, int count,
153              int after)
154           {
155           } // end method beforeTextChanged
156        }; // end amountEditTextWatcher
157     } // end class MainActivity
```

Fig. 3.16 | Anonymous inner class that implements interface TextWatcher to respond to the events of the amountEditText.

CharSequence s, which contains a copy of amountEditText's text. The other parameters indicate that the count characters starting at start *replaced* previous text of length before.

Line 133 converts the user input from amountEditText to a double. We allow users to enter only whole numbers in pennies, so we divide the converted value by 100.0 to get the actual bill amount—e.g., if the user enters 2495, the bill amount is 24.95. Lines 142–143 call updateStandard and updateCustom to recalculate and display the tips and totals.

Other Methods of the **amountEditTextWatcher** *TextWatcher*
This app does *not* need to know what changes are about to be made to the text (before-TextChanged) or that the text has already been changed (afterTextChanged), so we simply override each of these TextWatcher interface methods with an *empty* body (lines 146–155) to *fulfill the interface contract*.

3.6 AndroidManifest.xml

In this section, you'll modify the AndroidManifest.xml file to specify that this app's Activity supports only a device's *portrait* orientation and that the *soft keypad* should *always* remain on the screen. You'll use the IDE's **Android Manifest** editor to specify these settings. To open the **Android Manifest** editor, double click the app's AndroidManifest.xml file in the **Package Explorer**. At the bottom of the editor, click the **Application** tab (Fig. 3.17), then select the MainActivity node in the **Application Nodes** section at the bottom of the window. This displays settings for the MainActivity in the **Attributes for com.deitel.tipcalculator.MainActivity** section.

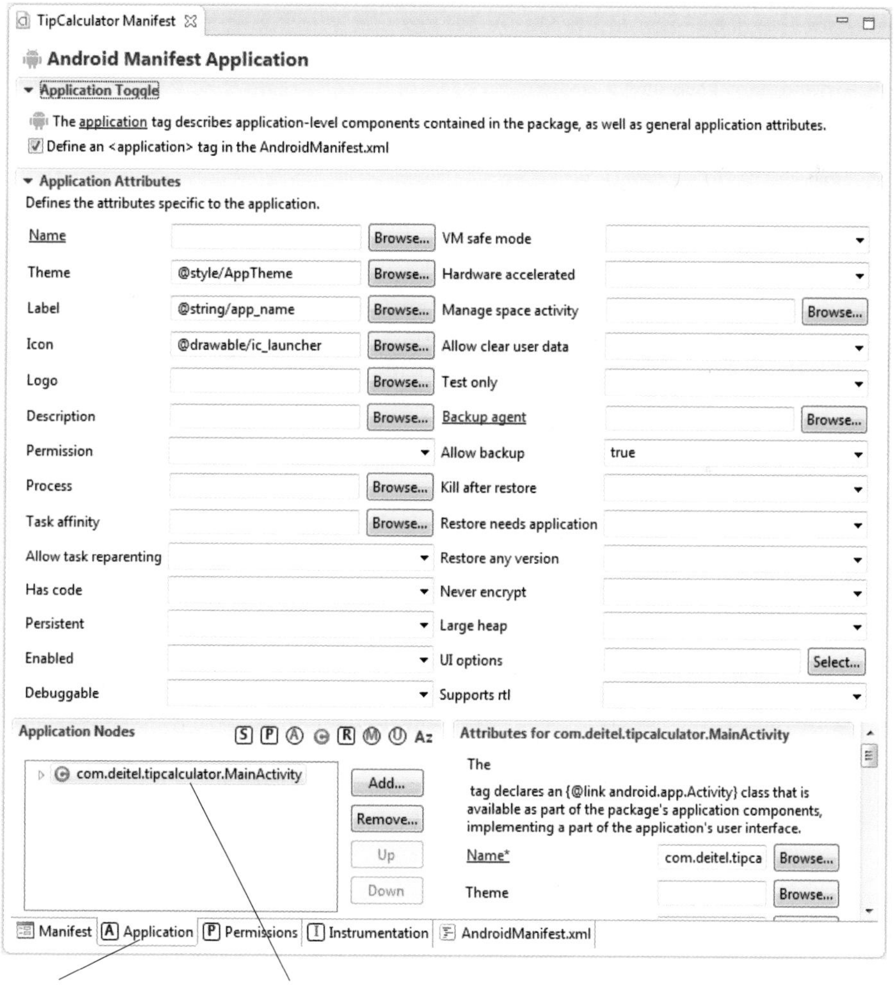

Application tab   Select this node to specify settings
                   for the app's MainActivity

Fig. 3.17 | **Android Manifest** editor's **Application** tab.

Configuring `MainActivity` for Portrait Orientation
In general, most apps should support *both* portrait and landscape orientations. In *portrait* orientation, the device's height is greater than its width. In *landscape orientation*, the device's width is greater than its height. In the **Tip Calculator** app, rotating the device to landscape orientation on a typical phone would cause the numeric keypad to obscure most of the **Tip Calculator**'s GUI. For this reason, you'll configure `MainActivity` to support *only* portrait orientation. In the **Android Manifest** editor's **Attributes for com.deitel.tipcalculator.MainActivity** section, scroll down to the **Screen orientation** option and select `portrait`.

Forcing the Soft Keypad to Always Display for `MainActivity`
In the **Tip Calculator** app, the soft keypad should be displayed immediately when the app executes and should remain on the screen at all times. In the **Android Manifest** editor's **Attributes for com.deitel.tipcalculator.MainActivity** section, scroll down to the **Window soft input mode** option and select `stateAlwaysVisible`. Note that this will *not* display the soft keyboard if a hard keyboard is present.

3.7 Wrap-Up

In this chapter, you created your first *interactive* Android app—the **Tip Calculator**. We overviewed the app's capabilities, then you test-drove it to calculate standard and custom tips based on the bill amount entered. You followed detailed step-by-step instructions to build the app's GUI using the Android Developer Tools IDE's **Graphical Layout** editor, **Outline** window and **Properties** window. We also walked through the code of the `Activity` subclass `MainActivity`, which defined the app's functionality.

In the app's GUI, you used a `GridLayout` to arrange the views into rows and columns. You displayed text in `TextView`s and received input from an `EditText` and a `SeekBar`.

The `MainActivity` class required many Java object-oriented programming capabilities, including classes, objects, methods, interfaces, anonymous inner classes and inheritance. We explained the notion of inflating the GUI from its XML file into its screen representation. You learned about Android's `Activity` class and part of the `Activity` lifecycle. In particular, you overrode the `onCreate` method to initialize the app when it's launched. In the `onCreate` method, you used `Activity` method `findViewById` to get references to each of the views that the app interacts with programmatically. You defined an anonymous inner class that implements the `TextWatcher` interface so the app can calculate new tips and totals as the user changes the text in the `EditText`. You also defined an anonymous inner class that implements the `OnSeekBarChangeListener` interface so the app can calculate a new custom tip and total as the user changes the custom tip percentage by moving the `SeekBar`'s thumb.

Finally, you opened the `AndroidManifest.xml` file in the IDE's **Android Manifest** editor to specify that the `MainActivity` supports only portrait orientation and that the `MainActivity` should always display the keypad.

Using the IDE's **Graphical Layout** editor, **Outline** window, **Properties** window and **Android Manifest** editor enabled you to build this app without manipulating the XML in the project's resource files and `AndroidManifest.xml` file.

In the next chapter, we introduce collections while building the **Twitter®️ Searches** app. Many mobile apps display lists of items. You'll do this by using a `ListActivity` containing a `ListView` that's bound to an `ArrayList<String>`. You'll also store app data as user preferences and learn how to launch the device's web browser to display a web page.

Twitter® Searches App

SharedPreferences, Collections, ImageButton, ListView, ListActivity, ArrayAdapter, Implicit Intents and AlertDialogs

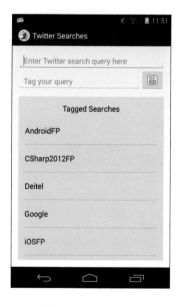

Objectives

In this chapter you'll:

- Support both portrait and landscape device orientations.
- Extend `ListActivity` to create an `Activity` that displays a list of items in a `ListView`.
- Enable users to interact with an app via an `ImageButton`.
- Manipulate collections of data.
- Use `SharedPreferences` to store key–value pairs of data associated with an app.
- Use a `SharedPreferences.Editor` to modify key-value pairs of data associated with an app.
- Use an `ArrayAdapter` to specify a `ListView`'s data.
- Use an `AlertDialog.Builder` object to create `AlertDialogs` that display options as `Buttons` or in a `ListView`.
- Use an implicit `Intent` to open a website in a browser.
- Use an implicit `Intent` to display an intent chooser containing a list of apps that can share text.
- Programmatically hide the soft keyboard.

4.1 Introduction

Twitter's search mechanism makes it easy to follow trending topics being discussed by more than 500 million Twitter users. Searches can be fine tuned using Twitter's *search operators* (overviewed in Section 4.2), often resulting in lengthy search strings that are time consuming and cumbersome to enter on a mobile device. The **Twitter Searches** app (Fig. 4.1) allows you to save your favorite search queries with short tag names that are easy to remember (Fig. 4.1(a)). You can then touch a tag name to quickly and easily follow tweets on a given topic (Fig. 4.1(b)). As you'll see, the app also allows you to *share, edit* and *delete* saved searches.

The app supports both portrait and landscape device orientations. In some apps, you'll do this by providing separate layouts for each orientation. In this app, we support both orientations by designing the GUI so that it can dynamically adjust GUI component sizes based on the current orientation.

First, you'll test-drive the app. Then we'll overview the technologies used to build it. Next, you'll design the app's GUI. Finally, we'll present the app's complete source code and walk through the code, discussing the app's new features in more detail.

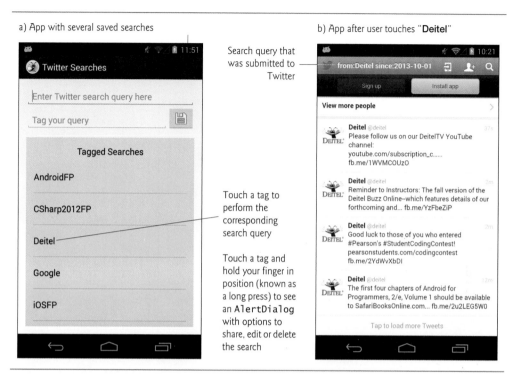

a) App with several saved searches

Search query that
was submitted to
Twitter

Touch a tag to
perform the
corresponding
search query

Touch a tag and
hold your finger in
position (known as
a long press) to see
an `AlertDialog`
with options to
share, edit or delete
the search

b) App after user touches "**Deitel**"

Fig. 4.1 | **Twitter Searches** app.

4.2 Test-Driving the App

In this section, you'll test-drive the **Twitter Searches** app. Open the Android Developer Tools IDE and import the **Twitter Searches** app project. As you did in Chapter 3, launch the Nexus 4 AVD—or connect your Android device to the computer—so that you can test the app. The screen captures we show in this chapter were taken on a Nexus 4 phone.

4.2.1 Importing the App and Running It

Perform the following steps to import the app into the IDE:

1. *Opening the Import dialog.* Select **File > Import....**

2. *Importing the Twitter Searches app's project.* Expand the **General** node and select **Existing Projects into Workspace**. Click **Next >** to proceed to the **Import Projects** step. Ensure that **Select root directory** is selected, then click **Browse....** Locate the `TwitterSearches` folder in the book's examples folder, select it and click **OK**. Ensure that **Copy projects into workspace** is *not* selected. Click **Finish** to import the project so that it appears in the **Package Explorer** window.

3. *Launching the Twitter Searches app.* Right click the `TwitterSearches` project in the **Package Explorer** window, then select **Run As > Android Application** to execute **Twitter Searches** in the AVD or on your device. This builds the project and runs the app (Fig. 4.2).

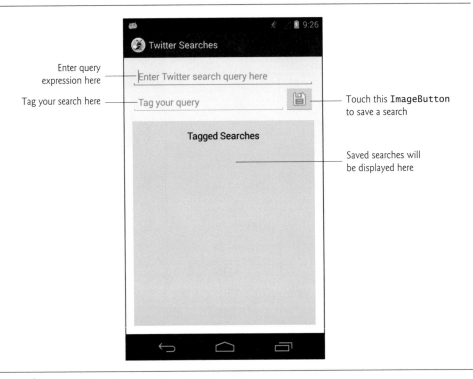

Enter query expression here

Tag your search here

Touch this ImageButton to save a search

Saved searches will be displayed here

Fig. 4.2 | **Twitter Searches** app when it first executes.

4.2.2 Adding a Favorite Search

Touch the top EditText, then enter from:deitel as the search query—the from: operator locates tweets from a specified Twitter account. Figure 4.3 shows several Twitter search operators—multiple operators can be used to construct more complex queries. A complete list can be found at

```
http://bit.ly/TwitterSearchOperators
```

Example	Finds tweets containing
deitel iOS6	Implicit *logical and* operator—Finds tweets containing deitel *and* iOS6.
deitel OR iOS6	Logical OR operator—Finds tweets containing deitel *or* iOS6 *or both*.
"how to program"	String in quotes("")—Finds tweets containing the exact phrase "how to program".
deitel ?	? (question mark)—Finds tweets asking questions about deitel.
deitel -sue	- (minus sign)—Finds tweets containing deitel but not sue.
deitel :)	:) (happy face)—Finds *positive attitude* tweets containing deitel.
deitel :(	:((sad face)—Finds *negative attitude* tweets containing deitel.

Fig. 4.3 | Some Twitter search operators. (Part 1 of 2.)

Example	Finds tweets containing
`since:2013-10-01`	Finds tweets that occurred *on or after* the specified date, which must be in the form YYYY-MM-DD.
`near:"New York City"`	Finds tweets that were sent near "New York City".
`from:deitel`	Finds tweets from the Twitter account @deitel.
`to:deitel`	Finds tweets to the Twitter account @deitel.

Fig. 4.3 | Some Twitter search operators. (Part 2 of 2.)

In the bottom `EditText` enter `Deitel` as the tag for the search query (Fig. 4.4(a)). This will be the *short name* displayed in a list in the app's **Tagged Searches** section. Touch the *save* (▣) button to save the search—the tag "**Deitel**" appears in the list under the **Tagged Searches** heading (Fig. 4.4(b)). When you save a search, the soft keyboard is dismissed so that you can see your list of saved searches—you'll learn how to programmatically hide the soft keyboard in Section 4.5.5.

a) Entering a Twitter search and search tag

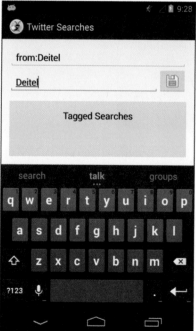

b) App after saving the search and search tag

Fig. 4.4 | Entering a Twitter search.

4.2.3 Viewing Twitter Search Results

To view the search results, touch the tag "**Deitel**." This launches the device's web browser and passes a URL that represents the saved search to the Twitter website. Twitter obtains the search query from the URL, then returns the tweets that match the query (if any) as a web page. The web browser then displays this results page (Fig. 4.5). When you're done viewing the results, touch the back button (⬅) to return to the **Twitter Searches** app where you can save more searches, and edit, delete and share previously saved searches.

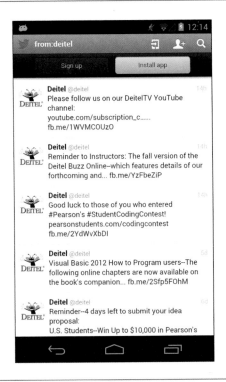

Fig. 4.5 | Viewing search results.

4.2.4 Editing a Search

You may also *share, edit* or *delete* a search. To see these options, *long press* the search's tag—that is, touch the tag and keep your finger on the screen. If you're using an AVD, click and hold the left mouse button on the search tag to perform a long press. When you long press "**Deitel**," the AlertDialog in Fig. 4.6(a) displays the **Share, Edit** and **Delete** options for the search tagged as "**Deitel**." If you don't wish to perform any of these tasks, touch **Cancel**.

To edit the search tagged as "**Deitel**," touch the dialog's **Edit** option. The app then loads the search's query and tag into the EditTexts for editing. Let's restrict our search to tweets since October 1, 2013 by adding since:2013-10-01 to the end of the query (Fig. 4.6(b)) in the top EditText. The since: operator restricts the search results to tweets that occurred *on or after* the specified date (in the form yyyy-mm-dd). Touch the *save* (📄) button to update the saved search, then view the updated results (Fig. 4.7) by touching **Deitel** in the **Tagged Searches** section of the app. [*Note:* Changing the tag name will create a *new* search—this is useful if you want to create a new query that's based on a previously saved query.]

a) Selecting **Edit** to edit an existing search   b) Editing the "**Deitel**" saved search

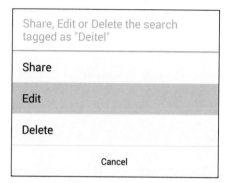 

Fig. 4.6 | Editing a saved search.

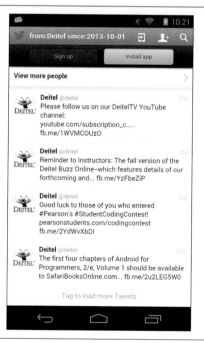

Fig. 4.7 | Viewing the updated "**Deitel**" search results.

4.2.5 Sharing a Search

Android makes it easy for you to share various types of information from an app via e-mail, instant messaging (SMS), Facebook, Google+, Twitter and more. In this app, you can share a favorite search by *long pressing* the search's tag and selecting **Share** from the `Alert-Dialog` that appears. This displays a so-called *intent chooser* (Fig. 4.8(a)), which can vary based on the type of content you're sharing and the apps that can handle that content. In this app we're sharing text, and the intent chooser on our phone (not the AVD) shows apps capable of handling text, such as **Facebook**, **Gmail**, **Google+**, **Messaging** (instant messaging) and **Twitter**. If no apps can handle the content, the intent chooser will display a message saying so. If only one app can handle the content, that app will launch without you having to select from the intent chooser which app to use. Figure 4.8(b) shows the Gmail app's **Compose** screen with the e-mail subject and body populated. Gmail also shows your e-mail address above the **To** field (we deleted the e-mail address for privacy in the screen capture).

a) Intent chooser showing share options

b) Gmail app **Compose** screen for an e-mail containing the "**Deitel**" search

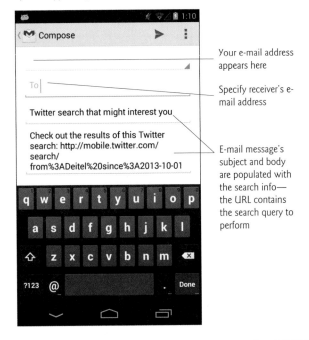

Fig. 4.8 | Sharing a search via e-mail.

4.2.6 Deleting a Search

To delete a search, *long press* the search's tag and select **Delete** from the `AlertDialog` that appears. The app prompts you to confirm that you'd like to delete the search (Fig. 4.9)—touching **Cancel** returns you to the main screen *without* deleting the search. Touching **Delete** deletes the search.

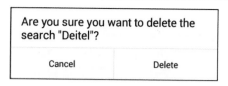

Are you sure you want to delete the
search "Deitel"?

| Cancel | Delete |

Fig. 4.9 | `AlertDialog` confirming a delete.

4.2.7 Scrolling Through Saved Searches

Figure 4.10 shows the app after we've saved 10 favorite searches—only five of which are currently visible. The app allows you to scroll through your favorite searches if there are more than can be displayed on the screen at once. The GUI component that displays the list of searches is a `ListView` (discussed in Section 4.3.1). To scroll, *drag* or *flick* your finger (or the mouse in an AVD) up or down in the list of **Tagged Searches**. Also, rotate the device to *landscape* orientation to see that the GUI dynamically adjusts.

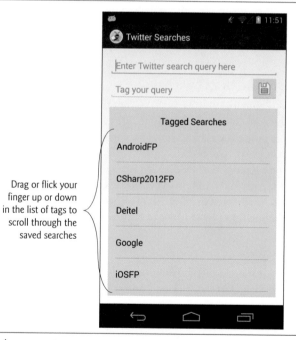

Fig. 4.10 | App with more searches than can be displayed on the screen.

4.3 Technologies Overview

This section introduces the features you'll use to build the **Twitter Searches** app.

4.3.1 `ListView`

Many mobile apps display lists of information. For example, an e-mail app displays a list of new e-mails, an address-book app displays a list of contacts, a news app displays a list of headlines, etc. In each case, the user touches an item in the list to see more information—e.g., the content of the selected e-mail, the details of the selected contact or the text of the selected news story. This app uses a `ListView` (package `android.widget`) to display a list of tagged searches that is *scrollable* if the complete list cannot be displayed on the screen. You can specify how to format each `ListView` item. For this app, we'll display each search's tag as a `String` in a `TextView`. In later apps, you'll completely customize the content that's displayed for each `ListView` item—displaying images, text and `Buttons`.

4.3.2 ListActivity

When an `Activity`'s primary task is to display a *scrollable* list of items, you can extend class `ListActivity` (package `android.app`), which uses a `ListView` that occupies the entire app as its default layout. `ListView` is a subclass of **AdapterView** (package `android.widget`)—a GUI component is bound to a data source via an **Adapter** object (package `android.widget`). In this app, we use an **ArrayAdapter** (package `android.widget`) to create an object that populates the `ListView` using data from an `ArrayList` collection object. This is known as data binding. Several types of `AdapterViews` can be bound to data using an `Adapter`. In Chapter 8, you'll learn how to bind database data to a `ListView`. For more details on data binding in Android and several tutorials, visit

```
http://developer.android.com/guide/topics/ui/binding.html
```

4.3.3 Customizing a ListActivity's Layout

A `ListActivity`'s default GUI contains only a `ListView` that fills the screen's client area between Android's top and bottom system bars (which were explained in Fig. 2.1). If a `ListActivity`'s GUI requires only the default `ListView`, then you do *not* need to define a separate layout for your `ListActivity` subclass.

The **Twitter Searches** app's `MainActivity` displays several GUI components. For this reason you'll define a *custom* layout for `MainActivity`. When customizing a `ListActivity` subclass's GUI, the layout *must* contain a `ListView` with its **Id** attribute set to `"@android:id/list"`—the name that class `ListActivity` uses to reference its `ListView`.

4.3.4 ImageButton

Users often touch buttons to initiate actions in a program. To save a search's query–tag pair in this app, you touch an **ImageButton** (package `android.widget`). `ImageButton` is a subclass of `ImageView` which provides additional capabilities that enable an image to be used like a `Button` object (package `android.widget`) to initiate an action.

4.3.5 SharedPreferences

You can have one or more files containing *key–value* pairs associated with each app—each *key* enables you to quickly look up a corresponding *value*. We use this capability to manipulate a file called `searches` in which we store the pairs of tags (the *keys*) and Twitter search queries (the *values*) that the user creates. To read the key–value pairs from this file we'll use **SharedPreferences** objects (package **android.content**). To modify the file's contents, we'll use **SharedPreferences.Editor** objects (package `android.content`). The keys in the file must be `Strings`, and the values can be `Strings` or primitive-type values.

This app reads the saved searches in the `Activity`'s `onCreate` method—this is acceptable only because the amount of data being loaded is small. When an app is launched, Android creates a main thread called the UI thread which handles all of the GUI interactions. All GUI processing must be performed in this thread. *Extensive input/output operations, such as loading data from files and databases should not be performed on the UI thread, because such operations can affect your app's responsiveness.* We'll show how to perform I/O in separate threads in later chapters.

4.3.6 Intents for Launching Other Activities

Android uses a technique known as **intent messaging** to communicate information between activities within one app or activities in separate apps. Each `Activity` can specify **intent filters** indicating *actions* the `Activity` is capable of handling. Intent filters are defined in the `AndroidManifest.xml` file. In fact, in each app so far, the IDE created an intent filter for the app's only `Activity` indicating that it could respond to the predefined action named `android.intent.action.MAIN`, which specifies that the `Activity` can be used to *launch* the app to begin its execution.

An **Intent** is used to launch an `Activity`—it indicates an *action* to be performed and the *data* on which to perform that action. In this app, when the user touches a search tag, we create a URL that contains the Twitter search query. We load the URL into a web browser by creating a new `Intent` for viewing a URL, then passing that `Intent` to the **`startActivity` method,** which our app inherits indirectly from class `Activity`. To view a URL, `startActivity` launches the device's web browser to display the content—in this app, the results of a Twitter search.

We also use an `Intent` and the `startActivity` method to display an **intent chooser**—a GUI that shows a list of apps that can handle the specified `Intent`. We use this when sharing a saved search to allow the user to choose how to share a search.

Implicit and Explicit *Intents*

The `Intents` used in this app are examples of **implicit `Intents`**—*we will not specify a component to display the web page but instead will allow Android to launch the most appropriate `Activity` based on the type of data.* If *multiple* activities can handle the action and data passed to `startActivity`, the system will display a *dialog* in which the user can select which activity to use. If the system cannot find an activity to handle the action, then method `startActivity` throws an `ActivityNotFoundException`. In general, it's a good practice to handle this exception. We chose not to in this app, because Android devices on which this app is likely to be installed will have a browser capable of displaying a web page. In future apps, we'll also use **explicit `Intents`**, which indicate the precise `Activity` to start. For a more information on `Intents`, visit

```
http://developer.android.com/guide/components/intents-filters.html
```

4.3.7 `AlertDialog`

You can display messages, options and confirmations to app users via **`AlertDialog`s**. While a dialog is displayed, the user cannot interact with the app—this is known as a **modal dialog**. As you'll see, you specify the settings for the dialog with an **`AlertDialog.Builder`** object, then use it to create the `AlertDialog`.

AlertDialogs can display buttons, checkboxes, radio buttons and lists of items that the user can touch to respond to the dialog's message. A standard AlertDialog may have up to three buttons that represent:

- A *negative* action—Cancels the dialog's specified action, often labeled with **Cancel** or **No**. This is the leftmost button when there are multiple buttons in the dialog.

- A *positive* action—Accepts the dialog's specified action, often labeled with **OK** or **Yes**. This is the rightmost button when there are multiple buttons in the dialog.

- A *neutral* action—This button indicates that the user does not want to cancel or accept the action specified by the dialog. For example, an app that asks the user to register to gain access to additional features might provide a **Remind Me Later** neutral button.

We use AlertDialogs in this app for several purposes:

- To display a message to the user if either or both of the query and tag EditTexts are empty. This dialog will contain only a positive button.

- To display the **Share**, **Edit** and **Delete** options for a search. This dialog will contain a list of options and a negative button.

- To have the user confirm before deleting a search—in case the user accidentally touched the **Delete** option for a search.

You can learn more about Android dialogs at:

```
http://developer.android.com/guide/topics/ui/dialogs.html
```

4.3.8 AndroidManifest.xml

As you learned in Chapter 3, the AndroidManifest.xml file is created for you when you create an app. For this app, we'll show you how to add a setting to the manifest that prevents the soft keyboard from displaying when the app first loads. For the complete details of AndroidManifest.xml, visit:

```
http://developer.android.com/guide/topics/manifest/
    manifest-intro.html
```

We'll cover various aspects of the AndroidManifest.xml file throughout the book.

4.4 Building the App's GUI

In this section, we'll build the GUI for the **Twitter Searches** app. We'll also create a second XML layout that the ListView will dynamically inflate and use to display each item.

4.4.1 Creating the Project

Recall that the Android Developer Tools IDE allows only *one* project with a given name per workspace, so before you create the new project, delete the TwitterSearches project that you test-drove in Section 4.2. To do so, right click it and select **Delete**. In the dialog that appears, ensure that **Delete project contents on disk** is *not* selected, then click **OK**. This removes the project from the workspace, but leaves the project's folder and files on disk in case you'd like to look at the original app again later.

Creating a New Blank App Project

Next, create a new **Android Application Project**. Specify the following values in the **New Android Project** dialog's first **New Android Application** step, then press **Next >**:

- **Application Name:** Twitter Searches
- **Project Name:** TwitterSearches
- **Package Name:** com.deitel.twittersearches
- **Minimum Required SDK:** API18: Android 4.3
- **Target SDK:** API19: Android 4.4
- **Compile With:** API19: Android 4.4
- **Theme:** Holo Light with Dark Action Bar

In the **New Android Project** dialog's second **New Android Application** step, leave the default settings, and press **Next >**. In the **Configure Launcher Icon** step, click the **Browse...** button, and select an app icon image (provided in the images folder with the book's examples), click the **Open** button, then press **Next >**. In the **Create Activity** step, select **Blank Activity**, then press **Next >**. In the **Blank Activity** step, leave the default settings and click **Finish** to create the project. In the **Graphical Layout** editor, select **Nexus 4** from the screen-type drop-down list (as in Fig. 2.12). Once again, we'll use this device as the basis for our design.

4.4.2 `activity_main.xml` Overview

As in Chapter 3, this app's `activity_main.xml` layout uses a `GridLayout` (Fig. 4.11). In this app, the `GridLayout` contains three rows and one column. Figure 4.12 shows the names of the app's GUI components.

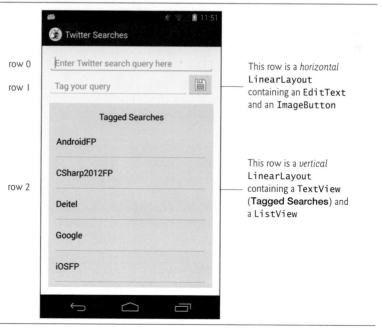

Fig. 4.11 | Rows and columns in the **Twitter Searches** app's `GridLayout`.

Fig. 4.12 | **Twitter Searches** GUI's components labeled with their **Id** property values.

4.4.3 Adding the GridLayout and Components

Using the techniques you learned in Chapter 3, you'll build the GUI in Figs. 4.11–4.12. All of the steps in the following subsections assume that you're working with the layout in the IDE's **Graphical Layout** editor. As a reminder, it's often easiest to select a particular GUI component in the **Outline** window.

You'll start with the basic layout and controls, then customize the controls' properties to complete the design. Use the **Outline** window to add components to the proper rows of the GridLayout. As you add GUI components, set their **Id**s as shown in Fig. 4.12—there are several components in this layout that do not require **Id**s, as they're never referenced from the app's Java code. Also, remember to define all your literal strings values in the strings.xml file (located in the app's res/values folder).

*Step 1: Changing from a **RelativeLayout** to a **GridLayout***
Follow the steps in Section 3.4.3 to remove the default TextView in the app's layout and to switch from a RelativeLayout to a GridLayout.

*Step 2: Configuring the **GridLayout***
In the **Outline** window, select the GridLayout and set the following properties—for each property that's nested in a node within the **Properties** window, we specify the node's name in parentheses following the property name:

- **Id**: @+id/gridLayout

- **Column Count** (**GridLayout** node): 1—Each GUI component nested directly in the `GridLayout` will be added as a new row.

The `GridLayout` fills the entire client area of the screen because the layout's **Width** and **Height** properties (in the **Layout Parameters** section of the **Properties** window) are each set to `match_parent` by the IDE.

By default, the IDE sets the **Padding Left** and **Padding Right** properties to `@dimen/activity_horizontal_margin`—a predefined dimension resource in the `dimens.xml` file of the project's `res/values` folder. This resource's value is `16dp`, so there will be a `16dp` space to the left and right of the `GridLayout`. The IDE created this resource when you created the app's project. Similarly, the IDE sets the **Padding Top** and **Padding Bottom** properties to `@dimen/activity_vertical_margin`—another predefined dimension resource with the value `16dp`. So there will be a `16dp` space above and below the `GridLayout`.

Look-and-Feel Observation 4.1

According to the Android design guidelines, 16dp is the recommended space between the edges of a device's touchable screen area and the app's content; however, many apps (such as games) use the full screen.

Step 3: Creating the GridLayout's First Row

This row contains only an `EditText`. Drag a **Plain Text** component from the **Palette**'s **Text Fields** section onto the `GridLayout` in the **Outline** window, then set its **Id** property to `@+id/queryEditText`. In the **Properties** window under the **TextView** node, delete the **Ems** property's value, which is not used in this app. Then use the **Properties** window to set the following properties:

- **Width** (**Layout Parameters** node): `wrap_content`

- **Height** (**Layout Parameters** node): `wrap_content`

- **Gravity** (**Layout Parameters** node): `fill_horizontal`—This ensures that when the user rotates the device, the `queryEditText` will fill all available horizontal space. We use similar **Gravity** settings for other GUI components to support both portrait and landscape orientations for this app's GUI.

- **Hint**: `@string/queryPrompt`—Create a `String` resource as you did in prior apps and give it the value `"Enter Twitter search query here"`. This attribute displays in an *empty* `EditText` a hint that helps the user understand the `EditText`'s purpose. This text is also spoken by Android TalkBack for users with visual impairments, so providing hints in your `EditText`s makes your app more accessible.

Look-and-Feel Observation 4.2

The Android design guidelines indicate that text displayed in your GUI should be brief, simple and friendly with the important words first. For details on the recommended writing style, see http://developer.android.com/design/style/writing.html.

- **IME Options** (**TextView** node): `actionNext`—This value indicates that `queryEditText`'s keyboard will contain a **Next** button that the user can touch to move the input focus to the next input component (i.e., the `tagEditText` in this app). This makes it easier for the user to fill in multiple input components in a form.

When the next component is another EditText, the appropriate keyboard is displayed without the user having to touch the EditText to give it the focus.

Step 4: Creating the GridLayout's Second Row

This row is a horizontal LinearLayout containing an EditText and an ImageButton. Perform the following tasks to build the row's GUI:

1. Drag a **LinearLayout (Horizontal)** component from the **Palette**'s **Layouts** section onto the GridLayout in the **Outline** window.

2. Drag a **Plain Text** component from the **Palette**'s **Text Fields** section onto the LinearLayout, then set the **Id** property to @+id/tagEditText.

3. Drag an **ImageButton** component from the **Palette**'s **Images & Media** section onto the LinearLayout. This displays the **Resource Chooser** dialog (Fig. 4.13), so that you can choose the button's image. By default, the dialog's **Project Resources** radio button is selected so that you can choose images from the project's resources (such images would be stored in your project's various res/drawable folders). In this app, we used the standard Android save icon (shown at the right side of Fig. 4.13). To do so, click the **System Resources** radio button, select ic_menu_save and click **OK**. Next, set the **Id** property to @+id/saveButton.

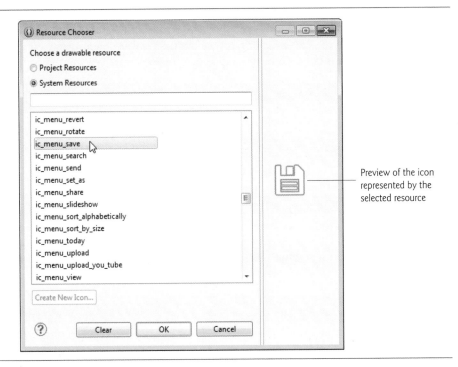

Fig. 4.13 | **Resource Chooser** dialog.

With the tagEditText selected, remove the **Ems** property's value from the **TextView** node in the **Properties** window. Then set the following properties:

- **Width** (**Layout Parameters** node): 0dp—The IDE recommends this value when you also set the **Weight** property, so that the IDE can lay out the components more efficiently.

- **Height** (**Layout Parameters** node): wrap_content

- **Gravity** (**Layout Parameters** node): bottom|fill_horizontal—This aligns the bottom of the tagEditText with the bottom of the saveButton and indicates that tagEditText should fill the available horizontal space.

- **Weight** (**Layout Parameters** node): 1—This makes the tagEditText more importance than the saveButton in this row. When Android lays out the row, the saveButton will occupy only the space it needs and the tagEditText will occupy all remaining horizontal space.

- **Hint**: @string/tagPrompt—Create a String resource with the value "Tag your query".

- **IME Options** (**TextView** node): actionDone—This value indicates that query-EditText's keyboard will contain a **Done** button that the user can touch to dismiss the keyboard from the screen.

With the saveButton selected, clear the value of the **Weight** property (**Layout Parameters** node) then set the following properties:

- **Width** (**Layout Parameters** node): wrap_content

- **Height** (**Layout Parameters** node): wrap_content

- **Content Description**: @string/saveDescription—Create a string resource with the value "Touch this button to save your tagged search".

Look-and-Feel Observation 4.3

Recall that it's considered a best practice in Android to ensure that every GUI component can be used with TalkBack. For components that don't have descriptive text, such as an ImageButton, provide text for the component's **Content Description** *property.*

Step 5: Creating the GridLayout's Third Row

This row is a vertical LinearLayout containing a TextView and a ListView. Perform the following tasks to build the row's GUI:

1. Drag a **LinearLayout (Vertical)** component from the **Palette**'s **Layouts** section onto the GridLayout in the **Outline** window.

2. Drag a **Medium Text** component from the **Palette**'s **Form Widgets** section onto the LinearLayout. This creates a TextView that's preconfigured to display text in the theme's medium-sized text font.

3. Drag a **ListView** component from the **Palette**'s **Composite** section onto the LinearLayout, then set the **Id** property to @android:id/list—recall that this is the required **Id** for the ListView in a ListActivity's custom layout.

With the vertical LinearLayout selected, set the following properties:

- **Height** (**Layout Parameters** node): 0dp—The actual height is determined by the **Gravity** property.

- **Gravity** (**Layout Parameters** node): fill—This tells the LinearLayout to fill all available horizontal and vertical space.
- **Top** (located in the **Layout Parameters** node's **Margins** node): @dimen/ activity_vertical_margin—This separates the top of the vertical LinearLayout from the horizontal LinearLayout in the GUI's second row.
- **Background** (**View** node): @android:color/holo_blue_bright—This is one of the predefined color resources in the app's Android theme.
- **Padding Left/Right** (**View** node): @dimen/activity_horizontal_margin—This ensures that the components in the vertical LinearLayout are inset by 16dp from the left and right edges of the layout.
- **Padding Top** (**View** node): @dimen/activity_vertical_margin—This ensures that the top component within the vertical LinearLayout is inset by 16dp from the top edge of the layout.

With the vertical TextView selected, set the following properties:

- **Width** (**Layout Parameters** node): match_parent
- **Height** (**Layout Parameters** node): wrap_content
- **Gravity** (**Layout Parameters** node): fill_horizontal—This makes the TextView fill the width of the vertical LinearLayout (minus the *padding* in the layout).
- **Gravity** (**TextView** node): center_horizontal—This centers the TextView's text.
- **Text**: @string/taggedSearches—Create a string resource with the value "Tagged Searches".
- **Padding Top** (**View** node): @dimen/activity_vertical_margin—This ensures that the top component within the vertical LinearLayout is inset by 16dp from the top edge of the layout.

With the ListView selected, set the following properties:

- **Width** (**Layout Parameters** node): match_parent
- **Height** (**Layout Parameters** node): 0dp—The IDE recommends this value when you also set the **Weight** property, so that the IDE can lay out the components more efficiently.
- **Weight** (**Layout Parameters** node): 1
- **Gravity** (**Layout Parameters** node): fill—The ListView should fill all available horizontal and vertical space.
- **Padding Top** (**View** node): @dimen/activity_vertical_margin—This ensures that the top component within the vertical LinearLayout is inset by 16dp from the top edge of the layout.
- **Top** and **Bottom** (located in the **Layout Parameters** node's **Margins** node): @dimen/ tagged_searches_padding—Create a new tagged_searches_padding dimension resource by clicking the ellipsis button to the right of the **Top** property. In the **Resource Chooser** dialog, click **New Dimension...** to create a new dimension resource. Specify tagged_searches_padding for the **Name** and 8dp for the **Value** and click **OK**, then select your new dimension resource and click **OK**. For the **Bottom** property, simply select this new dimension resource. These properties ensure that there is

an 8dp margin between the TextView and the top of the ListView and between the bottom of the ListView and the bottom of the vertical LinearLayout.

4.4.4 Graphical Layout Editor Toolbar

You've now completed the MainActivity's GUI. The **Graphical Layout** editor's toolbar (Fig. 4.14) contains various buttons that enable you to preview the design for other screen sizes and orientations. In particular, you can view thumbnail images of many screen sizes and orientations by clicking the down arrow next to the ⓓ button and selecting either **Preview Representative Sample** or **Preview All Screen Sizes**. For each thumbnail, there are + and – buttons that you can click to zoom in and out. Figure 4.14 overviews some of the buttons in the **Graphical Layout** editor's toolbar.

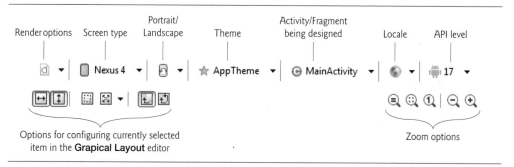

Fig. 4.14 | Canvas configuration options.

Option	Description
Render options	View one design screen at a time or see your design on a variety of screen sizes all at once.
Screen type	Android runs on a wide variety of devices, so the **Graphical Layout** editor comes with many device configurations that represent various screen sizes and resolutions that you can use to design your GUI. In this book, we use the predefined **Nexus 4**, **Nexus 7** and **Nexus 10** screens, depending on the app. In Fig. 4.14, we selected **Nexus 4**.
Portrait/Landscape	Toggles the design area between *portrait* and *landscape* orientations.
Theme	Can be used to set the theme for the GUI.
Activity/Fragment being designed	Shows the Activity or Fragment class that corresponds to the GUI being designed.
Locale	For *internationalized* apps (Section 2.8), allows you to select a specific localization, so that you can see, for example, what your design looks like with different language strings.
API level	Specifies the target API level for the design. With each new API level, there have typically been new GUI features. The **Graphical Layout** editor window shows only features that are available in the selected API level.

Fig. 4.15 | Explanation of the canvas configuration options.

4.4.5 ListView Item's Layout: `list_item.xml`

When populating a `ListView` with data, you must specify the format that's applied to each list item. Each list item in this app displays the `String` tag name for one saved search. To specify each list item's formatting, you'll create a new layout that contains only a `TextView` with the appropriate formatting. Perform the following steps:

1. In the **Package Explorer** window, expand the project's `res` folder, then right click the `layout` folder and select **New > Other...** to display the **New** dialog.

2. In the **Android** node, select **Android XML Layout File** and click **Next >** to display the dialog in Fig. 4.16, then configure the file as shown. The new layout's file name is `list_item.xml` and the root element in the layout is a `TextView`.

3. Click **Finish** to create the file.

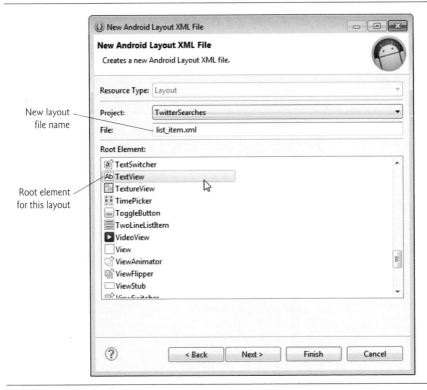

Fig. 4.16 | Creating a new `list_item.xml` layout in the **New Android Layout XML File** dialog.

The IDE opens the new layout in the **Graphical Layout** editor. Select the `TextView` in the **Outline** window, then set the following properties:

- **Id: @+id/textView**—GUI component **Id**s begin with a lowercase first letter by convention.

- **Height (Layout Parameters** node): `?android:attr/listPreferredItemHeight`— This value is a predefined Android resource that represents a list item's preferred height for responding properly to user touches with a minimal chance of touching the wrong item.

Look-and-Feel Observation 4.4

The Android design guidelines specify that the minimum recommended size for a touchable item on the screen is 48dp-by-48dp. For more information on GUI sizing and spacing, see `http://developer.android.com/design/style/metrics-grids.html`.

- **Gravity** (**Layout Parameters** node): `center_vertical`—The `TextView` should be centered vertically within the `ListView` item.

- **Text Appearance** (**TextView** node): `?android:attr/textAppearanceMedium`— This is the predefined theme resource that specifies the font size for medium-sized text.

List Items That Display Multiple Pieces of Data

If a list item should display multiple pieces of data, you'll need a list-item layout that consists of multiple elements, and each element will need an `android:id` attribute.

Other Predefined Android Resources

There are many predefined Android resources like the ones used to set the **Height** and **Text Appearance** for a list item. You can view the complete list at:

> `http://developer.android.com/reference/android/R.attr.html`

To use a value in your layouts, specify it in the format

> `?android:attr/`*resourceName*

4.5 Building the MainActivity Class

Figures 4.17–4.27 implement the **Twitter Searches** app's logic in the class `MainActivity`, which extends `ListActivity`. The default code for class `MainActivity` included an `onCreateOptionsMenu` method, which we removed because it's not used in this app—we'll discuss `onCreateOptionsMenu` in Chapter 5. Throughout this section, we assume that you create the necessary `String` resources as you encounter them in the code descriptions.

4.5.1 package and import Statements

Figure 4.17 shows the app's `package` and `import` statements. The `package` statement (inserted in line 4 by the IDE when you created the project) indicates that the class in this file is part of the `com.deitel.twittersearches` package. Lines 6–26 import the classes and interfaces the app uses.

```
1   // MainActivity.java
2   // Manages your favorite Twitter searches for easy
3   // access and display in the device's web browser
4   package com.deitel.twittersearches;
5
```

Fig. 4.17 | MainActivity's package and import statements. (Part 1 of 2.)

```
 6   import java.util.ArrayList;
 7   import java.util.Collections;
 8
 9   import android.app.AlertDialog;
10   import android.app.ListActivity;
11   import android.content.Context;
12   import android.content.DialogInterface;
13   import android.content.Intent;
14   import android.content.SharedPreferences;
15   import android.net.Uri;
16   import android.os.Bundle;
17   import android.view.View;
18   import android.view.View.OnClickListener;
19   import android.view.inputmethod.InputMethodManager;
20   import android.widget.AdapterView;
21   import android.widget.AdapterView.OnItemClickListener;
22   import android.widget.AdapterView.OnItemLongClickListener;
23   import android.widget.ArrayAdapter;
24   import android.widget.EditText;
25   import android.widget.ImageButton;
26   import android.widget.TextView;
27
```

Fig. 4.17 | MainActivity's package and import statements. (Part 2 of 2.)

Lines 6–7 import the ArrayList and Collections classes from the java.util package. We use class ArrayList to maintain the list of tags for the saved searches, and class Collections to *sort* the tags so they appear in alphabetical order. Of the remaining import statements, we consider only those for the features introduced in this chapter:

- Class AlertDialog of package android.app (line 9) is used to display dialogs.

- Class ListActivity of package android.app (line 10) is MainActivity's superclass, which provides the app's ListView and methods for manipulating it.

- Class **Context** of package **android.content** (line 11) provides access to information about the environment in which the app is running and allows you to use various Android services. We'll be using a constant from this class when we programmatically hide the soft keyboard after the user saves a search.

- Class **DialogInterface** of package android.content (line 12) contains the nested interface **OnClickListener**. We implement this interface to handle the events that occur when the user touches a button on an AlertDialog.

- Class Intent of package android.content (line 13) is used to create an object that specifies an *action* to be performed and the *data* to be acted upon—Android uses Intents to launch the appropriate activities. We'll use this class to launch the device's web browser to display Twitter search results and to display an *intent chooser* so the user can choose how to share a search.

- Class SharedPreferences of package android.content (line 14) is used to manipulate *persistent key–value pairs* that are stored in files associated with the app.

- Class **Uri** of package **android.net** (line 15) enables us to convert a URL into the format required by an Intent that launches the device's web browser.

- Class **View** of package **android.view** (line 17) is used in various event-handling methods to represent the GUI component that the user interacted with to initiate an event.

- Class View contains the nested interface **OnClickListener** (line 18). We implement this interface to handle the event raised when the user touches the Image-Button for saving a search.

- Class **InputMethodManager** of package **android.view.inputmethod** (line 19) enables us to hide the soft keyboard when the user saves a search.

- Package android.widget (lines 20–26) contains the GUI components and layouts that are used in Android GUIs. Class **AdapterView** (line 20) is the base class of ListView and is used when setting up the ListView's adapter (which supplies the ListView's items). You implement interface **AdapterView.OnItemClickListener** (line 21) to respond when the user *touches* an item in a ListView. You implement interface **AdapterView.OnItemLongClickListener** (line 22) to respond when the user *long presses* an item in a ListView. Class **ArrayAdapter** (line 23) is used to *bind* items to a ListView. Class ImageButton (line 25) represents a button that displays an image.

4.5.2 Extending `ListActivity`

MainActivity (Figs. 4.18–4.27) is the **Twitter Searches** app's only Activity class. When you created the TwitterSearches project, the IDE generated MainActivity as a subclass of Activity and provided the shell of an overridden onCreate method, which every Activity subclass *must* override. We changed the superclass to ListActivity (Fig. 4.18, line 28). When you make this change, the IDE does not recognize class ListActivity, so you must update your import statements. In the IDE, you can use **Source > Organize Imports** to update the import statements. Eclipse underlines any class or interface name that it does not recognize. In this case, if you hover the mouse over the class or interface name, a list of *quick fixes* will be displayed. If the IDE recognizes the name, it will suggest the missing import statement you need to add—simply click the name to add it.

```
28   public class MainActivity extends ListActivity
29   {
```

Fig. 4.18 | Class MainActivity is a subclass of ListActivity.

4.5.3 Fields of Class `MainActivity`

Figure 4.19 contains class MainActivity's static and instance variables. The String constant SEARCHES (line 31) represents the name of the file that will store the searches on the device. Lines 33–34 declare EditTexts that we'll use to access the queries and tags that the user enters. Line 35 declares the SharedPreferences instance variable savedSearches, which will be used to manipulate the *key–value pairs* representing the user's saved searches. Line 36 declares the ArrayList<String> that will store the sorted tag names for the user's searches. Line 37 declares the ArrayAdapter<String> that uses the contents of the Array-List<String> as the source of the items displayed in MainActivity's ListView.

> **Good Programming Practice 4.1**
>
> *For readability and modifiability, use* String *constants to represent filenames (and other* String *literals) that do not need to be localized, and thus are not defined in* strings.xml.

```
30      // name of SharedPreferences XML file that stores the saved searches
31      private static final String SEARCHES = "searches";
32
33      private EditText queryEditText; // EditText where user enters a query
34      private EditText tagEditText; // EditText where user tags a query
35      private SharedPreferences savedSearches; // user's favorite searches
36      private ArrayList<String> tags; // list of tags for saved searches
37      private ArrayAdapter<String> adapter; // binds tags to ListView
38
```

Fig. 4.19 | Fields of class MainActivity.

4.5.4 Overriding Activity Method onCreate

The onCreate method (Fig. 4.20) is called by the system:

- when the app *loads*

- if the app's process was *killed* by the operating system while the app was in the background, and the app is then *restored*

- each time the configuration changes, such as when the user *rotates* the device or *opens* or *closes* a physical keyboard.

The method initializes the Activity's instance variables and GUI components—we keep it simple so the app loads quickly. Line 43 makes the *required* call to the superclass's on-Create method. As in the previous app, the call to setContentView (line 44) passes the constant R.layout.activity_main to *inflate the GUI* from activity_main.xml.

```
39      // called when MainActivity is first created
40      @Override
41      protected void onCreate(Bundle savedInstanceState)
42      {
43         super.onCreate(savedInstanceState);
44         setContentView(R.layout.activity_main);
45
46         // get references to the EditTexts
47         queryEditText = (EditText) findViewById(R.id.queryEditText);
48         tagEditText = (EditText) findViewById(R.id.tagEditText);
49
50         // get the SharedPreferences containing the user's saved searches
51         savedSearches = getSharedPreferences(SEARCHES, MODE_PRIVATE);
52
53         // store the saved tags in an ArrayList then sort them
54         tags = new ArrayList<String>(savedSearches.getAll().keySet());
55         Collections.sort(tags, String.CASE_INSENSITIVE_ORDER);
56
```

Fig. 4.20 | Overriding Activity method onCreate. (Part 1 of 2.)

```
57          // create ArrayAdapter and use it to bind tags to the ListView
58          adapter = new ArrayAdapter<String>(this, R.layout.list_item, tags);
59          setListAdapter(adapter);
60
61          // register listener to save a new or edited search
62          ImageButton saveButton =
63             (ImageButton) findViewById(R.id.saveButton);
64          saveButton.setOnClickListener(saveButtonListener);
65
66          // register listener that searches Twitter when user touches a tag
67          getListView().setOnItemClickListener(itemClickListener);
68
69          // set listener that allows user to delete or edit a search
70          getListView().setOnItemLongClickListener(itemLongClickListener);
71      } // end method onCreate
72
```

Fig. 4.20 | Overriding Activity method onCreate. (Part 2 of 2.)

Getting References to the EditTexts
Lines 47–48 obtain references to the queryEditText and tagEditText to initialize the corresponding instance variables.

Getting a SharedPreferences Object
Line 51 uses the method **getSharedPreferences** (inherited from class Context) to get a SharedPreferences object that can read existing *tag–query pairs* (if any) from the SEARCHES file. The first argument indicates the name of the file that contains the data. The second argument specifies the accessibility of the file and can be set to one of the following options:

- **MODE_PRIVATE**—The file is accessible *only* to this app. In most cases, you'll use this option.

- **MODE_WORLD_READABLE**—Any app on the device can *read* from the file.

- **MODE_WORLD_WRITABLE**—Any app on the device can *write* to the file.

These constants can be combined with the bitwise OR operator (|). We aren't reading a lot of data in this app, so it's fast enough to load the searches in onCreate.

Performance Tip 4.1
Lengthy data access should not be done in the UI thread; otherwise, the app will display an Application Not Responding (ANR) dialog—typically after five seconds of preventing the user from interacting with the app. For information on designing responsive apps, see http://developer.android.com/guide/practices/design/responsiveness.html.

Getting the Keys Stored in the SharedPreferences Object
We'd like to display the search tags alphabetically so the user can easily find a search to perform. First, line 54 gets the Strings representing the keys in the SharedPreferences object and stores them in tags (an ArrayList<String>). SharedPreferences method **getAll** returns all the saved searches as a Map (package java.util)—a collection of key–value pairs. We then call method **keySet** on that object to get all the keys as a Set (package java.util)—a collection of unique values. The result is used to initialize tags.

Sorting the ArrayList of Tags

Line 55 uses **Collections.sort** to sort tags. Since the user could enter tags using mixtures of uppercase and lowercase letters, we chose to perform a *case-insensitive sort* by passing the predefined Comparator<String> object **String.CASE_INSENSITIVE_ORDER** as the second argument to Collections.sort.

Using an ArrayAdapter to Populate the ListView

To display the results in a ListView we create a new ArrayAdapter<String> object (line 58) which maps the contents tags to TextViews that are displayed in MainActivity's ListView. The ArrayAdapter<String>'s constructor receives:

- the Context (this) in which the ListView is displayed—this is the MainActivity

- the resource ID (R.layout.list_item) of the layout that's used to display each item in the ListView

- a List<String> containing the items to display—tags is an ArrayList<String>, which implements interface List<String>, so tags is a List<String>.

Line 59 uses inherited ListActivity method **setListAdapter** to bind the ListView to the ArrayAdapter, so that the ListView can display the data.

Registering Listeners for the saveButton and ListView

Lines 62–63 obtain a reference to the saveButton and line 64 registers its listener—instance variable saveButtonListener refers to an *anonymous-inner-class object* that implements interface OnClickListener (Fig. 4.21). Line 67 uses inherited ListActivity method **getListView** to get a reference to this activity's ListView, then registers the ListView's OnItemClickListener—instance variable itemClickListener refers to an *anonymous inner class object* that implements this interface (Fig. 4.24). Similarly, line 70 registers the ListView's OnItemLongClickListener—instance variable itemLongClickListener refers to an *anonymous-inner-class object* that implements this interface (Fig. 4.25).

4.5.5 Anonymous Inner Class That Implements the saveButton's OnClickListener to Save a New or Updated Search

Figure 4.21 declares and initializes instance variable saveButtonListener, which refers to an *anonymous inner class object* that implements interface OnClickListener. Line 64 (Fig. 4.20) registered saveButtonListener as saveButtons's event handler. Lines 76–109 override interface OnClickListener's onClick method. If the user entered a query *and* a tag (lines 80–81), lines 83–84 call method addTaggedSearch (Fig. 4.23) to store the tag–query pair and lines 85–86 clear the two EditTexts. Lines 88–90 hide the soft keyboard.

```
73    // saveButtonListener saves a tag-query pair into SharedPreferences
74    public OnClickListener saveButtonListener = new OnClickListener()
75    {
76        @Override
77        public void onClick(View v)
78        {
```

Fig. 4.21 | Anonymous inner class that implements the saveButton's OnClickListener to save a new or updated search. (Part 1 of 2.)

```
79                  // create tag if neither queryEditText nor tagEditText is empty
80                  if (queryEditText.getText().length() > 0 &&
81                      tagEditText.getText().length() > 0)
82                  {
83                      addTaggedSearch(queryEditText.getText().toString(),
84                          tagEditText.getText().toString());
85                      queryEditText.setText(""); // clear queryEditText
86                      tagEditText.setText(""); // clear tagEditText
87
88                      ((InputMethodManager) getSystemService(
89                          Context.INPUT_METHOD_SERVICE)).hideSoftInputFromWindow(
90                          tagEditText.getWindowToken(), 0);
91                  }
92                  else // display message asking user to provide a query and a tag
93                  {
94                      // create a new AlertDialog Builder
95                      AlertDialog.Builder builder =
96                          new AlertDialog.Builder(MainActivity.this);
97
98                      // set dialog's title and message to display
99                      builder.setMessage(R.string.missingMessage);
100
101                     // provide an OK button that simply dismisses the dialog
102                     builder.setPositiveButton(R.string.OK, null);
103
104                     // create AlertDialog from the AlertDialog.Builder
105                     AlertDialog errorDialog = builder.create();
106                     errorDialog.show(); // display the modal dialog
107                 }
108         } // end method onClick
109     }; // end OnClickListener anonymous inner class
110
```

Fig. 4.21 | Anonymous inner class that implements the saveButton's OnClickListener to save a new or updated search. (Part 2 of 2.)

Configuring an AlertDialog

If the user did not enter a query *and* a tag, lines 92–108 display an AlertDialog indicating that the user must enter both. An AlertDialog.Builder object (lines 95–96) helps you configure and create an AlertDialog. The argument to the constructor is the Context in which the dialog will be displayed—in this case, the MainActivity, which we refer to via its this reference. To access this from an *anonymous inner class*, you must fully qualify this with the outer class's name. Line 99 sets the dialog's message with the String resource R.string.missingMessage ("Enter both a Twitter search query and a tag").

Look-and-Feel Observation 4.5

You can set an AlertDialog's title (which appears above the dialog's message) with AlertDialog.Builder method setTitle. According to the Android design guidelines for dialogs (http://developer.android.com/design/building-blocks/dialogs.html), most dialogs do not need titles. A dialog should display a title for "a high-risk operation involving potential loss of data, connectivity, extra charges, and so on." Also, dialogs that display lists of options use the title to specify the dialog's purpose.

Adding *String Resources to* strings.xml

To create String resources like R.string.missingMessage, open the strings.xml file located in the project's res/values folder. The IDE shows this file in a *resource editor* that has two tabs—**Resources** and **strings.xml**. In the **Resources** tab, you can click **Add...** to display the dialog in Fig. 4.22. Selecting **String** and clicking **OK** displays **Name** and **Value** textfields where you can enter a new String resource's name (e.g., missingMessage) and value. Save your strings.xml file after making changes. You can also use the resource editor's **Resource** tab to select an existing String resource to change its name and value.

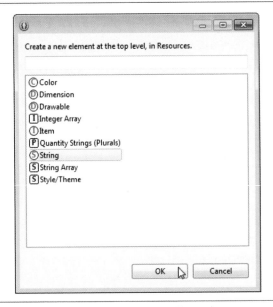

Fig. 4.22 | Adding a String resource.

Specifying the AlertDialog's Positive Button

In this AlertDialog, we need only one button that allows the user to acknowledge the message. We specify this as the dialog's *positive* button (Fig. 4.21, line 102)—touching this button indicates that the user acknowledges the message displayed in the dialog. Method setPositiveButton receives the button's label (specified with the String resource R.string.OK) and a reference to the button's event handler. For this dialog, we don't need to respond to the event, so we specify null for the event handler. When the user touches the button, the dialog is simply dismissed from the screen.

Creating and Showing the AlertDialog

You create the AlertDialog by calling the AlertDialog.Builder's create method (line 105) and display the *modal dialog* by calling AlertDialog's show method (line 106).

4.5.6 addTaggedSearch Method

The event handler in Fig. 4.21 calls MainActivity method addTaggedSearch (Fig. 4.23) to add a new search to savedSearches or to modify an existing search.

```
111     // add new search to the save file, then refresh all Buttons
112     private void addTaggedSearch(String query, String tag)
113     {
114        // get a SharedPreferences.Editor to store new tag/query pair
115        SharedPreferences.Editor preferencesEditor = savedSearches.edit();
116        preferencesEditor.putString(tag, query); // store current search
117        preferencesEditor.apply(); // store the updated preferences
118
119        // if tag is new, add to and sort tags, then display updated list
120        if (!tags.contains(tag))
121        {
122           tags.add(tag); // add new tag
123           Collections.sort(tags, String.CASE_INSENSITIVE_ORDER);
124           adapter.notifyDataSetChanged(); // rebind tags to ListView
125        }
126     }
127
```

Fig. 4.23 | addTaggedSearch method of class MainActivity.

Editing a *SharedPreferences* Object's Contents
To change a SharedPreferences object's contents, you must first call its **edit** method to obtain a SharedPreferences.Editor object (line 115), which can add key–value pairs to, remove key–value pairs from, and modify the value associated with a particular key in a SharedPreferences file. Line 116 calls SharedPreferences.Editor method **putString** to save the search's tag (the key) and query (the corresponding value)—if the tag already exists in the SharedPreferences this updates the value. Line 117 *commits* the changes by calling SharedPreferences.Editor method **apply** to make the changes to the file.

Notifying the *ArrayAdapter* That Its Data Has Changed
When the user adds a new search, the ListView should be updated to display it. Lines 120–125 determine whether a new tag was added. If so, lines 122–123 add the new search's tag to tags, then sort tags. Line 124 calls the ArrayAdapter's **notifyDataSet-Changed** method to indicate that the underlying data in tags has changed. The adapter then notifies the ListView to update its list of displayed items.

4.5.7 Anonymous Inner Class That Implements the ListView's OnItemClickListener to Display Search Results
Figure 4.24 declares and initializes instance variable itemClickListener, which refers to an *anonymous inner-class object* that implements interface OnItemClickListener. Line 67 (Fig. 4.20) registered itemClickListener as the ListView's event handler that responds when the user *touches* an item in the ListView. Lines 131–145 override interface OnItemClickListener's onItemClick method. The method's arguments are:

- The AdapterView where the user touched an item. The ? in AdapterView<?> is a *wildcard* in Java generics indicating method onItemClick can receive an AdapterView that displays *any* type of data—in this case, a ListView<String>.

- The View that the user touched in the AdapterView—in this case, the TextView that displays a search tag.

- The *zero-based* index number of the item the user touched.

- The row ID of the item that was touched—this is used primarily for data obtained from a database (as you'll do in Chapter 8).

```
128    // itemClickListener launches web browser to display search results
129    OnItemClickListener itemClickListener = new OnItemClickListener()
130    {
131       @Override
132       public void onItemClick(AdapterView<?> parent, View view,
133          int position, long id)
134       {
135          // get query string and create a URL representing the search
136          String tag = ((TextView) view).getText().toString();
137          String urlString = getString(R.string.searchURL) +
138             Uri.encode(savedSearches.getString(tag, ""), "UTF-8");
139
140          // create an Intent to launch a web browser
141          Intent webIntent = new Intent(Intent.ACTION_VIEW,
142             Uri.parse(urlString));
143
144          startActivity(webIntent); // launches web browser to view results
145       }
146    }; // end itemClickListener declaration
147
```

Fig. 4.24 | Anonymous inner class that implements the ListView's OnItemClickListener to display search results.

Getting *String Resources*

Line 136 gets the text of the View that the user touched in the ListView. Lines 137–138 create a String containing the Twitter search URL and the query to perform. First, line 137 calls Activity's inherited method **getString** with one argument to get the String resource named searchURL, which contains the Twitter search page's URL:

```
http://mobile.twitter.com/search/
```

As with all the String resources in this app, you should add this resource to strings.xml.

Getting *Strings from a SharedPreferences Object*

We append the result of line 138 to the search URL to complete the urlString. Shared-Preferences method **getString** returns the query associated with the tag. If the tag does not already exist, the second argument ("" in this case) is returned. Line 138 passes the query to Uri method encode, which *escapes* any special URL characters (such as ?, /, :, etc.) and returns a so-called *URL-encoded* String. This is important to ensure that the Twitter web server that receives the request can parse the URL properly to obtain the search query.

Creating an *Intent to Launch the Device's Web Browser*

Lines 141–142 create a new Intent, which we'll use to *launch* the device's *web browser* and display the search results. Intents can be used to launch other activities in the same app or in other apps. The first argument of Intent's constructor is a constant describing the *action* to perform. **Intent.ACTION_VIEW** indicates that we'd like to display a representation of the data. Many constants are defined in the Intent class describing actions such as *searching, choosing, sending* and *playing*. The second argument (line 142) is a **Uri** (uniform resource identifier) representing the *data* on which we want to perform the action. Class Uri's **parse method** converts a String representing a URL (uniform resource locator) to a Uri.

Starting an *Activity* for an *Intent*

Line 144 passes the Intent to the inherited Activity method startActivity, which starts an Activity that can perform the specified *action* on the given *data*. In this case, because we've specified to view a URI, the Intent launches the device's web browser to display the corresponding web page. This page shows the results of the supplied Twitter search.

4.5.8 Anonymous Inner Class That Implements the ListView's OnItemLongClickListener to Share, Edit or Delete a Search

Figure 4.25 declares and initializes instance variable itemLongClickListener, which refers to an *anonymous inner-class object* that implements interface OnItemLongClickListener. Line 70 (Fig. 4.20) registered itemLongClickListener as the ListView's event handler that responds when the user long presses an item in the ListView. Lines 153–210 override interface OnItemLongClickListener's onItemLongClick method.

```
148    // itemLongClickListener displays a dialog allowing the user to delete
149    // or edit a saved search
150    OnItemLongClickListener itemLongClickListener =
151       new OnItemLongClickListener()
152       {
153          @Override
154          public boolean onItemLongClick(AdapterView<?> parent, View view,
155             int position, long id)
156          {
157             // get the tag that the user long touched
158             final String tag = ((TextView) view).getText().toString();
159
160             // create a new AlertDialog
161             AlertDialog.Builder builder =
162                new AlertDialog.Builder(MainActivity.this);
163
164             // set the AlertDialog's title
165             builder.setTitle(
166                getString(R.string.shareEditDeleteTitle, tag));
167
168             // set list of items to display in dialog
169             builder.setItems(R.array.dialog_items,
170                new DialogInterface.OnClickListener()
171                {
172                   // responds to user touch by sharing, editing or
173                   // deleting a saved search
```

Fig. 4.25 | Anonymous inner class that implements the ListView's OnItemLongClickListener to share, edit or delete. (Part 1 of 2.)

```
174                @Override
175                public void onClick(DialogInterface dialog, int which)
176                {
177                   switch (which)
178                   {
179                      case 0: // share
180                         shareSearch(tag);
181                         break;
182                      case 1: // edit
183                         // set EditTexts to match chosen tag and query
184                         tagEditText.setText(tag);
185                         queryEditText.setText(
186                            savedSearches.getString(tag, ""));
187                         break;
188                      case 2: // delete
189                         deleteSearch(tag);
190                         break;
191                   }
192                }
193             } // end DialogInterface.OnClickListener
194          ); // end call to builder.setItems
195
196          // set the AlertDialog's negative Button
197          builder.setNegativeButton(getString(R.string.cancel),
198             new DialogInterface.OnClickListener()
199             {
200                // called when the "Cancel" Button is clicked
201                public void onClick(DialogInterface dialog, int id)
202                {
203                   dialog.cancel(); // dismiss the AlertDialog
204                }
205             }
206          ); // end call to setNegativeButton
207
208          builder.create().show(); // display the AlertDialog
209          return true;
210       } // end method onItemLongClick
211    }; // end OnItemLongClickListener declaration
212
```

Fig. 4.25 | Anonymous inner class that implements the `ListView`'s `OnItemLongClickLis-tener` to share, edit or delete. (Part 2 of 2.)

final *Local Variables for Use in Anonymous Inner Classes*

Line 158 gets the text of the item the user *long pressed* and assigns it to `final` local variable `tag`. Any local variable or method parameter that will be used in an anonymous inner class *must* be declared `final`.

AlertDialog *That Displays a List of Items*

Lines 161–166 create an `AlertDialog.Builder` and set the dialog's title to a formatted `String` in which `tag` replaces the format specifier in the resource `R.string.shareEdit-DeleteTitle` (which represents `"Share, Edit or Delete the search tagged as \"%s\""`).

Line 166 calls Activity's inherited method getString that receives *multiple arguments*—this first is a String resource ID representing a *format String* and the remaining arguments are the values that should replace the format specifiers in the format String. In addition to buttons, an AlertDialog can display a list of items in a ListView. Lines 169–194 specify that the dialog should display the array of Strings R.array.dialog_items (which represents the Strings "Share", "Edit" and "Delete") and define an anonymous inner class to respond when the user touches an item in the list.

Adding a *String* Array Resource to *strings.xml*

The array of Strings is defined as a String array resource in the strings.xml file. To add a String array resource to strings.xml:

1. Follow the steps in Section 4.5.5 to add a String resource, but select **String Array** rather than **String** in the dialog of Fig. 4.22, then click **OK**.

2. Specify the array's name (dialog_items) in the **Name** textfield.

3. Select the array in the list of resources at the left side of the resource editor.

4. Click Add... then click OK to add a new **Item** to the array.

5. Specify the new **Item**'s value in the **Value** textfield.

Perform these steps for the items Share, Edit and Delete (in that order), then save the strings.xml file.

Event Handler for the Dialog's List of Items

The anonymous inner class in lines 170–193 determines which item the user selected in the dialog's list and performs the appropriate action. If the user selects **Share**, shareSearch is called (line 180). If the user selects **Edit**, lines 184–186 display the search's query and tag in the EditTexts. If the user selects **Delete**, deleteSearch is called (line 189).

Configuring the Negative Button and Displaying the Dialog

Lines 197–206 configure the dialog's *negative* button to dismiss the dialog if the user decides not to share, edit or delete the search. Line 208 creates and shows the dialog.

4.5.9 shareSearch Method

Method shareSearch (Fig. 4.26) is called by the event handler in Fig. 4.25 when the user selects to share a search. Lines 217–218 create a String representing the search to share. Lines 221–227 create and configure an Intent that allows the user to send the search URL using an Activity that can handle the Intent.**ACTION_SEND** (line 222).

```
213    // allows user to choose an app for sharing a saved search's URL
214    private void shareSearch(String tag)
215    {
216        // create the URL representing the search
217        String urlString = getString(R.string.searchURL) +
218            Uri.encode(savedSearches.getString(tag, ""), "UTF-8");
219
```

Fig. 4.26 | shareSearch method of class MainActivity. (Part 1 of 2.)

```
220        // create Intent to share urlString
221        Intent shareIntent = new Intent();
222        shareIntent.setAction(Intent.ACTION_SEND);
223        shareIntent.putExtra(Intent.EXTRA_SUBJECT,
224           getString(R.string.shareSubject));
225        shareIntent.putExtra(Intent.EXTRA_TEXT,
226           getString(R.string.shareMessage, urlString));
227        shareIntent.setType("text/plain");
228
229        // display apps that can share text
230        startActivity(Intent.createChooser(shareIntent,
231           getString(R.string.shareSearch)));
232     }
233
```

Fig. 4.26 | shareSearch method of class MainActivity. (Part 2 of 2.)

*Adding Extras to an **Intent***

An Intent includes a Bundle of *extras*—additional information that's passed to the Activity that handles the Intent. For example, an e-mail Activity can receive *extras* representing the e-mail's subject, CC and BCC addresses, and the body text. Lines 223–226 use Intent method **putExtra** to add an extra as a key–value pair to the Intent's Bundle. The method's first argument is a String key representing the purpose of the extra and the second argument is the corresponding extra data. Extras may be primitive type values, primitive type arrays, entire Bundle objects and more—see class Intent's documentation for a complete list of the putExtra overloads.

The extra at lines 223–224 specifies an e-mail's subject with the String resource R.string.shareSubject ("Twitter search that might interest you"). For an Activity that does *not* use a subject (such as sharing on a social network), this extra is *ignored*. The extra at lines 225–226 represents the text to share—a formatted String in which the urlString is substituted into the String resource R.string.shareMessage ("Check out the results of this Twitter search: %s"). Line 227 sets the Intent's MIME type to text/plain—such data can be handled by any Activity capable of sending plain text messages.

Displaying an Intent Chooser

To display the *intent chooser* shown in Fig. 4.8(a), we pass the Intent and a String title to Intent's static **createChooser** method (line 230). The resource R.string.shareSearch ("Share Search to:") is used as the intent chooser's title. It's important to set this title to remind the user to select an appropriate Activity. You cannot control the apps installed on a user's phone or the Intent filters that can launch those apps, so it's possible that incompatible activities could appear in the chooser. Method createChooser returns an Intent that we pass to startActivity to display the intent chooser.

4.5.10 deleteSearch Method

The event handler in Fig. 4.25 calls method deleteSearch (Figure 4.27) when the user long presses a search tag and selects **Delete**. Before deleting the search, the app displays an AlertDialog to confirm the delete operation. Lines 241–242 set the dialog's title to a formatted String in which tag replaces the format specifier in the String resource

R.string.confirmMessage ("Are you sure you want to delete the search \"%s\"?"). Lines 245–254 configure the dialog's negative button to dismiss the dialog. The String resource R.string.cancel represents "Cancel". Lines 257–275 configure the dialog's positive button to remove the search. The String resource R.string.delete represents "Delete". Line 263 removes the tag from the tags collection, and lines 266–269 use a SharedPreferences.Editor to remove the search from the app's SharedPreferences. Line 272 then notifies the ArrayAdapter that the underlying data has changed so that the ListView can update its displayed list of items.

```
234   // deletes a search after the user confirms the delete operation
235   private void deleteSearch(final String tag)
236   {
237      // create a new AlertDialog
238      AlertDialog.Builder confirmBuilder = new AlertDialog.Builder(this);
239
240      // set the AlertDialog's message
241      confirmBuilder.setMessage(
242         getString(R.string.confirmMessage, tag));
243
244      // set the AlertDialog's negative Button
245      confirmBuilder.setNegativeButton(getString(R.string.cancel),
246         new DialogInterface.OnClickListener()
247         {
248            // called when "Cancel" Button is clicked
249            public void onClick(DialogInterface dialog, int id)
250            {
251               dialog.cancel(); // dismiss dialog
252            }
253         }
254      ); // end call to setNegativeButton
255
256      // set the AlertDialog's positive Button
257      confirmBuilder.setPositiveButton(getString(R.string.delete),
258         new DialogInterface.OnClickListener()
259         {
260            // called when "Cancel" Button is clicked
261            public void onClick(DialogInterface dialog, int id)
262            {
263               tags.remove(tag); // remove tag from tags
264
265               // get SharedPreferences.Editor to remove saved search
266               SharedPreferences.Editor preferencesEditor =
267                  savedSearches.edit();
268               preferencesEditor.remove(tag); // remove search
269               preferencesEditor.apply(); // saves the changes
270
271               // rebind tags ArrayList to ListView to show updated list
272               adapter.notifyDataSetChanged();
273            }
274         } // end OnClickListener
275      ); // end call to setPositiveButton
```

Fig. 4.27 | deleteSearch method of class MainActivity. (Part 1 of 2.)

```
276
277          confirmBuilder.create().show(); // display AlertDialog
278     } // end method deleteSearch
279   } // end class MainActivity
```

Fig. 4.27 | deleteSearch method of class MainActivity. (Part 2 of 2.)

4.6 AndroidManifest.xml

In Section 3.6, you made two changes to the AndroidManifest.xml file:

- The first indicated that the **Tip Calculator** app supported only portrait orientation.

- The second forced the soft keyboard to be displayed when the app started executing so that the user could immediately enter a bill amount in the **Tip Calculator** app.

This app supports both portrait and landscape orientations. No changes are required to indicate this, because all apps support both orientations by default.

In this app, most users will launch this app so that they can perform one of their saved searches. When the first GUI component in the GUI is an EditText, Android gives that component the focus when the app loads. As you know, when an EditText receives the focus, its corresponding soft keyboard is displayed (unless a hardware keyboard is present). In this app, we want to prevent the soft keyboard from being displayed unless the user touches one of the app's EditTexts. To do so, follow the steps in Section 3.6 for setting the **Window soft input mode** option, but set its value to stateAlwaysHidden.

4.7 Wrap-Up

In this chapter, you created the **Twitter Searches** app. First you designed the GUI. We introduced the ListView component for displaying a scrollable list of items and used it to display the arbitrarily large list of saved searches. Each search was associated with an item in the ListView that the user could touch to pass the search to the device's web browser. You also learned how to create String resources for use in your Java code.

We stored the search tag–query pairs in a SharedPreferences file associated with the app and showed how to programmatically *hide* the soft keyboard. We also used a Shared-Preferences.Editor object to store values in, modify values in and remove values from a SharedPreferences file. In response to the user touching a search tag, we loaded a Uri into the device's web browser by creating a new Intent and passing it to Context's start-Activity method. You also used an Intent to display an intent chooser allowing the user to select an Activity for sharing a search.

You used AlertDialog.Builder objects to configure and create AlertDialogs for displaying messages to the user. Finally, we discussed the AndroidManifest.xml file and showed you how to configure the app so that the soft keyboard is not displayed when the app is launched.

In Chapter 5, you'll build the **Flag Quiz** app in which the user is shown a graphic of a country's flag and must guess the country from 3, 6 or 9 choices. You'll use a menu and checkboxes to customize the quiz, limiting the flags and countries chosen to specific regions of the world.

5

Flag Quiz App

Fragments, Menus, Preferences, AssetManager, Tweened Animations, Handler, Toasts, Explicit Intents, Layouts for Multiple Device Orientations

Objectives

In this chapter you'll:

- Use Fragments to make better use of available screen real estate in an Activity's GUI on phones and tablets.

- Display an options menu on the action bar to enable users to configure the app's preferences.

- Use a PreferenceFragment to automatically manage and persist an app's user preferences.

- Use an app's assets subfolders to organize image resources and manipulate them with an AssetManager.

- Define an animation and apply it to a View.

- Use a Handler to schedule a future task to perform on the GUI thread.

- Use Toasts to display messages briefly to the user.

- Launch a specific Activity with an explicit Intent.

- Use various collections from the java.util package.

- Define layouts for multiple device orientations.

- Use Android's logging mechanism to log error messages.

Outline

5.1 Introduction

The **Flag Quiz** app tests your ability to correctly identify 10 country flags (Fig. 5.1). Initially, the app presents a flag image and three guess Buttons representing the possible country answers—one matches the flag and the others are randomly selected, nonduplicated incorrect answers. The app displays the user's progress throughout the quiz, showing the question number (out of 10) in a TextView above the current flag image. As you'll see, the app also allows you to control the quiz difficulty by specifying whether to display three, six or nine guess Buttons, and by choosing the world regions that should be included in the quiz. These options are displayed differently based on the device that's running the app and the orientation of the device—the app supports portrait orientation on *any* device, but landscape orientation only on tablets. In portrait orientation, the app displays on the action bar an *options menu* containing a **Settings** menu item. When the user selects this item, the app

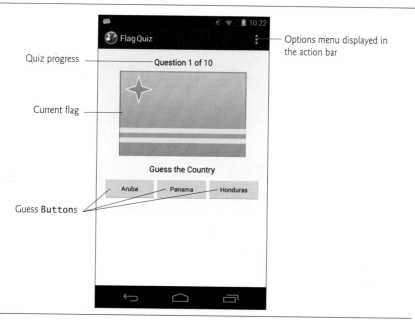

Quiz progress

Current flag

Guess **Buttons**

Options menu displayed in
the action bar

Fig. 5.1 | **Flag Quiz** app running on a smartphone in portrait orientation.

displays an `Activity` for setting the number of guess `Buttons` and the world regions to use in the quiz. On a tablet in landscape orientation (Fig. 5.2), the app uses a different layout that displays the app's settings at the left side of the screen and the quiz at the right side.

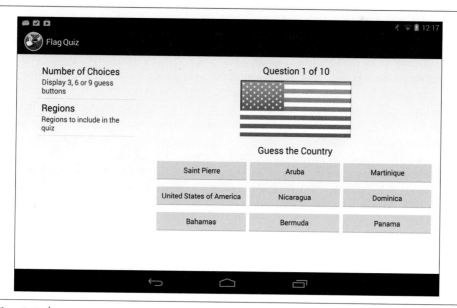

Fig. 5.2 | **Flag Quiz** app running on a tablet in landscape orientation.

First, you'll test-drive the app. Then we'll overview the technologies used to build it. Next, you'll design the app's GUI. Finally, we'll present the app's complete source code and walk through the code, discussing the app's new features in more detail.

5.2 Test-Driving the Flag Quiz App

You'll now test-drive the Flag Quiz app. Open the IDE and import the Flag Quiz app project. You can test this app on a phone AVD, tablet AVD or actual device. The screen captures in this chapter were taken on a Nexus 4 phone and a Nexus 7 tablet.

5.2.1 Importing the App and Running It

Perform the following steps to import the app into the IDE:

1. *Opening the Import dialog.* Select File > Import....

2. *Importing the Flag Quiz app's project.* Expand the General node and select Existing Projects into Workspace. Click Next > to proceed to the Import Projects step. Ensure that Select root directory is selected, then click Browse.... Locate the FlagQuiz folder in the book's examples folder, select it and click OK. Ensure that Copy projects into workspace is *not* selected. Click Finish to import the project so that it appears in the Package Explorer window.

3. *Launching the Flag Quiz app.* Right click the FlagQuiz project and select Run As > Android Application to execute the app in the AVD or on a device. This builds the project and runs the app (Fig. 5.1 or Fig. 5.2).

5.2.2 Configuring the Quiz

When you first install and run the app, the quiz is configured to display three guess Buttons and to select flags from *all* of the world's regions. For this test-drive, you'll change the app's options to select flags only from North America and you'll keep the app's default setting of three guess Buttons per flag. On a phone, a tablet or AVD in portrait orientation, touch the *options menu* icon (█, Fig. 5.1) on the action bar to open the menu, then select Settings so you can view the app's options in the Flag Quiz Settings screen (Fig. 5.3(a)). On a tablet device or tablet AVD in *landscape* orientation, the app's settings options appear at the left side of the screen (Fig. 5.2). Touch Number of Choices to display the dialog (Fig. 5.3(b)) for selecting the number of Buttons that should be displayed with each flag. (On a tablet device or tablet AVD in landscape orientation, the entire app is grayed out and the dialog appears in the center of the screen.) By default, 3 is selected. To make the quiz more challenging, you can select 6 or 9 and touch OK; otherwise, touch Cancel to return to the Flag Quiz Settings screen. We used the default setting of three guess Buttons for this test-drive.

Next, touch Regions (Fig. 5.4(a)) to display the checkboxes representing the world regions (Fig. 5.4(b)). By default, all regions are enabled when the app is first executed, so any of the world's flags can be selected randomly for the quiz. Touch the checkboxes next to Africa, Asia, Europe, Oceania and South America to uncheck them—this excludes those regions' countries from the quiz. Touch OK to reset the quiz with the updated settings. On a phone, a tablet or AVD in portrait orientation, touch the back button (◰) to return to the quiz. On a tablet device or tablet AVD in landscape orientation, a quiz with the updated settings is immediately displayed at the right side of the screen.

a) Menu with the user touching **Number of Choices**   b) Dialog showing options for number of choices

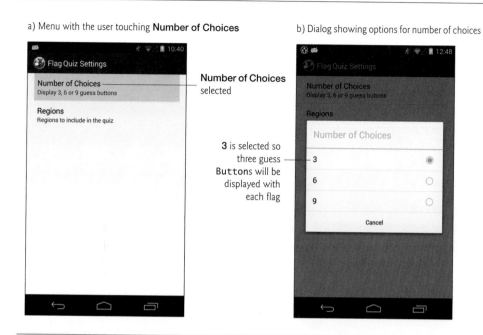

Fig. 5.3 | **Flag Quiz** settings screen and the **Number of Choices** dialog.

a) Menu with the user touching **Regions**   b) Dialog showing regions

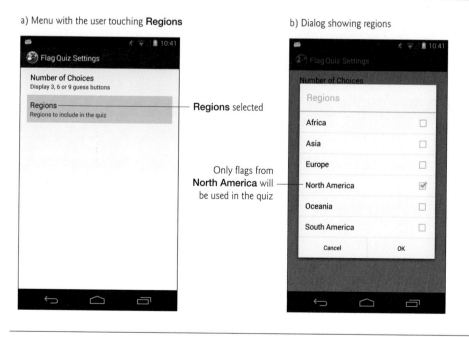

Fig. 5.4 | **Flag Quiz** settings screen and the **Regions** dialog.

5.2.3 Taking the Quiz

A new quiz starts with the number of answer choices you selected and flags from only the North America region. Work through the quiz by touching the guess Button for the country that you think matches each flag.

Making a Correct Selection
If the choice is correct (Fig. 5.5(a)), the app disables all the answer Buttons and displays the country name in green followed by an exclamation point at the bottom of the screen (Fig. 5.5(b)). After a short delay, the app loads the next flag and displays a new set of answer Buttons.

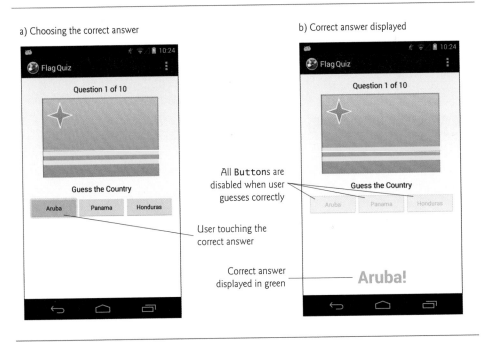

Fig. 5.5 | User choosing the correct answer and the correct answer displayed.

User Making an Incorrect Selection
If you select incorrectly (Fig. 5.6(a)), the app disables the corresponding country name Button, uses an animation to *shake* the flag and displays Incorrect! in red at the bottom of the screen (Fig. 5.6(b)). Keep guessing until you get the correct answer for that flag.

Completing the Quiz
After you select the 10 correct country names, a popup AlertDialog displays over the app and shows your total number of guesses and the percentage of correct answers (Fig. 5.7). When you touch the dialog's Reset Quiz Button, a new quiz begins based on the current quiz options.

a) Choosing an incorrect answer

b) **Incorrect!** displayed

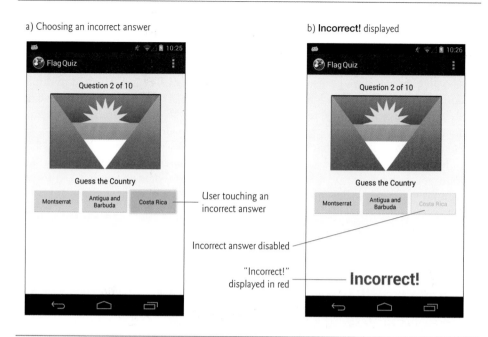

Fig. 5.6 | Disabled incorrect answer in the **Flag Quiz** app.

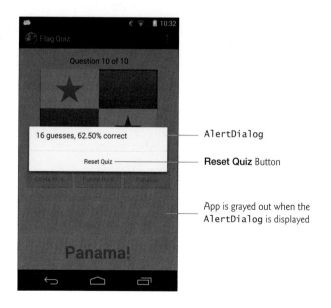

Fig. 5.7 | Results displayed after quiz completion.

5.3 Technologies Overview

This section introduces the features you'll use to build the **Flag Quiz** app.

5.3.1 Menus

When you create an app's project in the IDE, the MainActivity is configured to display an options menu (⋮) at the right side of the action bar. The menu contains a **Settings** menu item that's typically used to display an app's settings to the user. In later apps, you'll learn how to create additional menu items and how to decide which items should be displayed directly on the action bar vs. in the options menu.

The options menu is an object of class **Menu** (package android.view). To specify Menu options, you override Activity's **onCreateOptionsMenu** method (Section 5.5.4) to add the options to the method's Menu argument. When the user selects a menu item, Activity method **onOptionsItemSelected** (Section 5.5.5) responds to the selection.

5.3.2 Fragments

A **fragment** typically represents a reusable portion of an Activity's user interface, but may also represent reusable program logic. This app uses fragments to create and manage portions of the app's GUI. You can combine several fragments to create user interfaces that take advantage of tablet screen sizes. You also can easily interchange fragments to make your GUIs more dynamic—you'll learn about this in Chapter 8.

Fragment (package android.app) is the base class of all fragments. The **Flag Quiz** app defines the following direct and indirect Fragment subclasses:

- Class QuizFragment (Section 5.6)—a direct subclass of Fragment—displays the quiz's GUI and defines the quiz's logic. Like an Activity, each Fragment has its own layout that's typically defined as a layout resource, but can be created dynamically. In Section 5.4.8, you'll build QuizFragment's GUI. You'll use the QuizFragment in MainActivity's layouts—one for devices in portrait orientation and one for tablet devices in landscape orientation.

- Class SettingsFragment (Section 5.7) is a subclass of **PreferenceFragment** (package **android.preference**), which can automatically maintain an app's user preferences in a SharedPreferences file on the device. As you'll see, you can create an XML file that describes the user preferences and class PreferenceFragment can use that XML file to build an appropriate preferences GUI (Figs. 5.3–5.4).

- When you finish a quiz, the QuizFragment creates an anonymous inner class that extends **DialogFragment** (package android.app) and uses it to display an Alert-Dialog containing the quiz results (Section 5.6.9).

Fragments *must* be hosted by an Activity—they cannot execute independently. When this app runs in landscape orientation on a tablet, the MainActivity hosts all of the Fragments. In portrait orientation (on any device), the SettingsActivity (Section 5.8) hosts the SettingsFragment and the MainActivity hosts the others.

Though Fragments were introduced in Android 3.0, Fragments and other more recent Android features can be used in earlier versions via the Android Support Library. For more information, visit:

```
http://developer.android.com/tools/support-library/index.html
```

5.3.3 Fragment Lifecycle Methods

Like an Activity, each Fragment has a *lifecycle* and provides methods that you can override to respond to lifecycle events. In this app, you'll override:

- **onCreate**—This method (which you'll override in class SettingsFragment) is called when a Fragment is created. The QuizFragment and SettingsFragment are created when their parent activities' layouts are inflated, and the DialogFragment that displays the quiz results is created when you complete a quiz.

- **onCreateView**—This method (which you'll override in class QuizFragment) is called after onCreate to build and return a View containing the Fragment's GUI. As you'll see, this method receives a **LayoutInflater**, which you'll use to programmatically inflate a Fragment's GUI from the components specified in a predefined XML layout.

We'll discuss other Fragment lifecycle methods as we encounter them throughout the book. For the complete lifecycle details, visit:

```
http://developer.android.com/guide/components/fragments.html
```

5.3.4 Managing Fragments

A parent Activity manages its Fragments with a **FragmentManager** (package android.app) that's returned by the Activity's **getFragmentManager** method. If the Activity needs to interact with a Fragment that's declared in the Activity's layout and has an Id, the Activity can call FragmentManager method **findFragmentById** to obtain a reference to the specified Fragment. As you'll see in Chapter 8, a FragmentManager can use **FragmentTransactions** (package android.app) to dynamically *add, remove* and *transition* between Fragments.

5.3.5 Preferences

In Section 5.2.2, you changed the app's settings to customize the quiz. A PreferenceFragment uses **Preference** objects (package android.preference) to manage these settings. This app uses Preference subclass **ListPreference** to manage the number of guess Buttons displayed for each flag and Preference subclass **MultiSelectListPreference** to manage the world regions to include in the quiz. A ListPreference's items are *mutually exclusive*, whereas any number of items can be selected in a MultiSelectListPreference. You'll use a **PreferenceManager** object (package android.preference) to access and interact with the app's preferences.

5.3.6 assets Folder

This app's flag images[1] are loaded into the app only when needed and are located in the app's **assets folder**. To add the images to the project, we dragged each region's folder from our file system onto the assets folder in the **Package Explorer**. The images are located in the images/FlagQuizImages folder with the book's examples.

Unlike an app's drawable folders, which require their image contents to be at the root level in each folder, the assets folder may contain files of any type and they can be organized in subfolders—we maintain the flag images for each region in a separate subfolder.

---

1. We obtained the images from www.free-country-flags.com.

Files in the `assets` subfolders are accessed via an **AssetManager** (package `android.content.res`), which can provide a list of all of the file names in a specified subfolder and can be used to access each asset.

5.3.7 Resource Folders

In Section 2.4.4, you learned about the `drawable`, `layout` and `values` subfolders of an app's `res` folder. In this app, you'll also use the `menu`, `anim` and `xml` resource folders. Figure 5.8 overviews these subfolders as well as the `animator`, `color` and `raw` subfolders.

Resource subfolder	Description
anim	Folder names that begin with `anim` contain XML files that define *tweened animations*, which can change an object's *transparency, size, position* and *rotation* over time. We'll define such an animation in Section 5.4.11 then play it in Section 5.6.9 to create a *shake effect* for visual feedback to the user.
animator	Folder names that begin with `animator` contain XML files that define *property animations*, which change the value of a property of an object over time. In Java, a property is typically implemented in a class as an instance variable with both *set* and *get* accessors.
color	Folder names that begin with `color` contain XML files that define a list of colors for various states, such as the states of a `Button` (*unpressed, pressed, enabled*, etc.).
raw	Folder names that begin with `raw` contain resource files (such as audio clips) that are read into an app as streams of bytes. We'll use such resources in Chapter 6 to play sounds.
menu	Folder names that begin with `menu` contain XML files that describe the contents of menus. When you create a project, the IDE automatically defines a menu with a **Settings** option.
xml	Folder names that begin with `xml` contain XML files that do not fit into the other resource categories. These are often raw XML data files used by the app. In Section 5.4.10, you'll create an XML file that represents the preferences displayed by this app's `SettingsFragment`.

Fig. 5.8 | Other subfolders within a project's `res` folder.

5.3.8 Supporting Different Screen Sizes and Resolutions

In Section 2.5.1 you learned that Android devices have various *screen sizes, resolutions* and *pixel densities* (dots per inch or DPI). You also learned that you typically provide images and other visual resources in multiple resolutions so Android can choose the best resource for a device's pixel density. Similarly, in Section 2.8, you learned how to provide string resources for different languages and regions. Android uses resource folders with *qualified names* to choose the appropriate images based on a device's pixel density and the correct language strings based on a device's locale and region settings. This mechanism also can be used to select resources from any of the resource folders discussed in Section 5.3.7.

For this app's MainActivity, you'll use size and orientation qualifiers to determine which layout to use—one for portrait orientation on phones and tablets and another for landscape orientation only on tablets. To do this, you'll define two MainActivity layouts:

- activity_main.xml in the project's res/layout folder is the default layout.
- activity_main.xml in the project's res/layout-large-land folder is used *only* on large devices (i.e., tablets) when the app is in landscape (land) orientation.

Qualified resource folder names have the format:

> *name-qualifiers*

where *qualifiers* consists of one or more qualifiers separated by dashes (-). There are 18 types of qualifiers that you can add to resource folder names. We'll explain other qualifiers as we use them throughout the book. For a complete description of all the res subfolder qualifiers and the rules for the order in which they must be defined in a folder's name, visit:

```
http://developer.android.com/guide/topics/resources/
    providing-resources.html#AlternativeResources
```

5.3.9 Determining the Screen Size

In this app, we display the Menu only when the app is running on a phone-sized device or when it's running on a tablet in portrait orientation (Section 5.5.4). To determine this, we'll use Android's **WindowManager** (package android.view) to obtain a **Display** object that contains the display's current width and height. This changes with the device's orientation—in portrait orientation, the device's width is less than its height.

5.3.10 Toasts for Displaying Messages

A **Toast** (package android.widget) briefly displays a message, then disappears from the screen. Toasts are often used to display minor error messages or informational messages, such as that the quiz will be reset after the user changes the app's preferences. When the user changes the preferences, we display a Toast to indicate that the quiz will start over. We also display a Toast to indicate that at least one region must be selected if the user deselects all regions—in this case, the app sets North America as the default region for the quiz.

5.3.11 Using a Handler to Execute a Runnable in the Future

When the user makes a correct guess, the app displays the correct answer for two seconds before displaying the next flag. To do this, we use a **Handler** (package android.os). Handler method **postDelayed** receives as arguments a Runnable to execute and a delay in milliseconds. After the delay has passed, the Handler's Runnable executes in the *same thread* that created the Handler. *Operations that interact with or modify the GUI must be performed in the GUI thread, because GUI components are not thread safe.*

5.3.12 Applying an Animation to a View

When the user makes an incorrect choice, the app shakes the flag by applying an **Animation** (package android.view.animation) to the ImageView. We use **AnimationUtils** static method **loadAnimation** to load the animation from an XML file that specifies the animation's options. We also specify the number of times the animation should repeat with `Animation` method **`setRepeatCount`** and perform the animation by calling `View` method **`startAnimation`** (with the `Animation` as an argument) on the `ImageView`.

5.3.13 Logging Exception Messages

When exceptions occur, you can *log* them for debugging purposes with Android's built-in logging mechanism. Android provides class **`Log`** (package `android.util`) with several `static` methods that represent messages of varying detail. Logged messages can be viewed in the **LogCat** tab at the bottom of the IDE as well as with the **Android logcat tool**. For more details on logging messages, visit

```
http://developer.android.com/reference/android/util/Log.html
```

5.3.14 Using an Explicit `Intent` to Launch Another `Activity` in the Same App

When this app runs in portrait orientation, the app's preferences are displayed in the `SettingsActivity` (Section 5.8). In Chapter 4, we showed how to use an *implicit* `Intent` to display a URL in the device's web browser. Section 5.5.5 shows how to use an *explicit* `Intent` to launch a specific `Activity` in the same app.

5.3.15 Java Data Structures

This app uses various data structures from the `java.util` package. The app dynamically loads the image file names for the enabled regions and stores them in an `ArrayList<String>`. We use `Collections` method `shuffle` to randomize the order of the image file names for each new game. We use a second `ArrayList<String>` to hold the image file names of the countries in the current quiz. We also use a **`Set<String>`** to store the world regions included in a quiz. We refer to the `ArrayList<String>` object with a variable of interface type `List<String>`—this is a good Java programming practice that enables you to change data structures easily without affecting the rest of your app's code.

5.4 Building the GUI and Resource Files

In this section, you'll create the project and configure the `String`, array, color, dimension, layout and animation resources used by the **Flag Quiz** app.

5.4.1 Creating the Project

Before you create the new project, delete the `FlagQuiz` project that you test-drove in Section 5.2 by right clicking it and selecting **Delete**. In the dialog that appears, ensure that **Delete project contents on disk** is *not* selected, then click **OK**.

Creating a New Blank App Project
Next, create a new **Android Application Project**. Specify the following values in the **New Android Project** dialog's first **New Android Application** step, then press **Next >**:

- **Application Name:** `Flag Quiz`
- **Project Name:** `FlagQuiz`
- **Package Name:** `com.deitel.flagquiz`

- **Minimum Required SDK:** API18: Android 4.3
- **Target SDK:** API19: Android 4.4
- **Compile With:** API19: Android 4.4
- **Theme:** Holo Light with Dark Action Bar

In the **New Android Project** dialog's second **New Android Application** step, leave the default settings, and press **Next >**. In the **Configure Launcher Icon** step, click the **Browse...** button, and select an app icon image (provided in the images folder with the book's examples), click the **Open** button, then press **Next >**. In the **Create Activity** step, select **Blank Activity**, then press **Next >**. In the **Blank Activity** step, leave the default settings and click **Finish** to create the project. In the **Graphical Layout** editor, select **Nexus 4** from the screen-type drop-down list. Once again, we'll use this device as the basis for our design.

5.4.2 `strings.xml` and Formatted `String` Resources

You created `String` resources in earlier chapters, so we show only a table (Fig. 5.9) of the `String` resource names and corresponding values here. Double click `strings.xml` in the `res/values` folder to display the resource editor for creating these `String` resources.

Resource name	Value
settings_activity	Flag Quiz Settings
number_of_choices	Number of Choices
number_of_choices_description	Display 3, 6 or 9 guess buttons
world_regions	Regions
world_regions_description	Regions to include in the quiz
guess_country	Guess the Country
results	%1$d guesses, %2$.02f%% correct
incorrect_answer	Incorrect!
default_region_message	Setting North America as the default region. One region must be selected.
restarting_quiz	Quiz will restart with your new settings
ok	OK
question	Question %1$d of %2$d
reset_quiz	Reset Quiz
image_description	Image of the current flag in the quiz
default_region	North_America

Fig. 5.9 | `String` resources used in the **Flag Quiz** app.

Format *Strings* as *String* Resources

The `results` and `question` resources are format `Strings` that are used with `String` method `format`. When a `String` resource contains multiple format specifiers you must number the format specifiers for localization purposes. In the `results` resource, the notation 1$ in %1$d indicates that `String` method `format`'s *first* argument after the format `String` should replace the format specifier %1$d. Similarly, 2$ in %2$.02f indicates that the *second* argument after the format String should replace the format specifier %2$.02f. The d in the first format specifier formats an integer and the f in the second one formats a floating-point number. In localized versions of strings.xml, the format specifiers %1$d and %2$.02f can be reordered as necessary to properly translate the String resource. The *first* argument after the format String will replace %1$d—regardless of where it appears in the format String—and the *second* argument will replace %2$.02f *regardless* of where they appear in the format String.

5.4.3 arrays.xml

In Section 4.5.8, you created a String array resource in the app's strings.xml file. Technically, all of your app's resources in the res/values folder can be defined in the *same* file. However, to make it easier to manage different types of resources, separate files are typically used for each. For example, array resources are normally defined in arrays.xml, colors in colors.xml, Strings in strings.xml and numeric values in values.xml. This app uses three String array resources that are defined in arrays.xml:

- regions_list specifies the names of the world regions with their words separated by underscores—these values are used to load image file names from the appropriate folders and as the selected values for the world regions the user selects in the SettingsFragment.

- regions_list_for_settings specifies the names of the world regions with their words separated by spaces—these values are used in the SettingsFragment to display the region names to the user.

- guesses_list specifies the Strings 3, 6 and 9—these values are used in the SettingsFragment to display the options for the number of guess Buttons to display.

Figure 5.10 shows the names and element values for these three array resources.

Array resource name	Values
regions_list	Africa, Asia, Europe, North_America, Oceania, South_America
regions_list_for_settings	Africa, Asia, Europe, North America, Oceania, South America
guesses_list	3, 6, 9

Fig. 5.10 | String array resources defined in arrays.xml.

To create the file and configure the array resources, perform the following steps:

1. In the project's res folder, right click the values folder, then select **New > Android XML File** to display the **New Android XML File** dialog. Because you right clicked the values folder, the dialog is preconfigured to add a **Values** resource file in the values folder.

2. Specify arrays.xml in the **File** field and click **Finish** to create the file.

3. If the IDE opens the new file in XML view, click the **Resources** tab at the bottom of the window to view the resource editor.

4. To create a `String` array resource, click **Add...**, select **String Array** and click **OK**.

5. In the **Name** field, enter `regions_list`, then save the file.

6. Select the new `String` array resource, then use the **Add** button to add items for each of the values shown for the array in Fig. 5.10.

7. Repeat Steps 4–6 for the `regions_list_for_settings` and `guesses_list` arrays. When you click **Add...** to create the additional **String Array** resources, you'll need to first select the radio button **Create a new element at the top level in Resources**.

5.4.4 `colors.xml`

This app displays correct answers in green and incorrect answers in red. As with any other resource, color resources should be defined in XML so that you can easily change colors without modifying your app's Java source code. Typically, colors are defined in a file name `colors.xml`, which you must create. As you learned in Section 3.4.5, colors are defined using the RGB or ARGB color schemes.

To create the file and configure the two color resources, perform the following steps:

1. In the project's `res` folder, right click the `values` folder, then select **New > Android XML File** to display the **New Android XML File** dialog.

2. Specify `colors.xml` in the **File** field and click **Finish** to create the file.

3. If the IDE opens the new file in XML view, click the **Resources** tab at the bottom of the window to view the resource editor.

4. To create a color resource, click **Add...**, select **Color** and click **OK**.

5. In the **Name** and **Value** fields that appear, enter `correct_answer` and `#00CC00`, respectively, then save the file.

6. Repeat Steps 4 and 5, but enter `incorrect_answer` and `#FF0000`.

5.4.5 `dimens.xml`

You created dimension resources in earlier chapters, so we show only a table (Fig. 5.11) of the dimension resource names and values here. Open `dimens.xml` in the `res/values` folder to display the resource editor for creating these resources. The `spacing` resource is used in the layouts as the spacing between various GUI components, and the `answer_size` resource specifies the font size for the `answerTextView`. Recall from Section 2.5.3 that font sizes should be specified in scale-independent pixels (`sp`) so that fonts in your app can also be scaled by the user's preferred font size (as specified in the device's settings).

Resource name	Value
`spacing`	8dp
`answer_size`	40sp

Fig. 5.11 | Dimension resources used in the **Flag Quiz** app.

5.4.6 `activity_settings.xml` Layout

In this section, you'll create the layout for the SettingsActivity (Section 5.8) that will display the SettingsFragment (Section 5.7). The SettingsActivity's layout will consist of only a LinearLayout containing the GUI for the SettingsFragment. As you'll see, when you add a Fragment to a layout, the IDE can create the Fragment's class for you. To create this layout, perform the following steps:

1. In the project's res folder, right click layout and select **New > Android XML File** to display the **New Android XML File** dialog. Because you right clicked the layout folder, the dialog is preconfigured to add a **Layout** resource file.

2. In the **File** field, enter `activity_settings.xml`.

3. In the **Root Element** section, select **LinearLayout** and click **Finish** to create the file.

4. From the **Palette**'s **Layouts** section, drag a **Fragment** onto the design area or onto the LinearLayout node in the **Outline** window.

5. The preceding step displays the **Choose Fragment Class** dialog. If you defined the Fragment class before its layout, you'd be able to select the class here. Click **Create New...** to display the **New Java Class** dialog.

6. Enter SettingsFragment in the dialog's **Name** field, change the **Superclass** field's value to `android.preference.PreferenceFragment` and click **Finish** to create the class. The IDE opens the Java file for the class, which you can close for now.

7. Save `activity_settings.xml`.

5.4.7 `activity_main.xml` Layout for Phone and Tablet Portrait Orientation

In this section, you'll create the layout for the MainActivity (Section 5.5) that will be used in portrait orientation on all devices. You'll define the landscape orientation layout for tablets in Section 5.4.9. To create this layout—which will display only the QuizFragment (Section 5.6)—perform the following steps:

1. In the project's res/layout folder, open `activity_main.xml`.

2. From the **Palette**'s **Layouts** section, drag a **Fragment** onto the RelativeLayout node in the **Outline** window.

3. In the **Choose Fragment Class** dialog, click **Create New...** to display the **New Java Class** dialog.

4. In the dialog's **Name** field, enter QuizFragment, then click **Finish** to create the class. The IDE opens the Java file for the class, which you can close for now.

5. In `activity_main.xml`, select the QuizFragment in the **Outline** window, then set its **Id** to `@+id/quizFragment` and, in the **Layout Parameters** properties, set **Width** and **Height** to `match_parent`.

6. Save `activity_main.xml`.

5.4.8 `fragment_quiz.xml` Layout

You'll typically define a layout for each of your Fragments. For each Fragment layout, you'll add a layout XML file to your app's res/layout folder(s) and specify which Fragment class the layout is associated with. Note that you do not need to define a layout for this app's SettingsFragment because its GUI is auto-generated by the inherited capabilities of class PreferenceFragment.

This section presents the QuizFragment's layout (fragment_quiz.xml). You'll define its layout file once in the app's res/layout folder, because we use the same layout for the QuizFragment on all devices and device orientations. Figure 5.12 shows the QuizFragment's GUI component names.

Fig. 5.12 | **Flag Quiz** GUI's components labeled with their **Id** property values.

*Creating **fragment_quiz.xml***

To create fragment_quiz.xml, perform the following steps:

1. In the project's res folder, right click the layout folder, then select **New > Android XML File** to display the **New Android XML File** dialog.

2. In the **File** field, enter fragment_quiz.xml.

3. In the **Root Element** section, select **LinearLayout (Vertical)** and click **Finish** to create the layout file.

4. Use the **Graphical Layout** editor and the **Outline** window to form the layout structure shown in Fig. 5.13. As you create the GUI components, set their **Id** properties. For the questionNumberTextView and guessCountryTextView, we used **Medium Text** components from the **Palette's Form Widgets** section. For the Buttons, we used **Small Button** components, which use a smaller font size so that they can fit more text.

5. Once you've completed Step 4, configure the GUI component properties with the values shown in Fig. 5.14. Setting flagImageView's **Height** to 0dp and **Weight**

Fig. 5.13 | Outline window for `fragment_quiz.xml`.

to 1 enables this component to resize vertically to occupy any remaining space not used by the other GUI components. Similarly, setting each Button's **Width** to 0dp and **Weight** to 1 enables the Buttons in a given LinearLayout to divide the horizontal space equally. The flagImageView's **Scale Type** value fitCenter scales the image to fill either the ImageView's width or height while maintaining the original image's aspect ratio. Setting the ImageView's **Adjust View Bounds** property to true indicates that the ImageView maintains the aspect ratio of its Drawable.

GUI component	Property	Value
questionNumberTextView	*Layout Parameters*	
	Width	wrap_content
	Height	wrap_content
	Gravity	center_horizontal
	Other Properties	
	Text	@string/question
flagImageView	*Layout Parameters*	
	Width	wrap_content
	Height	0dp
	Gravity	center
	Weight	1
	Margins	
	Left/Right	@dimen/activity_horizontal_margin
	Top/Bottom	@dimen/activity_vertical_margin
	Other Properties	
	Adjust View Bounds	true
	Content Desctiption	@string/image_description
	Scale Type	fitCenter

Fig. 5.14 | Property values for the GUI components in `fragment_quiz.xml`. (Part 1 of 2.)

GUI component	Property	Value
guessCountryTextView	*Layout Parameters*	
	Width	wrap_content
	Height	wrap_content
	Gravity	center_horizontal
	Other Properties	
	Text	@string/guess_country
LinearLayouts	*Layout Parameters*	
	Width	match_parent
	Height	wrap_content
	Margins	
	Bottom	@dimen/spacing
Buttons	*Layout Parameters*	
	Width	0dp
	Height	fill_parent
	Weight	1
answerTextView	*Layout Parameters*	
	Width	wrap_content
	Height	wrap_content
	Gravity	center|bottom
	Other Properties	
	Gravity	center_horizontal
	Text Size	@dimen/answer_size
	Text Style	bold

Fig. 5.14 | Property values for the GUI components in `fragment_quiz.xml`. (Part 2 of 2.)

5.4.9 `activity_main.xml` Layout for Tablet Landscape Orientation

In Section 5.4.7, you defined MainActivity's portrait-orientation layout, which contained only the QuizFragment. You'll now define MainActivity's landscape-orientation layout for tablets, which will contain both the SettingsFragment and the QuizFragment. To create the layout, perform the following steps:

1. Right click the project's res folder, then select **New > Folder**. In the **Folder name** field enter layout-large-land and click **Finish**. The qualifiers large and land ensure that any layouts defined in this folder will be used only on large devices on which the app is running in landscape orientation.

2. Right click the layout-large-land folder, then select **New > Android XML File** to display the **New Android XML File** dialog, then enter activity_main.xml in **File** field. In the **Root Element** section, select **LinearLayout (Horizontal)** and click **Finish** to create the layout file.

3. Select the LinearLayout and set its **Base Aligned** property to false.

4. From the **Layouts** section of the **Graphical Layout** editor, drag a **Fragment** onto the LinearLayout node in the **Outline** window. In the **Choose Fragment Class** dialog, select SettingsFragment and click **OK**.

5. Repeat Step 5, but select QuizFragment and click **OK**.

6. Select the SettingsFragment node in the **Outline** window. In the **Layout Parameters** section set **Width** to 0dp, **Height** to match_parent and **Weight** to 1.

7. Select the QuizFragment node in the **Outline** window. In the **Layout Parameters** section set **Width** to 0dp, **Height** to match_parent and **Weight** to 2.

Because the QuizFragment's **Weight** is 2 and the SettingsFragment's is 1, the QuizFragment will occupy two-thirds of the layout's horizontal space.

5.4.10 preferences.xml for Specifying the App's Settings

In this section, you'll create the preferences.xml file that the SettingsFragment uses to display the app's preferences. To create the file:

1. Right click the project's res folder, then select **New > Folder**, in the **Folder name** field enter xml and click **Finish**.

2. Right click the xml folder, then select **New > Android XML File** to display the **New Android XML File** dialog.

3. In the **File** text field, enter the name preferences.xml.

4. Ensure that the **Resource Type** is set to **Preference** and the **Root Element** is **PreferenceScreen**, which represents a screen in which preferences are displayed.

5. Click **Finish** to create the file. If the IDE displays the raw XML, click the **Structure** tab at the bottom of the window to configure the preferences.

6. At the left side of the window, select **PreferenceScreen**, then click **Add...**.

7. In the dialog that appears, select **ListPreference**, then click **OK**. This preference will display a list of mutually exclusive options.

8. At the left side of the window, select **PreferenceScreen**, then click **Add...**.

9. In the dialog that appears, select **MultiSelectListPreference**, then click **OK**. This preference will display a list of options in which multiple items can be selected. All of the selected items are saved as the value of such a preference.

10. Select the **ListPreference**, then configure the properties in Fig. 5.15.

11. Select the **MultiSelectListPreference**, then configure the properties in Fig. 5.16.

12. Save and close preferences.xml.

Property	Value	Description
Entries	@array/guesses_list	An array of Strings that will be displayed in the list of options.
Entry values	@array/guesses_list	An array of the values associated with the options in the **Entries** property. The selected entry's value will be stored in the app's SharedPreferences.

Fig. 5.15 | ListPreference property values. (Part 1 of 2.)

Property	Value	Description
Key	pref_numberOfChoices	The name of the preference stored in the app's SharedPreferences.
Title	@string/number_of_choices	The title of the preference displayed in the GUI.
Summary	@string/number_of_choices_description	A summary description of the preference that's displayed below its title.
Persistent	true	Whether the preference should persist after the app terminates—if true, class PreferenceFragment immediately persists the preference value each time it changes.
Default value	3	The item in the **Entries** property that's selected by default.

Fig. 5.15 | ListPreference property values. (Part 2 of 2.)

Property	Value	Description
Entries	@array/regions_list_for_settings	An array of Strings that will be displayed in the list of options.
Entry values	@array/regions_list	An array of the values associated with the options in the **Entries** property. The selected entries' values will *all* be stored in the app's SharedPreferences.
Key	pref_regionsToInclude	The name of the preference stored in the app's SharedPreferences.
Title	@string/world_regions	The title of the preference displayed in the GUI.
Summary	@string/world_regions_description	A summary description of the preference that's displayed below its title.
Persistent	true	Whether the preference should persist after the app terminates.
Default value	@array/regions_list	An array of the default values for this preference—in this case, all of the regions will be selected by default.

Fig. 5.16 | MultiSelectListPreference property values.

5.4.11 Creating the Flag Shake Animation

In this section, you'll create the animation that shakes the flag when the user guesses incorrectly. We'll show how this animation is used by the app in Section 5.6.9. To create the animation:

1. Right click the project's res folder, then select **New > Folder**, in the **Folder name** field enter anim and click **Finish**.

2. Right click the anim folder, then select **New > Android XML File** to display the **New Android XML File** dialog.

3. In the **File** text field, enter the name incorrect_shake.xml.

4. Ensure that the **Resource Type** is Tween Animation and the **Root Element** is set.

5. Click **Finish** to create the file. The file opens immediately in **XML** view.

6. Unfortunately, the IDE does not provide an editor for animations, so you must modify the XML contents of the file as shown in Fig. 5.17.

```
 1    <?xml version="1.0" encoding="utf-8"?>
 2
 3    <set xmlns:android="http://schemas.android.com/apk/res/android"
 4       android:interpolator="@android:anim/decelerate_interpolator">
 5
 6       <translate android:fromXDelta="0" android:toXDelta="-5%p"
 7          android:duration="100"/>
 8
 9       <translate android:fromXDelta="-5%p" android:toXDelta="5%p"
10          android:duration="100" android:startOffset="100"/>
11
12       <translate android:fromXDelta="5%p" android:toXDelta="-5%p"
13          android:duration="100" android:startOffset="200"/>
14    </set>
```

Fig. 5.17 | Shake animation (incorrect_shake.xml) that's applied to the flag when the user guesses incorrectly.

In this example, we use **View animations** to create a *shake effect* that consists of three animations in an **animation set** (lines 3–14)—a collection of animations that make up a larger animation. Animation sets may contain any combination of **tweened animations**—**alpha** (transparency), **scale** (resize), **translate** (move) and **rotate**. Our shake animation consists of a series of three translate animations. A translate animation moves a View within its parent. Android also supports *property animations* in which you can animate any property of any object.

The first translate animation (lines 6–7) moves a View from a starting location to an ending position over a specified period of time. The **android:fromXDelta** attribute is the View's offset when the animation starts and the **android:toXDelta** attribute is the View's offset when the animation ends. These attributes can have

- absolute values (in pixels)
- a percentage of the animated View's size
- a percentage of the animated View's *parent's* size.

For the android:fromXDelta attribute, we specified an absolute value of 0. For the android:toXDelta attribute, we specified the value -5%p, which indicates that the View should move to the *left* (due to the minus sign) by 5% of the parent's width (indicated by the p). If we wanted to move by 5% of the View's width, we would leave out the p. The **android:duration attribute** specifies how long the animation lasts in milliseconds. So the animation in lines 6–7 will move the View to the left by 5% of its parent's width in 100 milliseconds.

The second animation (lines 9–10) continues from where the first finished, moving the View from the -5%p offset to a %5p offset in 100 milliseconds. By default, animations in an animation set are applied simultaneously (i.e., in parallel), but you can use the **android:startOffset** attribute to specify the number of milliseconds into the future at which an animation should begin. This can be used to sequence the animations in a set. In this case, the second animation starts 100 milliseconds after the first. The third animation (lines 12–13) is the same as the second, but in the reverse direction, and it starts 200 milliseconds after the first animation.

5.5 MainActivity Class

Class MainActivity (Figs. 5.18–Fig. 5.23) hosts the app's QuizFragment when the app is running in portrait orientation, and hosts both the SettingsFragment and QuizFragment when the app is running on a tablet in landscape orientation.

5.5.1 package Statement, import Statements and Fields

Figure 5.18 shows the MainActivity package statement, import statements and fields. Lines 6–21 import the various Java and Android classes and interfaces that the app uses. We've highlighted the new import statements, and we discuss the corresponding classes and interfaces in Section 5.3 and as they're encountered in Sections 5.5.2–5.5.6.

```
 1   // MainActivity.java
 2   // Hosts the QuizFragment on a phone and both the
 3   // QuizFragment and SettingsFragment on a tablet
 4   package com.deitel.flagquiz;
 5
 6   import java.util.Set;
 7
 8   import android.app.Activity;
 9   import android.content.Intent;
10   import android.content.SharedPreferences;
11   import android.content.SharedPreferences.OnSharedPreferenceChangeListener;
12   import android.content.pm.ActivityInfo;
13   import android.content.res.Configuration;
14   import android.graphics.Point;
15   import android.os.Bundle;
16   import android.preference.PreferenceManager;
17   import android.view.Display;
18   import android.view.Menu;
19   import android.view.MenuItem;
20   import android.view.WindowManager;
21   import android.widget.Toast;
```

Fig. 5.18 | MainActivity package statement, import statements and fields. (Part 1 of 2.)

```
22
23   public class MainActivity extends Activity
24   {
25      // keys for reading data from SharedPreferences
26      public static final String CHOICES = "pref_numberOfChoices";
27      public static final String REGIONS = "pref_regionsToInclude";
28
29      private boolean phoneDevice = true; // used to force portrait mode
30      private boolean preferencesChanged = true; // did preferences change?
31
```

Fig. 5.18 | MainActivity package statement, import statements and fields. (Part 2 of 2.)

Lines 26–27 define constants for the preference keys you created in Section 5.4.10. You'll use these to access the corresponding preference values. The boolean variable phoneDevice (line 29) specifies whether the app is running on a phone—if so, the app will allow only portrait orientation. The boolean variable preferencesChanged (line 30) specifies whether the app's preferences have changed—if so, the MainActivity's onStart lifecycle method (Section 5.5.3) will call the QuizFragment's methods updateGuessRows (Section 5.6.4) and updateRegions (Section 5.6.5) to reconfigure the quiz based on the user's new settings. We set this boolean to true initially so that when the app first executes the quiz is configured using the default preferences.

5.5.2 Overridden Activity Method onCreate

Overridden Activity method onCreate (Fig. 5.19) calls setContentView (line 36) to set MainActivity's GUI. Android chooses the activity_main.xml file from the res/layout folder if the app is running in portrait orientation or res/layout-large-land if the app is running on a tablet in landscape orientation.

```
32      @Override
33      protected void onCreate(Bundle savedInstanceState)
34      {
35         super.onCreate(savedInstanceState);
36         setContentView(R.layout.activity_main);
37
38         // set default values in the app's SharedPreferences
39         PreferenceManager.setDefaultValues(this, R.xml.preferences, false);
40
41         // register listener for SharedPreferences changes
42         PreferenceManager.getDefaultSharedPreferences(this).
43            registerOnSharedPreferenceChangeListener(
44               preferenceChangeListener);
45
46         // determine screen size
47         int screenSize = getResources().getConfiguration().screenLayout &
48            Configuration.SCREENLAYOUT_SIZE_MASK;
49
```

Fig. 5.19 | MainActivity overridden Activity method onCreate. (Part 1 of 2.)

```
50          // if device is a tablet, set phoneDevice to false
51          if (screenSize == Configuration.SCREENLAYOUT_SIZE_LARGE ||
52              screenSize == Configuration.SCREENLAYOUT_SIZE_XLARGE )
53              phoneDevice = false; // not a phone-sized device
54
55          // if running on phone-sized device, allow only portrait orientation
56          if (phoneDevice)
57              setRequestedOrientation(
58                  ActivityInfo.SCREEN_ORIENTATION_PORTRAIT);
59      } // end method onCreate
60
```

Fig. 5.19 | MainActivity overridden Activity method onCreate. (Part 2 of 2.)

Setting the Default Preference Values and Registering a Change Listener
When you install and launch the app for the first time, line 39 sets the app's *default preferences* by calling PreferenceManager method **setDefaultValues**—this creates and initializes the app's SharedPreferences file using the default values that you specified in preferences.xml. The method requires three arguments:

- the preferences' Context—the Activity (this) for which you are setting the default preferences

- the resource ID for the preferences XML file (R.xml.preferences) that you created in Section 5.4.10

- a boolean indicating whether the default values should be reset each time method setDefaultValues is called—false indicates that the default preference values should be set only the first time this method is called.

Each time the user changes the app's preferences, MainActivity should call QuizFragment's methods updateGuessRows or updateRegions (based on which preference changed) to reconfigure the quiz. MainActivity registers an OnSharedPreferenceChangedListener (lines 42–44) so that it will be notified each time a preference changes. PreferenceManager method **getDefaultSharedPreferences** returns a reference to the SharedPreferences object representing the app's preferences, and SharedPreferences method **registerOnSharedPreferenceChangeListener** registers the listener, which is defined in Section 5.5.6.

Configuring a Phone Device for Portrait Orientation
Lines 47–53 determine whether the app is running on a tablet or a phone. Inherited method **getResources** returns the app's **Resources** object (package android.content.res) that can be used to access an app's resources and determine information about the app's environment. Resources method **getConfiguration** returns a **Configuration** object (package android.content.res) that contains public instance variable screenLayout, which you can use to determine the device's screen-size category. To do so, first you combine the value of screenLayout with Configuration.SCREENLAYOUT_SIZE_MASK using the bitwise AND (&) operator. Then, you compare the result to the Configuration constants SCREENLAYOUT_SIZE_LARGE and SCREENLAYOUT_SIZE_XLARGE (lines 51–52). If either is a match, the app is running on a tablet-sized device. Finally, if the device is a phone, lines 57–58 call inherited Activity method **setRequestedOrientation** to force the app to display MainActivity in only portrait orientation.

5.5.3 Overridden `Activity` Method `onStart`

Overridden `Activity` lifecycle method **onStart** (Fig. 5.20) is called in two scenarios:

- When the app first executes, `onStart` is called after `onCreate`. We use `onStart` in this case to ensure that the quiz is configured correctly based on the app's default preferences when the app is installed and executes for the first time or based on the user's updated preferences when the app is launched subsequently.

- When the app is running in portrait orientation and the user opens the `Settings-Activity`, the `MainActivity` is *paused* while the `SettingsActivity` is displayed. When the user returns to the `MainActivity`, `onStart` is called again. We use `on-Start` in this case to ensure that the quiz is reconfigured properly if the user made any preference changes.

In both cases, if `preferencesChanged` is true, `onStart` calls `QuizFragment`'s `update-GuessRows` (Section 5.6.4) and `updateRegions` (Section 5.6.5) methods to reconfigure the quiz. To get a reference to the `QuizFragment` so we can call its methods, lines 71–72 use inherited `Activity` method `getFragmentManager` to get the `FragmentManager`, then call its `findFragmentById` method. Next, lines 73–76 call `QuizFragment`'s `updateGuessRows` and `updateRegions` methods, passing the app's `SharedPreferences` object as an argument so those methods can load the current preferences. Line 77 resets the quiz.

```
61     // called after onCreate completes execution
62     @Override
63     protected void onStart()
64     {
65         super.onStart();
66
67         if (preferencesChanged)
68         {
69             // now that the default preferences have been set,
70             // initialize QuizFragment and start the quiz
71             QuizFragment quizFragment = (QuizFragment)
72                 getFragmentManager().findFragmentById(R.id.quizFragment);
73             quizFragment.updateGuessRows(
74                 PreferenceManager.getDefaultSharedPreferences(this));
75             quizFragment.updateRegions(
76                 PreferenceManager.getDefaultSharedPreferences(this));
77             quizFragment.resetQuiz();
78             preferencesChanged = false;
79         }
80     } // end method onStart
81
```

Fig. 5.20 | MainActivity overridden `Activity` method `onStart`.

5.5.4 Overridden `Activity` Method `onCreateOptionsMenu`

We override `Activity` method `onCreateOptionsMenu` (Fig. 5.21) to initialize `Activity`'s standard options menu. The system passes in the `Menu` object where the options will appear. In this app, we want to show the menu only when the app is running in portrait orientation. Lines 87–88 use the `WindowManager` to get a `Display` object that contains the screen's current width and height, which changes based on the device's orientation. If the width is less than the height, then the device is in portrait orientation. Line 89 creates a Point object to store the current width and height, then line 90 calls Display method getRealSize, which stores the screen's width and height in the Point's public instance variables x and y, respectively. If the width is less than the height (line 93), line 95 creates the menu from menu.xml—the default menu resource that the IDE configured when you created the project. Inherited Activity method **getMenuInflater** returns a **MenuInflater** on which we call **inflate** with two arguments—the resource ID of the menu resource that populates the menu and the Menu object in which the menu items will be placed. Returning true from onCreateOptionsMenu indicates that the menu should be displayed.

```
82      // show menu if app is running on a phone or a portrait-oriented tablet
83      @Override
84      public boolean onCreateOptionsMenu(Menu menu)
85      {
86          // get the default Display object representing the screen
87          Display display = ((WindowManager)
88              getSystemService(WINDOW_SERVICE)).getDefaultDisplay();
89          Point screenSize = new Point(); // used to store screen size
90          display.getRealSize(screenSize); // store size in screenSize
91
92          // display the app's menu only in portrait orientation
93          if (screenSize.x < screenSize.y) // x is width, y is height
94          {
95              getMenuInflater().inflate(R.menu.main, menu); // inflate the menu
96              return true;
97          }
98          else
99              return false;
100     } // end method onCreateOptionsMenu
101
```

Fig. 5.21 | MainActivity overridden Activity method onCreateOptionsMenu.

5.5.5 Overridden Activity Method onOptionsItemSelected

Method onOptionsItemSelected (Fig. 5.22) is called when a menu item is selected. In this app, the default menu provided by the IDE when you created the project contains only the **Settings** menu item, so if this method is called, the user selected **Settings**. Line 106 creates an explicit Intent for launching the SettingsActivity. The Intent constructor used here receives the Context from which the Activity will be launched and the class representing the Activity to launch (SettingsActivity.class). We then pass this Intent to the inherited Activity method startActivity to launch the Activity.

```
102     // displays SettingsActivity when running on a phone
103     @Override
104     public boolean onOptionsItemSelected(MenuItem item)
105     {
```

Fig. 5.22 | MainActivity overridden Activity method onOptionsItemSelected. (Part 1 of 2.)

```
106          Intent preferencesIntent = new Intent(this, SettingsActivity.class);
107          startActivity(preferencesIntent);
108          return super.onOptionsItemSelected(item);
109       }
110
```

Fig. 5.22 | MainActivity overridden Activity method onOptionsItemSelected. (Part 2 of 2.)

5.5.6 Anonymous Inner Class That Implements OnSharedPreferenceChangeListener

The preferenceChangeListener (Fig. 5.23) is an anonymous-inner-class object that implements the OnSharedPreferenceChangeListener interface. This object was registered in method onCreate to listen for changes to the app's SharedPreferences. When a change occurs, method onSharedPreferenceChanged sets preferencesChanged to true (line 120), then gets a reference to the QuizFragment (lines 122–123) so that the quiz can be reset with the new preferences. If the CHOICES preference changed, lines 127–128 call the QuizFragment's updateGuessRows and resetQuiz methods.

```
111      // listener for changes to the app's SharedPreferences
112      private OnSharedPreferenceChangeListener preferenceChangeListener =
113         new OnSharedPreferenceChangeListener()
114      {
115         // called when the user changes the app's preferences
116         @Override
117         public void onSharedPreferenceChanged(
118            SharedPreferences sharedPreferences, String key)
119         {
120            preferencesChanged = true; // user changed app settings
121
122            QuizFragment quizFragment = (QuizFragment)
123               getFragmentManager().findFragmentById(R.id.quizFragment);
124
125            if (key.equals(CHOICES)) // # of choices to display changed
126            {
127               quizFragment.updateGuessRows(sharedPreferences);
128               quizFragment.resetQuiz();
129            }
130            else if (key.equals(REGIONS)) // regions to include changed
131            {
132               Set<String> regions =
133                  sharedPreferences.getStringSet(REGIONS, null);
134
135               if (regions != null && regions.size() > 0)
136               {
137                  quizFragment.updateRegions(sharedPreferences);
138                  quizFragment.resetQuiz();
139               }
140               else // must select one region--set North America as default
141               {
```

Fig. 5.23 | Anonymous Inner class that implements OnSharedPreferenceChangeListener. (Part 1 of 2.)

```
142          SharedPreferences.Editor editor = sharedPreferences.edit();
143          regions.add(
144             getResources().getString(R.string.default_region));
145          editor.putStringSet(REGIONS, regions);
146          editor.commit();
147          Toast.makeText(MainActivity.this,
148             R.string.default_region_message,
149             Toast.LENGTH_SHORT).show();
150       }
151    }
152
153    Toast.makeText(MainActivity.this,
154       R.string.restarting_quiz, Toast.LENGTH_SHORT).show();
155    } // end method onSharedPreferenceChanged
156 }; // end anonymous inner class
157 } // end class MainActivity
```

Fig. 5.23 | Anonymous Inner class that implements OnSharedPreferenceChangeListener. (Part 2 of 2.)

If the REGIONS preference changed, lines 132–133 get the Set<String> containing the enabled regions. SharedPreferences method **getStringSet** returns a Set<String> for the specified key. The quiz must have at least one region enabled, so if the Set<String> is not empty, lines 137–138 call the QuizFragment's updateRegions and resetQuiz methods. Otherwise, lines 142–146 update the REGIONS preference with North America set as the default region, and lines 147–149 use a Toast to indicate that the default region was set. Toast method **makeText** receives as arguments the Context on which the Toast is displayed, the message to display and the duration for which the Toast will be displayed. Toast method show displays the Toast. Regardless of which preference changed, lines 153–154 display a Toast indicating that the quiz will be reset with the new preferences. Figure 5.24 shows the Toast that appears after the user changes the app's preferences.

Fig. 5.24 | Toast displayed after a preference is changed.

5.6 QuizFragment Class

Class QuizFragment (Figs. 5.25–5.34) builds the **Flag Quiz**'s GUI and implements the quiz's logic.

5.6.1 package Statement and import Statements

Figure 5.25 shows the QuizFragment package statement and import statements. Lines 5–33 import the various Java and Android classes and interfaces that the app uses. We've highlighted the new import statements, and we discuss the corresponding classes and interfaces in Section 5.3 and as they're encountered in Sections 5.6.2–5.6.10.

```
 1   // QuizFragment.java
 2   // Contains the Flag Quiz logic
 3   package com.deitel.flagquiz;
 4
 5   import java.io.IOException;
 6   import java.io.InputStream;
 7   import java.security.SecureRandom;
 8   import java.util.ArrayList;
 9   import java.util.Collections;
10   import java.util.List;
11   import java.util.Set;
12
13   import android.app.AlertDialog;
14   import android.app.Dialog;
15   import android.app.DialogFragment;
16   import android.app.Fragment;
17   import android.content.DialogInterface;
18   import android.content.SharedPreferences;
19   import android.content.res.AssetManager;
20   import android.graphics.drawable.Drawable;
21   import android.os.Bundle;
22   import android.os.Handler;
23   import android.util.Log;
24   import android.view.LayoutInflater;
25   import android.view.View;
26   import android.view.View.OnClickListener;
27   import android.view.ViewGroup;
28   import android.view.animation.Animation;
29   import android.view.animation.AnimationUtils;
30   import android.widget.Button;
31   import android.widget.ImageView;
32   import android.widget.LinearLayout;
33   import android.widget.TextView;
34
```

Fig. 5.25 | QuizFragment package statement, import statements.

5.6.2 Fields

Figure 5.26 lists class QuizFragment's static and instance variables. The constant TAG (line 38) is used when we log error messages using class Log (Fig. 5.31) to distinguish this Activity's error messages from others that are being written to the device's log. The constant FLAGS_IN_QUIZ (line 40) represents the number of flags in the quiz.

```
35   public class QuizFragment extends Fragment
36   {
37      // String used when logging error messages
38      private static final String TAG = "FlagQuiz Activity";
39
40      private static final int FLAGS_IN_QUIZ = 10;
41
```

Fig. 5.26 | QuizFragment fields. (Part 1 of 2.)

```
42    private List<String> fileNameList; // flag file names
43    private List<String> quizCountriesList; // countries in current quiz
44    private Set<String> regionsSet; // world regions in current quiz
45    private String correctAnswer; // correct country for the current flag
46    private int totalGuesses; // number of guesses made
47    private int correctAnswers; // number of correct guesses
48    private int guessRows; // number of rows displaying guess Buttons
49    private SecureRandom random; // used to randomize the quiz
50    private Handler handler; // used to delay loading next flag
51    private Animation shakeAnimation; // animation for incorrect guess
52
53    private TextView questionNumberTextView; // shows current question #
54    private ImageView flagImageView; // displays a flag
55    private LinearLayout[] guessLinearLayouts; // rows of answer Buttons
56    private TextView answerTextView; // displays Correct! or Incorrect!
57
```

Fig. 5.26 | QuizFragment fields. (Part 2 of 2.)

Variable fileNameList (line 42) holds the flag image file names for the currently enabled geographic regions. Variable quizCountriesList (line 43) holds the flag file names for the countries used in the current quiz. Variable regionsSet (line 44) stores the geographic regions that are enabled.

Variable correctAnswer (line 45) holds the flag file name for the current flag's correct answer. Variable totalGuesses (line 46) stores the total number of correct and incorrect guesses the player has made so far. Variable correctAnswers (line 47) is the number of correct guesses so far; this will eventually be equal to FLAGS_IN_QUIZ if the user completes the quiz. Variable guessRows (line 48) is the number of three-Button LinearLayouts displaying the flag answer choices.

Variable random (line 49) is the random-number generator used to randomly pick the flags to include in the quiz and which Button in the three-Button LinearLayouts represents the correct answer. When the user selects a correct answer and the quiz is not over, we use the Handler object handler (line 50) to load the next flag after a short delay.

The Animation shakeAnimation (line 51) holds the dynamically inflated *shake animation* that's applied to the flag image when an incorrect guess is made. Lines 53–56 contain variables that we use to manipulate various GUI components programmatically.

5.6.3 Overridden Fragment Method onCreateView

QuizFragment's onCreateView method (Fig. 5.27) inflates the GUI and initializes most of the QuizFragment's instance variables—guessRows and regionsSet are initialized when the MainActivity calls QuizFragment's updateGuessRows and updateRegions methods. After calling the superclass's onCreateView method (line 63), we inflate the QuizFragment's GUI (line 64–65) using the LayoutInflater that method onCreateView receives as an argument. The LayoutInflater's **inflate** method receives three arguments:

- the layout resource ID indicating the layout to inflate

- the ViewGroup (layout object) in which the Fragment will be displayed, which is received as onCreateView's second argument

- a boolean indicating whether or not the inflated GUI needs to be attached to the ViewGroup in the second argument—false means that the Fragment was declared in the parent Activity's layout and true indicates that you're dynamically creating the Fragment and its GUI should be attached.

Method inflate returns a reference to a View that contains the inflated GUI. We store that in local variable view so that it can be returned by onCreateView after the QuizFragment's other instance variables are initialized.

```
58    // configures the QuizFragment when its View is created
59    @Override
60    public View onCreateView(LayoutInflater inflater, ViewGroup container,
61       Bundle savedInstanceState)
62    {
63       super.onCreateView(inflater, container, savedInstanceState);
64       View view =
65          inflater.inflate(R.layout.fragment_quiz, container, false);
66
67       fileNameList = new ArrayList<String>();
68       quizCountriesList = new ArrayList<String>();
69       random = new SecureRandom();
70       handler = new Handler();
71
72       // load the shake animation that's used for incorrect answers
73       shakeAnimation = AnimationUtils.loadAnimation(getActivity(),
74          R.anim.incorrect_shake);
75       shakeAnimation.setRepeatCount(3); // animation repeats 3 times
76
77       // get references to GUI components
78       questionNumberTextView =
79          (TextView) view.findViewById(R.id.questionNumberTextView);
80       flagImageView = (ImageView) view.findViewById(R.id.flagImageView);
81       guessLinearLayouts = new LinearLayout[3];
82       guessLinearLayouts[0] =
83          (LinearLayout) view.findViewById(R.id.row1LinearLayout);
84       guessLinearLayouts[1] =
85          (LinearLayout) view.findViewById(R.id.row2LinearLayout);
86       guessLinearLayouts[2] =
87          (LinearLayout) view.findViewById(R.id.row3LinearLayout);
88       answerTextView = (TextView) view.findViewById(R.id.answerTextView);
89
90       // configure listeners for the guess Buttons
91       for (LinearLayout row : guessLinearLayouts)
92       {
93          for (int column = 0; column < row.getChildCount(); column++)
94          {
95             Button button = (Button) row.getChildAt(column);
96             button.setOnClickListener(guessButtonListener);
97          }
98       }
99
```

Fig. 5.27 | QuizFragment overridden Fragment method onCreateView. (Part I of 2.)

```
100         // set questionNumberTextView's text
101         questionNumberTextView.setText(
102            getResources().getString(R.string.question, 1, FLAGS_IN_QUIZ));
103         return view; // returns the fragment's view for display
104      } // end method onCreateView
105
```

Fig. 5.27 | QuizFragment overridden Fragment method onCreateView. (Part 2 of 2.)

Lines 67–68 create ArrayList<String> objects that will store the flag image file names for the currently enabled geographical regions and the names of the countries in the current quiz, respectively. Line 69 creates the SecureRandom object for randomizing the quiz's flags and guess Buttons. Line 70 creates the Handler object handler, which we'll use to delay by two seconds the appearance of the next flag after the user correctly guesses the current flag.

Lines 73–74 dynamically load the *shake animation* that will be applied to the flag when an incorrect guess is made. AnimationUtils static method loadAnimation loads the animation from the XML file represented by the constant R.anim.incorrect_shake. The first argument indicates the Context containing the resources that will be animated—inherited Fragment method getActivity returns the Activity that hosts this Fragment. Activity is an indirect subclass of Context. Line 75 specifies the number of times the animation should repeat with Animation method setRepeatCount.

Lines 78–88 get references to various GUI components that we'll programmatically manipulate. Lines 91–98 get each guess Button from the three guessLinearLayouts and register guessButtonListener (Section 5.6.9) as the OnClickListener.

Lines 101–102 set the text in questionNumberTextView to the String returned by String static method format. The first argument to format is the String resource R.string.question, which is a format String containing placeholders for two integer values (as described in Section 5.4.2). Inherited Fragment method **getResources** returns a Resources object (package android.content.res) that can be used to load resources. We then call that object's **getString** method to load the R.string.question resource, which represents the String

```
    Question %1$d of %2$d
```

Line 103 returns the QuizFragment's GUI.

5.6.4 Method updateGuessRows

Method updateGuessRows (Fig. 5.28) is called from the app's MainActivity when the app is launched and each time the user changes the number of guess Buttons to display with each flag. Lines 110–111 use the method's SharedPreferences argument to get the String for the key MainActivity.CHOICES—a constant containing the name of the preference in which the SettingsFragment stores the number of guess Buttons to display. Line 112 converts the preference's value to an int and divides it by 3 to determine the value for guessRows, which indicates how many of the guessLinearLayouts should be displayed—each with three guess Buttons. Next, lines 115–116 hide all of the guessLinearLayouts, so that lines 119–120 can show the appropriate guessLinearLayouts based on the value of guessRows.

```
106    // update guessRows based on value in SharedPreferences
107    public void updateGuessRows(SharedPreferences sharedPreferences)
108    {
109        // get the number of guess buttons that should be displayed
110        String choices =
111            sharedPreferences.getString(MainActivity.CHOICES, null);
112        guessRows = Integer.parseInt(choices) / 3;
113
114        // hide all guess button LinearLayouts
115        for (LinearLayout layout : guessLinearLayouts)
116            layout.setVisibility(View.INVISIBLE);
117
118        // display appropriate guess button LinearLayouts
119        for (int row = 0; row < guessRows; row++)
120            guessLinearLayouts[row].setVisibility(View.VISIBLE);
121    }
122
```

Fig. 5.28 | QuizFragment method updateGuessRows.

5.6.5 Method updateRegions

Method updateRegions (Fig. 5.29) is called from the app's MainActivity when the app is launched and each time the user changes the world regions that should be included in the quiz. Lines 126–127 use the method's SharedPreferences argument to get the names of all of the enabled regions as a Set<String>. MainActivity.REGIONS is a constant containing the name of the preference in which the SettingsFragment stores the enabled world regions.

```
123    // update world regions for quiz based on values in SharedPreferences
124    public void updateRegions(SharedPreferences sharedPreferences)
125    {
126        regionsSet =
127            sharedPreferences.getStringSet(MainActivity.REGIONS, null);
128    }
129
```

Fig. 5.29 | QuizFragment method updateRegions.

5.6.6 Method resetQuiz

Method resetQuiz (Fig. 5.30) sets up and starts a quiz. Recall that the images for the game are stored in the app's assets folder. To access this folder's contents, the method gets the app's AssetManager (line 134) by calling the parent Activity's **getAssets** method. Next, line 135 clears the fileNameList to prepare to load image file names for only the enabled geographical regions. Lines 140–147 iterate through all the enabled world regions. For each, we use the AssetManager's list method (line 143) to get an array of the flag image file names, which we store in the String array paths. Lines 145–146 remove the .png extension from each file name and place the names in the fileNameList. AssetManager's list method throws IOExceptions, which are *checked* exceptions (so you must catch or declare the exception). If an exception occurs because the app is unable to access the assets folder, lines 149–152 catch the exception and *log* it for debugging purposes with Android's built-in logging mechanism. Log static method **e** is used to log error messages. You can see the complete list of Log methods at

http://developer.android.com/reference/android/util/Log.html

```
130    // set up and start the next quiz
131    public void resetQuiz()
132    {
133       // use AssetManager to get image file names for enabled regions
134       AssetManager assets = getActivity().getAssets();
135       fileNameList.clear(); // empty list of image file names
136
137       try
138       {
139          // loop through each region
140          for (String region : regionsSet)
141          {
142             // get a list of all flag image files in this region
143             String[] paths = assets.list(region);
144
145             for (String path : paths)
146                fileNameList.add(path.replace(".png", ""));
147          }
148       }
149       catch (IOException exception)
150       {
151          Log.e(TAG, "Error loading image file names", exception);
152       }
153
154       correctAnswers = 0; // reset the number of correct answers made
155       totalGuesses = 0; // reset the total number of guesses the user made
156       quizCountriesList.clear(); // clear prior list of quiz countries
157
158       int flagCounter = 1;
159       int numberOfFlags = fileNameList.size();
160
161       // add FLAGS_IN_QUIZ random file names to the quizCountriesList
162       while (flagCounter <= FLAGS_IN_QUIZ)
163       {
164          int randomIndex = random.nextInt(numberOfFlags);
165
166          // get the random file name
167          String fileName = fileNameList.get(randomIndex);
168
169          // if the region is enabled and it hasn't already been chosen
170          if (!quizCountriesList.contains(fileName))
171          {
172             quizCountriesList.add(fileName); // add the file to the list
173             ++flagCounter;
174          }
175       }
```

Fig. 5.30 | QuizFragment method resetQuiz. (Part I of 2.)

```
176
177        loadNextFlag(); // start the quiz by loading the first flag
178     } // end method resetQuiz
179
```

Fig. 5.30 | QuizFragment method resetQuiz. (Part 2 of 2.)

Next, lines 154–156 reset the counters for the number of correct guesses the user has made (correctAnswers) and the total number of guesses the user has made (totalGuesses) to 0 and clear the quizCountriesList.

Lines 162–175 add FLAGS_IN_QUIZ (10) randomly selected file names to the quizCountriesList. We get the total number of flags, then randomly generate the index in the range 0 to one less than the number of flags. We use this index to select one image file name from fileNamesList. If the quizCountriesList does not already contain that file name, we add it to quizCountriesList and increment the flagCounter. We repeat this process until FLAGS_IN_QUIZ unique file names have been selected. Then line 177 calls loadNextFlag (Fig. 5.31) to load the quiz's first flag.

5.6.7 Method loadNextFlag

Method loadNextFlag (Fig. 5.31) loads and displays the next flag and the corresponding set of answer Buttons. The image file names in quizCountriesList have the format

> *regionName-countryName*

without the .png extension. If a *regionName* or *countryName* contains multiple words, they're separated by underscores (_).

```
180     // after the user guesses a correct flag, load the next flag
181     private void loadNextFlag()
182     {
183        // get file name of the next flag and remove it from the list
184        String nextImage = quizCountriesList.remove(0);
185        correctAnswer = nextImage; // update the correct answer
186        answerTextView.setText(""); // clear answerTextView
187
188        // display current question number
189        questionNumberTextView.setText(
190           getResources().getString(R.string.question,
191              (correctAnswers + 1), FLAGS_IN_QUIZ));
192
193        // extract the region from the next image's name
194        String region = nextImage.substring(0, nextImage.indexOf('-'));
195
196        // use AssetManager to load next image from assets folder
197        AssetManager assets = getActivity().getAssets();
198
199        try
200        {
```

Fig. 5.31 | QuizFragment method loadNextFlag. (Part 1 of 2.)

```
201        // get an InputStream to the asset representing the next flag
202        InputStream stream =
203           assets.open(region + "/" + nextImage + ".png");
204
205        // load the asset as a Drawable and display on the flagImageView
206        Drawable flag = Drawable.createFromStream(stream, nextImage);
207        flagImageView.setImageDrawable(flag);
208     }
209     catch (IOException exception)
210     {
211        Log.e(TAG, "Error loading " + nextImage, exception);
212     }
213
214     Collections.shuffle(fileNameList); // shuffle file names
215
216     // put the correct answer at the end of fileNameList
217     int correct = fileNameList.indexOf(correctAnswer);
218     fileNameList.add(fileNameList.remove(correct));
219
220     // add 3, 6, or 9 guess Buttons based on the value of guessRows
221     for (int row = 0; row < guessRows; row++)
222     {
223        // place Buttons in currentTableRow
224        for (int column = 0;
225           column < guessLinearLayouts[row].getChildCount(); column++)
226        {
227           // get reference to Button to configure
228           Button newGuessButton =
229              (Button) guessLinearLayouts[row].getChildAt(column);
230           newGuessButton.setEnabled(true);
231
232           // get country name and set it as newGuessButton's text
233           String fileName = fileNameList.get((row * 3) + column);
234           newGuessButton.setText(getCountryName(fileName));
235        }
236     }
237
238     // randomly replace one Button with the correct answer
239     int row = random.nextInt(guessRows); // pick random row
240     int column = random.nextInt(3); // pick random column
241     LinearLayout randomRow = guessLinearLayouts[row]; // get the row
242     String countryName = getCountryName(correctAnswer);
243     ((Button) randomRow.getChildAt(column)).setText(countryName);
244  } // end method loadNextFlag
245
```

Fig. 5.31 | QuizFragment method loadNextFlag. (Part 2 of 2.)

Line 184 removes the first name from quizCountriesList and stores it in nextImage. We also save this in correctAnswer so it can be used later to determine whether the user made a correct guess. Next, we clear the answerTextView and display the current question number in the questionNumberTextView (lines 189–191) using the formatted String resource R.string.question.

Line 194 extracts from nextImage the region to be used as the assets subfolder name from which we'll load the image. Next we get the AssetManager, then use it in the try statement to open an InputStream (package java.io) to read bytes from the flag image's file. We use that stream as an argument to class **Drawable**'s static method **createFrom-Stream**, which creates a Drawable object (package android.graphics.drawable). The Drawable is set as flagImageView's item to display by calling its **setImageDrawable** method. If an exception occurs, we log it for debugging purposes (line 211).

Next, line 214 shuffles the fileNameList, and lines 217–218 locate the correctAnswer and move it to the end of the fileNameList—later we'll insert this answer randomly into the one of the guess Buttons.

Lines 221–236 iterate through the Buttons in the guessLinearLayouts for the current number of guessRows. For each Button:

- lines 228–229 get a reference to the next Button
- line 230 enables the Button
- line 233 gets the flag file name from the fileNameList
- line 234 sets Button's text with the country name that's returned by method get-CountryName (Section 5.6.8)

Lines 239–243 pick a random row (based on the current number of guessRows) and column, then set the text of the corresponding Button.

5.6.8 Method getCountryName

Method getCountryName (Fig. 5.32) parses the country name from the image file name. First, we get a substring starting from the dash (-) that separates the region from the country name. Then we call String method replace to replace the underscores (_) with spaces.

```
246     // parses the country flag file name and returns the country name
247     private String getCountryName(String name)
248     {
249         return name.substring(name.indexOf('-') + 1).replace('_', ' ');
250     }
251
```

Fig. 5.32 | QuizFragment method getCountryName.

5.6.9 Anonymous Inner Class That Implements OnClickListener

Lines 91–98 (Fig. 5.27) registered guessButtonListener (Fig. 5.33) as the event-handling object for each guess Button. Instance variable guessButtonListener refers to an anonymous inner class object that implements interface OnClickListener to respond to Button events. The method receives the clicked Button as parameter v. We get the Button's text (line 259) and the parsed country name (line 260), then increment total-Guesses.

If the guess is correct (line 263), we increment correctAnswers. Next, we set the answerTextView's text to the country name and change its color to the color represented by the constant R.color.correct_answer (green), and we call our utility method disableButtons (Section 5.6.10) to disable all the answer Buttons.

```
252    // called when a guess Button is touched
253    private OnClickListener guessButtonListener = new OnClickListener()
254    {
255        @Override
256        public void onClick(View v)
257        {
258            Button guessButton = ((Button) v);
259            String guess = guessButton.getText().toString();
260            String answer = getCountryName(correctAnswer);
261            ++totalGuesses; // increment number of guesses the user has made
262
263            if (guess.equals(answer)) // if the guess is correct
264            {
265                ++correctAnswers; // increment the number of correct answers
266
267                // display correct answer in green text
268                answerTextView.setText(answer + "!");
269                answerTextView.setTextColor(
270                    getResources().getColor(R.color.correct_answer));
271
272                disableButtons(); // disable all guess Buttons
273
274                // if the user has correctly identified FLAGS_IN_QUIZ flags
275                if (correctAnswers == FLAGS_IN_QUIZ)
276                {
277                    // DialogFragment to display quiz stats and start new quiz
278                    DialogFragment quizResults =
279                        new DialogFragment()
280                        {
281                            // create an AlertDialog and return it
282                            @Override
283                            public Dialog onCreateDialog(Bundle bundle)
284                            {
285                                AlertDialog.Builder builder =
286                                    new AlertDialog.Builder(getActivity());
287                                builder.setCancelable(false);
288
289                                builder.setMessage(
290                                    getResources().getString(R.string.results,
291                                    totalGuesses, (1000 / (double) totalGuesses)));
292
293                                // "Reset Quiz" Button
294                                builder.setPositiveButton(R.string.reset_quiz,
295                                    new DialogInterface.OnClickListener()
296                                    {
297                                        public void onClick(DialogInterface dialog,
298                                            int id)
299                                        {
300                                            resetQuiz();
301                                        }
302                                    } // end anonymous inner class
303                                ); // end call to setPositiveButton
```

Fig. 5.33 | Anonymous inner class that implements OnClickListener. (Part 1 of 2.)

```
304
305                      return builder.create(); // return the AlertDialog
306                  } // end method onCreateDialog
307              }; // end DialogFragment anonymous inner class
308
309          // use FragmentManager to display the DialogFragment
310          quizResults.show(getFragmentManager(), "quiz results");
311      }
312      else // answer is correct but quiz is not over
313      {
314          // load the next flag after a 1-second delay
315          handler.postDelayed(
316              new Runnable()
317              {
318                  @Override
319                  public void run()
320                  {
321                      loadNextFlag();
322                  }
323              }, 2000); // 2000 milliseconds for 2-second delay
324      }
325  }
326  else // guess was incorrect
327  {
328      flagImageView.startAnimation(shakeAnimation); // play shake
329
330      // display "Incorrect!" in red
331      answerTextView.setText(R.string.incorrect_answer);
332      answerTextView.setTextColor(
333          getResources().getColor(R.color.incorrect_answer));
334      guessButton.setEnabled(false); // disable incorrect answer
335  }
336  }
337  }; // end guessButtonListener
338
```

Fig. 5.33 | Anonymous inner class that implements OnClickListener. (Part 2 of 2.)

If correctAnswers is FLAGS_IN_QUIZ (line 275), the quiz is over. Lines 278–307 create a new anonymous inner class that extends DialogFragment and will be used to display the quiz results. The DialogFragment's **onCreateDialog** method uses an Alert-Dialog.Builder to configure and create an AlertDialog, then returns it. When the user touches the dialog's **Reset Quiz** Button, method resetQuiz is called to start a new game (line 300). To display the DialogFragment, line 310 calls its **show** method, passing as arguments the FragmentManager returned by getFragmentManager and a String. The second argument can be used with FragmentManager method **getFragmentByTag** to get a reference to the DialogFragment at a later time—we don't use this capability in this app.

If correctAnswers is less than FLAGS_IN_QUIZ, then lines 315–323 call the postDelayed method of Handler object handler. The first argument defines an anonymous inner class that implements the Runnable interface—this represents the task to perform (loadNextFlag) some number of milliseconds into the future. The second argument is the delay in milliseconds (2000). If the guess is incorrect, line 328 invokes flagImageView's start-

Animation method to play the shakeAnimation that was loaded in method onCreateView. We also set the text on answerTextView to display "Incorrect!" in red (lines 331–333), then disable the guessButton that corresponds to the incorrect answer.

5.6.10 Method disableButtons

Method disableButtons (Fig. 5.34) iterates through the guess Buttons and disables them.

```
339     // utility method that disables all answer Buttons
340     private void disableButtons()
341     {
342        for (int row = 0; row < guessRows; row++)
343        {
344           LinearLayout guessRow = guessLinearLayouts[row];
345           for (int i = 0; i < guessRow.getChildCount(); i++)
346              guessRow.getChildAt(i).setEnabled(false);
347        }
348     }
349  } // end class FlagQuiz
```

Fig. 5.34 | QuizFragment method disableButtons.

5.7 SettingsFragment Class

Class SettingsFragment (Fig. 5.35) extends PreferenceFragment, which provides capabilities for managing the app's settings. Overridden method onCreate (lines 11–16) is called when the SettingsFragment is created—either by the SettingsActivity when the app is running in portrait orientation or by the MainActivity when the app is running on a tablet in landscape orientation. Line 15 uses inherited PreferenceFragment method **addPreferencesFromResource** to build the preferences GUI. The argument is the resource ID for the preferences.xml file you created in Section 5.4.10.

```
1   // SettingsFragment.java
2   // Subclass of PreferenceFragment for managing app settings
3   package com.deitel.flagquiz;
4
5   import android.os.Bundle;
6   import android.preference.PreferenceFragment;
7
8   public class SettingsFragment extends PreferenceFragment
9   {
10     // creates preferences GUI from preferences.xml file in res/xml
11     @Override
12     public void onCreate(Bundle savedInstanceState)
13     {
14        super.onCreate(savedInstanceState);
15        addPreferencesFromResource(R.xml.preferences); // load from XML
16     }
17  } // end class SettingsFragment
```

Fig. 5.35 | Subclass of PreferenceFragment for managing app settings.

5.8 SettingsActivity Class

Class SettingsActivity (Fig. 5.36) hosts the SettingsFragment when the app is running in portrait orientation. To create this class, right click the package (com.deitel.flagquiz) and select **New > Class** to display the **New Java Class** dialog. Set the new class's **Name** to SettingsActivity, set its **Superclass** to android.app.Activity and click **Finish**.

Overridden method onCreate (lines 11–16) calls Activity method setContentView to inflate the GUI defined by activity_settings.xml (Section 5.4.6)—represented by the resource R.layout.activity_settings.

```
 1   // SettingsActivity.java
 2   // Activity to display SettingsFragment on a phone
 3   package com.deitel.flagquiz;
 4
 5   import android.app.Activity;
 6   import android.os.Bundle;
 7
 8   public class SettingsActivity extends Activity
 9   {
10      // use FragmentManager to display SettingsFragment
11      @Override
12      protected void onCreate(Bundle savedInstanceState)
13      {
14         super.onCreate(savedInstanceState);
15         setContentView(R.layout.activity_settings);
16      }
17   } // end class SettingsActivity
```

Fig. 5.36 | Activity to display SettingsFragment on a phone.

5.9 AndroidManifest.xml

Each Activity in an app must be declared in the app's AndroidManifest.xml file; otherwise, Android will not know that the Activity exists and will not be able to launch it. When you created the app, the IDE declared its MainActivity in AndroidManifest.xml. To declare the app's SettingsActivity:

1. Open AndroidManifest.xml and click the **Application** tab at the bottom of the manifest editor.

2. In the **Application Nodes** section, click **Add...**, select **Activity** from the dialog that appears and click **OK**.

3. In the **Application Nodes** section, select the new **Activity** node to display its attributes in the **Attributes for Activity** section.

4. In the **Name** field, enter .SettingsActivity. The dot (.) before SettingsActivity is shorthand notation for the app's package name (com.deitel.flagquiz).

5. In the **Label** field, enter @string/settings_activity—this string resource is displayed in the action bar when the SettingsActivity is running.

For complete manifest file details, visit http://developer.android.com/guide/topics/manifest/manifest-intro.html.

5.10 Wrap-Up

In this chapter, you built a **Flag Quiz** app that tests a user's ability to correctly identify country flags. A key feature of this chapter was using Fragments to create portions of an Activity's GUI. You used two activities to display the QuizFragment and the SettingsFragment when the app was running in portrait orientation, and one Activity to display both Fragments when the app was running on a tablet in landscape orientation—thus, making better use of the available screen real estate. You used a subclass of PreferenceFragment to automatically maintain and persist the app's settings and a subclass of DialogFragment to display an AlertDialog to the user. We discussed portions of a Fragment's lifecycle and showed how to use the FragmentManager to obtain a reference to a Fragment so that you could interact with it programmatically.

In portrait orientation, you used the app's action menu to enable the user to display the SettingsActivity containing the SettingsFragment. To launch the SettingsActivity, you used an explicit Intent.

We showed how to use Android's WindowManager to obtain a Display object so that you could determine whether the app was running on a tablet in landscape orientation. In this case, you prevented the menu from displaying because the SettingsFragment was already on the screen.

We demonstrated how to manage a large number of image resources using subfolders in the app's assets folder and how to access those resources via an AssetManager. You created a Drawable from an image's bytes by reading them from an InputStream, then displayed the Drawable in an ImageView.

You learned about additional subfolders of the app's res folder—menu for storing menu resource files, anim for storing animation resource files and xml for storing raw XML data files. We also discussed how to use qualifiers to create a folder for storing a layout that should be used only on large devices in landscape orientation.

You used Toasts to display minor error messages or informational messages that appear on the screen briefly. To display the next flag in the quiz after a short delay, you used a Handler, which executes a Runnable after a specified number of milliseconds. You learned that a Handler's Runnable executes in the thread that created the Handler (the GUI thread in this app).

We defined an Animation in XML and applied it to the app's ImageView when the user guessed incorrectly to provide visual feedback to the user. You learned how to log exceptions for debugging purposes with Android's built-in logging mechanism and class Log. You also used additional classes and interfaces from the java.util package, including List, ArrayList, Collections and Set.

In Chapter 6, you'll create a **Cannon Game** using multithreading and frame-by-frame animation. You'll handle touch gestures to fire a cannon. You'll also learn how to create a game loop that updates the display as fast as possible to create smooth animations and to make the game feel like it executes at the same speed regardless of a given device's processor speed. We'll also show how to perform simple collision detection.

6

Cannon Game App

Listening for Touches, Manual Frame-By-Frame Animation, Graphics, Sound, Threading, SurfaceView and SurfaceHolder

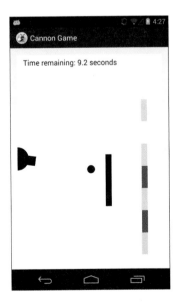

Objectives

In this chapter you'll:

- Create a simple game app that's easy to code and fun to play.

- Create a custom SurfaceView subclass for displaying the game's graphics from a separate thread of execution.

- Draw graphics using Paints and a Canvas.

- Override View's onTouchEvent method to fire a cannonball when the user touches the screen.

- Perform simple collision detection.

- Add sound to your app using a SoundPool and the AudioManager.

- Override Fragment lifecycle methods onPause and onDestroy.

6.1 Introduction

The **Cannon Game** app challenges you to destroy a seven-piece target before a ten-second time limit expires (Fig. 6.1). The game consists of four visual components—a *cannon* that you control, a *cannonball*, the *target* and a *blocker* that defends the target. You aim and fire the cannon by *touching* the screen—the cannon then aims at the touched point and fires the cannonball in a straight line in that direction. At the end of the game, the app displays an `AlertDialog` indicating whether you won or lost, and showing the number of shots fired and the elapsed time (Fig. 6.2).

The game begins with a *10-second time limit*. Each time you destroy a target section, a three-second time bonus is *added* to your remaining time, and each time you hit the blocker, a two-second time penalty is *subtracted* from your remaining time. You win by destroying all seven target sections before you run out of time—if the timer reaches zero, you lose.

When you fire the cannon, the game plays a *firing sound*. When a cannonball hits a target piece, a *glass-breaking sound* plays and that piece of the target disappears. When the cannonball hits the blocker, a *hit sound* plays and the cannonball bounces back. The blocker cannot be destroyed. The target and blocker move *vertically* at different speeds, changing direction when they hit the top or bottom of the screen.

[*Note:* Due to performance issues with the Android Emulator, you should test this app on an Android device.]

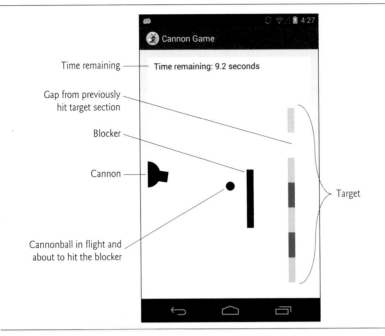

Time remaining
Gap from previously hit target section
Blocker
Cannon
Cannonball in flight and about to hit the blocker
Target

Fig. 6.1 | Completed **Cannon Game** app.

a) `AlertDialog` displayed after user destroys all seven target sections

b) `AlertDialog` displayed when game ends before user destroys all seven target sections

Fig. 6.2 | **Cannon Game** app `AlertDialog`s showing a win and a loss.

6.2 Test-Driving the Cannon Game App

Opening and Running the App

Open Eclipse and import the **Cannon Game** app project. Perform the following steps:

1. *Open the Import dialog.* Select **File > Import...** to open the **Import** dialog.

2. *Import the Cannon Game app's project.* In the **Import** dialog, expand the **General** node and select **Existing Projects into Workspace**, then click **Next >** to proceed to the **Import Projects** step. Ensure that **Select root directory** is selected, then click the **Browse...** button. In the **Browse for Folder** dialog, locate the CannonGame folder in the book's examples folder, select it and click **OK**. Click **Finish** to import the project into Eclipse. The project now appears in the **Package Explorer** window at the left side of the Eclipse window.

3. *Launch the Cannon Game app.* In Eclipse, right click the CannonGame project in the **Package Explorer** window, then select **Run As > Android Application** from the menu that appears.

Playing the Game

Tap the screen to aim and fire the cannon. You can fire a cannonball only if there is not another cannonball on the screen. If you're running this in an AVD, the mouse is your "finger." Try to destroy the target as fast as you can—the game ends if the timer runs out or you destroy all seven target pieces.

6.3 Technologies Overview

This section presents the new technologies that we use in the **Cannon Game** app in the order they're encountered in the chapter.

6.3.1 Attaching a Custom View to a Layout

You can create a *custom view* by extending class View or one of its subclasses, as we do with class CannonView (Section 6.8), which extends SurfaceView (discussed shortly). To add a custom component to a layout's XML file, you must provide its *fully qualified* name (i.e., its package and class name), so the custom View's class must exist before you add it to the layout. We demonstrate how to create the CannonView class and add it to a layout in Section 6.4.3.

6.3.2 Using the Resource Folder raw

Media files, such as the sounds used in the **Cannon Game** app, are placed in the app's resource folder **res/raw**. Section 6.4.5 discusses how to create this folder. You'll then drag the app's sound files into it.

6.3.3 Activity and Fragment Lifecycle Methods

When a Fragment is attached to an Activity as we did in Chapter 5 and will do in this chapter, its lifecycle is tied to that of its parent Activity. There are six Activity lifecycle methods that have corresponding Fragment lifecycle methods—onCreate, onStart, on-Resume, onPause, onStop and onDestroy. When the system calls these methods on an Activity, it will also call these corresponding methods (and potentially other Fragment lifecycle methods) on all of the Activity's attached Fragments.

This app uses Fragment lifecycle methods onPause and onDestroy. An Activity's **onPause** method is called when *another* Activity receives the focus, which pauses the one that loses the focus and sends it to the background. When an Activity hosts Fragments and the Activity is paused, all of its Fragments' **onPause** methods are called. In this app, the CannonView is displayed in a CannonGameFragment (Section 6.7). We override onPause to suspend game play in the CannonView so that the game does not continue executing when the user cannot interact with it—this saves battery power. Many Activity lifecycle methods have corresponding methods in a Fragment's lifecycle.

When an Activity is shut down, its **onDestroy** method is called, which in turn calls the **onDestroy** methods of all the Fragments hosted by the Activity. We use this method in the CannonFragment to *release* the CannonView's sound resources.

We discuss other Activity and Fragment lifecycle methods as we need them. For more information on the complete Activity lifecycle, visit:

```
http://developer.android.com/reference/android/app/Activity.html
    #ActivityLifecycle
```

and for more information about the complete Fragment lifecycle, visit:

```
http://developer.android.com/guide/components/fragments.html
    #Lifecycle
```

6.3.4 Overriding View Method onTouchEvent

Users interact with this app by touching the device's screen. A *touch* aligns the cannon to face the touch point on the screen, then fires the cannon. To process simple touch events for the CannonView, you'll override View method **onTouchEvent** (Section 6.8.13), then use constants from class **MotionEvent** (package android.view) to test which type of event occurred and process it accordingly.

6.3.5 Adding Sound with SoundPool and AudioManager

An app's sound effects are managed with a **SoundPool** (package android.media), which can be used to *load*, *play* and *unload* sounds. Sounds are played using one of Android's audio streams for *alarms, music, notifications, phone rings, system sounds, phone calls* and more. The Android documentation recommends that games use the *music audio stream* to play sounds. We use the Activity's **setVolumeControlStream** method to specify that the game's volume can be controlled with the device's volume keys. The method receives a constant from class **AudioManager** (package android.media), which provides access to the device's volume and phone ringer controls.

6.3.6 Frame-by-Frame Animation with Threads, SurfaceView and SurfaceHolder

This app *performs its animations manually* by updating the game elements from a separate thread of execuion. To do this, we use a subclass of Thread with a run method that directs our custom CannonView to update the positions of the game's elements, then draws them. The run method drives the *frame-by-frame animations*—this is known as the **game loop**.

Normally, all updates to an app's user interface must be performed in the GUI thread of execution. In Android, it's important to minimize the amount of work you do in the GUI thread to ensure that the GUI remains responsive and does not display ANR (Application Not Responding) dialogs. However, games often require complex logic that should be performed in separate threads of execution and those threads often need to draw to the screen. For such cases, Android provides class **SurfaceView**—a subclass of View to which a thread can draw, then indicate that the results should be displayed in the GUI thread. You manipulate a SurfaceView via an object of class **SurfaceHolder**, which enables you to obtain a Canvas on which you can draw graphics. Class SurfaceHolder also provides methods that give a thread *exclusive access* to the Canvas for drawing—only one thread at a time can draw to a SurfaceView. Each SurfaceView subclass should implement the interface **SurfaceHolder.Callback**, which contains methods that are called when the SurfaceView is *created, changed* (e.g., its size or orientation changes) or *destroyed*.

6.3.7 Simple Collision Detection

The CannonView performs simple *collision detection* to determine whether the cannonball has collided with any of the CannonView's edges, with the blocker or with a section of the target. These techniques are presented in Section 6.8. Game-development frameworks typically provide more sophisticated "pixel-perfect" collision-detection capabilities. There are many open-source game-development frameworks available.

6.3.8 Drawing Graphics Using Paint and Canvas

We use methods of class **Canvas** (package android.graphics) to draw text, lines and circles. Canvas methods draw on a View's **Bitmap**. Each drawing method in class Canvas uses an object of class **Paint** (package android.graphics) to specify drawing characteristics, including color, line thickness, font size and more. These capabilities are presented with the drawGameElements method in Section 6.8. For more details on the drawing characteristics you can specify with a Paint object, visit

```
http://developer.android.com/reference/android/graphics/Paint.html
```

6.4 Building the App's GUI and Resource Files

In this section, you'll create the app's resource files and main.xml layout file.

6.4.1 Creating the Project

Begin by creating a new Android project named CannonGame. Specify the following values in the **New Android Project** dialog:

- **Application Name:** Cannon Game
- **Project Name:** CannonGame
- **Package Name:** com.deitel.cannongame
- **Minimum Required SDK:** API18: Android 4.3
- **Target SDK:** API19: Android 4.4
- **Compile With:** API19: Android 4.4
- **Theme:** Holo Light with Dark Action Bar

In the **New Android Project** dialog's second **New Android Application** step, leave the default settings, and press **Next >**. In the **Configure Launcher Icon** step, select an app icon image, then press **Next >**. In the **Create Activity** step, select **Blank Activity**, then press **Next >**. In the **Blank Activity** step, leave the default settings and click **Finish** to create the project. Switch to the activity_main.xml tab in the editor. In the **Graphical Layout** editor, select **Nexus 4** from the screen-type drop-down list and delete the TextView containing "Hello world!"

Configure the App for Portrait Orientation

The cannon game is designed to work best in portrait orientation. Follow the steps you performed in Section 3.6 to set the app's screen orientation to portrait.

6.4.2 strings.xml

You created String resources in earlier chapters, so we show only a table (Fig. 6.3) of the String resource names and corresponding values here. Double click strings.xml in the res/values folder to display the resource editor for creating these String resources.

Resource name	Value
results_format	Shots fired: %1$d\nTotal time: %2$.1f
reset_game	Reset Game
win	You win!
lose	You lose!
time_remaining_format	Time remaining: %.1f seconds

Fig. 6.3 | String resources used in the **Cannon Game** app.

6.4.3 fragment_game.xml

The fragment_game.xml layout for the CannonGameFragment contains a FrameLayout that displays the CannonView. A **FrameLayout** is designed to display only one View—in this case, the CannonView. In this section, you'll create CannonGameFragment's layout and the CannonView class. To add the fragment_game.xml layout, perform the following steps:

1. Expand the project's res/layout node in the **Package Explorer**.

2. Right click the layout folder and select **New > Android XML File** to display the **New Android XML File** dialog.

3. In the dialog's **File** field, enter fragment_game.xml

4. In the **Root Element** section, select **FrameLayout**, then click **Finish**.

5. From the **Palette**'s **Advanced** section, drag a **view** (with a lowercase **v**) onto the design area.

6. The previous step displays the **Choose Custom View Class** dialog. In that dialog, click **Create New...** to display the **New Java Class** dialog.

7. In the **Name** field, enter CannonView. In the **Superclass** field, change the superclass from android.view.View to android.view.SurfaceView. Ensure that **Constructors from superclass** is checked, then click **Finish**. This creates and opens CannonView.java. We'll be using only the two-argument constructor, so delete the other two. Save and close CannonView.java.

8. In fragment_game.xml, select **view1** in the **Outline** window. In the **Properties** window's **Layout Parameters** section, set **Width** and **Height** to match_parent.

9. In the **Outline** window, right click **view1**, select **Edit ID…**, rename view1 as cannonView and click **OK**.

10. Save fragment_game.xml.

6.4.4 activity_main.xml

The activity_main.xml layout for this app's MainActivity contains only the Cannon-GameFragment. To add this Fragment to the layout:

1. Open activity_main.xml in the **Graphical Layout** editor.

2. From the **Palette**'s **Layouts** section, drag a **Fragment** onto the design area or onto the RelativeLayout node in the **Outline** window.

3. The preceding step displays the **Choose Fragment Class** dialog. Click **Create New…** to display the **New Java Class** dialog.

4. Enter CannonGameFragment in the dialog's **Name** field, change the **Superclass** field's value to android.app.Fragment and click **Finish** to create the class. The IDE opens the Java file for the class, which you can close for now.

5. Save activity_main.xml.

6.4.5 Adding the Sounds to the App

As we mentioned previously, sound files are stored in the app's res/raw folder. This app uses three sound files—blocker_hit.wav, target_hit.wav and cannon_fire.wav—which are located with the book's examples in the sounds folder. To add these files to your project:

1. Right click the app's res folder, then select **New > Folder**.

2. Specify the folder name raw and click **Finish** to create the folder.

3. Drag the sound files into the res/raw folder.

6.5 Class Line Maintains a Line's Endpoints

This app consists of four classes:

- Line (Fig. 6.4)
- MainActivity (the Activity subclass; Section 6.6)
- CannonGameFragment (Section 6.7), and
- CannonView (Section 6.8)

In this section, we discuss class Line, which represents a line's starting and ending Points. Objects of this class define the game's blocker and target. To add class Line to the project:

1. Expand the project's src node in the **Package Explorer**.

2. Right click the package (com.deitel.cannongame) and select **New > Class** to display the **New Java Class** dialog.

3. In the dialog's **Name** field, enter Line and click **Finish**.

4. Enter the code in Fig. 6.4 into the Line.java file. The default Point constructor sets a Point's public x and y instance variables to 0.

```
1   // Line.java
2   // Class Line represents a line with two endpoints.
3   package com.deitel.cannongame;
4
5   import android.graphics.Point;
6
7   public class Line
8   {
9      public Point start = new Point(); // start Point--(0,0) by default
10     public Point end = new Point(); // end Point--(0,0) by default
11  } // end class Line
```

Fig. 6.4 | Class Line represents a line with two endpoints.

6.6 MainActivity Subclass of Activity

Class MainActivity (Fig. 6.5) is host for the **Cannon Game** app's CannonGameFragment. In this app, we override only Activity method onCreate, which inflates the GUI.

```
1   // MainActivity.java
2   // MainActivity displays the CannonGameFragment
3   package com.deitel.cannongame;
4
5   import android.app.Activity;
6   import android.os.Bundle;
7
8   public class MainActivity extends Activity
9   {
10     // called when the app first launches
11     @Override
12     public void onCreate(Bundle savedInstanceState)
13     {
14        super.onCreate(savedInstanceState); // call super's onCreate method
15        setContentView(R.layout.activity_main); // inflate the layout
16     }
17  } // end class MainActivity
```

Fig. 6.5 | MainActivity displays the CannonGameFragment.

6.7 CannonGameFragment Subclass of Fragment

Class CannonGameFragment (Fig. 6.6) overrides four Fragment methods:

- onCreateView (lines 17–28)—As you learned in Section 5.3.3, this method is called after a Fragment's onCreate method to build and return a View containing the Fragment's GUI. Lines 22–23 inflate the GUI. Line 26 gets a reference to the CannonGameFragment's CannonView so that we can call its methods.

- onActivityCreated (lines 31–38)—This method is called after the Fragment's host Activity is created. Line 37 calls the Activity's setVolumeControlStream method to allow the game's audio volume to be controlled by the device's volume keys.

- onPause (lines 41–46)—When the MainActivity is sent to the *background* (and thus, paused), the CannonGameFragment's method onPause executes. Line 45 calls the CannonView's stopGame method (Section 6.8.11) to stop the game loop.

- onDestroy (lines 49–54)—When the MainActivity is destroyed, its onDestroy method calls the CannonGameFragment's onDestroy. Line 46 calls the CannonView's releaseResources method (Section 6.8.11) to release the sound resources.

```java
 1  // CannonGameFragment.java
 2  // CannonGameFragment creates and manages a CannonView
 3  package com.deitel.cannongame;
 4
 5  import android.app.Fragment;
 6  import android.media.AudioManager;
 7  import android.os.Bundle;
 8  import android.view.LayoutInflater;
 9  import android.view.View;
10  import android.view.ViewGroup;
11
12  public class CannonGameFragment extends Fragment
13  {
14     private CannonView cannonView; // custom view to display the game
15
16     // called when Fragment's view needs to be created
17     @Override
18     public View onCreateView(LayoutInflater inflater, ViewGroup container,
19        Bundle savedInstanceState)
20     {
21        super.onCreateView(inflater, container, savedInstanceState);
22        View view =
23           inflater.inflate(R.layout.fragment_game, container, false);
24
25        // get the CannonView
26        cannonView = (CannonView) view.findViewById(R.id.cannonView);
27        return view;
28     }
29
30     // set up volume control once Activity is created
31     @Override
32     public void onActivityCreated(Bundle savedInstanceState)
33     {
34        super.onActivityCreated(savedInstanceState);
35
36        // allow volume keys to set game volume
37        getActivity().setVolumeControlStream(AudioManager.STREAM_MUSIC);
38     }
39
40     // when MainActivity is paused, CannonGameFragment terminates the game
41     @Override
42     public void onPause()
43     {
```

Fig. 6.6 | CannonGameFragment creates and manages a CannonView. (Part I of 2.)

```
44          super.onPause();
45          cannonView.stopGame(); // terminates the game
46       }
47
48       // when MainActivity is paused, CannonGameFragment releases resources
49       @Override
50       public void onDestroy()
51       {
52          super.onDestroy();
53          cannonView.releaseResources();
54       }
55    } // end class CannonGameFragment
```

Fig. 6.6 | CannonGameFragment creates and manages a CannonView. (Part 2 of 2.)

6.8 CannonView Subclass of View

Class CannonView (Figs. 6.7–6.20) is a custom subclass of View that implements the **Cannon Game**'s logic and draws game objects on the screen.

6.8.1 package and import Statements

Figure 6.7 lists the package statement and the import statements for class CannonView. Section 6.3 discussed the key new classes and interfaces that class CannonView uses. We've highlighted them in Fig. 6.7.

```
 1   // CannonView.java
 2   // Displays and controls the Cannon Game
 3   package com.deitel.cannongame;
 4
 5   import android.app.Activity;
 6   import android.app.AlertDialog;
 7   import android.app.Dialog;
 8   import android.app.DialogFragment;
 9   import android.content.Context;
10   import android.content.DialogInterface;
11   import android.graphics.Canvas;
12   import android.graphics.Color;
13   import android.graphics.Paint;
14   import android.graphics.Point;
15   import android.media.AudioManager;
16   import android.media.SoundPool;
17   import android.os.Bundle;
18   import android.util.AttributeSet;
19   import android.util.Log;
20   import android.util.SparseIntArray;
21   import android.view.MotionEvent;
22   import android.view.SurfaceHolder;
23   import android.view.SurfaceView;
24
```

Fig. 6.7 | CannonView class's package and import statements.

6.8.2 Instance Variables and Constants

Figure 6.8 lists the large number of class CannonView's constants and instance variables. Most are self documenting, but we'll explain each as we encounter it in the discussion.

```
25   public class CannonView extends SurfaceView
26      implements SurfaceHolder.Callback
27   {
28      private static final String TAG = "CannonView"; // for logging errors
29
30      private CannonThread cannonThread; // controls the game loop
31      private Activity activity; // to display Game Over dialog in GUI thread
32      private boolean dialogIsDisplayed = false;
33
34      // constants for game play
35      public static final int TARGET_PIECES = 7; // sections in the target
36      public static final int MISS_PENALTY = 2; // seconds deducted on a miss
37      public static final int HIT_REWARD = 3; // seconds added on a hit
38
39      // variables for the game loop and tracking statistics
40      private boolean gameOver; // is the game over?
41      private double timeLeft; // time remaining in seconds
42      private int shotsFired; // shots the user has fired
43      private double totalElapsedTime; // elapsed seconds
44
45      // variables for the blocker and target
46      private Line blocker; // start and end points of the blocker
47      private int blockerDistance; // blocker distance from left
48      private int blockerBeginning; // blocker top-edge distance from top
49      private int blockerEnd; // blocker bottom-edge distance from top
50      private int initialBlockerVelocity; // initial blocker speed multiplier
51      private float blockerVelocity; // blocker speed multiplier during game
52
53      private Line target; // start and end points of the target
54      private int targetDistance; // target distance from left
55      private int targetBeginning; // target distance from top
56      private double pieceLength; // length of a target piece
57      private int targetEnd; // target bottom's distance from top
58      private int initialTargetVelocity; // initial target speed multiplier
59      private float targetVelocity; // target speed multiplier
60
61      private int lineWidth; // width of the target and blocker
62      private boolean[] hitStates; // is each target piece hit?
63      private int targetPiecesHit; // number of target pieces hit (out of 7)
64
65      // variables for the cannon and cannonball
66      private Point cannonball; // cannonball image's upper-left corner
67      private int cannonballVelocityX; // cannonball's x velocity
68      private int cannonballVelocityY; // cannonball's y velocity
69      private boolean cannonballOnScreen; // whether cannonball on the screen
70      private int cannonballRadius; // cannonball's radius
71      private int cannonballSpeed; // cannonball's speed
72      private int cannonBaseRadius; // cannon base's radius
```

Fig. 6.8 | CannonView class's fields. (Part 1 of 2.)

```
73    private int cannonLength; // cannon barrel's length
74    private Point barrelEnd; // the endpoint of the cannon's barrel
75    private int screenWidth;
76    private int screenHeight;
77
78    // constants and variables for managing sounds
79    private static final int TARGET_SOUND_ID = 0;
80    private static final int CANNON_SOUND_ID = 1;
81    private static final int BLOCKER_SOUND_ID = 2;
82    private SoundPool soundPool; // plays sound effects
83    private SparseIntArray soundMap; // maps IDs to SoundPool
84
85    // Paint variables used when drawing each item on the screen
86    private Paint textPaint; // Paint used to draw text
87    private Paint cannonballPaint; // Paint used to draw the cannonball
88    private Paint cannonPaint; // Paint used to draw the cannon
89    private Paint blockerPaint; // Paint used to draw the blocker
90    private Paint targetPaint; // Paint used to draw the target
91    private Paint backgroundPaint; // Paint used to clear the drawing area
92
```

Fig. 6.8 | CannonView class's fields. (Part 2 of 2.)

6.8.3 Constructor

Figure 6.9 shows class CannonView's constructor. When a View is inflated, its constructor is called with a Context and an AttributeSet as arguments. The Context is the Activity that displays the CannonGameFragment containing the CannonView, and the **AttributeSet** (package android.util) contains the CannonView attribute values that are set in the layout's XML document. These arguments are passed to the superclass constructor (line 96) to ensure that the custom View is properly configured with the values of any standard View attributes specified in the XML. Line 97 stores a reference to the MainActivity so we can use it at the end of a game to display an AlertDialog from the Activity's GUI thread.

```
93    // public constructor
94    public CannonView(Context context, AttributeSet attrs)
95    {
96       super(context, attrs); // call superclass constructor
97       activity = (Activity) context; // store reference to MainActivity
98
99       // register SurfaceHolder.Callback listener
100      getHolder().addCallback(this);
101
102      // initialize Lines and Point representing game items
103      blocker = new Line(); // create the blocker as a Line
104      target = new Line(); // create the target as a Line
105      cannonball = new Point(); // create the cannonball as a Point
106
107      // initialize hitStates as a boolean array
108      hitStates = new boolean[TARGET_PIECES];
```

Fig. 6.9 | CannonView constructor. (Part 1 of 2.)

```
109
110      // initialize SoundPool to play the app's three sound effects
111      soundPool = new SoundPool(1, AudioManager.STREAM_MUSIC, 0);
112
113      // create Map of sounds and pre-load sounds
114      soundMap = new SparseIntArray(3); // create new SparseIntArray
115      soundMap.put(TARGET_SOUND_ID,
116         soundPool.load(context, R.raw.target_hit, 1));
117      soundMap.put(CANNON_SOUND_ID,
118         soundPool.load(context, R.raw.cannon_fire, 1));
119      soundMap.put(BLOCKER_SOUND_ID,
120         soundPool.load(context, R.raw.blocker_hit, 1));
121
122      // construct Paints for drawing text, cannonball, cannon,
123      // blocker and target; these are configured in method onSizeChanged
124      textPaint = new Paint();
125      cannonPaint = new Paint();
126      cannonballPaint = new Paint();
127      blockerPaint = new Paint();
128      targetPaint = new Paint();
129      backgroundPaint = new Paint();
130   } // end CannonView constructor
131
```

Fig. 6.9 | CannonView constructor. (Part 2 of 2.)

Registering the *SurfaceHolder.Callback Listener*

Line 100 registers this (i.e., the CannonView) as the object that implements SurfaceHold-er.Callback to receive the method calls that indicate when the SurfaceView is *created*, *updated* and *destroyed*. Inherited SurfaceView method **getHolder** returns the Surface-Holder object for managing the SurfaceView, and SurfaceHolder method **addCallback** stores the object that implements interface SurfaceHolder.Callback.

Creating the *blocker, target* and *cannonball*

Lines 103–105 create the blocker and target as Lines and the cannonball as a Point. Next, we create boolean array hitStates to keep track of which of the target's seven pieces have been hit (and thus should not be drawn).

Configuring the *SoundPool and Loading the Sounds*

Lines 111–120 configure the sounds that we use in the app. First, we create the SoundPool that's used to load and play the app's sound effects. The constructor's first argument represents the maximum number of simultaneous sound streams that can play at once. We play only one sound at a time, so we pass 1. The second argument specifies which audio stream will be used to play the sounds. There are seven sound streams identified by constants in class AudioManager, but the documentation for class SoundPool recommends using the stream for playing music (AudioManager.STREAM_MUSIC) for sound in games. The last argument represents the sound quality, but the documentation indicates that this value is not currently used and 0 should be specified as the default value.

Line 114 creates a SparseIntArray (soundMap), which maps integer keys to integer values. SparseIntArray is similar to—but more efficient than—a HashMap<Integer, Integer> for small numbers of key–value pairs. In this case, we map the sound keys (defined in Fig. 6.8, lines 79–81) to the loaded sounds' IDs, which are represented by the return values of the SoundPool's **load method** (called in Fig. 6.9, lines 116, 118 and 120). Each sound ID can be used to *play* a sound (and later to return its resources to the system). Sound-Pool method load receives three arguments—the application's Context, a resource ID representing the sound file to load and the sound's priority. According to the documentation for this method, the last argument is not currently used and should be specified as 1.

Creating the *Paint Objects Used to Draw Game Elements*
Lines 124–129 create the Paint objects that are used when drawing the game's elements. We configure these in method onSizeChanged (Section 6.8.4), because some of the Paint settings depend on scaling the game elements based on the device's screen size.

6.8.4 Overriding View Method onSizeChanged

Figure 6.10 overrides class View's **onSizeChanged method**, which is called whenever the View's size changes, including when the View is first added to the View hierarchy as the layout is inflated. This app always displays in *portrait mode*, so onSizeChanged is called only once when the activity's onCreate method inflates the GUI. The method receives the View's new width and height and its old width and height—when this method is called the first time, the old width and height are 0. The calculations performed here *scale* the game's on-screen elements based on the device's pixel width and height. We arrived at our scaling factors via trial and error, choosing values that made the game elements look nice on the screen. Lines 170–175 configure the Paint objects that are used to specify drawing characteristics for the game's elements. After the calculations, line 177 calls method newGame (Fig. 6.11).

```
132    // called by surfaceChanged when the size of the SurfaceView changes,
133    // such as when it's first added to the View hierarchy
134    @Override
135    protected void onSizeChanged(int w, int h, int oldw, int oldh)
136    {
137        super.onSizeChanged(w, h, oldw, oldh);
138
139        screenWidth = w; // store CannonView's width
140        screenHeight = h; // store CannonView's height
141        cannonBaseRadius = h / 18; // cannon base radius 1/18 screen height
142        cannonLength = w / 8; // cannon length 1/8 screen width
143
144        cannonballRadius = w / 36; // cannonball radius 1/36 screen width
145        cannonballSpeed = w * 3 / 2; // cannonball speed multiplier
146
147        lineWidth = w / 24; // target and blocker 1/24 screen width
148
149        // configure instance variables related to the blocker
150        blockerDistance = w * 5 / 8; // blocker 5/8 screen width from left
151        blockerBeginning = h / 8; // distance from top 1/8 screen height
152        blockerEnd = h * 3 / 8; // distance from top 3/8 screen height
153        initialBlockerVelocity = h / 2; // initial blocker speed multiplier
154        blocker.start = new Point(blockerDistance, blockerBeginning);
155        blocker.end = new Point(blockerDistance, blockerEnd);
```

Fig. 6.10 | Overridden onSizeChanged method. (Part 1 of 2.)

```
156
157        // configure instance variables related to the target
158        targetDistance = w * 7 / 8; // target 7/8 screen width from left
159        targetBeginning = h / 8; // distance from top 1/8 screen height
160        targetEnd = h * 7 / 8; // distance from top 7/8 screen height
161        pieceLength = (targetEnd - targetBeginning) / TARGET_PIECES;
162        initialTargetVelocity = -h / 4; // initial target speed multiplier
163        target.start = new Point(targetDistance, targetBeginning);
164        target.end = new Point(targetDistance, targetEnd);
165
166        // endpoint of the cannon's barrel initially points horizontally
167        barrelEnd = new Point(cannonLength, h / 2);
168
169        // configure Paint objects for drawing game elements
170        textPaint.setTextSize(w / 20); // text size 1/20 of screen width
171        textPaint.setAntiAlias(true); // smoothes the text
172        cannonPaint.setStrokeWidth(lineWidth * 1.5f); // set line thickness
173        blockerPaint.setStrokeWidth(lineWidth); // set line thickness
174        targetPaint.setStrokeWidth(lineWidth); // set line thickness
175        backgroundPaint.setColor(Color.WHITE); // set background color
176
177        newGame(); // set up and start a new game
178    } // end method onSizeChanged
179
```

Fig. 6.10 | Overridden onSizeChanged method. (Part 2 of 2.)

6.8.5 Method newGame

Method newGame (Fig. 6.11) resets the instance variables that are used to control the game. If variable gameOver is true, which occurs only *after* the first game completes, line 203 resets gameOver and lines 204–205 create a new CannonThread and start it to begin the *game loop* that controls the game. You'll learn more about this in Section 6.8.14.

```
180    // reset all the screen elements and start a new game
181    public void newGame()
182    {
183        // set every element of hitStates to false--restores target pieces
184        for (int i = 0; i < TARGET_PIECES; i++)
185            hitStates[i] = false;
186
187        targetPiecesHit = 0; // no target pieces have been hit
188        blockerVelocity = initialBlockerVelocity; // set initial velocity
189        targetVelocity = initialTargetVelocity; // set initial velocity
190        timeLeft = 10; // start the countdown at 10 seconds
191        cannonballOnScreen = false; // the cannonball is not on the screen
192        shotsFired = 0; // set the initial number of shots fired
193        totalElapsedTime = 0.0; // set the time elapsed to zero
194
195        // set the start and end Points of the blocker and target
196        blocker.start.set(blockerDistance, blockerBeginning);
197        blocker.end.set(blockerDistance, blockerEnd);
```

Fig. 6.11 | CannonView method newGame. (Part 1 of 2.)

```
198        target.start.set(targetDistance, targetBeginning);
199        target.end.set(targetDistance, targetEnd);
200
201        if (gameOver) // starting a new game after the last game ended
202        {
203           gameOver = false; // the game is not over
204           cannonThread = new CannonThread(getHolder()); // create thread
205           cannonThread.start(); // start the game loop thread
206        } // end if
207     } // end method newGame
208
```

Fig. 6.11 | CannonView method newGame. (Part 2 of 2.)

6.8.6 Method updatePositions

Method updatePositions (Fig. 6.12) is called by the CannonThread's run method (Section 6.8.14) to update the on-screen elements' positions and to perform simple *collision detection*. The new locations of the game elements are calculated based on the elapsed time in milliseconds between the previous and current animation frames. This enables the game to update the amount by which each game element moves based on the device's *refresh rate*. We discuss this in more detail when we cover game loops in Section 6.8.14.

```
209     // called repeatedly by the CannonThread to update game elements
210     private void updatePositions(double elapsedTimeMS)
211     {
212        double interval = elapsedTimeMS / 1000.0; // convert to seconds
213
214        if (cannonballOnScreen) // if there is currently a shot fired
215        {
216           // update cannonball position
217           cannonball.x += interval * cannonballVelocityX;
218           cannonball.y += interval * cannonballVelocityY;
219
220           // check for collision with blocker
221           if (cannonball.x + cannonballRadius > blockerDistance &&
222              cannonball.x - cannonballRadius < blockerDistance &&
223              cannonball.y + cannonballRadius > blocker.start.y &&
224              cannonball.y - cannonballRadius < blocker.end.y)
225           {
226              cannonballVelocityX *= -1; // reverse cannonball's direction
227              timeLeft -= MISS_PENALTY; // penalize the user
228
229              // play blocker sound
230              soundPool.play(soundMap.get(BLOCKER_SOUND_ID), 1, 1, 1, 0, 1f);
231           }
232           // check for collisions with left and right walls
233           else if (cannonball.x + cannonballRadius > screenWidth ||
234              cannonball.x - cannonballRadius < 0)
235           {
```

Fig. 6.12 | CannonView method updatePositions. (Part 1 of 3.)

```
236                cannonballOnScreen = false; // remove cannonball from screen
237            }
238            // check for collisions with top and bottom walls
239            else if (cannonball.y + cannonballRadius > screenHeight ||
240                cannonball.y - cannonballRadius < 0)
241            {
242                cannonballOnScreen = false; // remove cannonball from screen
243            }
244            // check for cannonball collision with target
245            else if (cannonball.x + cannonballRadius > targetDistance &&
246                cannonball.x - cannonballRadius < targetDistance &&
247                cannonball.y + cannonballRadius > target.start.y &&
248                cannonball.y - cannonballRadius < target.end.y)
249            {
250                // determine target section number (0 is the top)
251                int section =
252                    (int) ((cannonball.y - target.start.y) / pieceLength);
253
254                // check if the piece hasn't been hit yet
255                if ((section >= 0 && section < TARGET_PIECES) &&
256                    !hitStates[section])
257                {
258                    hitStates[section] = true; // section was hit
259                    cannonballOnScreen = false; // remove cannonball
260                    timeLeft += HIT_REWARD; // add reward to remaining time
261
262                    // play target hit sound
263                    soundPool.play(soundMap.get(TARGET_SOUND_ID), 1,
264                        1, 1, 0, 1f);
265
266                    // if all pieces have been hit
267                    if (++targetPiecesHit == TARGET_PIECES)
268                    {
269                        cannonThread.setRunning(false); // terminate thread
270                        showGameOverDialog(R.string.win); // show winning dialog
271                        gameOver = true;
272                    }
273                }
274            }
275        }
276
277        // update the blocker's position
278        double blockerUpdate = interval * blockerVelocity;
279        blocker.start.y += blockerUpdate;
280        blocker.end.y += blockerUpdate;
281
282        // update the target's position
283        double targetUpdate = interval * targetVelocity;
284        target.start.y += targetUpdate;
285        target.end.y += targetUpdate;
286
```

Fig. 6.12 | CannonView method updatePositions. (Part 2 of 3.)

```
287        // if the blocker hit the top or bottom, reverse direction
288        if (blocker.start.y < 0 || blocker.end.y > screenHeight)
289           blockerVelocity *= -1;
290
291        // if the target hit the top or bottom, reverse direction
292        if (target.start.y < 0 || target.end.y > screenHeight)
293           targetVelocity *= -1;
294
295        timeLeft -= interval; // subtract from time left
296
297        // if the timer reached zero
298        if (timeLeft <= 0.0)
299        {
300           timeLeft = 0.0;
301           gameOver = true; // the game is over
302           cannonThread.setRunning(false); // terminate thread
303           showGameOverDialog(R.string.lose); // show the losing dialog
304        }
305     } // end method updatePositions
306
```

Fig. 6.12 | CannonView method updatePositions. (Part 3 of 3.)

Elapsed Time Since the Last Animation Frame
Line 212 converts the elapsed time since the last animation frame from milliseconds to seconds. This value is used to modify the positions of various game elements.

Checking for Collisions with the Blocker
Line 214 checks whether the cannonball is on the screen. If it is, we update its position by adding the distance it should have traveled since the last timer event. This is calculated by multiplying its velocity by the amount of time that passed (lines 217–218). Lines 221–224 check whether the cannonball has *collided* with the blocker. We perform simple *collision detection*, based on the rectangular boundary of the cannonball. There are four conditions that must be met if the cannonball is in contact with the blocker:

- The cannonball's *x*-coordinate plus the cannonball's radius must be greater than the blocker's distance from the left edge of the screen (blockerDistance) (line 221). This means that the cannonball has reached the blocker's distance from the left edge of the screen.

- The cannonball's *x*-coordinate minus the cannonball's radius must also be less than the blocker's distance from the left edge of the screen (line 222). This ensures that the cannonball has not yet passed the blocker.

- Part of the cannonball must be lower than the top of the blocker (line 223).

- Part of the cannonball must be higher than the bottom of the blocker (line 224).

If all these conditions are met, we *reverse* the cannonball's direction on the screen (line 226), *penalize* the user by *subtracting* MISS_PENALTY from timeLeft, then call soundPool's **play method** to play the blocker hit sound—BLOCKER_SOUND_ID is used as the soundMap key to locate the sound's ID in the SoundPool.

Checking Whether the Cannonball Left the Screen
We remove the cannonball if it reaches any of the screen's edges. Lines 233–237 test whether the cannonball has *collided* with the left or right wall and, if it has, remove the cannonball from the screen. Lines 239–243 remove the cannonball if it collides with the top or bottom of the screen.

Checking for Collisions with the Target
We then check whether the cannonball has hit the target (lines 245–248). These conditions are similar to those used to determine whether the cannonball collided with the blocker. If the cannonball hit the target, lines 251–252 determine which *section* has been hit—dividing the distance between the cannonball and the bottom of the target by the length of a piece. This expression evaluates to 0 for the topmost section and 6 for the bottommost. We check whether that section was previously hit, using the hitStates array (line 256). If it wasn't, we set the corresponding hitStates element to true and remove the cannonball from the screen. We then add HIT_REWARD to timeLeft, increasing the game's time remaining, and play the target hit sound (TARGET_SOUND_ID). We increment targetPiecesHit, then determine whether it's equal to TARGET_PIECES (line 267). If so, the game is over, so we terminate the CannonThread by calling its setRunning method with the argument false, invoke method showGameOverDialog with the String resource ID representing the winning message and set gameOver to true.

Updating the Blocker and Target Positions
Now that all possible cannonball collisions have been checked, the blocker and target positions must be updated. Lines 278–280 change the blocker's position by multiplying blockerVelocity by the amount of time that has passed since the last update, and adding that value to the current *x*- and *y*-coordinates. Lines 283–285 do the same for the target. If the blocker has collided with the top or bottom wall, its direction is *reversed* by multiplying its velocity by -1 (lines 288–289). Lines 292–293 perform the same check and adjustment for the full length of the target, including any sections that have already been destroyed.

Updating the Time Left and Determining Whether Time Ran Out
We decrease timeLeft by the time that has passed since the prior animation frame (line 295). If timeLeft has reached zero, the game is over—we set timeLeft to 0.0 just in case it was negative; otherwise, sometimes a negative final time would display on the screen). Then we set gameOver to true, terminate the CannonThread by calling its setRunning method with the argument false and call method showGameOverDialog with the String resource ID representing the losing message.

6.8.7 Method fireCannonball

When the user *touches* the screen, method onTouchEvent (Section 6.8.13) calls fireCannonball (Fig. 6.13). If there's already a cannonball on the screen, the method *returns immediately*. Line 313 calls alignCannon to aim the cannon at the *touch point* and get the cannon's angle. Lines 316–317 "load the cannon" (that is, position the cannonball inside the cannon). Then, lines 320 and 323 calculate the horizontal and vertical components of the cannonball's velocity. Next, we set cannonballOnScreen to true so that the cannonball will be drawn by method drawGameElements (Fig. 6.15) and increment shotsFired. Finally, we play the cannon's firing sound (represented by the CANNON_SOUND_ID).

```
307    // fires a cannonball
308    public void fireCannonball(MotionEvent event)
309    {
310       if (cannonballOnScreen) // if a cannonball is already on the screen
311          return; // do nothing
312
313       double angle = alignCannon(event); // get the cannon barrel's angle
314
315       // move the cannonball to be inside the cannon
316       cannonball.x = cannonballRadius; // align x-coordinate with cannon
317       cannonball.y = screenHeight / 2; // centers ball vertically
318
319       // get the x component of the total velocity
320       cannonballVelocityX = (int) (cannonballSpeed * Math.sin(angle));
321
322       // get the y component of the total velocity
323       cannonballVelocityY = (int) (-cannonballSpeed * Math.cos(angle));
324       cannonballOnScreen = true; // the cannonball is on the screen
325       ++shotsFired; // increment shotsFired
326
327       // play cannon fired sound
328       soundPool.play(soundMap.get(CANNON_SOUND_ID), 1, 1, 1, 0, 1f);
329    } // end method fireCannonball
330
```

Fig. 6.13 | CannonView method fireCannonball.

6.8.8 Method alignCannon

Method alignCannon (Fig. 6.14) aims the cannon at the point where the user touched the screen. Line 335 gets the *x*- and *y*-coordinates of the *touch* from the MotionEvent argument. We compute the vertical distance of the touch from the center of the screen. If this is not zero, we calculate cannon barrel's angle from the horizontal (line 345). If the touch is on the lower-half of the screen we adjust the angle by Math.PI (line 349). We then use the cannonLength and the angle to determine the *x*- and *y*-coordinate values for the endpoint of the cannon's barrel—this is used to draw a line from the cannon base's center at the left edge of the screen to the cannon's barrel endpoint.

```
331    // aligns the cannon in response to a user touch
332    public double alignCannon(MotionEvent event)
333    {
334       // get the location of the touch in this view
335       Point touchPoint = new Point((int) event.getX(), (int) event.getY());
336
337       // compute the touch's distance from center of the screen
338       // on the y-axis
339       double centerMinusY = (screenHeight / 2 - touchPoint.y);
340
341       double angle = 0; // initialize angle to 0
342
```

Fig. 6.14 | CannonView method alignCannon. (Part 1 of 2.)

```
343        // calculate the angle the barrel makes with the horizontal
344        if (centerMinusY != 0) // prevent division by 0
345           angle = Math.atan((double) touchPoint.x / centerMinusY);
346
347        // if the touch is on the lower half of the screen
348        if (touchPoint.y > screenHeight / 2)
349           angle += Math.PI; // adjust the angle
350
351        // calculate the endpoint of the cannon barrel
352        barrelEnd.x = (int) (cannonLength * Math.sin(angle));
353        barrelEnd.y =
354           (int) (-cannonLength * Math.cos(angle) + screenHeight / 2);
355
356        return angle; // return the computed angle
357     } // end method alignCannon
358
```

Fig. 6.14 | CannonView method alignCannon. (Part 2 of 2.)

6.8.9 Method drawGameElements

The method drawGameElements (Fig. 6.15) draws the *cannon, cannonball, blocker* and *target* on the SurfaceView using the Canvas that the CannonThread (Section 6.8.14) obtains from the SurfaceView's SurfaceHolder.

```
359     // draws the game to the given Canvas
360     public void drawGameElements(Canvas canvas)
361     {
362        // clear the background
363        canvas.drawRect(0, 0, canvas.getWidth(), canvas.getHeight(),
364           backgroundPaint);
365
366        // display time remaining
367        canvas.drawText(getResources().getString(
368           R.string.time_remaining_format, timeLeft), 30, 50, textPaint);
369
370        // if a cannonball is currently on the screen, draw it
371        if (cannonballOnScreen)
372           canvas.drawCircle(cannonball.x, cannonball.y, cannonballRadius,
373              cannonballPaint);
374
375        // draw the cannon barrel
376        canvas.drawLine(0, screenHeight / 2, barrelEnd.x, barrelEnd.y,
377           cannonPaint);
378
379        // draw the cannon base
380        canvas.drawCircle(0, (int) screenHeight / 2,
381           (int) cannonBaseRadius, cannonPaint);
382
383        // draw the blocker
384        canvas.drawLine(blocker.start.x, blocker.start.y, blocker.end.x,
385           blocker.end.y, blockerPaint);
```

Fig. 6.15 | CannonView method drawGameElements. (Part 1 of 2.)

```
386
387        Point currentPoint = new Point(); // start of current target section
388
389        // initialize currentPoint to the starting point of the target
390        currentPoint.x = target.start.x;
391        currentPoint.y = target.start.y;
392
393        // draw the target
394        for (int i = 0; i < TARGET_PIECES; i++)
395        {
396           // if this target piece is not hit, draw it
397           if (!hitStates[i])
398           {
399              // alternate coloring the pieces
400              if (i % 2 != 0)
401                 targetPaint.setColor(Color.BLUE);
402              else
403                 targetPaint.setColor(Color.YELLOW);
404
405              canvas.drawLine(currentPoint.x, currentPoint.y, target.end.x,
406                 (int) (currentPoint.y + pieceLength), targetPaint);
407           }
408
409           // move currentPoint to the start of the next piece
410           currentPoint.y += pieceLength;
411        }
412     } // end method drawGameElements
413
```

Fig. 6.15 | CannonView method drawGameElements. (Part 2 of 2.)

*Clearing the **Canvas** with Method **drawRect***

First, we call Canvas's **drawRect** method (lines 363–364) to clear the Canvas so that all the game elements can be displayed in their new positions. The method receives as arguments the rectangle's upper-left x-y coordinates, the rectangle's width and height, and the Paint object that specifies the drawing characteristics—recall that backgroundPaint sets the drawing color to white.

*Displaying the Time Remaining with **Canvas** Method **drawText***

Next, we call Canvas's **drawText** method (lines 367–368) to display the time remaining in the game. We pass as arguments the String to be displayed, the x- and y-coordinates at which to display it and the textPaint (configured in lines 170–171) to describe how the text should be rendered (that is, the text's font size, color and other attributes).

*Drawing the Cannonball with **Canvas** Method **drawCircle***

If the cannonball is on the screen, lines 372–373 use Canvas's **drawCircle** method to draw the cannonball in its current position. The first two arguments represent the coordinates of the circle's *center*. The third argument is the circle's *radius*. The last argument is the Paint object specifying the circle's drawing characteristics.

Drawing the Cannon Barrel, Blocker and Target with **Canvas** *Method* **drawLine**

We use Canvas's **drawLine** method to display the cannon *barrel* (lines 376–377), the *blocker* (lines 384–385) and the *target pieces* (lines 405–406). This method receives five parameters—the first four represent the *x-y* coordinates of the line's start and end, and the last is the Paint object specifying the line's characteristics, such as its thickness.

Drawing the Cannon Base with **Canvas** *Method* **drawCircle**

Lines 380–381 use Canvas's drawCircle method to draw the cannon's half-circle base by drawing a circle that's centered at the left edge of the screen—because a circle is displayed based on its center point, half of this circle is drawn off the left side of the SurfaceView.

Drawing the Target Sections with **Canvas** *Method* **drawLine**

Lines 390–411 draw the target sections. We iterate through the sections, drawing each in the correct color—blue for the odd-numbered pieces and yellow for the others. Only those sections that haven't been hit are displayed.

6.8.10 Method showGameOverDialog

When the game ends, the showGameOverDialog method (Fig. 6.16) displays a Dialog-Fragment (using the techniques you learned in Section 5.6.9) containing an AlertDialog that indicates whether the player won or lost, the number of shots fired and the total time elapsed. The call to method setPositiveButton (lines 433–444) creates a reset button for starting a new game.

```
414    // display an AlertDialog when the game ends
415    private void showGameOverDialog(final int messageId)
416    {
417       // DialogFragment to display quiz stats and start new quiz
418       final DialogFragment gameResult =
419          new DialogFragment()
420          {
421             // create an AlertDialog and return it
422             @Override
423             public Dialog onCreateDialog(Bundle bundle)
424             {
425                // create dialog displaying String resource for messageId
426                AlertDialog.Builder builder =
427                   new AlertDialog.Builder(getActivity());
428                builder.setTitle(getResources().getString(messageId));
429
430                // display number of shots fired and total time elapsed
431                builder.setMessage(getResources().getString(
432                   R.string.results_format, shotsFired, totalElapsedTime));
433                builder.setPositiveButton(R.string.reset_game,
434                   new DialogInterface.OnClickListener()
435                   {
436                      // called when "Reset Game" Button is pressed
437                      @Override
438                      public void onClick(DialogInterface dialog, int which)
439                      {
```

Fig. 6.16 | CannonView method showGameOverDialog. (Part 1 of 2.)

```
440                        dialogIsDisplayed = false;
441                        newGame(); // set up and start a new game
442                     }
443                  } // end anonymous inner class
444               ); // end call to setPositiveButton
445
446               return builder.create(); // return the AlertDialog
447            } // end method onCreateDialog
448         }; // end DialogFragment anonymous inner class
449
450         // in GUI thread, use FragmentManager to display the DialogFragment
451      activity.runOnUiThread(
452         new Runnable() {
453            public void run()
454            {
455               dialogIsDisplayed = true;
456               gameResult.setCancelable(false); // modal dialog
457               gameResult.show(activity.getFragmentManager(), "results");
458            }
459         } // end Runnable
460      ); // end call to runOnUiThread
461   } // end method showGameOverDialog
462
```

Fig. 6.16 | CannonView method showGameOverDialog. (Part 2 of 2.)

The onClick method of the button's listener indicates that the dialog is no longer displayed and calls newGame to set up and start a new game. A dialog must be displayed from the GUI thread, so lines 451–460 call Activity method **runOnUiThread** to specify a Runnable that should execute in the GUI thread as soon as possible. The argument is an object of an anonymous inner class that implements Runnable. The Runnable's run method indicates that the dialog is displayed and then displays it.

6.8.11 Methods stopGame and releaseResources

Class CannonGameFragment's onPause and onDestroy methods (Section 6.7) call class CannonView's stopGame and releaseResources methods (Fig. 6.17), respectively. Method stopGame (lines 464–468) is called from the main Activity to stop the game when the Activity's onPause method is called—for simplicity, we don't store the game's state in this example. Method releaseResources (lines 471–475) calls the SoundPool's **release method** to release the resources associated with the SoundPool.

```
463      // stops the game; called by CannonGameFragment's onPause method
464      public void stopGame()
465      {
466         if (cannonThread != null)
467            cannonThread.setRunning(false); // tell thread to terminate
468      }
469
```

Fig. 6.17 | CannonView methods stopGame and releaseResources. (Part 1 of 2.)

```
470    // releases resources; called by CannonGame's onDestroy method
471    public void releaseResources()
472    {
473       soundPool.release(); // release all resources used by the SoundPool
474       soundPool = null;
475    }
476
```

Fig. 6.17 | CannonView methods stopGame and releaseResources. (Part 2 of 2.)

6.8.12 Implementing the SurfaceHolder.Callback Methods

Figure 6.18 implements the **surfaceChanged**, **surfaceCreated** and **surfaceDestroyed** methods of interface SurfaceHolder.Callback. Method surfaceChanged has an empty body in this app because the app is *always* displayed in *portrait orientation*. This method is called when the SurfaceView's size or orientation changes, and would typically be used to redisplay graphics based on those changes. Method surfaceCreated (lines 485–494) is called when the SurfaceView is created—e.g., when the app first loads or when it resumes from the background. We use surfaceCreated to create and start the CannonThread to begin the game loop. Method surfaceDestroyed (lines 497–515) is called when the SurfaceView is destroyed—e.g., when the app terminates. We use the method to ensure that the CannonThread terminates properly. First, line 502 calls CannonThread's setRunning method with false as an argument to indicate that the thread should *stop*, then lines 504–515 wait for the thead to *terminate*. This ensures that no attempt is made to draw to the SurfaceView once surfaceDestroyed completes execution.

```
477    // called when surface changes size
478    @Override
479    public void surfaceChanged(SurfaceHolder holder, int format,
480       int width, int height)
481    {
482    }
483
484    // called when surface is first created
485    @Override
486    public void surfaceCreated(SurfaceHolder holder)
487    {
488       if (!dialogIsDisplayed)
489       {
490          cannonThread = new CannonThread(holder); // create thread
491          cannonThread.setRunning(true); // start game running
492          cannonThread.start(); // start the game loop thread
493       }
494    }
495
496    // called when the surface is destroyed
497    @Override
498    public void surfaceDestroyed(SurfaceHolder holder)
499    {
```

Fig. 6.18 | Implementing the SurfaceHolder.Callback methods. (Part 1 of 2.)

```
500        // ensure that thread terminates properly
501        boolean retry = true;
502        cannonThread.setRunning(false); // terminate cannonThread
503
504        while (retry)
505        {
506           try
507           {
508              cannonThread.join(); // wait for cannonThread to finish
509              retry = false;
510           }
511           catch (InterruptedException e)
512           {
513              Log.e(TAG, "Thread interrupted", e);
514           }
515        }
516     } // end method surfaceDestroyed
517
```

Fig. 6.18 | Implementing the `SurfaceHolder.Callback` methods. (Part 2 of 2.)

6.8.13 Overriding View Method onTouchEvent

In this example, we override `View` method `onTouchEvent` (Fig. 6.19) to determine when the user touches the screen. The `MotionEvent` parameter contains information about the event that occurred. Line 523 uses the `MotionEvent`'s `getAction` method to determine which type of touch event occurred. Then, lines 526–527 determine whether the user touched the screen (`MotionEvent.ACTION_DOWN`) or dragged a finger across the screen (`MotionEvent.ACTION_MOVE`). In either case, line 529 calls the cannonView's `fireCannonball` method to aim and fire the cannon toward that touch point. Line 532 then returns `true` to indicate that the touch event was handled.

```
518        // called when the user touches the screen in this Activity
519        @Override
520        public boolean onTouchEvent(MotionEvent e)
521        {
522           // get int representing the type of action which caused this event
523           int action = e.getAction();
524
525           // the user user touched the screen or dragged along the screen
526           if (action == MotionEvent.ACTION_DOWN ||
527              action == MotionEvent.ACTION_MOVE)
528           {
529              fireCannonball(e); // fire the cannonball toward the touch point
530           }
531
532           return true;
533        } // end method onTouchEvent
534
```

Fig. 6.19 | Overriding `View` method `onTouchEvent`. .

6.8.14 CannonThread: Using a Thread to Create a Game Loop

Figure 6.20 defines a subclass of Thread which updates the game. The thread maintains a reference to the SurfaceView's SurfaceHolder (line 538) and a boolean indicating whether the thread is *running*. The class's run method (lines 556–587) drives the *frame-by-frame animations*—this is known as the *game loop*. Each update of the game elements on the screen is performed based on the number of milliseconds that have passed since the last update. Line 559 gets the system's current time in milliseconds when the thread begins running. Lines 561–586 loop until threadIsRunning is false.

```
535    // Thread subclass to control the game loop
536    private class CannonThread extends Thread
537    {
538        private SurfaceHolder surfaceHolder; // for manipulating canvas
539        private boolean threadIsRunning = true; // running by default
540
541        // initializes the surface holder
542        public CannonThread(SurfaceHolder holder)
543        {
544            surfaceHolder = holder;
545            setName("CannonThread");
546        }
547
548        // changes running state
549        public void setRunning(boolean running)
550        {
551            threadIsRunning = running;
552        }
553
554        // controls the game loop
555        @Override
556        public void run()
557        {
558            Canvas canvas = null; // used for drawing
559            long previousFrameTime = System.currentTimeMillis();
560
561            while (threadIsRunning)
562            {
563                try
564                {
565                    // get Canvas for exclusive drawing from this thread
566                    canvas = surfaceHolder.lockCanvas(null);
567
568                    // lock the surfaceHolder for drawing
569                    synchronized(surfaceHolder)
570                    {
571                        long currentTime = System.currentTimeMillis();
572                        double elapsedTimeMS = currentTime - previousFrameTime;
573                        totalElapsedTime += elapsedTimeMS / 1000.0;
574                        updatePositions(elapsedTimeMS); // update game state
575                        drawGameElements(canvas); // draw using the canvas
```

Fig. 6.20 | Runnable that updates the game every TIME_INTERVAL milliseconds. (Part 1 of 2.)

```
576                          previousFrameTime = currentTime; // update previous time
577                      }
578                  }
579              finally
580              {
581                  // display canvas's contents on the CannonView
582                  // and enable other threads to use the Canvas
583                  if (canvas != null)
584                      surfaceHolder.unlockCanvasAndPost(canvas);
585              }
586          } // end while
587      } // end method run
588  } // end nested class CannonThread
589  } // end class CannonView
```

Fig. 6.20 | `Runnable` that updates the game every `TIME_INTERVAL` milliseconds. (Part 2 of 2.)

First we obtain the `Canvas` for drawing on the `SurfaceView` by calling `SurfaceHolder` method `lockCanvas` (line 566). Only one thread at a time can draw to a `SurfaceView`. To ensure this, you must first *lock* the `SurfaceHolder` by specifying it as the expression in the parentheses of a `synchronized` block (line 569). Next, we get the current time in milliseconds, then calculate the elapsed time and add that to the total time so far—this will be used to help display the amount of time left in the game. Line 574 calls method `update-Positions` to move all the game elements, passing the elapsed time in milliseconds as an argument. This ensures that the game operates at the same speed *regardless of how fast the device is*. If the time between frames is larger (i.e, the device is slower), the game elements will move further when each frame of the animation is displayed. If the time between frames is smaller (i.e, the device is faster), the game elements will move less when each frame of the animation is displayed. Finally, line 575 draws the game elements using the `SurfaceView`'s `Canvas` and line 576 stores the `currentTime` as the `previousFrameTime` to prepare to calculate the elapsed time between this animation frame and the *next*.

6.9 Wrap-Up

In this chapter, you created the **Cannon Game** app, which challenges the player to destroy a seven-piece target before a 10-second time limit expires. The user aims and fires the cannon by touching the screen. To draw on the screen from a separate thread, you created a custom view by extending class `SurfaceView`. You learned that custom component class names must be fully qualified in the XML layout element that represents the component. We presented additional `Fragment` lifecycle methods. You learned that method `onPause` is called when a `Fragment` is paused and method `onDestroy` is called when the `Fragment` is destroyed. You handled touches by overriding `View`'s `onTouchEvent` method. You added sound effects to the app's `res/raw` folder and managed them with a `SoundPool`. You also used the system's `AudioManager` service to obtain the device's current music volume and use it as the playback volume.

This app manually performs its animations by updating the game elements on a `SurfaceView` from a separate thread of execution. To do this, you extended class `Thread` and created a `run` method that displays graphics by calling methods of class `Canvas`. You used the SurfaceView's SurfaceHolder to obtain the appropriate Canvas. You also learned how to build a game loop that controls a game based on the amount of time that has elapsed between animation frames, so that the game will operate at the same overall speed on all devices, regardless of their processor speeds.

In Chapter 7, we present the **Doodlz** app, which uses Android's graphics capabilities to turn a device's screen into a *virtual canvas*. You'll also learn about Android 4.4's new immersive mode and printing capabilities.

Doodlz App

Two-Dimensional Graphics, Canvas, Bitmap, Accelerometer, SensorManager, Multitouch Events, MediaStore, Printing, Immersive Mode

Objectives

In this chapter you'll:

- Detect when the user touches the screen, moves a finger across the screen and removes a finger from the screen.
- Process multiple touches so the user can draw with multiple fingers at once.
- Use a SensorManager and the accelerometer to detect motion events.
- Use a Paint object to specify the color and width of a line.
- Use Path objects to store each line's data and use a Canvas to draw each line into a Bitmap.
- Create a menu and display menu items on the action bar.
- Use Android 4.4's immersive mode to enable the user to draw on the entire screen.
- Use Android 4.4's printing framework and the Android Support Library's PrintHelper class to enable the user to print a drawing.

Outline

7.1 Introduction

The **Doodlz** app (Fig. 7.1) enables you to paint by dragging one or more fingers across the screen. The app uses Android 4.4's *immersive mode* so that you can draw on the entire screen—the device's *system bars* and *action bar* toggle between displayed and hidden when you tap the screen.

Fig. 7.1 | **Doodlz** app with a finished drawing.

The app's options enable you to set the drawing color and line width. The **Choose Color** dialog (Fig. 7.2(a)) provides *alpha (transparency)*, red, green and blue SeekBars (i.e., sliders) that allow you to select the ARGB color (introduced in Section 1.9). As you move each SeekBar's thumb, the updated color is displayed below the SeekBars. The **Choose Line Width** dialog (Fig. 7.2(b)) provides a single SeekBar that controls the thickness of the line that you'll draw. Additional menu items (Fig. 7.3) in the app's *options menu* allow you to turn your finger into an eraser (**Eraser**), to clear the screen (**Clear**), to save the current drawing into your device's **Gallery** (**Save**) and, on Android 4.4 devices, to print the current drawing. Depending on your device's screen size, some or all of the app's menu items are displayed directly on the action bar—any that do not fit are displayed in the options menu. At any point, you can *shake* the device to clear the entire drawing from the screen. You test-drove this app in Section 1.9, so we do not present a test drive in this chapter. Though this app works in AVDs, the capabilities are more fluid on actual devices. [*Note:* Due to a **Gallery** app bug at the time of this writing, on some devices you might need to take a picture with the device's camera app before you'll be able to save properly from the **Doodlz** app.]

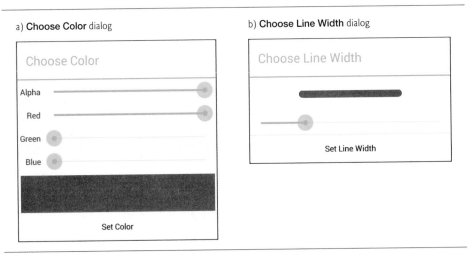

Fig. 7.2 | **Choose Color** and **Choose Line Width** dialogs for the **Doodlz** app.

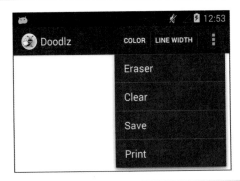

Fig. 7.3 | **Doodlz** app additional menu options as displayed on an Android 4.4 phone.

7.2 Technologies Overview

This section presents the new technologies that we use in the **Doodlz** app.

7.2.1 Using SensorManager to Listen for Accelerometer Events

In this app, you can shake the device to erase the current drawing. Most devices have an **accelerometer** that allows apps to detect movement. Other sensors currently supported by Android include gravity, gyroscope, light, linear acceleration, magnetic field, orientation, pressure, proximity, rotation vector and temperature. The list of **Sensor** constants representing these sensor types can be found at:

```
http://developer.android.com/reference/android/hardware/Sensor.html
```

We'll discuss in Section 7.5 the accelerometer and sensor event handling. For a complete discussion of Android's other sensors, see the *Sensors Overview* at

```
http://developer.android.com/guide/topics/sensors/
    sensors_overview.html
```

7.2.2 Custom DialogFragments

Several previous apps have used `AlertDialog`s in `DialogFragment`s to display information to the user or to ask questions and receive responses from the user in the form of `Button` clicks. The `AlertDialog`s you've used so far were created using anonymous inner classes that extended `DialogFragment` and displayed only text and buttons. `AlertDialog`s may also contain custom `View`s. In this app, you'll define three subclasses of `DialogFragment`:

- `ColorDialogFragment` (Section 7.7) displays an `AlertDialog` with a custom `View` containing GUI components for previewing and selecting a new ARGB drawing color.

- `LineWidthDialogFragment` (Section 7.8) displays an `AlertDialog` with a custom `View` containing GUI components for previewing and selecting the line thickness.

- `EraseImageDialogFragment` (Section 7.9) displays a standard `AlertDialog` asking the user to confirm whether the entire image should be erased.

For the `ColorDialogFragment` and `EraseImageDialogFragment`, you'll inflate the custom `View` from a layout resource file. In each of the three `DialogFragment` subclasses, you'll also override the following `Fragment` lifecycle methods:

- **onAttach**—The first `Fragment` lifecycle method called when a `Fragment` is attached to a parent `Activity`.

- **onDetach**—The last `Fragment` lifecycle method called when a `Fragment` is about to be detached from a parent `Activity`.

Preventing Multiple Dialogs from Appearing at the Same Time
It's possible that the event handler for the shake event could try to display the confirmation dialog for erasing an image when another dialog is already on the screen. To prevent this, you'll use `onAttach` and `onDetach` to set the value of a `boolean` that indicates whether a dialog is on the screen. When the `boolean`'s value is `true`, we will not allow the event handler for the shake event to display a dialog.

7.2.3 Drawing with Canvas and Bitmap

This app draws lines onto **Bitmaps** (package android.graphics). You can associate a Canvas with a Bitmap, then use the Canvas to draw on the Bitmap, which can then be displayed on the screen (Section 7.6). A Bitmap can also be saved into a file—we'll use this capability to store drawings in the device's gallery when you touch the **Save** option.

7.2.4 Processing Multiple Touch Events and Storing Lines in Paths

You can drag one or more fingers across the screen to draw. The app stores the information for each *individual* finger as a **Path** object (package android.graphics) that represents line segments and curves. You process *touch events* by overriding the View method **onTouchEvent** (Section 7.6). This method receives a **MotionEvent** (package android.view) that contains the type of touch event that occurred and the ID of the finger (i.e., pointer) that generated the event. We use the IDs to distinguish the different fingers and add information to the corresponding Path objects. We use the type of the touch event to determine whether the user has *touched* the screen, *dragged* across the screen or *lifted a finger* from the screen.

7.2.5 Android 4.4 Immersive Mode

Android 4.4 introduces a new full-screen **immersive mode** (Section 7.6) that enables an app to take advantage of the entire screen, but still allows the user to access the system bars when necessary. In this app, you'll use this mode when the app is running on an Android 4.4 or higher device.

7.2.6 GestureDetector and SimpleOnGestureListener

This app uses a **GestureDetector** (package android.view) to hide or show the device's system bars and the app's action bar. A GestureDetector allows an app to react to user interactions such as *flings*, *single taps*, *double taps*, *long presses* and *scrolls* by implementing the methods of interfaces **GestureDetector.OnGestureListener** and **GestureDetector.OnDoubleTapListener** interfaces. Class **GestureDetector.SimpleOnGestureListener** is an *adapter class* that implements all the methods of these two interfaces, so you can extend this class and override just the method(s) you need from these interfaces. In Section 7.6, you'll initialize a GestureDetector with a SimpleOnGestureListener, which will handle the *single-tap* event that hides or shows the system bars and action bar.

7.2.7 Saving the Drawing to the Device's Gallery

The app provides a **Save** option that allows the user to save a drawing into the device's gallery—the default location in which photos taken with the device are stored. A **ContentResolver** (package android.content) enables the app to read data from and store data on a device. You'll use a ContentResolver (Section 7.6) and the method **insertImage** of class MediaStore.Images.Media to save an image into the device's **Gallery**. The **MediaStore** manages media files (images, audio and video) stored on a device.

7.2.8 Android 4.4 Printing and the Android Support Library's `PrintHelper` Class

Android 4.4 now includes a printing framework. In this app, we use class `PrintHelper` (Section 7.6) to print the current drawing. Class `PrintHelper` provides a user interface for selecting a printer, has a method for determining whether a given device supports printing and provides a method for printing a `Bitmap`. `PrintHelper` is part of the *Android Support Library*—a set of libraries that are commonly used to provide new Android features for use in older Android versions. The libraries also include additional convenience features, like class `PrintHelper`, that support specific Android versions.

7.3 Building the App's GUI and Resource Files

In this section, you'll create the **Doodlz** app's resource files, GUI layout files and classes.

7.3.1 Creating the Project

Begin by creating a new Android project named `Doodlz`. Specify the following values in the **New Android Project** dialog, then press **Finish**:

- **Application Name:** `Doodlz`
- **Project Name:** `Doodlz`
- **Package Name:** `com.deitel.doodlz`
- **Minimum Required SDK:** `API18: Android 4.3`
- **Target SDK:** `API19: Android 4.4`
- **Compile With:** `API19: Android 4.4`
- **Theme:** `Holo Light with Dark Action Bar`

In the **New Android Project** dialog's second **New Android Application** step, leave the default settings, and press **Next >**. In the **Configure Launcher Icon** step, select an app icon image, then press **Next >**. In the **Create Activity** step, select **Blank Activity**, then press **Next >**. In the **Blank Activity** step, leave the default settings and click **Finish** to create the project. In the **Graphical Layout** editor, select **Nexus 4** from the screen-type drop-down list and delete the `TextView` containing "Hello world!"

The new project will automatically be configured to use the current version of the Android Support Library. If you're updating an existing project, you can add the latest version of the Android Support Library to your project. For details, visit:

```
http://developer.android.com/tools/support-library/index.html
http://developer.android.com/tools/support-library/setup.html
```

7.3.2 `strings.xml`

You created `String` resources in earlier chapters, so we show only a table of the `String` resource names and corresponding values here (Fig. 7.4). Double click `strings.xml` in the `res/values` folder to display the resource editor for creating these `String` resources.

Resource name	Value
app_name	Doodlz
button_erase	Erase Image
button_cancel	Cancel
button_set_color	Set Color
button_set_line_width	Set Line Width
line_imageview_description	This displays the line thickness
label_alpha	Alpha
label_red	Red
label_green	Green
label_blue	Blue
menuitem_clear	Clear
menuitem_color	Color
menuitem_eraser	Eraser
menuitem_line_width	Line Width
menuitem_save	Save
menuitem_print	Print
message_erase	Erase the drawing?
message_error_saving	There was an error saving the image
message_saved	Your painting has been saved to the Gallery
message_error_printing	Your device does not support printing
title_color_dialog	Choose Color
title_line_width_dialog	Choose Line Width

Fig. 7.4 | String resources used in the **Doodlz** app.

7.3.3 dimens.xml

Figure 7.5 shows a table of the dimension resource names and values that we added to dimens.xml. Open dimens.xml in the res/values folder to display the resource editor for creating these resources. The line_imageview_height resource specifies the height of the ImageView that previews the line width in the LineWidthDialogFragment, and the color_view_height resource specifies height of the View that previews the drawing color in the ColorDialogFragment.

Resource name	Value
line_imageview_height	50dp
color_view_height	80dp

Fig. 7.5 | Dimension resources used in the **Doodlz** app.

7.3.4 Menu for the DoodleFragment

In Chapter 5, you used the default menu provided by the IDE to display the **Flag Quiz** app's **Settings** menu item. You will not use the default menu in this app, so you can delete the main.xml file in your project's res/menu folder. In this app, you'll define your own menu for the DoodleFragment.

Menus for Different Android Versions

You'll provide two versions of the DoodleFragment's menu—one for Android 4.3 and earlier devices and one for Android 4.4 and higher devices. Printing is available only in Android 4.4 and higher, so only the menu for such devices will include a **Print** option. To support separate menus, you'll define one menu resource in the res/menu folder and a separate menu resource in the res/menu-v19 folder—19 is the Android API version that corresponds to Android 4.4. Android will choose the menu resource in the res/menu-v19 folder when the app is running on Android 4.4 and higher devices. To create the res/menu-v19 folder, right click the res folder, select **New > Folder**, specify the **Folder name** menu-v19 and click **Finish**.

Menu for Android 4.3 and Earlier Versions

To create the menu resource for Android 4.3 and earlier versions:

1. Right click the res/menu folder and select **New > Android XML File.**

2. In the dialog that appears, name the file doodle_fragment_menu.xml and click **Finish.** The IDE opens the file in the editor for menu resources.

3. Click **Add...**, click the editor's **Layout** tab in the dialog that appears, select **Item** and click **OK.** The IDE highlights the new item and displays its attributes to the right.

4. Change its **Id** to @+id/color, its **Title** to @string/menuitem_color and its **Show as action** to ifRoom. The value ifRoom indicates that Android should display the menu item on the action bar if there's room available; otherwise, the menu item will appear in the options menu at the right side of the action bar. Other **Show as action** values can be found at http://developer.android.com/guide/topics/resources/menu-resource.html.

5. Repeat Steps 3 and 4 for the lineWidth, eraser, clear and save items in Fig. 7.6. Note that when you click **Add...** for each additional menu item, you'll need to select **Create a new element at the top level in Menu** in the dialog that appears.

6. Save and close doodle_fragment_menu.xml.

Id	Title
@+id/lineWidth	@string/menuitem_line_width
@+id/eraser	@string/menuitem_eraser
@+id/clear	@string/menuitem_clear
@+id/save	@string/menuitem_save

Fig. 7.6 | Additional menu items for the DoodleFragment.

Menu for Android 4.4 and Higher Versions

To create the menu resource for Android 4.4 and higher devices:

1. Copy doodle_fragment_menu.xml from res/menu, paste it into res/menu-v19 and open the file.

2. Click **Add...**, select **Create a new element at the top level in Menu** in the dialog that appears, then select **Item** and click **OK**.

3. Change the new item's **Id** to @+id/print, its **Title** to @string/menuitem_print and its **Show as action** to ifRoom.

7.3.5 activity_main.xml Layout for MainActivity

The activity_main.xml layout for this app's MainActivity contains only the Doodle-Fragment. To add this Fragment to the layout:

1. Open activity_main.xml in the **Graphical Layout** editor.

2. From the **Palette**'s **Layouts** section, drag a **Fragment** onto the design area or onto the RelativeLayout node in the **Outline** window.

3. The preceding step displays the **Choose Fragment Class** dialog. Click **Create New...** to display the **New Java Class** dialog.

4. Enter DoodleFragment in the dialog's **Name** field, change the **Superclass** field's value to android.app.Fragment and click **Finish** to create the class. The IDE opens the Java file for the class, which you can close for now.

5. Change the new Fragment's **Id** to @+id/doodleFragment, then save the layout.

7.3.6 fragment_doodle.xml Layout for DoodleFragment

The fragment_doodle.xml layout for the DoodleFragment contains a FrameLayout that displays the DoodleView. In this section, you'll create DoodleFragment's layout and the DoodleView class. To add the fragment_doodle.xml layout:

1. Expand the project's res/layout node in the **Package Explorer**.

2. Right click the layout folder and select **New > Android XML File** to display the **New Android XML File** dialog.

3. In the dialog's **File** field, enter fragment_doodle.xml

4. In the **Root Element** section, select **FrameLayout**, then click **Finish**.

5. From the **Palette**'s **Advanced** section, drag a **view** (with a lowercase **v**) onto the design area.

6. The previous step displays the **Choose Custom View Class** dialog. In that dialog, click **Create New...** to display the **New Java Class** dialog.

7. In the **Name** field, enter DoodleView. Ensure that **Constructors from superclass** is checked, then click **Finish**. This creates and opens DoodleView.java. We'll be using only the two-argument constructor, so delete the other two. Save and close DoodleView.java.

8. In fragment_doodle.xml, select **view1** in the **Outline** window. In the **Properties** window's **Layout Parameters** section, set **Width** and **Height** to match_parent.

9. In the **Outline** window, right click **view1**, select **Edit ID...**, rename `view1` as `doodleView` and click **OK**.

10. Save and close `fragment_doodle.xml`.

7.3.7 `fragment_color.xml` Layout for `ColorDialogFragment`

The `fragment_color.xml` layout for the `ColorDialogFragment` contains a `GridLayout` that displays a GUI for selecting and previewing a new drawing color. In this section, you'll create `ColorDialogFragment`'s layout and the `ColorDialogFragment` class. To add the `fragment_color.xml` layout:

1. Expand the project's res/layout node in the **Package Explorer**.

2. Right click the `layout` folder and select **New > Android XML File** to display the **New Android XML File** dialog.

3. In the dialog's **File** field, enter `fragment_color.xml`

4. In the **Root Element** section, select **GridLayout**, then click **Finish**.

5. In the **Outline** window, select the **GridLayout** and change its **Id** value to `@+id/colorDialogGridLayout`.

6. Using the **Graphical Layout** editor's **Palette**, drag **TextViews**, **SeekBars** and a **View** onto the `colorDialogGridLayout` node in the **Outline** window. Drag the items in the order they're listed in Fig. 7.7 and set each item's **Id** as shown in the figure.

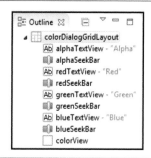

Fig. 7.7 | **Outline** view for `fragment_color.xml`.

7. After completing Step 6, configure the GUI component properties with the values shown in Fig. 7.8, then save and close `fragment_color.xml`.

GUI component	Property	Value
`colorDialogGridLayout`	Column Count	2
	Orientation	vertical
	Use Default Margins	true

Fig. 7.8 | Property values for the GUI components in `fragment_color.xml`. (Part I of 3.)

GUI component	Property	Value
alphaTextView	*Layout Parameters*	
	Column	0
	Gravity	right|center_vertical
	Row	0
	Other Properties	
	Text	@string/label_alpha
alphaSeekBar	*Layout Parameters*	
	Column	1
	Gravity	fill_horizontal
	Row	0
	Other Properties	
	Max	255
redTextView	*Layout Parameters*	
	Column	0
	Gravity	right|center_vertical
	Row	1
	Other Properties	
	Text	@string/label_red
redSeekBar	*Layout Parameters*	
	Column	1
	Gravity	fill_horizontal
	Row	1
	Other Properties	
	Max	255
greenTextView	*Layout Parameters*	
	Column	0
	Gravity	right|center_vertical
	Row	2
	Other Properties	
	Text	@string/label_green
greenSeekBar	*Layout Parameters*	
	Column	1
	Gravity	fill_horizontal
	Row	2
	Other Properties	
	Max	255
blueTextView	*Layout Parameters*	
	Column	0
	Gravity	right|center_vertical
	Row	3
	Other Properties	
	Text	@string/label_blue

Fig. 7.8 | Property values for the GUI components in fragment_color.xml. (Part 2 of 3.)

GUI component	Property	Value
blueSeekBar	*Layout Parameters*	
	Column	1
	Gravity	fill_horizontal
	Row	3
	Other Properties	
	Max	255
colorView	*Layout Parameters*	
	Height	@dimen/color_view_height
	Column	0
	Column Span	2
	Gravity	fill_horizontal

Fig. 7.8 | Property values for the GUI components in `fragment_color.xml`. (Part 3 of 3.)

Adding Class *ColorDialogFragment* to the Project

To add class `ColorDialogFragment` to the project:

1. Right click the package `com.deitel.doodlz` in the project's `src` folder and select **New > Class** to display the **New Java Class** dialog.

2. In the **Name** field, enter `ColorDialogFragment`.

3. In the **Superclass** field, change the superclass to `android.app.DialogFragment`.

4. Click **Finish** to create the class.

7.3.8 fragment_line_width.xml Layout for LineWidthDialogFragment

The `fragment_line_width.xml` layout for the `LineWidthDialogFragment` contains a GridLayout that displays a GUI for selecting and previewing a new line thickness. In this section, you'll create `LineWidthDialogFragment`'s layout and the `LineWidthDialogFragment` class. To add the `fragment_line_width.xml` layout:

1. Expand the project's `res/layout` node in the **Package Explorer**.

2. Right click the `layout` folder and select **New > Android XML File** to display the **New Android XML File** dialog.

3. In the dialog's **File** field, enter `fragment_line_width.xml`

4. In the **Root Element** section, select **GridLayout**, then click **Finish**.

5. In the **Outline** window, select the **GridLayout** and change its **Id** value to `@+id/lineWidthDialogGridLayout`.

6. Using the **Graphical Layout** editor's **Palette**, drag an **ImageView** and a **SeekBar** onto the `lineWidthDialogGridLayout` node in the **Outline** window so that the window appears as shown in Fig. 7.9. Set each item's **Id** as shown in the figure.

7. After completing Step 6, configure the GUI component properties with the values shown in Fig. 7.10, then save and close `fragment_line_width.xml`.

Fig. 7.9 | **Outline** view for `fragment_line_width.xml`.

GUI component	Property	Value

`lineWidthDialog-`
`GridLayout`
	Column Count
	Orientation
	Use Default Margins
		1
		`vertical`
		`true`

`widthImageView`	*Layout Parameters*
	    Height
	    Gravity
	Other Properties
	    Content Description
		
		`@dimen/line_imageview_height`
		`fill_horizontal`
		
		`@string/line_imageview_description`

`widthSeekBar`	*Layout Parameters*
	    Gravity
	Other Properties
	    Max
		
		`fill_horizontal`
		
		50

Fig. 7.10 | Property values for the GUI components in `fragment_line_width.xml`.

Adding Class LineWidthDialogFragment to the Project

To add class `LineWidthDialogFragment` to the project:

1. Right click the package `com.deitel.doodlz` in the project's `src` folder and select **New > Class** to display the **New Java Class** dialog.

2. In the **Name** field, enter `LineWidthDialogFragment`.

3. In the **Superclass** field, change the superclass to `android.app.DialogFragment`.

4. Click **Finish** to create the class.

7.3.9 Adding Class EraseImageDialogFragment

The `EraseImageDialogFragment` does not require a layout resource as it will display a simple `AlertDialog` containing text. To add class `EraseImageDialogFragment` to the project:

1. Right click the package `com.deitel.doodlz` in the project's `src` folder and select **New > Class** to display the **New Java Class** dialog.

2. In the **Name** field, enter `EraseImageDialogFragment`.

3. In the **Superclass** field, change the superclass to `android.app.DialogFragment`.

4. Click **Finish** to create the class.

7.4 MainActivity Class

This app consists of six classes:

- MainActivity (Fig. 7.11)—Serves as the parent Activity for this app's Fragments.

- DoodleFragment (Section 7.5)—Manages the DoodleView and accelerometer event handling.

- DoodleView (Section 7.6)—Provides the drawing, saving and printing capabilities.

- ColorDialogFragment (Section 7.7)—A DialogFragment that's displayed when the user taps **COLOR** to set the drawing color.

- LineWidthDialogFragment (Section 7.8)—A DialogFragment that's displayed when the user taps **LINE WIDTH** to set the line width.

- EraseImageDialogFragment (Section 7.9)—A DialogFragment that's displayed when the user taps **CLEAR** or shakes the device to erase the current drawing.

Class MainActivity's onCreate method (Fig. 7.11) inflates the GUI (line 16), then uses the techniques you learned in Section 5.2.2 to determine the device's size and set MainActivity's orientation. If this app is running on an extra large device (line 24), we set the orientation to landscape (lines 25–26); otherwise, we set it to portrait (lines 28–29).

```
 1   // MainActivity.java
 2   // Sets MainActivity's layout
 3   package com.deitel.doodlz;
 4
 5   import android.app.Activity;
 6   import android.content.pm.ActivityInfo;
 7   import android.content.res.Configuration;
 8   import android.os.Bundle;
 9
10   public class MainActivity extends Activity
11   {
12      @Override
13      protected void onCreate(Bundle savedInstanceState)
14      {
15         super.onCreate(savedInstanceState);
16         setContentView(R.layout.activity_main);
17
18         // determine screen size
19         int screenSize =
20            getResources().getConfiguration().screenLayout &
21            Configuration.SCREENLAYOUT_SIZE_MASK;
22
23         // use landscape for extra large tablets; otherwise, use portrait
24         if (screenSize == Configuration.SCREENLAYOUT_SIZE_XLARGE)
25            setRequestedOrientation(
26               ActivityInfo.SCREEN_ORIENTATION_LANDSCAPE);
```

Fig. 7.11 | MainActivity class. (Part 1 of 2.)

```
27          else
28             setRequestedOrientation(
29                ActivityInfo.SCREEN_ORIENTATION_PORTRAIT);
30       }
31    } // end class MainActivity
```

Fig. 7.11 | MainActivity class. (Part 2 of 2.)

7.5 DoodleFragment Class

Class DoodleFragment (Figs. 7.12–7.19) displays the DoodleView (Section 7.6), manages the menu options displayed on the action bar and in the options menu and manages the sensor event handling for the app's *shake-to-erase* feature.

package Statement, import Statements and Fields

Section 7.2 discussed the key new classes and interfaces that class DoodleFragment uses. We've highlighted these classes and interfaces in Fig. 7.12. DoodleView variable doodleView (line 22) represents the drawing area. The float variables declared in lines 23–25 are used to calculate changes in the device's acceleration to determine when a *shake event* occurs (so we can ask whether the user would like to erase the drawing), and the constant in line 29 is used to ensure that small movements are *not* interpreted as shakes—we picked this constant via trial and error by shaking the app on several devices. Line 26 defines a boolean variable with the default value false that will be used throughout this class to specify when there's a dialog displayed on the screen. We use this to prevent multiple dialogs from being displayed at the same time—for example, if the **Choose Color** dialog is displayed and the user accidentally shakes the device, the dialog for erasing the image should *not* be displayed.

```
1   // DoodleFragment.java
2   // Fragment in which the DoodleView is displayed
3   package com.deitel.doodlz;
4
5   import android.app.Fragment;
6   import android.content.Context;
7   import android.graphics.Color;
8   import android.hardware.Sensor;
9   import android.hardware.SensorEvent;
10  import android.hardware.SensorEventListener;
11  import android.hardware.SensorManager;
12  import android.os.Bundle;
13  import android.view.LayoutInflater;
14  import android.view.Menu;
15  import android.view.MenuInflater;
16  import android.view.MenuItem;
17  import android.view.View;
```

Fig. 7.12 | DoodleFragment class package statement, import statements and fields. (Part 1 of 2.)

```
18   import android.view.ViewGroup;
19
20   public class DoodleFragment extends Fragment
21   {
22      private DoodleView doodleView; // handles touch events and draws
23      private float acceleration;
24      private float currentAcceleration;
25      private float lastAcceleration;
26      private boolean dialogOnScreen = false;
27
28      // value used to determine whether user shook the device to erase
29      private static final int ACCELERATION_THRESHOLD = 100000;
30
```

Fig. 7.12 | DoodleFragment class package statement, import statements and fields. (Part 2 of 2.)

Overriding Fragment Method onCreateView

Method onCreateView (Fig. 7.13) inflates the DoodleFragment's GUI and initializes the instance variables. Like an Activity, a Fragment can place items in the app's action bar and options menu. To do so, the Fragment must call its setHasOptionsMenu method with the argument true. If the parent Activity also has options menu items, then both the Activity's and the Fragment's items will be placed on the action bar and in the options menu (based on their settings).

```
31      // called when Fragment's view needs to be created
32      @Override
33      public View onCreateView(LayoutInflater inflater, ViewGroup container,
34         Bundle savedInstanceState)
35      {
36         super.onCreateView(inflater, container, savedInstanceState);
37         View view =
38            inflater.inflate(R.layout.fragment_doodle, container, false);
39
40         setHasOptionsMenu(true); // this fragment has menu items to display
41
42         // get reference to the DoodleView
43         doodleView = (DoodleView) view.findViewById(R.id.doodleView);
44
45         // initialize acceleration values
46         acceleration = 0.00f;
47         currentAcceleration = SensorManager.GRAVITY_EARTH;
48         lastAcceleration = SensorManager.GRAVITY_EARTH;
49         return view;
50      }
51
```

Fig. 7.13 | Overriding Fragment method onCreateView.

Line 43 gets a reference to the DoodleView, then lines 46–48 initialize the instance variables that help calculate acceleration changes to determine whether the user shook the device. We initially set variables `currentAcceleration` and `lastAcceleration` to SensorManager's `GRAVITY_EARTH` constant, which represents the acceleration due to gravity on earth. SensorManager also provides constants for other planets in the solar system, for the moon and for several other entertaining values, which you can see at:

```
http://developer.android.com/reference/android/hardware/
    SensorManager.html
```

Methods *onStart* and *enableAccelerometerListening*

Accelerometer listening should be enabled only when the `DoodleFragment` is on the screen. For this reason, we override `Fragment` lifecycle method **onStart** (Fig. 7.14, lines 53–58), which calls method `enableAccelerometerListening` (lines 61–72) to begin listening for accelerometer events. A SensorManager is used to register listeners for accelerometer events.

```
52    // start listening for sensor events
53    @Override
54    public void onStart()
55    {
56        super.onStart();
57        enableAccelerometerListening(); // listen for shake
58    }
59
60    // enable listening for accelerometer events
61    public void enableAccelerometerListening()
62    {
63        // get the SensorManager
64        SensorManager sensorManager =
65            (SensorManager) getActivity().getSystemService(
66                Context.SENSOR_SERVICE);
67
68        // register to listen for accelerometer events
69        sensorManager.registerListener(sensorEventListener,
70            sensorManager.getDefaultSensor(Sensor.TYPE_ACCELEROMETER),
71            SensorManager.SENSOR_DELAY_NORMAL);
72    }
73
```

Fig. 7.14 | Methods onStart and enableAccelerometerListening.

Method `enableAccelerometerListening` first uses `Activity`'s `getSystemService` method to retrieve the system's `SensorManager` service, which enables the app to interact with the device's sensors. Lines 69–71 then register to receive accelerometer events using SensorManager's **registerListener** method, which receives three arguments:

- The SensorEventListener that responds to the events (defined in Fig. 7.16)

- A Sensor object representing the type of sensor data the app wishes to receive— this is retrieved by calling SensorManager's **getDefaultSensor** method and passing a Sensor-type constant (Sensor.TYPE_ACCELEROMETER in this app).

- A rate at which sensor events should be delivered to the app. We chose SENSOR_DELAY_NORMAL to receive sensor events at the default rate—a faster rate can be used to get more accurate data, but this is also more CPU and battery intensive.

Methods *onPause* and *disableAccelerometerListening*

To ensure that accelerometer listening is disabled when the DoodleFragment is not on the screen, we override Fragment lifecycle method onPause (Fig. 7.15, lines 75–80), which calls method disableAccelerometerListening (lines 83–93). Method disableAccelerometerListening uses class SensorManager's **unregisterListener** method to stop listening for accelerometer events.

```
74      // stop listening for sensor events
75      @Override
76      public void onPause()
77      {
78         super.onPause();
79         disableAccelerometerListening(); // stop listening for shake
80      }
81
82      // disable listening for accelerometer events
83      public void disableAccelerometerListening()
84      {
85         // get the SensorManager
86         SensorManager sensorManager =
87            (SensorManager) getActivity().getSystemService(
88               Context.SENSOR_SERVICE);
89
90         // stop listening for accelerometer events
91         sensorManager.unregisterListener(sensorEventListener,
92            sensorManager.getDefaultSensor(Sensor.TYPE_ACCELEROMETER));
93      }
94
```

Fig. 7.15 | Methods onPause and disableAccelerometerListening.

Anonymous Inner Class That Implements Interface *SensorEventListener to Process Accelerometer Events*

Figure 7.16 overrides SensorEventListener method **onSensorChanged** (lines 100–125) to process accelerometer events. If the user moves the device, this method determines whether the movement was enough to be considered a shake. If so, line 123 calls method confirmErase (Fig. 7.17) to display an EraseImageDialogFragment (Section 7.9) and confirm whether the user really wants to erase the image. Interface SensorEventListener also contains method onAccuracyChanged (lines 128–131)—we don't use this method in this app, so we provide an empty body because the method is required by the interface.

```
95      // event handler for accelerometer events
96      private SensorEventListener sensorEventListener =
97         new SensorEventListener()
98         {
```

Fig. 7.16 | Anonymous inner class that implements interface SensorEventListener to process accelerometer events. (Part 1 of 2.)

```
 99            // use accelerometer to determine whether user shook device
100            @Override
101            public void onSensorChanged(SensorEvent event)
102            {
103               // ensure that other dialogs are not displayed
104               if (!dialogOnScreen)
105               {
106                  // get x, y, and z values for the SensorEvent
107                  float x = event.values[0];
108                  float y = event.values[1];
109                  float z = event.values[2];
110
111                  // save previous acceleration value
112                  lastAcceleration = currentAcceleration;
113
114                  // calculate the current acceleration
115                  currentAcceleration = x * x + y * y + z * z;
116
117                  // calculate the change in acceleration
118                  acceleration = currentAcceleration *
119                     (currentAcceleration - lastAcceleration);
120
121                  // if the acceleration is above a certain threshold
122                  if (acceleration > ACCELERATION_THRESHOLD)
123                     confirmErase();
124               }
125            } // end method onSensorChanged
126
127            // required method of interface SensorEventListener
128            @Override
129            public void onAccuracyChanged(Sensor sensor, int accuracy)
130            {
131            }
132         }; // end anonymous inner class
133
```

Fig. 7.16 | Anonymous inner class that implements interface `SensorEventListener` to process accelerometer events. (Part 2 of 2.)

The user can shake the device even when dialogs are already displayed on the screen. For this reason, onSensorChanged first checks whether a dialog is displayed (line 104). This test ensures that no other dialogs are displayed; otherwise, onSensorChanged simply returns. This is important because the sensor events occur in a different thread of execution. Without this test, we'd be able to display the confirmation dialog for erasing the image when another dialog is on the screen.

The **SensorEvent** parameter contains information about the sensor change that occurred. For accelerometer events, this parameter's values array contains three elements representing the acceleration (in *meter/second²*) in the *x* (left/right), *y* (up/down) and *z* (forward/backward) directions. A description and diagram of the coordinate system used by the SensorEvent API is available at:

developer.android.com/reference/android/hardware/SensorEvent.html

This link also describes the real-world meanings for a SensorEvent's *x, y* and *z* values for each different Sensor.

Lines 107–109 store the acceleration values. It's important to handle sensor events quickly or to copy the event data (as we did here) because the array of sensor values is *reused* for each sensor event. Line 112 stores the last value of currentAcceleration. Line 115 sums the squares of the x, y and z acceleration values and stores them in currentAcceleration. Then, using the currentAcceleration and lastAcceleration values, we calculate a value (acceleration) that can be compared to our ACCELERATION_THRESHOLD constant. If the value is greater than the constant, the user moved the device enough for this app to consider the movement a shake. In this case, we call method confirmErase.

Method confirmErase

Method confirmErase (Fig. 7.17) simply creates an EraseImageDialogFragment (Section 7.9) and uses the DialogFragment method show to display it.

```
134    // confirm whether image should be erased
135    private void confirmErase()
136    {
137       EraseImageDialogFragment fragment = new EraseImageDialogFragment();
138       fragment.show(getFragmentManager(), "erase dialog");
139    }
140
```

Fig. 7.17 | Method confirmErase displays an EraseImageDialogFragment.

Overridden Fragment *Methods* onCreateOptionsMenu *and* onOptionsItemSelected

Figure 7.18 overrides Fragment's **onCreateOptionsMenu** method (lines 142–147) to add the options to the method's Menu argument using the method's MenuInflater argument. When the user selects a menu item, Fragment method **onOptionsItemSelected** (lines 150–180) responds to the selection.

```
141    // display this fragment's menu items
142    @Override
143    public void onCreateOptionsMenu(Menu menu, MenuInflater inflater)
144    {
145       super.onCreateOptionsMenu(menu, inflater);
146       inflater.inflate(R.menu.doodle_fragment_menu, menu);
147    }
148
149    // handle choice from options menu
150    @Override
151    public boolean onOptionsItemSelected(MenuItem item)
152    {
```

Fig. 7.18 | Overridden Fragment methods onCreateOptionsMenu and onOptionsItemSelected. (Part 1 of 2.)

```
153        // switch based on the MenuItem id
154        switch (item.getItemId())
155        {
156           case R.id.color:
157              ColorDialogFragment colorDialog = new ColorDialogFragment();
158              colorDialog.show(getFragmentManager(), "color dialog");
159              return true; // consume the menu event
160           case R.id.lineWidth:
161              LineWidthDialogFragment widthdialog =
162                 new LineWidthDialogFragment();
163              widthdialog.show(getFragmentManager(), "line width dialog");
164              return true; // consume the menu event
165           case R.id.eraser:
166              doodleView.setDrawingColor(Color.WHITE); // line color white
167              return true; // consume the menu event
168           case R.id.clear:
169              confirmErase(); // confirm before erasing image
170              return true; // consume the menu event
171           case R.id.save:
172              doodleView.saveImage(); // save the current image
173              return true; // consume the menu event
174           case R.id.print:
175              doodleView.printImage(); // print the current images
176              return true; // consume the menu event
177        } // end switch
178
179        return super.onOptionsItemSelected(item); // call super's method
180     } // end method onOptionsItemSelected
181
```

Fig. 7.18 | Overridden Fragment methods onCreateOptionsMenu and onOptionsItemSelected. (Part 2 of 2.)

We use the MenuItem argument's **getItemID** method (line 154) to get the resource ID of the selected menu item, then take different actions based on the selection. The actions are as follows:

- For R.id.color, lines 157–158 create and show a ColorDialogFragment (Section 7.7) to allow the user to select a new drawing color.

- For R.id.lineWidth, lines 161–163 create and show a LineWidthDialogFragment (Section 7.8) to allow the user to select a new drawing color.

- For R.id.eraser, line 166 sets the doodleView's drawing color to white, which effectively turns the user's fingers into *erasers*.

- For R.id.clear, line 169 calls method confirmErase (Fig. 7.17) to display an EraseImageDialogFragment (Section 7.9) and confirm whether the user really wants to erase the image.

- For R.id.save, line 172 calls doodleView's saveImage method to save the painting as an image stored in the device's **Gallery**.

- For R.id.print, line 175 calls doodleView's printImage method to allow the user to save the image as a PDF or to print the image.

*Methods **getDoodleView** and **setDialogOnScreen***
Methods getDoodleView and setDialogOnScreen (Fig. 7.19) are called by methods of the
app's DialogFragment subclasses. Method getDoodleView returns a reference to this
Fragment's DoodleView so that a DialogFragment can set the drawing color, set the line
width or clear the image. Method setDialogOnScreen is called by Fragment lifecycle
methods of the app's DialogFragment subclasses to indicate when a dialog is on the screen.

```
182    // returns the DoodleView
183    public DoodleView getDoodleView()
184    {
185       return doodleView;
186    }
187
188    // indicates whether a dialog is displayed
189    public void setDialogOnScreen(boolean visible)
190    {
191       dialogOnScreen = visible;
192    }
193 }
```

Fig. 7.19 | Methods getDoodleView and setDialogOnScreen.

7.6 DoodleView Class

The DoodleView class (Figs. 7.20–7.33) processes the user's touches and draws the corresponding lines.

***DooldleView** package Statement and **import** Statements*
Figure 7.20 lists class DoodleView's package statement, import statements and fields. The
new classes and interfaces are highlighted here. Many of these were discussed in
Section 7.2 and the rest are discussed as we use them throughout class DoodleView.

```
1   // DoodleView.java
2   // Main View for the Doodlz app.
3   package com.deitel.doodlz;
4
5   import java.util.HashMap;
6   import java.util.Map;
7
8   import android.content.Context;
9   import android.graphics.Bitmap;
10  import android.graphics.Canvas;
11  import android.graphics.Color;
12  import android.graphics.Paint;
13  import android.graphics.Path;
14  import android.graphics.Point;
15  import android.os.Build;
16  import android.provider.MediaStore;
17  import android.support.v4.print.PrintHelper;
```

Fig. 7.20 | DooldleView package statement and import statements. (Part 1 of 2.)

```
18    import android.util.AttributeSet;
19    import android.view.GestureDetector;
20    import android.view.GestureDetector.SimpleOnGestureListener;
21    import android.view.Gravity;
22    import android.view.MotionEvent;
23    import android.view.View;
24    import android.widget.Toast;
25
```

Fig. 7.20 | `DoodleView` package statement and `import` statements. (Part 2 of 2.)

DoodleView static *and Instance Variables*

Class `DoodleView`'s `static` and instance variables (Fig. 7.21, lines 30–43) are used to manage the data for the set of lines that the user is currently drawing and to draw those lines. Line 38 creates the `pathMap`, which maps each finger ID (known as a pointer) to a corresponding `Path` object for the lines currently being drawn. Lines 39–40 create the `previousPointMap`, which maintains the last point for each finger—as each finger moves, we draw a line from its current point to its previous point. We discuss the other fields as we use them in class `DoodleView`.

```
26    // the main screen that is painted
27    public class DoodleView extends View
28    {
29       // used to determine whether user moved a finger enough to draw again
30       private static final float TOUCH_TOLERANCE = 10;
31
32       private Bitmap bitmap; // drawing area for display or saving
33       private Canvas bitmapCanvas; // used to draw on bitmap
34       private final Paint paintScreen; // used to draw bitmap onto screen
35       private final Paint paintLine; // used to draw lines onto bitmap
36
37       // Maps of current Paths being drawn and Points in those Paths
38       private final Map<Integer, Path> pathMap = new HashMap<Integer, Path>();
39       private final Map<Integer, Point> previousPointMap =
40          new HashMap<Integer, Point>();
41
42       // used to hide/show system bars
43       private GestureDetector singleTapDetector;
44
```

Fig. 7.21 | `DoodleView` static and instance variables.

DoodleView *Constructor*

The constructor (Fig. 7.22) initializes several of the class's instance variables—the two `Map`s are initialized in their declarations in Fig. 7.21. Line 49 creates the `Paint` object `paintScreen` that will be used to display the user's drawing on the screen and line 52 creates the `Paint` object `paintLine` that specifies the settings for the line(s) the user is currently drawing. Lines 53–57 specify the settings for the `paintLine` object. We pass `true` to `Paint`'s **setAntiAlias** method to enable *anti-aliasing* which smooths the edges of the lines. Next, we set the `Paint`'s style to `Paint.Style.STROKE` with `Paint`'s **setStyle** method. The style can be STROKE, FILL or FILL_AND_STROKE for a line, a filled shape without a border and a filled shape with a border, respectively. The default option is Paint.Style.FILL. We set the line's width using Paint's setStrokeWidth method. This sets the app's *default line width* to five pixels. We also use Paint's setStrokeCap method to round the ends of the lines with Paint.Cap.ROUND. Lines 60–61 create a GestureDetector that uses the singleTapListener to check for single-tap events.

```
45    // DoodleView constructor initializes the DoodleView
46    public DoodleView(Context context, AttributeSet attrs)
47    {
48        super(context, attrs); // pass context to View's constructor
49        paintScreen = new Paint(); // used to display bitmap onto screen
50
51        // set the initial display settings for the painted line
52        paintLine = new Paint();
53        paintLine.setAntiAlias(true); // smooth edges of drawn line
54        paintLine.setColor(Color.BLACK); // default color is black
55        paintLine.setStyle(Paint.Style.STROKE); // solid line
56        paintLine.setStrokeWidth(5); // set the default line width
57        paintLine.setStrokeCap(Paint.Cap.ROUND); // rounded line ends
58
59        // GestureDetector for single taps
60        singleTapDetector =
61            new GestureDetector(getContext(), singleTapListener);
62    }
63
```

Fig. 7.22 | DoodleView constructor.

Overridden View Method onSizeChanged

The DoodleView's size is not determined until it's inflated and added to the MainActivity's View hierarchy; therefore, we can't determine the size of the drawing Bitmap in on-Create. So, we override View method onSizeChanged (Fig. 7.23), which is called when the DoodleView's size changes—e.g., when it's added to an Activity's View hierarchy or when the user rotates the device. In this app, onSizeChanged is called only when the DoodleView is added to the Doodlz Activity's View hierarchy, because the app always displays in *portrait* on phones and small tablets, and in *landscape* on large tablets.

```
64    // Method onSizeChanged creates Bitmap and Canvas after app displays
65    @Override
66    public void onSizeChanged(int w, int h, int oldW, int oldH)
67    {
68        bitmap = Bitmap.createBitmap(getWidth(), getHeight(),
69            Bitmap.Config.ARGB_8888);
70        bitmapCanvas = new Canvas(bitmap);
71        bitmap.eraseColor(Color.WHITE); // erase the Bitmap with white
72    }
73
```

Fig. 7.23 | Overridden View method onSizeChanged.

Bitmap's static **createBitmap** method creates a Bitmap of the specified width and height—here we use the DoodleView's width and height as the Bitmap's dimensions. The last argument to createBitmap is the Bitmap's encoding, which specifies how each pixel in the Bitmap is stored. The constant Bitmap.Config.ARGB_8888 indicates that each pixel's color is stored in four bytes (one byte each for the alpha, red, green and blue values) of the pixel's color. Next, we create a new Canvas that's used to draw shapes directly to the Bitmap. Finally, we use Bitmap's eraseColor method to fill the Bitmap with white pixels—the default Bitmap background is black.

DoodleView *Methods* clear, setDrawingColor, getDrawingColor, setLine-Width *and* getLineWidth

Figure 7.24 defines methods clear (lines 75–81), setDrawingColor (lines 84–87), get-DrawingColor (lines 90–93), setLineWidth (lines 96–99) and getLineWidth (lines 102–105), which are called from the DoodleFragment. Method clear, which we use in the EraseImageDialogFragment, empties the pathMap and previousPointMap, erases the Bitmap by setting all of its pixels to white, then calls the inherited View method **invalidate** to indicate that the View needs to be redrawn. Then, the system automatically determines when the View's onDraw method should be called. Method setDrawingColor changes the current drawing color by setting the color of the Paint object paintLine. Paint's setColor method receives an int that represents the new color in ARGB format. Method getDrawingColor returns the current color, which we use in the ColorDialog-Fragment. Method setLineWidth sets paintLine's stroke width to the specified number of pixels. Method getLineWidth returns the current stroke width, which we use in the LineWidthDialogFragment.

```
74    // clear the painting
75    public void clear()
76    {
77       pathMap.clear(); // remove all paths
78       previousPointMap.clear(); // remove all previous points
79       bitmap.eraseColor(Color.WHITE); // clear the bitmap
80       invalidate(); // refresh the screen
81    }
82
83    // set the painted line's color
84    public void setDrawingColor(int color)
85    {
86       paintLine.setColor(color);
87    }
88
89    // return the painted line's color
90    public int getDrawingColor()
91    {
92       return paintLine.getColor();
93    }
94
```

Fig. 7.24 | DoodleView methods clear, setDrawingColor, getDrawingColor, setLine-Width and getLineWidth. (Part 1 of 2.)

```
 95      // set the painted line's width
 96      public void setLineWidth(int width)
 97      {
 98         paintLine.setStrokeWidth(width);
 99      }
100
101      // return the painted line's width
102      public int getLineWidth()
103      {
104         return (int) paintLine.getStrokeWidth();
105      }
106
```

Fig. 7.24 | DoodleView methods clear, setDrawingColor, getDrawingColor, setLine-Width and getLineWidth. (Part 2 of 2.)

Overridden View Method onDraw

When a View needs to be *redrawn*, its **onDraw** method is called. Figure 7.25 overrides onDraw to display bitmap (the Bitmap that contains the drawing) on the DoodleView by calling the Canvas argument's **drawBitmap** method. The first argument is the Bitmap to draw, the next two arguments are the *x-y* coordinates where the upper-left corner of the Bitmap should be placed on the View and the last argument is the Paint object that specifies the drawing characteristics. Lines 115–116 then loop through and display the Paths that are currently being drawn. For each Integer key in the pathMap, we pass the corresponding Path to Canvas's **drawPath** method to draw the Path using the paintLine object, which defines the line *width* and *color*.

```
107      // called each time this View is drawn
108      @Override
109      protected void onDraw(Canvas canvas)
110      {
111         // draw the background screen
112         canvas.drawBitmap(bitmap, 0, 0, paintScreen);
113
114         // for each path currently being drawn
115         for (Integer key : pathMap.keySet())
116            canvas.drawPath(pathMap.get(key), paintLine); // draw line
117      }
118
```

Fig. 7.25 | Overridden View method onDraw.

DoodleView Methods hideSystemBars and showSystemBars

This app uses Android 4.4's new *immersive mode* to allow users to draw on the entire screen. When the user taps the screen, a GestureDetector's SimplyOnGestureListener (Fig. 7.27) determines whether the system bars and action bar are displayed. If so, method hideSystemBars (Fig. 7.26, lines 120–130) is called; otherwise, method showSystemBars (Fig. 7.26, lines 133–140) is called. For this app, we enable immersive mode only for Android 4.4. So, both methods first check whether the version of Android running on the device—Build.VERSION_SDK_INT—is greater than or equal to the constant for Android

4.4 (API level 19)—Build.VERSION_CODES_KITKAT. If so, both methods use View method **setSystemUiVisibility** to configure the system bars and action bar. To hide the system bars and action bar and place the UI into immersive mode, you pass to setSystemUi-Visibility the constants that are combined via the bitwise OR (|) operator in lines 124–129. To show the system bars and action bar, you pass to setSystemUiVisibility the constants that are combined in lines 137–139. These combinations of View constants ensure that the DoodleView is *not* resized each time the system bars and action bar are hidden and redisplayed. Instead, the system bars and action bar *overlay* the DoodleView—that is, part of the DoodleView is temporarily hidden when the system bars and action bar are on the screen. The constant View.SYSTEM_UI_FLAG_IMMERSIVE is new in Android 4.4. For more information on immersive mode, visit:

http://developer.android.com/training/system-ui/immersive.html

```
119    // hide system bars and action bar
120    public void hideSystemBars()
121    {
122       if (Build.VERSION.SDK_INT >= Build.VERSION_CODES.KITKAT)
123          setSystemUiVisibility(
124             View.SYSTEM_UI_FLAG_LAYOUT_STABLE |
125             View.SYSTEM_UI_FLAG_LAYOUT_HIDE_NAVIGATION |
126             View.SYSTEM_UI_FLAG_LAYOUT_FULLSCREEN |
127             View.SYSTEM_UI_FLAG_HIDE_NAVIGATION |
128             View.SYSTEM_UI_FLAG_FULLSCREEN |
129             View.SYSTEM_UI_FLAG_IMMERSIVE);
130    }
131
132    // show system bars and action bar
133    public void showSystemBars()
134    {
135       if (Build.VERSION.SDK_INT >= Build.VERSION_CODES.KITKAT)
136          setSystemUiVisibility(
137             View.SYSTEM_UI_FLAG_LAYOUT_STABLE |
138             View.SYSTEM_UI_FLAG_LAYOUT_HIDE_NAVIGATION |
139             View.SYSTEM_UI_FLAG_LAYOUT_FULLSCREEN);
140    }
141
```

Fig. 7.26 | DoodleView methods hideSystemBars and showSystemBars.

*Anonymous Inner Class that Implements Interface **SimpleOnGestureListener***
Figure 7.27 creates the SimpleOnGestureListener named singleTapListener, which was registered at lines 60–61 (Fig. 7.14) with the GestureDetector. Recall that SimpleOnGestureListener is an adapter class that implements interfaces OnGestureListener and OnDoubleTapListener. The methods simply return false—indicating that the events were *not handled*. We override only the **onSingleTap** method (lines 146–155), which is called when the user taps the screen. We determine whether the system bars and app bar are displayed (lines 149–150) by calling method View method **getSystemUiVisibilty** and combining its result with the constant View.SYSTEM_UI_FLAG_HIDE_NAVIGATION. If the result is 0, the system bars and app bar are currently displayed, so we call method hideSystemBars;

otherwise, we call showSystemBars. Returning true indicates that the single-tap event has been handled.

```
142    // create SimpleOnGestureListener for single tap events
143    private SimpleOnGestureListener singleTapListener =
144       new SimpleOnGestureListener()
145       {
146          @Override
147          public boolean onSingleTapUp(MotionEvent e)
148          {
149             if ((getSystemUiVisibility() &
150                View.SYSTEM_UI_FLAG_HIDE_NAVIGATION) == 0)
151                hideSystemBars();
152             else
153                showSystemBars();
154             return true;
155          }
156       };
157
```

Fig. 7.27 | Anonymous inner class that implements interface SimpleOnGestureListener.

Overridden View Method onTouchEvent

Method onTouchEvent (Fig. 7.28) is called when the View receives a touch event. Android supports *multitouch*—that is, having multiple fingers touching the screen. At any time, the user can touch the screen with more fingers or remove fingers from the screen. For this reason, each finger—known as a *pointer*—has a unique ID that identifies it across touch events. We'll use that ID to locate the corresponding Path objects that represent each line currently being drawn. These Paths are stored in pathMap.

```
158    // handle touch event
159    @Override
160    public boolean onTouchEvent(MotionEvent event)
161    {
162       // get the event type and the ID of the pointer that caused the event
163       // if a single tap event occurred on KitKat or higher device
164       if (singleTapDetector.onTouchEvent(event))
165          return true;
166
167       int action = event.getActionMasked(); // event type
168       int actionIndex = event.getActionIndex(); // pointer (i.e., finger)
169
170       // determine whether touch started, ended or is moving
171       if (action == MotionEvent.ACTION_DOWN ||
172          action == MotionEvent.ACTION_POINTER_DOWN)
173       {
174          touchStarted(event.getX(actionIndex), event.getY(actionIndex),
175             event.getPointerId(actionIndex));
176       }
```

Fig. 7.28 | Overridden View method onTouchEvent. (Part 1 of 2.)

```
177          else if (action == MotionEvent.ACTION_UP ||
178             action == MotionEvent.ACTION_POINTER_UP)
179          {
180             touchEnded(event.getPointerId(actionIndex));
181          }
182          else
183          {
184             touchMoved(event);
185          }
186
187          invalidate(); // redraw
188          return true;
189       } // end method onTouchEvent
190
```

Fig. 7.28 | Overridden View method onTouchEvent. (Part 2 of 2.)

When a touch event occurs, line 164 calls the GestureDetector (singleTapDetector) method onTouchEvent to first determine if the touch event was a tap to hide or show the system bars and app bar. If the motion event was a tap, the method returns immediately.

MotionEvent's **getActionMasked** method (line 167) returns an int representing the MotionEvent type, which you can use with constants from class MotionEvent to determine how to handle each event. MotionEvent's **getActionIndex** method (line 168) returns an integer index representing which finger caused the event. This index is *not* the finger's unique ID—it's simply the index at which that finger's information is located in this MotionEvent object. To get the finger's unique ID that persists across MotionEvents until the user removes that finger from the screen, we'll use MotionEvent's **getPointerID** method (lines 175 and 180), passing the finger index as an argument.

If the action is MotionEvent.ACTION_DOWN or MotionEvent.ACTION_POINTER_DOWN (lines 171–172), the user *touched the screen with a new finger*. The first finger to touch the screen generates a MotionEvent.ACTION_DOWN event, and all other fingers generate MotionEvent.ACTION_POINTER_DOWN events. For these cases, we call the touchStarted method (Fig. 7.29) to store the initial coordinates of the touch. If the action is MotionEvent.ACTION_UP or MotionEvent.ACTION_POINTER_UP, the user *removed a finger from the screen*, so we call method touchEnded (Fig. 7.31) to draw the completed Path to the bitmap so that we have a permanent record of that Path. For all other touch events, we call method touchMoved (Fig. 7.30) to draw the lines. After the event is processed, line 187 calls the inherited View method invalidate to redraw the screen, and line 188 returns true to indicate that the event has been processed.

touchStarted *Method of Class* DoodleView

The touchStarted method (Fig. 7.29) is called when a finger first *touches* the screen. The coordinates of the touch and its ID are supplied as arguments. If a Path already exists for the given ID (line 198), we call Path's **reset** method to *clear* any existing points so we can *reuse* the Path for a new stroke. Otherwise, we create a new Path, add it to pathMap, then add a new Point to the previousPointMap. Lines 213–215 call Path's **moveTo** method to set the Path's starting coordinates and specify the new Point's x and y values.

```
191    // called when the user touches the screen
192    private void touchStarted(float x, float y, int lineID)
193    {
194        Path path; // used to store the path for the given touch id
195        Point point; // used to store the last point in path
196
197        // if there is already a path for lineID
198        if (pathMap.containsKey(lineID))
199        {
200            path = pathMap.get(lineID); // get the Path
201            path.reset(); // reset the Path because a new touch has started
202            point = previousPointMap.get(lineID); // get Path's last point
203        }
204        else
205        {
206            path = new Path();
207            pathMap.put(lineID, path); // add the Path to Map
208            point = new Point(); // create a new Point
209            previousPointMap.put(lineID, point); // add the Point to the Map
210        }
211
212        // move to the coordinates of the touch
213        path.moveTo(x, y);
214        point.x = (int) x;
215        point.y = (int) y;
216    } // end method touchStarted
217
```

Fig. 7.29 | touchStarted method of class DoodleView.

touchMoved *Method of Class* **DoodleView**

The touchMoved method (Fig. 7.30) is called when the user moves one or more fingers across the screen. The system MotionEvent passed from onTouchEvent contains touch information for multiple moves on the screen if they occur at the same time. MotionEvent method **getPointerCount** (line 222) returns the number of touches this MotionEvent describes. For each, we store the finger's ID (line 225) in pointerID, and store the finger's corresponding index in this MotionEvent (line 226) in pointerIndex. Then we check whether there's a corresponding Path in the pathMap HashMap (line 229). If so, we use MotionEvent's getX and getY methods to get the last coordinates for this *drag* event for the specified pointerIndex. We get the corresponding Path and last Point for the pointerID from each respective HashMap, then calculate the difference between the last point and the current point—we want to update the Path *only* if the user has moved a distance that's greater than our TOUCH_TOLERANCE constant. We do this because many devices are sensitive enough to generate MotionEvents indicating small movements when the user is attempting to hold a finger motionless on the screen. If the user moved a finger further than the TOUCH_TOLERANCE, we use Path's **quadTo** method (lines 248–249) to add a geometric curve (specifically a *quadratic Bezier curve*) from the previous Point to the new Point. We then update the most recent Point for that finger.

```
218    // called when the user drags along the screen
219    private void touchMoved(MotionEvent event)
220    {
221       // for each of the pointers in the given MotionEvent
222       for (int i = 0; i < event.getPointerCount(); i++)
223       {
224          // get the pointer ID and pointer index
225          int pointerID = event.getPointerId(i);
226          int pointerIndex = event.findPointerIndex(pointerID);
227
228          // if there is a path associated with the pointer
229          if (pathMap.containsKey(pointerID))
230          {
231             // get the new coordinates for the pointer
232             float newX = event.getX(pointerIndex);
233             float newY = event.getY(pointerIndex);
234
235             // get the Path and previous Point associated with
236             // this pointer
237             Path path = pathMap.get(pointerID);
238             Point point = previousPointMap.get(pointerID);
239
240             // calculate how far the user moved from the last update
241             float deltaX = Math.abs(newX - point.x);
242             float deltaY = Math.abs(newY - point.y);
243
244             // if the distance is significant enough to matter
245             if (deltaX >= TOUCH_TOLERANCE || deltaY >= TOUCH_TOLERANCE)
246             {
247                // move the path to the new location
248                path.quadTo(point.x, point.y, (newX + point.x) / 2,
249                   (newY + point.y) / 2);
250
251                // store the new coordinates
252                point.x = (int) newX;
253                point.y = (int) newY;
254             }
255          }
256       }
257    } // end method touchMoved
258
```

Fig. 7.30 | touchMoved method of class DoodleView.

touchEnded *Method of Class* **DoodleView**

The touchEnded method (Fig. 7.31) is called when the user lifts a finger from the screen. The method receives the ID of the finger (lineID) for which the touch just ended as an argument. Line 262 gets the corresponding Path. Line 263 calls the bitmapCanvas's draw-Path method to draw the Path on the Bitmap object named bitmap before we call Path's reset method to clear the Path. Resetting the Path does not erase its corresponding painted line from the screen, because those lines have already been drawn to the bitmap that's displayed to the screen. The lines that are currently being drawn by the user are displayed on top of that bitmap.

```
259    // called when the user finishes a touch
260    private void touchEnded(int lineID)
261    {
262       Path path = pathMap.get(lineID); // get the corresponding Path
263       bitmapCanvas.drawPath(path, paintLine); // draw to bitmapCanvas
264       path.reset(); // reset the Path
265    }
266
```

Fig. 7.31 | touchEnded method of class DoodleView.

DoodleView *Method* saveImage

Method saveImage (Fig. 7.32) saves the current drawing to a file in the device's gallery. Line 271 creates a filename for the image, then lines 274–276 store the image in the device's **Gallery** by calling class MediaStore.Images.Media's insertImage method. The method receives four arguments:

- a ContentResolver that the method uses to locate where the image should be stored on the device
- the Bitmap to store
- the name of the image
- a description of the image

Method insertImage returns a String representing the image's location on the device, or null if the image could not be saved. Lines 278–295 check whether the image was saved and display an appropriate Toast.

```
267    // save the current image to the Gallery
268    public void saveImage()
269    {
270       // use "Doodlz" followed by current time as the image name
271       String name = "Doodlz" + System.currentTimeMillis() + ".jpg";
272
273       // insert the image in the device's gallery
274       String location = MediaStore.Images.Media.insertImage(
275          getContext().getContentResolver(), bitmap, name,
276          "Doodlz Drawing");
277
278       if (location != null) // image was saved
279       {
280          // display a message indicating that the image was saved
281          Toast message = Toast.makeText(getContext(),
282             R.string.message_saved, Toast.LENGTH_SHORT);
283          message.setGravity(Gravity.CENTER, message.getXOffset() / 2,
284             message.getYOffset() / 2);
285          message.show();
286       }
287       else
288       {
```

Fig. 7.32 | DoodleView method saveImage. (Part 1 of 2.)

```
289          // display a message indicating that the image was saved
290          Toast message = Toast.makeText(getContext(),
291             R.string.message_error_saving, Toast.LENGTH_SHORT);
292          message.setGravity(Gravity.CENTER, message.getXOffset() / 2,
293             message.getYOffset() / 2);
294          message.show();
295       }
296    } // end method saveImage
297
```

Fig. 7.32 | DoodleView method saveImage. (Part 2 of 2.)

DoodleView *Method* printImage

On Android 4.4 and higher devices, method printImage (Fig. 7.33) uses the Android Support Library's PrintHelper class to print the current drawing. Line 301 first confirms that printing support is available on the device. If so, line 304 creates a PrintHelper object. Next, line 307 specifies the image's *scale mode*—PrintHelper.SCALE_MODE_FIT indicates that the image should fit within the printable area of the paper. There's also the scale mode PrintHelper.SCALE_MODE_FILL, which causes the image to fill the paper, possibly cutting off a portion of the image. Finally, line 308 calls PrintHelper method **printBitmap**, passing as arguments the print job name (used by the printer to identify the print) and the Bitmap containing the image to print. This displays Android's print dialog, which allows the user to choose whether to save the image as a PDF document on the device or to print the image to an available printer.

```
298      // print the current image
299      public void printImage()
300      {
301         if (PrintHelper.systemSupportsPrint())
302         {
303            // use Android Support Library's PrintHelper to print image
304            PrintHelper printHelper = new PrintHelper(getContext());
305
306            // fit image in page bounds and print the image
307            printHelper.setScaleMode(PrintHelper.SCALE_MODE_FIT);
308            printHelper.printBitmap("Doodlz Image", bitmap);
309         }
310         else
311         {
312            // display message indicating that system does not allow printing
313            Toast message = Toast.makeText(getContext(),
314               R.string.message_error_printing, Toast.LENGTH_SHORT);
315            message.setGravity(Gravity.CENTER, message.getXOffset() / 2,
316               message.getYOffset() / 2);
317            message.show();
318         }
319      }
320   } // end class DoodleView
```

Fig. 7.33 | DoodleView method printImage.

7.7 ColorDialogFragment Class

Class ColorDialogFragment (Figs. 7.34–7.38) extends DialogFragment to create an AlertDialog for setting the drawing color. The class's instance variables (lines 19–24) are used to reference the GUI controls for selecting the new color, displaying a preview of it and storing the color as a 32-bit int value that represents the color's ARGB values.

```java
1   // ColorDialogFragment.java
2   // Allows user to set the drawing color on the DoodleView
3   package com.deitel.doodlz;
4
5   import android.app.Activity;
6   import android.app.AlertDialog;
7   import android.app.Dialog;
8   import android.app.DialogFragment;
9   import android.content.DialogInterface;
10  import android.graphics.Color;
11  import android.os.Bundle;
12  import android.view.View;
13  import android.widget.SeekBar;
14  import android.widget.SeekBar.OnSeekBarChangeListener;
15
16  // class for the Select Color dialog
17  public class ColorDialogFragment extends DialogFragment
18  {
19     private SeekBar alphaSeekBar;
20     private SeekBar redSeekBar;
21     private SeekBar greenSeekBar;
22     private SeekBar blueSeekBar;
23     private View colorView;
24     private int color;
25
```

Fig. 7.34 | ColorDialogFragment's package statement, import statements and instance variables.

Overridden DialogFragment Method onCreateDialog

Method onCreateDialog (Fig. 7.35) inflates the custom View (lines 32–34) defined by fragment_color.xml containing the GUI for selecting a color, then attaches that View to the AlertDialog by calling AlertDialog.Builder's setView method (line 35). Lines 42–50 get references to the dialog's SeekBars and colorView. Next, lines 53–56 register colorChangedListener (Fig. 7.38) as the listener for the SeekBars' events.

```java
26     // create an AlertDialog and return it
27     @Override
28     public Dialog onCreateDialog(Bundle bundle)
29     {
30        AlertDialog.Builder builder =
31           new AlertDialog.Builder(getActivity());
```

Fig. 7.35 | Overridden DialogFragment method onCreateDialog. (Part 1 of 2.)

```
32          View colorDialogView =
33             getActivity().getLayoutInflater().inflate(
34                R.layout.fragment_color, null);
35          builder.setView(colorDialogView); // add GUI to dialog
36
37          // set the AlertDialog's message
38          builder.setTitle(R.string.title_color_dialog);
39          builder.setCancelable(true);
40
41          // get the color SeekBars and set their onChange listeners
42          alphaSeekBar = (SeekBar) colorDialogView.findViewById(
43             R.id.alphaSeekBar);
44          redSeekBar = (SeekBar) colorDialogView.findViewById(
45             R.id.redSeekBar);
46          greenSeekBar = (SeekBar) colorDialogView.findViewById(
47             R.id.greenSeekBar);
48          blueSeekBar = (SeekBar) colorDialogView.findViewById(
49             R.id.blueSeekBar);
50          colorView = colorDialogView.findViewById(R.id.colorView);
51
52          // register SeekBar event listeners
53          alphaSeekBar.setOnSeekBarChangeListener(colorChangedListener);
54          redSeekBar.setOnSeekBarChangeListener(colorChangedListener);
55          greenSeekBar.setOnSeekBarChangeListener(colorChangedListener);
56          blueSeekBar.setOnSeekBarChangeListener(colorChangedListener);
57
58          // use current drawing color to set SeekBar values
59          final DoodleView doodleView = getDoodleFragment().getDoodleView();
60          color = doodleView.getDrawingColor();
61          alphaSeekBar.setProgress(Color.alpha(color));
62          redSeekBar.setProgress(Color.red(color));
63          greenSeekBar.setProgress(Color.green(color));
64          blueSeekBar.setProgress(Color.blue(color));
65
66          // add Set Color Button
67          builder.setPositiveButton(R.string.button_set_color,
68             new DialogInterface.OnClickListener()
69             {
70                public void onClick(DialogInterface dialog, int id)
71                {
72                   doodleView.setDrawingColor(color);
73                }
74             }
75          ); // end call to setPositiveButton
76
77          return builder.create(); // return dialog
78       } // end method onCreateDialog
79
```

Fig. 7.35 | Overridden `DialogFragment` method `onCreateDialog`. (Part 2 of 2.)

Line 59 calls method getDoodleFragment (Fig. 7.36) to get a reference to the Doo-dleFragment, then calls the DoodleFragment's getDoodleView method to get the Doo-dleView. Lines 60–64 get the DoodleView's current drawing color, then use it to set each

SeekBar's value. Color's static methods **alpha**, **red**, **green** and **blue** extract the ARGB values from the color, and SeekBar's setProgress method positions the thumbs. Lines 67–75 configure the AlertDialog's positive button to set the DoodleView's new drawing color. Line 77 returns the AlertDialog.

Method *getDoodleFragment*

Method getDoodleFragment (Fig. 7.36) simply uses the FragmentManager to get a reference to the DoodleFragment.

```
80     // gets a reference to the DoodleFragment
81     private DoodleFragment getDoodleFragment()
82     {
83         return (DoodleFragment) getFragmentManager().findFragmentById(
84             R.id.doodleFragment);
85     }
86
```

Fig. 7.36 | Method getDoodleFragment.

Overridden *Fragment Lifecycle Methods* onAttach *and* onDetach

When the ColorDialogFragment is added to a parent Activity, method onAttach (Fig. 7.37, lines 88–96) is called. Line 92 gets a reference to the DoodleFragment. If that reference is not null, line 95 calls DoodleFragment's setDialogOnScreen method to indicate that the **Choose Color** dialog is now displayed. When the ColorDialogFragment is removed from a parent Activity, method onDetach (lines 99–107) is called. Line 106 calls DoodleFragment's setDialogOnScreen method to indicate that the **Choose Color** dialog is no longer on the screen.

```
87      // tell DoodleFragment that dialog is now displayed
88      @Override
89      public void onAttach(Activity activity)
90      {
91          super.onAttach(activity);
92          DoodleFragment fragment = getDoodleFragment();
93
94          if (fragment != null)
95              fragment.setDialogOnScreen(true);
96      }
97
98      // tell DoodleFragment that dialog is no longer displayed
99      @Override
100     public void onDetach()
101     {
102         super.onDetach();
103         DoodleFragment fragment = getDoodleFragment();
104
105         if (fragment != null)
106             fragment.setDialogOnScreen(false);
107     }
108
```

Fig. 7.37 | Overridden Fragment lifecycle methods onAttach and onDetach.

*Anonymous Inner Class That Implements Interface **OnSeekBarChangeListener** to Respond to the Events of the Alpha, Red, Green and Blue **SeekBars***

Figure 7.38 defines an anonymous inner class that implements interface OnSeekBar-ChangeListener to respond to events when the user adjusts the SeekBars in the **Choose Color** Dialog. This was registered as the SeekBars' event handler in Fig. 7.35 (lines 53–56). Method onProgressChanged (lines 115–123) is called when the position of a Seek-Bar's thumb changes. If the user moved a SeekBar's thumb (line 118), lines 119–121 store the new color. Class Color's **static** method **argb** combines the SeekBars' values into a Color and returns the appropriate color as an int. We then use class View's **setBackgroundColor** method to update the colorView with a color that matches the current state of the SeekBars.

```
109     // OnSeekBarChangeListener for the SeekBars in the color dialog
110     private OnSeekBarChangeListener colorChangedListener =
111        new OnSeekBarChangeListener()
112     {
113        // display the updated color
114        @Override
115        public void onProgressChanged(SeekBar seekBar, int progress,
116           boolean fromUser)
117        {
118           if (fromUser) // user, not program, changed SeekBar progress
119              color = Color.argb(alphaSeekBar.getProgress(),
120                 redSeekBar.getProgress(), greenSeekBar.getProgress(),
121                 blueSeekBar.getProgress());
122           colorView.setBackgroundColor(color);
123        }
124
125        @Override
126        public void onStartTrackingTouch(SeekBar seekBar) // required
127        {
128        }
129
130        @Override
131        public void onStopTrackingTouch(SeekBar seekBar) // required
132        {
133        }
134     }; // end colorChanged
135  } // end class ColorDialogFragment
```

Fig. 7.38 | Anonymous inner class that implements interface OnSeekBarChangeListener to respond to the events of the alpha, red, green and blue SeekBars.

7.8 LineWidthDialogFragment Class

Class LineWidthDialogFragment (Fig. 7.39) extends DialogFragment to create an Alert-Dialog for setting the line width. The class is similar to class ColorDialogFragment, so we discuss only the key differences here. The class's only instance variable is an ImageView (line 22) in which we draw a line showing the current line-width setting.

```java
 1   // LineWidthDialogFragment.java
 2   // Allows user to set the drawing color on the DoodleView
 3   package com.deitel.doodlz;
 4
 5   import android.app.Activity;
 6   import android.app.AlertDialog;
 7   import android.app.Dialog;
 8   import android.app.DialogFragment;
 9   import android.content.DialogInterface;
10   import android.graphics.Bitmap;
11   import android.graphics.Canvas;
12   import android.graphics.Paint;
13   import android.os.Bundle;
14   import android.view.View;
15   import android.widget.ImageView;
16   import android.widget.SeekBar;
17   import android.widget.SeekBar.OnSeekBarChangeListener;
18
19   // class for the Select Color dialog
20   public class LineWidthDialogFragment extends DialogFragment
21   {
22      private ImageView widthImageView;
23
24      // create an AlertDialog and return it
25      @Override
26      public Dialog onCreateDialog(Bundle bundle)
27      {
28         AlertDialog.Builder builder =
29            new AlertDialog.Builder(getActivity());
30         View lineWidthDialogView = getActivity().getLayoutInflater().inflate(
31            R.layout.fragment_line_width, null);
32         builder.setView(lineWidthDialogView); // add GUI to dialog
33
34         // set the AlertDialog's message
35         builder.setTitle(R.string.title_line_width_dialog);
36         builder.setCancelable(true);
37
38         // get the ImageView
39         widthImageView = (ImageView) lineWidthDialogView.findViewById(
40            R.id.widthImageView);
41
42         // configure widthSeekBar
43         final DoodleView doodleView = getDoodleFragment().getDoodleView();
44         final SeekBar widthSeekBar = (SeekBar)
45            lineWidthDialogView.findViewById(R.id.widthSeekBar);
46         widthSeekBar.setOnSeekBarChangeListener(lineWidthChanged);
47         widthSeekBar.setProgress(doodleView.getLineWidth());
48
49         // add Set Line Width Button
50         builder.setPositiveButton(R.string.button_set_line_width,
51            new DialogInterface.OnClickListener()
52            {
```

Fig. 7.39 | Class LineWidthDialogFragment. (Part 1 of 3.)

```
53              public void onClick(DialogInterface dialog, int id)
54              {
55                  doodleView.setLineWidth(widthSeekBar.getProgress());
56              }
57          }
58      ); // end call to setPositiveButton
59
60      return builder.create(); // return dialog
61  } // end method onCreateDialog
62
63  // gets a reference to the DoodleFragment
64  private DoodleFragment getDoodleFragment()
65  {
66      return (DoodleFragment) getFragmentManager().findFragmentById(
67          R.id.doodleFragment);
68  }
69
70  // tell DoodleFragment that dialog is now displayed
71  @Override
72  public void onAttach(Activity activity)
73  {
74      super.onAttach(activity);
75      DoodleFragment fragment = getDoodleFragment();
76
77      if (fragment != null)
78          fragment.setDialogOnScreen(true);
79  }
80
81  // tell DoodleFragment that dialog is no longer displayed
82  @Override
83  public void onDetach()
84  {
85      super.onDetach();
86      DoodleFragment fragment = getDoodleFragment();
87
88      if (fragment != null)
89          fragment.setDialogOnScreen(false);
90  }
91
92  // OnSeekBarChangeListener for the SeekBar in the width dialog
93  private OnSeekBarChangeListener lineWidthChanged =
94      new OnSeekBarChangeListener()
95      {
96          Bitmap bitmap = Bitmap.createBitmap(
97              400, 100, Bitmap.Config.ARGB_8888);
98          Canvas canvas = new Canvas(bitmap); // associate with Canvas
99
100         @Override
101         public void onProgressChanged(SeekBar seekBar, int progress,
102             boolean fromUser)
103         {
```

Fig. 7.39 | Class `LineWidthDialogFragment`. (Part 2 of 3.)

```
104                // configure a Paint object for the current SeekBar value
105                Paint p = new Paint();
106                p.setColor(
107                   getDoodleFragment().getDoodleView().getDrawingColor());
108                p.setStrokeCap(Paint.Cap.ROUND);
109                p.setStrokeWidth(progress);
110
111                // erase the bitmap and redraw the line
112                bitmap.eraseColor(
113                   getResources().getColor(android.R.color.transparent));
114                canvas.drawLine(30, 50, 370, 50, p);
115                widthImageView.setImageBitmap(bitmap);
116             }
117
118             @Override
119             public void onStartTrackingTouch(SeekBar seekBar) // required
120             {
121             }
122
123             @Override
124             public void onStopTrackingTouch(SeekBar seekBar)  // required
125             {
126             }
127       }; // end lineWidthChanged
128 }
```

Fig. 7.39 | Class LineWidthDialogFragment. (Part 3 of 3.)

Method onCreateDialog

Method onCreateDialog (lines 25–61) inflates the custom View (lines 30–31) defined by fragment_line_width.xml that displays the GUI for selecting the line width, then attaches that View to the AlertDialog by calling AlertDialog.Builder's setView method (line 32). Lines 39–40 get a reference to the ImageView in which the sample line will be drawn. Next, lines 43–47 get a reference to the widthSeekBar, register lineWidthChanged (lines 93–127) as the SeekBar's listener and set the SeekBar's current value to the current line width. Lines 50–58 define the dialog's positive button to call the DoodleView's setLineWidth method when the user touches the **Set Line Width** button. Line 60 returns the AlertDialog for display.

Anonymous Inner Class That Implements Interface OnSeekBarChangeListener to Respond to the Events of the widthSeekBar

Lines 93–127 define the lineWidthChanged OnSeekBarChangeListener that responds to events when the user adjusts the SeekBar in the **Choose Line Width** dialog. Lines 96–97 create a Bitmap on which to display a sample line representing the selected line thickness. Line 98 creates a Canvas for drawing on the Bitmap. Method onProgressChanged (lines 100–116) draws the sample line based on the current drawing color and the SeekBar's value. First, lines 105–109 configure a Paint object for drawing the sample line. Class Paint's **setStrokeCap** method (line 108) specifies the appearance of the line ends—in this case, they're rounded (Paint.Cap.ROUND). Lines 112–113 clear bitmap's background to the predefined Android color android.R.color.transparent with Bitmap method

eraseColor. We use canvas to draw the sample line. Finally, line 115 displays bitmap in the widthImageView by passing it to ImageView's **setImageBitmap** method.

7.9 EraseImageDialogFragment Class

Class EraseImageDialogFragment (Fig. 7.40) extends DialogFragment to create an AlertDialog that confirms whether the user really wants to erase the entire image. The class is similar to class ColorDialogFragment and LineWidthDialogFragment, so we discuss only method onCreateDialog (lines 16–41) here. The method creates an AlertDialog with **Erase Image** and **Cancel** button. Lines 27–35 configure the **Erase Image** button as the positive button—when the user touches this, line 32 in the button's listener calls the DoodleView's clear method to erase the image. Line 38 configures **Cancel** as the negative button—when the user touches this, the dialog is dismissed. Line 40 returns the Alert-Dialog.

```java
 1  // EraseImageDialogFragment.java
 2  // Allows user to erase image
 3  package com.deitel.doodlz;
 4
 5  import android.app.Activity;
 6  import android.app.AlertDialog;
 7  import android.app.Dialog;
 8  import android.app.DialogFragment;
 9  import android.content.DialogInterface;
10  import android.os.Bundle;
11
12  //class for the Select Color dialog
13  public class EraseImageDialogFragment extends DialogFragment
14  {
15     // create an AlertDialog and return it
16     @Override
17     public Dialog onCreateDialog(Bundle bundle)
18     {
19        AlertDialog.Builder builder =
20           new AlertDialog.Builder(getActivity());
21
22        // set the AlertDialog's message
23        builder.setMessage(R.string.message_erase);
24        builder.setCancelable(false);
25
26        // add Erase Button
27        builder.setPositiveButton(R.string.button_erase,
28           new DialogInterface.OnClickListener()
29           {
30              public void onClick(DialogInterface dialog, int id)
31              {
32                 getDoodleFragment().getDoodleView().clear(); // clear image
33              }
34           }
35        ); // end call to setPositiveButton
```

Fig. 7.40 | Class EraseImageDialogFragment. (Part I of 2.)

```
36
37          // add Cancel Button
38          builder.setNegativeButton(R.string.button_cancel, null);
39
40          return builder.create(); // return dialog
41      } // end method onCreateDialog
42
43      // gets a reference to the DoodleFragment
44      private DoodleFragment getDoodleFragment()
45      {
46          return (DoodleFragment) getFragmentManager().findFragmentById(
47              R.id.doodleFragment);
48      }
49
50      // tell DoodleFragment that dialog is now displayed
51      @Override
52      public void onAttach(Activity activity)
53      {
54          super.onAttach(activity);
55          DoodleFragment fragment = getDoodleFragment();
56
57          if (fragment != null)
58              fragment.setDialogOnScreen(true);
59      }
60
61      // tell DoodleFragment that dialog is no longer displayed
62      @Override
63      public void onDetach()
64      {
65          super.onDetach();
66          DoodleFragment fragment = getDoodleFragment();
67
68          if (fragment != null)
69              fragment.setDialogOnScreen(false);
70      }
71  } // end class EraseImageDialogFragment
```

Fig. 7.40 | Class EraseImageDialogFragment. (Part 2 of 2.)

7.10 Wrap-Up

In this chapter, you built the **Doodlz** app which enables users to paint by dragging one or more fingers across the screen. You implemented a shake-to-erase feature by using Android's SensorManager to register a SensorEventListener that responds to accelerometer events, and you learned that Android supports many other sensors.

You created subclasses of DialogFragment that displayed custom Views in AlertDialogs. You also overrode the Fragment lifecycle methods onAttach and onDetach, which are called when a Fragment is attached to or detached from a parent Activity, respectively.

We showed how to associate a Canvas with a Bitmap, then use the Canvas to draw on the Bitmap. We demonstrated how to handle multitouch events so the user can draw with multiple fingers at the same time. You stored the information for each individual finger as a Path. You processed the touch events by overriding the View method onTouchEvent, which receives a MotionEvent containing the event type and the ID of the pointer that generated the event. We used the IDs to distinguish among the fingers and add information to the corresponding Path objects.

You used Android 4.4's new full-screen immersive mode that enables an app to take advantage of the entire screen, but still allows the user to access the system bars and action bar when necessary. To toggle immersive mode, you used a GestureDetector to determine when the user single-tapped the screen.

You used a ContentResolver and the MediaStore.Images.Media.insertImage method to save an image into the device's **Gallery.** Finally, we showed how to use the new Android 4.4 printing framework to allow users to print their drawings. You used the Android Support Library's PrintHelper class to print a BitmapBitmap. The PrintHelper displayed a user interface for selecting a printer or saving the image into a PDF document.

In Chapter 8, we build the database-driven **Address Book** app, which provides quick and easy access to stored contact information and the ability to add contacts, delete contacts and edit existing contacts. You'll learn how to dynamically swap Fragments in a GUI and once again provide layouts that optimize screen real estate on phones and tablets.

8

Address Book App

ListFragment, FragmentTransactions and the Fragment Back Stack, Threading and AsyncTasks, CursorAdapter, SQLite and GUI Styles

Objectives

In this chapter you'll:

- Use a `ListFragment` to display and manage a `ListView`.
- Use `FragmentTransaction`s and the back stack to dynamically attach `Fragment`s to and detach `Fragment`s from the GUI.
- Create and open SQLite databases using a `SQLiteOpenHelper`, and insert, delete and query data in a SQLite database using a `SQLiteDatabase` object.
- Use a `SimpleCursorAdapter` to bind database query results to a `ListView`'s items.
- Use a `Cursor` to manipulate database query results.
- Use multithreading and `AsyncTasks` to perform database operations outside the GUI thread and maintain application responsiveness.
- Define styles containing common GUI attributes and values, then apply them to multiple GUI components.

8.1 Introduction

The **Address Book** app (Fig. 8.1) provides convenient access to contact information that's stored in a SQLite database on the device. You can scroll through an alphabetical contact list and can view a contact's details by touching the contact's name.

a) Contact list with **Paul** selected

b) Details for the contact **Paul**

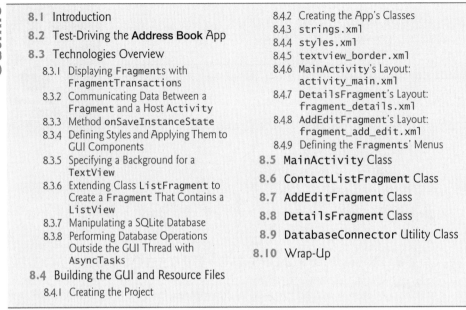
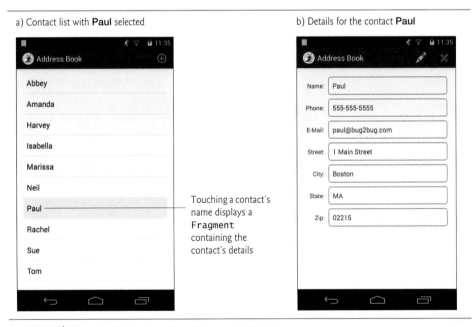

Touching a contact's name displays a **Fragment** containing the contact's details

Fig. 8.1 | Contact list and a selected contact's details.

When a contact's details are displayed, touching *edit* (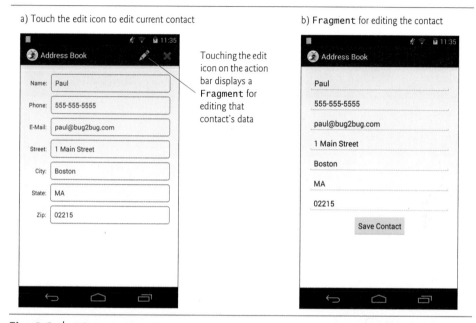) displays a `Fragment` containing prepopulated `EditTexts` for editing the contact's data (Fig. 8.2), and touching *delete* (■) displays a `DialogFragment` asking the user to confirm the deletion (Fig. 8.3).

a) Touch the edit icon to edit current contact   b) `Fragment` for editing the contact

Touching the edit icon on the action bar displays a `Fragment` for editing that contact's data

Fig. 8.2 | Editing a contact's data.

a) Touch the delete icon to delete current contact   b) Confirmation dialog for deleting contact

Touching the delete icon on the action bar displays a dialog asking the user to confirm the deletion

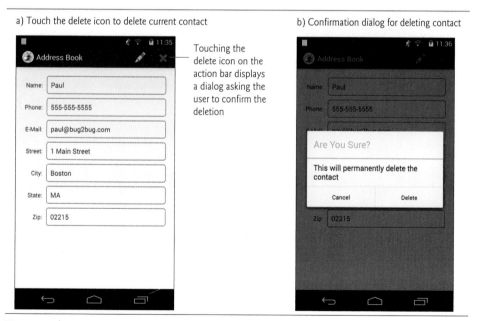

Fig. 8.3 | Deleting a contact from the database.

When viewing the contact list, touching *add* (⊕) displays a Fragment containing EditTexts that you can use to add the new contact's data (Fig. 8.4). When editing an existing contact or adding a new one, you touch the **Save Contact** Button to save the contact's data. Figure 8.5 shows the app running on a tablet in landscape orientation. On tablets, the contact list is always displayed at the app's left side.

a) Touch the add icon to add a new contact

b) **Fragment** for adding the contact

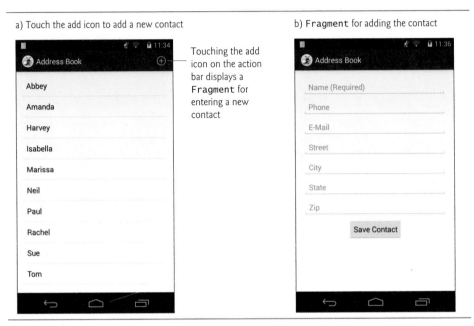

Touching the add icon on the action bar displays a **Fragment** for entering a new contact

Fig. 8.4 | Adding a contact to the database.

a) In landscape orientation on a phone or tablet, the action bar icons are displayed with their text

Fig. 8.5 | **Address Book** running in landscape on a tablet.

8.2 Test-Driving the Address Book App

Opening and Running the App

Open Eclipse and import the **Address Book** app project. Perform the following steps:

1. *Open the Import Dialog.* Select **File > Import...** to open the **Import** dialog.

2. *Import the Address Book app's project.* In the **Import** dialog, expand the **General** node and select **Existing Projects into Workspace**, then click **Next >** to proceed to the **Import Projects** step. Ensure that **Select root directory** is selected, then click the **Browse...** button. In the **Browse for Folder** dialog, locate the AddressBook folder in the book's examples folder, select it and click **OK**. Click **Finish** to import the project into Eclipse. The project now appears in the **Package Explorer** window at the left side of the Eclipse window.

3. *Launch the Address Book app.* In Eclipse, right click the AddressBook project in the **Package Explorer** window, then select **Run As > Android Application** from the menu that appears.

Adding a Contact

The first time you run the app, the contact list will be empty and will display **No Contacts** in the center of the screen. Touch 🔵 on the action bar to display the screen for adding a new entry. After adding the contact's information, touch the **Save Contact** Button to store the contact in the database and return to the app's main screen. If you choose not to add the contact, you can simply touch the device's back button to return to the main screen. Add more contacts if you wish. On a tablet, after adding a contact, the new contact's details will be displayed to the right of the contact list, as in Fig. 8.5.

Viewing a Contact

Touch the name of the contact you just added in the contacts list to view that contact's details. On a tablet, the details are displayed to the right of the contact list.

Editing a Contact

While viewing the contact's details, touch 🖊 on the action bar to display a screen of EditTexts that are prepopulated with the contact's data. Edit the data as necessary, then touch the **Save Contact** Button to store the updated contact information in the database and return to the app's main screen. On a tablet, after editing a contact, the new contact's details will be displayed to the right of the contact list.

Deleting a Contact

While viewing the contact's details, touch ⬛ on the action bar to delete the contact. A dialog will be displayed asking you to confirm this action. If you do, the contact will be removed from the database and the app will display the updated contact list.

8.3 Technologies Overview

This section presents the new technologies that we use in the **Address Book** app in the order in which they're encountered throughout the chapter.

8.3.1 Displaying Fragments with FragmentTransactions

In earlier apps that used Fragments, you declared each Fragment in an Activity's layout or, for a DialogFragment, called its show method to create it. The **Flag Quiz** app demonstrated how to use multiple activities to host each of the app's Fragments on a phone device. In this app, you'll use only one Activity to host all of the app's Fragments. On a phone-sized device, you'll display one Fragment at a time. On a tablet, you'll always display the Fragment containing the list of contacts and display the Fragments for viewing, adding and editing contacts as necessary at the app's right side. You'll use the FragmentManager and FragmentTransactions to dynamically display Fragments. In addition, you'll use Android's Fragment back stack—a data structure that stores Fragments in last-in-first-out (LIFO) order—to provide automatic support for the Android system bar's back button and to allow the app to remove Fragments in the reverse order from which they were added.

8.3.2 Communicating Data Between a Fragment and a Host Activity

To communicate data between Fragments and a host Activity or the Activity's other Fragments, it's considered best practice to do so through the host Activity—this makes the Fragments more reusable, because they do not refer to one another directly. Typically, each Fragment defines an *interface* of *callback methods* that are implemented in the host Activity. We'll use this technique to enable this app's MainActivity to be notified when the user selects a contact to display, touches an action bar item (⊕, ✎ or ✖), or finishes editing an existing contact or adding a new one.

8.3.3 Method onSaveInstanceState

onSaveInstanceState is called by the system when the configuration of the device changes during the app's execution—for example, when the user rotates the device or slides out a keyboard on a device with a hard keyboard. This method can be used to save state information that you'd like to restore when the app's onCreate method is called as part of the configuration change. When an app is simply placed into the background, perhaps so the user can answer a phone call or when the user starts another app, the app's GUI components will automatically save their contents for when the app is brought back to the foreground (provided that the system does not kill the app). We use onSaveInstanceState in Fig. 8.47.

8.3.4 Defining Styles and Applying Them to GUI Components

You can define common GUI component attribute–value pairs as **style** resources (Section 8.4.4). You can then apply the styles to all components that share those values (Section 8.4.7) by using the **style attribute**. Any subsequent changes you make to a style are automatically applied to all GUI components that use the style. We use this to style the TextViews that display a contact's information.

8.3.5 Specifying a Background for a TextView

By default TextViews do not have a border. To define one, you can specify a Drawable as the value for the TextView's android:background attribute. The Drawable could be an image, but in this app you'll define a Drawable as a shape in a resource file (Section 8.4.5). The resource file for such a Drawable is defined in one or more of the app's drawable folders—in this app, textview_border.xml is defined in the drawable-mdpi folder.

8.3.6 Extending Class ListFragment to Create a Fragment That Contains a ListView

When a Fragment's primary task is to display a scrollable list of items, you can extend class ListFragment (package android.app, Section 8.6)—this is nearly identical to extending ListActivity, as you did in Chapter 4. A ListFragment uses a ListView as its default layout. In this app, rather than an ArrayAdapter, we'll use a **CursorAdapter** (package android.widget) to display the results of a database query in the ListView.

8.3.7 Manipulating a SQLite Database

The contact information is stored in a SQLite database. According to www.sqlite.org, SQLite is one of the world's most widely deployed database engines. Each Fragment in this app interacts with a SQLite database via utility class DatabaseConnector (Section 8.9). That class uses a nested subclass of **SQLiteOpenHelper** (package **android.database.sqlite**), which simplifies creating the database and enables you to obtain a **SQLiteDatabase** object (package android.database.sqlite) for manipulating a database's contents. Database queries are performed with Structured Query Language (SQL) and query results are managed via a **Cursor** (package **android.database**).

8.3.8 Performing Database Operations Outside the GUI Thread with AsyncTasks

You should perform *long-running operations* or operations that *block* execution until they complete (e.g., file and database access) *outside* the GUI thread. This helps maintain application responsiveness and avoid *Activity Not Responding (ANR) dialogs* that appear when Android thinks the GUI is not responsive. When we need a database operation's results in the GUI thread, we'll use a subclass of **AsyncTask** (package android.os) to perform the operation in one thread and receive the results in the GUI thread. The details of creating and manipulating threads are handled for you by class AsyncTask, as are communicating the results from the AsyncTask to the GUI thread.

8.4 Building the GUI and Resource Files

In this section, you'll create the **Address Book** app's additional Java source-code files, resource files and GUI layout files.

8.4.1 Creating the Project

Begin by creating a new Android project. Specify the following values in the **New Android Project** dialog, then press **Finish**:

- **Application Name:** Address Book
- **Project Name:** AddressBook
- **Package Name:** com.deitel.addressbook
- **Minimum Required SDK:** API18: Android 4.3
- **Target SDK:** API19: Android 4.4
- **Compile With:** API19: Android 4.4
- **Theme:** Holo Light with Dark Action Bar

In the **New Android Project** dialog's second **New Android Application** step, leave the default settings, and press **Next >**. In the **Configure Launcher Icon** step, select an app icon image, then press **Next >**. In the **Create Activity** step, select **Blank Activity**, then press **Next >**. In the **Blank Activity** step, leave the default settings and click **Finish** to create the project. In the **Graphical Layout** editor, select **Nexus 4** from the screen-type drop-down list and delete the TextView containing "Hello world!"

8.4.2 Creating the App's Classes

This app consists of five classes:

- Class MainActivity (Section 8.5) manages the app's fragments and coordinates the interactions between them.

- Class ContactListFragment (Section 8.6) is a subclass of ListFragment that displays the contacts' names and provides a menu item for adding a new contact.

- Class AddEditFragment (Section 8.7) is a subclass of Fragment that provides a GUI for adding a new contact or editing an existing one.

- Class DetailsFragment (Section 8.8) is a subclass of Fragment that displays one contact's data and provides menu items for editing and deleting that contact.

- Class DatabaseConnector (Section 8.9) is a subclass of **Object** that manages this app's interactions with a SQLite database.

Class MainActivity is created by the IDE when you create your project. As you've done in prior projects, you must add the other classes to the project's com.deitel.addressbook package in the src folder. To do so for each class, right click the package and select **New > Class**, then specify the class's name and superclass.

8.4.3 strings.xml

Figure 8.6 shows this app's String resource names and corresponding values. Double click strings.xml in the res/values folder to display the resource editor for creating these String resources.

Resource name	Value
no_contacts	No Contacts
menuitem_add	Add
menuitem_edit	Edit
menuitem_delete	Delete
button_save_contact	Save Contact
hint_name	Name (Required)
hint_email	E-Mail
hint_phone	Phone
hint_street	Street
hint_city	City

Fig. 8.6 | String resources used in the **Address Book** app. (Part 1 of 2.)

Resource name	Value
hint_state	State
hint_zip	Zip
label_name	Name:
label_email	E-Mail:
label_phone	Phone:
label_street	Street:
label_city	City:
label_state	State:
label_zip	Zip:
confirm_title	Are You Sure?
confirm_message	This will permanently delete the contact
ok	OK
error_message	You must enter a contact name
button_cancel	Cancel
button_delete	Delete

Fig. 8.6 | `String` resources used in the **Address Book** app. (Part 2 of 2.)

8.4.4 `styles.xml`

In this section, you'll define the styles for the `DetailsFragment`'s `TextView`s that display a contact's information (Section 8.4.7). Like other resources, style resources are placed in the app's `res/values` folder. When you create a project, the IDE creates a `styles.xml` file containing predefined styles. Each new style you create specifies a name that's used to apply that style to GUI components and one or more items specifying property values to apply. To create the new styles:

1. In the app's `res/values` folder, open the `styles.xml` file and ensure that the **Resources** tab is selected at the bottom of the editor window.

2. Click **Add...**, then select **Style/Theme** and click **OK** to create a new style.

3. Set the style's **Name** to `ContactLabelTextView` and save the file.

4. With the `ContactLabelTextView` style selected, click **Add...**, then click **OK** to add an **Item** to the style. Set the **Name** and **Value** attributes for the new **Item** and save the file. Repeat this step for each **Name** and **Value** in Fig. 8.7.

Name	Value
android:layout_width	wrap_content
android:layout_height	wrap_content
android:layout_gravity	right|center_vertical

Fig. 8.7 | `ContactLabelTextView` style attributes.

5. Repeat Steps 2 and 3 to create a style named `ContactTextView`—when you click **Add...**, you'll need to select **Create a new element at the top level in Resources**. Then repeat Step 4 for each **Name** and **Value** in Fig. 8.8. When you're done, save and close `styles.xml`.

Name	Value
android:layout_width	wrap_content
android:layout_height	wrap_content
android:layout_gravity	fill_horizontal
android:textSize	16sp
android:background	@drawable/textview_border

Fig. 8.8 | `ContactTextView` style attributes.

8.4.5 `textview_border.xml`

The `style` `ContactTextView` that you created in the preceding section defines the appearance of the `TextView`s that are used to display a contact's details. You specified a `Drawable` (i.e., an image or graphic) named `@drawable/textview_border` as the value for the `TextView`'s `android:background` attribute. In this section, you'll define that `Drawable` in the app's `res/drawable-mdpi` folder. If a `Drawable` is defined in only one of the project's drawable folders, Android will use that `Drawable` on *all* device sizes and resolutions. To define the `Drawable`:

1. Right click the `res/drawable-mdpi` folder and select **New > Android XML File**.

2. Specify `textview_border.xml` as the **File** name and select **shape** as the root element, then click **Finish**.

3. At the time of this writing, the IDE does not provide an editor for creating Drawables, so enter the XML code in Fig. 8.9 into the file.

```
1  <?xml version="1.0" encoding="utf-8"?>
2  <shape xmlns:android="http://schemas.android.com/apk/res/android"
3      android:shape="rectangle" >
4      <corners android:radius="5dp"/>
5      <stroke android:width="1dp" android:color="#555"/>
6      <padding android:top="10dp" android:left="10dp" android:bottom="10dp"
7          android:right="10dp"/>
8  </shape>
```

Fig. 8.9 | XML representation of a `Drawable` that's used to place a border on a `TextView`.

The **shape element**'s element's `android:shape` attribute (line 3) can have the value `"rectangle"` (used in this example), `"oval"`, `"line"` or `"ring"`. The **corners** element (line 4) specifies the rectangle's corner radius, which rounds the corners. The **stroke** element (line 5) defines the rectangle's line width and line color. The **padding** element (lines 6–7) specifies the spacing around the content in the element to which this `Drawable` is applied. You must specify the top, left, right and bottom padding amounts separately. The complete details of defining shapes can be viewed at:

```
http://developer.android.com/guide/topics/resources/
    drawable-resource.html#Shape
```

8.4.6 MainActivity's Layout: activity_main.xml

You'll provide two layouts for MainActivity—one for phone-sized devices in the res/layout folder and one for tablet-sized devices in the res/layout-large folder. You'll need to add the layout-large folder.

Phone Layout: *activity_main.xml in res/layout*

For the phone layout, open activity_main.xml in the res/layout folder. Right click the RelativeLayout in the **Outline** window, then select **Change Layout...** and change the layout to a FrameLayout. Set the FrameLayout's **Id** to @id/fragmentContainer. This FrameLayout will be used on phones to display the app's Fragments.

Tablet Layout: *activity_main.xml in res/layout-large*

For the tablet layout, create a new activity_main.xml layout in the res/layout-large folder. This layout should use a horizontal LinearLayout containing a ContactListFragment and an empty FrameLayout. Use the techniques you learned in Section 5.4.9 to add the ContactListFragment to the layout, then add the FrameLayout. Set the following properties:

- For the LinearLayout set **Weight Sum** to 3—this will help allocate the horizontal space to the ContactListFragment and FrameLayout.

- For the Fragment, set the **Id** to @+id/contactListFragment, the **Width** to 0, the **Height** to match_parent, the **Weight** to 1 and the **Right** margin to @dimen/activity_horizontal_margin.

- For the FrameLayout set the **Id** to @+id/rightPaneContainer, the **Width** to 0, the **Height** to match_parent and the **Weight** to 2.

Setting the LinearLayout's **Weight Sum** to 3, then setting the ContactListFragment's and FrameLayout's **Weight**s to 1 and 2, respectively, indicates that the ContactListFragment should occupy one-third of the LinearLayout's width and the FrameLayout should occupy the remaining two-thirds.

8.4.7 DetailsFragment's Layout: fragment_details.xml

When the user touches a contact in the MainActivity, the app displays the DetailsFragment (Fig. 8.10). This Fragment's layout (fragment_details.xml) consists of a ScrollView containing a vertical GridLayout with two columns of TextViews. A **ScrollView** is a **ViewGroup** that can contain other Views (like a layout) and that lets users *scroll* through content too large to display on the screen. We use a ScrollView here to ensure that the user can scroll through a contact's details if a device does not have enough vertical space to show all the TextViews in Fig. 8.10. Follow the steps in Section 5.4.8 to create the fragment_details.xml file, but use a ScrollView as the **Root Element**. After creating the file, set the ScrollView's **Id** to @+id/detailsScrollView and add a GridLayout to the ScrollView.

Fig. 8.10 | DetailsFragment's GUI components labeled with their id property values.

GridLayout Settings

For the GridLayout, we set the **Width** to match_parent, **Height** to wrap_content, **Column Count** to 2 and **Use Default Margins** to true. The **Height** value enables the parent Scroll-View to determine the GridLayout's actual height and decide whether to provide scrolling. Add TextViews to the GridLayout as shown in Fig. 8.10.

Left Column TextView Settings

For each TextView in the left column set the TextView's **Id** property as specified in Fig. 8.10 and set:

- **Row** to a value from 0–6 depending on the row.
- **Column** to 0.
- **Text** to the appropriate String resource from strings.xml.
- **Style** (located in the **View** category) to @style/ContactLabelTextView—style resources are specified using the syntax @style/*styleName*.

Right Column TextView Settings

For each TextView in the right column set the TextView's **Id** property as specified in Fig. 8.10 and set:

- **Row** to a value from 0–6 depending on the row.
- **Column** to 1.
- **Style** (located in the **View** category) to @style/ContactTextView.

8.4.8 AddEditFragment's Layout: fragment_add_edit.xml

When the user touches the action bar items  or , the MainActivity displays the Add-EditFragment (Fig. 8.11) with a layout (fragment_add_edit.xml) that uses a ScrollView containing a one-column vertical GridLayout. Be sure to set the ScrollView's **Id** to @+id/addEditScrollView. If the AddEditFragment is displayed to add a new contact, the EditTexts will be empty and will display *hints* (Fig. 8.4). Otherwise, they'll display the contact's data that was passed to the AddEditFragment by the MainActivity. Each EditText specifies the **Input Type** and **IME Options** properties. For devices that display a soft keyboard, the **Input Type** specifies which keyboard to display when the user touches the corresponding EditText. This enables us to *customize the keyboard* to the specific type of data the user must enter in a given EditText. We use the **IME Options** property to display a **Next** button on the soft keyboards for the nameEditText, emailEditText, phoneEditText, streetEditText, cityEditText and stateEditText. When one of these has the focus, touching this Button transfers the focus to the next EditText. If the zipEditText has the focus, you can hide the soft keyboard by touching the keyboard's **Done** Button.

Fig. 8.11 | AddEditFragment's GUI components labeled with their id property values. This GUI's root component is a ScrollView that contains a vertical GridLayout.

GridLayout *Settings*

For the GridLayout, we set the **Width** to match_parent, **Height** to wrap_content, **Column Count** to 1 and **Use Default Margins** to true. Add the components shown in Fig. 8.11.

EditText *Settings*

For each EditText, set the TextView's **Id** property as specified in Fig. 8.11 and set:

- **Width** to match_parent.
- **Height** to wrap_content.

- **Hint** to the appropriate `String` resource from `strings.xml`.

- **IME Options** to `actionNext` for all `EditTexts` except `zipEditText`, which should have the value `actionDone`.

- **Style** (located in the **View** category) to `@style/ContactLabelTextView`—style resources are specified using the syntax `@style/`*styleName*.

Set the `EditTexts`' **Input Type** properties to display appropriate keyboards as follows:

- `nameEditText`: `textPersonName|textCapWords`—for entering names and starts each word with a capital letter.

- `phoneEditText`: `phone`—for entering phone numbers.

- `emailEditText`: `textEmailAddress`—for entering an e-mail address.

- `streetEditText`: `textPostalAddress|textCapWords`—for entering an address and starts each word with a capital letter.

- `cityEditText`: `textPostalAddress|textCapWords`.

- `stateEditText`: `textPostalAddress|textCapCharacters`—ensures that state abbreviations are displayed in capital letters.

- `zipEditText`: `number`—for entering numbers.

8.4.9 Defining the Fragments' Menus

You'll now use the techniques you learned in Section 7.3.4 to create two menu resource files in the app's res/menu folder:

- `fragment_contact_list_menu.xml` defines the menu item for adding a contact.

- `fragment_details_menu.xml` defines the menu items for editing an existing contact and deleting a contact.

When both the `ContactListFragment` and the `DetailsFragment` are displayed on a tablet at the same time, all of the menu items are displayed.

Figures 8.12–8.13 show the settings for the menu items in the two menu resource files. Each menu item's **Order in category** values determines the order in which the menu items appear on the action bar. For each menu item's **Icon** value, we specified a standard Android icon. You can see the complete set of standard icons in the Android SDK's platforms folder under each platform version's data/res/drawable-hdpi folder. To refer to these icons in your menus or layouts, prefix them with `@android:drawable/`*icon_name*.

Name	Value
Id	@id/action_add
Order in category	0
Title	@string/menuitem_add
Icon	@android:drawable/ic_menu_add
Show as action	ifRoom|withText

Fig. 8.12 | Menu item for `fragment_contact_list_menu.xml`.

Name	Value
Edit menu item	
Id	@id/action_edit
Order in category	1
Title	@string/menuitem_edit
Icon	@android:drawable/ic_menu_edit
Show as action	ifRoom|withText
Delete menu item	
Id	@id/action_delete
Order in category	2
Title	@string/menuitem_delete
Icon	@android:drawable/ic_delete
Show as action	ifRoom|withText

Fig. 8.13 | Menu item for `fragment_details_menu.xml`.

8.5 MainActivity Class

Class `MainActivity` (Figs. 8.14–8.23) manages the app's fragments and coordinates the interactions between them. On phones, `MainActivity` displays one Fragment at a time, starting with the `ContactListFragment`. On tablets, `MainActivity` always displays the `ContactListFragment` at the left of the layout and, depending on the context, displays either the `DetailsFragment` or the `AddEditFragment` in the right two-thirds of the layout.

***MainActivity* package** *Statement,* **import** *statements and Fields*
Class `MainActivity` (Fig. 8.14) uses class `FragmentTransaction` (imported at line 6) to add and remove the app's Fragments. `MainActivity` implements three interfaces:

- `ContactListFragment.ContactListFragmentListener` contains callback methods that the `ContactListFragment` uses to tell the `MainActivity` when the user selects a contact in the contact list or adds a new contact.

- `DetailsFragment.DetailsFragmentListener` contains callback methods that the `DetailsFragment` uses to tell the `MainActivity` when the user deletes a contact or wishes to edit an existing contact.

- `AddEditFragment.AddEditFragmentListener` contains callback methods that the `AddEditFragment` uses to tell the `MainActivity` when the user finishes adding a new contact or editing an existing one.

The constant `ROW_ID` (line 15) is used as a key in a key–value pair that's passed between the `MainActivity` and its Fragments. The instance variable `contactListFragment` (line 17) is used to tell the `ContactListFragment` to update the displayed list of contacts after a contact is added or deleted.

```
1   // MainActivity.java
2   // Hosts Address Book app's fragments
3   package com.deitel.addressbook;
4
5   import android.app.Activity;
6   import android.app.FragmentTransaction;
7   import android.os.Bundle;
8
9   public class MainActivity extends Activity
10      implements ContactListFragment.ContactListFragmentListener,
11         DetailsFragment.DetailsFragmentListener,
12         AddEditFragment.AddEditFragmentListener
13  {
14      // keys for storing row ID in Bundle passed to a fragment
15      public static final String ROW_ID = "row_id";
16
17      ContactListFragment contactListFragment; // displays contact list
18
```

Fig. 8.14 | MainActivity package statement, import statements and fields.

MainActivity Overridden onCreate Method

Method onCreate (Fig. 8.15) inflates MainActivity's GUI and, if the app is running on a phone-sized device, displays a ContactListFragment. As you'll see in Section 8.6, you can configure a Fragment to be retained across configuration changes, such as when the user rotates the device. If the Activity is being restored after being shut down or recreated from a configuration change, savedInstanceState will not be null. In this case, we simply return (line 28) because the ContactListFragment already exists—on a phone, it would have been retained and on a tablet, it's part of the MainActivity's layout that was inflated in line 24.

```
19      // display ContactListFragment when MainActivity first loads
20      @Override
21      protected void onCreate(Bundle savedInstanceState)
22      {
23         super.onCreate(savedInstanceState);
24         setContentView(R.layout.activity_main);
25
26         // return if Activity is being restored, no need to recreate GUI
27         if (savedInstanceState != null)
28            return;
29
30         // check whether layout contains fragmentContainer (phone layout);
31         // ContactListFragment is always displayed
32         if (findViewById(R.id.fragmentContainer) != null)
33         {
34            // create ContactListFragment
35            contactListFragment = new ContactListFragment();
36
```

Fig. 8.15 | MainActivity overridden onCreate method. (Part I of 2.)

```
37              // add the fragment to the FrameLayout
38              FragmentTransaction transaction =
39                 getFragmentManager().beginTransaction();
40              transaction.add(R.id.fragmentContainer, contactListFragment);
41              transaction.commit(); // causes ContactListFragment to display
42          }
43      }
44
```

Fig. 8.15 | MainActivity overridden onCreate method. (Part 2 of 2.)

If the R.id.fragmentContainer exists in MainActivity's layout (line 32), then the app is running on a phone. In this case, line 35 creates the ContactListFragment, then lines 38–41 use a FragmentTransaction to add the ContactListFragment to the user interface. Lines 38–39 call FragmentManager's **beginTransaction** method to obtain a FragmentTransaction. Next, line 40 uses FragmentTransaction method **add** to specify that, when the FragmentTransaction completes, the ContactListFragment should be attached to the View with the ID specified as the first argument. Finally, line 41 uses FragmentTransaction method **commit** to finalize the transaction and display the ContactListFragment.

MainActivity Overridden *onResume* Method

Method onResume (Fig. 8.16) determines whether contactListFragment is null—if so, the app is running on a tablet, so lines 55–57 use the FragmentManager to get a reference to the existing ContactListFragment in MainActivity's layout.

```
45      // called when MainActivity resumes
46      @Override
47      protected void onResume()
48      {
49          super.onResume();
50
51          // if contactListFragment is null, activity running on tablet,
52          // so get reference from FragmentManager
53          if (contactListFragment == null)
54          {
55              contactListFragment =
56                 (ContactListFragment) getFragmentManager().findFragmentById(
57                     R.id.contactListFragment);
58          }
59      }
60
```

Fig. 8.16 | MainActivity overridden onResume method.

MainActivity Method *onContactSelected*

Method onContactSelected (Fig. 8.17) from the ContactListFragment.ContactListFragmentListener interface is called by the ContactListFragment to notify the MainActivity when the user selects a contact to display. If the app is running on a phone (line 65), line 66 calls method displayContact (Fig. 8.18), which replaces the ContactListFragment in the fragmentContainer (defined in Section 8.4.6) with the DetailsFragment that shows the contact's information. On a tablet, line 69 calls the FragmentManager's **popBackStack** method to *pop* (remove) the top Fragment on the back stack, then line 70 calls displayContact, which replaces the contents of the rightPaneContainer (defined in Section 8.4.6) with the DetailsFragment that shows the contact's information.

```
61    // display DetailsFragment for selected contact
62    @Override
63    public void onContactSelected(long rowID)
64    {
65       if (findViewById(R.id.fragmentContainer) != null) // phone
66          displayContact(rowID, R.id.fragmentContainer);
67       else // tablet
68       {
69          getFragmentManager().popBackStack(); // removes top of back stack
70          displayContact(rowID, R.id.rightPaneContainer);
71       }
72    }
73
```

Fig. 8.17 | MainActivity method onContactSelected.

MainActivity *Method* displayContact

Method displayContact (Fig. 8.18) creates the DetailsFragment that displays the selected contact and uses a FragmentTransaction to attach it to the GUI. You can pass arguments to a Fragment by placing them in a Bundle of key–value pairs—we do this to pass the selected contact's rowID so that the DetailsFragment knows which contact to get from the database. Line 80 creates the Bundle. Line 81 calls its **putLong** method to store a key–value pair containing the ROW_ID (a String) as the key and the rowID (a long) as the value. Line 82 passes the Bundle to the Fragment's **setArguments** method—the Fragment can then extract the information from the Bundle (as you'll see in Section 8.8). Lines 85–86 get a FragmentTransaction, then line 87 calls FragmentTransaction method **replace** to specify that, when the FragmentTransaction completes, the DetailsFragment should replace the contents of the View with the ID specified as the first argument. Line 88 calls FragmentTransaction method **addToBackStack** to *push* (add) the DetailsFragment onto the back stack. This allows the user to touch the back button to pop the Fragment from the back stack and allows MainActivity to programmatically pop the Fragment from the back stack.

```
74    // display a contact
75    private void displayContact(long rowID, int viewID)
76    {
77       DetailsFragment detailsFragment = new DetailsFragment();
78
79       // specify rowID as an argument to the DetailsFragment
80       Bundle arguments = new Bundle();
81       arguments.putLong(ROW_ID, rowID);
82       detailsFragment.setArguments(arguments);
```

Fig. 8.18 | MainActivity method displayContact. (Part 1 of 2.)

```
83
84        // use a FragmentTransaction to display the DetailsFragment
85        FragmentTransaction transaction =
86           getFragmentManager().beginTransaction();
87        transaction.replace(viewID, detailsFragment);
88        transaction.addToBackStack(null);
89        transaction.commit(); // causes DetailsFragment to display
90     }
91
```

Fig. 8.18 | MainActivity method displayContact. (Part 2 of 2.)

MainActivity *Method* onAddContact

Method onAddContact (Fig. 8.19) from the ContactListFragment.ContactListFragmentListener interface is called by the ContactListFragment to notify the MainActivity when the user chooses to add a new contact. If the layout contains the fragmentContainer, line 97 calls displayAddEditFragment (Fig. 8.20) to display the AddEditFragment in the fragmentContainer; otherwise, line 99 calls displayAddEditFragment to display the Fragment in the rightPaneContainer. The second argument is a Bundle. Specifying null indicates that a new contact is being added.

```
92        // display the AddEditFragment to add a new contact
93        @Override
94        public void onAddContact()
95        {
96           if (findViewById(R.id.fragmentContainer) != null) // phone
97              displayAddEditFragment(R.id.fragmentContainer, null);
98           else // tablet
99              displayAddEditFragment(R.id.rightPaneContainer, null);
100    }
101
```

Fig. 8.19 | MainActivity method onAddContact.

MainActivity *Method* displayAddEditFragment

Method displayAddEditFragment (Fig. 8.20) receives a View's resource ID specifying where to attach the AddEditFragment and a Bundle of key–value pairs. If the second argument is null, a new contact is being added; otherwise, the Bundle contains the data to display in the AddEditFragment for editing. Line 105 creates the AddEditFragment. If the Bundle argument is not null, line 108 uses it to set the Fragment's arguments. Lines 111–115 then create the FragmentTransaction, replace the contents of the View with the specified resource ID, add the Fragment to the back stack and commit the transaction.

```
102       // display fragment for adding a new or editing an existing contact
103       private void displayAddEditFragment(int viewID, Bundle arguments)
104       {
105          AddEditFragment addEditFragment = new AddEditFragment();
```

Fig. 8.20 | MainActivity Method displayAddEditFragment. (Part 1 of 2.)

```
106
107        if (arguments != null) // editing existing contact
108           addEditFragment.setArguments(arguments);
109
110        // use a FragmentTransaction to display the AddEditFragment
111        FragmentTransaction transaction =
112           getFragmentManager().beginTransaction();
113        transaction.replace(viewID, addEditFragment);
114        transaction.addToBackStack(null);
115        transaction.commit(); // causes AddEditFragment to display
116     }
117
```

Fig. 8.20 | MainActivity Method displayAddEditFragment. (Part 2 of 2.)

MainActivity *Method* onContactDeleted

Method onContactDeleted (Fig. 8.21) from the DetailsFragment.DetailsFragmentListener interface is called by the DetailsFragment to notify the MainActivity when the user deletes a contact. In this case, line 122 pops the DetailsFragment from the back stack. If the app is running on a tablet, line 125 calls the contactListFragment's updateContactList method to reload the contacts.

```
118        // return to contact list when displayed contact deleted
119        @Override
120        public void onContactDeleted()
121        {
122           getFragmentManager().popBackStack(); // removes top of back stack
123
124           if (findViewById(R.id.fragmentContainer) == null) // tablet
125              contactListFragment.updateContactList();
126        }
127
```

Fig. 8.21 | MainActivity method onContactDeleted.

MainActivity *Method* onEditContact

Method onEditContact (Fig. 8.22) from the DetailsFragment.DetailsFragmentListener interface is called by the DetailsFragment to notify the MainActivity when the user touches the menu item to edit a contact. The DetailsFragment passes a Bundle containing the contact's data so that it can be displayed in the AddEditFragment's EditTexts for editing. If the layout contains the fragmentContainer, line 133 calls displayAddEditFragment to display the AddEditFragment in the fragmentContainer; otherwise, line 135 calls displayAddEditFragment to display the AddEditFragment in the rightPaneContainer.

```
128        // display the AddEditFragment to edit an existing contact
129        @Override
130        public void onEditContact(Bundle arguments)
131        {
```

Fig. 8.22 | MainActivity method onEditContact. (Part 1 of 2.)

```
132        if (findViewById(R.id.fragmentContainer) != null) // phone
133            displayAddEditFragment(R.id.fragmentContainer, arguments);
134        else // tablet
135            displayAddEditFragment(R.id.rightPaneContainer, arguments);
136    }
137
```

Fig. 8.22 | MainActivity method onEditContact. (Part 2 of 2.)

MainActivity Method onAddEditCompleted

Method onAddEditCompleted (Fig. 8.23) from the AddEditFragment.AddEditFragment-Listener interface is called by the AddEditFragment to notify the MainActivity when the user saves a new contact or saves changes to an existing one. Line 142 pops the AddEditFragment from the back stack. If the app is running on a tablet (line 144), line 146 pops the back stack again to remove the DetailsFragment (if there is one). Then line 147 updates the contact list in the ContactListFragment and line 150 displays the new or updated contact's details in the rightPaneContainer.

```
138        // update GUI after new contact or updated contact saved
139        @Override
140        public void onAddEditCompleted(long rowID)
141        {
142            getFragmentManager().popBackStack(); // removes top of back stack
143
144            if (findViewById(R.id.fragmentContainer) == null) // tablet
145            {
146                getFragmentManager().popBackStack(); // removes top of back stack
147                contactListFragment.updateContactList(); // refresh contacts
148
149                // on tablet, display contact that was just added or edited
150                displayContact(rowID, R.id.rightPaneContainer);
151            }
152        }
153    }
```

Fig. 8.23 | MainActivity method onAddEditCompleted.

8.6 ContactListFragment Class

Class ContactListFragment (Figs. 8.24–8.33) extends ListFragment to display the contact list in a ListView and provides a menu item for adding a new contact.

ContactListFragment package Statement and import Statements

Figure 8.24 lists ContactListFragment's package statement and import statements. We've highlighted the imports for the new classes and interfaces.

```
 1   // ContactListFragment.java
 2   // Displays the list of contact names
 3   package com.deitel.addressbook;
 4
 5   import android.app.Activity;
 6   import android.app.ListFragment;
 7   import android.database.Cursor;
 8   import android.os.AsyncTask;
 9   import android.os.Bundle;
10   import android.view.Menu;
11   import android.view.MenuInflater;
12   import android.view.MenuItem;
13   import android.view.View;
14   import android.widget.AdapterView;
15   import android.widget.AdapterView.OnItemClickListener;
16   import android.widget.CursorAdapter;
17   import android.widget.ListView;
18   import android.widget.SimpleCursorAdapter;
19
```

Fig. 8.24 | ContactListFragment package statement and import statements.

ContactListFragmentListener *Interface and* ContactListFragment *Instance Variables*

Figure 8.25 begins class ContactListFragment's declaration. Lines 23–30 declare the nested interface ContactListFragmentListener, which contains the callback methods that MainActivity implements to be notified when the user selects a contact (line 26) and when the user touches the menu item to add a new contact (line 29). Line 32 declares instance variable listener which will refer to the object (MainActivity) that implements the interface. Instance variable contactListView (line 34) will refer to the ContactListFragment's built-in ListView, so we can interact with it programmatically. Instance variable contactAdapter will refer to the CursorAdapter that populates the AddressBook's ListView.

```
20   public class ContactListFragment extends ListFragment
21   {
22      // callback methods implemented by MainActivity
23      public interface ContactListFragmentListener
24      {
25         // called when user selects a contact
26         public void onContactSelected(long rowID);
27
28         // called when user decides to add a contact
29         public void onAddContact();
30      }
31
32      private ContactListFragmentListener listener;
33
```

Fig. 8.25 | ContactListFragmentListener interface and ContactListFragment instance variables. (Part 1 of 2.)

```
34      private ListView contactListView; // the ListActivity's ListView
35      private CursorAdapter contactAdapter; // adapter for ListView
36
```

Fig. 8.25 | ContactListFragmentListener interface and ContactListFragment instance variables. (Part 2 of 2.)

ContactListFragment *Overridden Methods* onAttach *and* onDetach

Class ContactListFragment overrides Fragment lifecycle methods onAttach and onDetach (Fig. 8.26) to set instance variable listener. In this app, listener refers to the host Activity (line 42) when the ContactListFragment is attached and is set to null (line 50) when the ContactListFragment is detached.

```
37      // set ContactListFragmentListener when fragment attached
38      @Override
39      public void onAttach(Activity activity)
40      {
41          super.onAttach(activity);
42          listener = (ContactListFragmentListener) activity;
43      }
44
45      // remove ContactListFragmentListener when Fragment detached
46      @Override
47      public void onDetach()
48      {
49          super.onDetach();
50          listener = null;
51      }
52
```

Fig. 8.26 | ContactListFragment overridden methods onAttach and onDetach.

ContactListFragment *Overridden Method* onViewCreated

Recall that class ListFragment already contains a ListView, so we don't need to inflate the GUI as in previous app's Fragments. However, class ContactListFragment has tasks that should be performed after its default layout is inflated. For this reason, ContactListFragment overrides Fragment lifecycle method **onViewCreated** (Fig. 8.27), which is called after onCreateView.

```
53      // called after View is created
54      @Override
55      public void onViewCreated(View view, Bundle savedInstanceState)
56      {
57          super.onViewCreated(view, savedInstanceState);
58          setRetainInstance(true); // save fragment across config changes
59          setHasOptionsMenu(true); // this fragment has menu items to display
60
```

Fig. 8.27 | ContactListFragment overridden method onViewCreated. (Part 1 of 2.)

```
61          // set text to display when there are no contacts
62          setEmptyText(getResources().getString(R.string.no_contacts));
63
64          // get ListView reference and configure ListView
65          contactListView = getListView();
66          contactListView.setOnItemClickListener(viewContactListener);
67          contactListView.setChoiceMode(ListView.CHOICE_MODE_SINGLE);
68
69          // map each contact's name to a TextView in the ListView layout
70          String[] from = new String[] { "name" };
71          int[] to = new int[] { android.R.id.text1 };
72          contactAdapter = new SimpleCursorAdapter(getActivity(),
73             android.R.layout.simple_list_item_1, null, from, to, 0);
74          setListAdapter(contactAdapter); // set adapter that supplies data
75       }
76
```

Fig. 8.27 | ContactListFragment overridden method onViewCreated. (Part 2 of 2.)

Line 58 calls Fragment method **setRetainInstance** with the argument true to indicate that the ContactListFragment should be retained rather than recreated when the host Activity is re-created on a configuration change (e.g., when the user rotates the device). Line 59 indicates that the ContactListFragment has menu items that should be displayed on the Activity's action bar (or in its options menu). ListFragment method **setEmptyText** (line 62) specifies the text to display ("No Contacts") when there are no items in the ListView's adapter.

Line 65 uses the inherited ListActivity method **getListView** to obtain a reference to the built-in ListView. Line 66 sets the ListView's OnItemClickListener to viewContactListener (Fig. 8.28), which responds when the user touches a contact in the ListView. Line 67 calls ListView method **setChoiceMode** to indicate that only one item can be selected at a time.

Configuring the CursorAdapter That Binds Database Data to the ListView

To display the Cursor's results in a ListView we create a new CursorAdapter object (lines 70–73) which exposes the Cursor's data in a manner that can be used by a ListView. **SimpleCursorAdapter** is a subclass of CursorAdapter that's designed to simplify mapping Cursor columns directly to TextViews or ImagesViews defined in your XML layouts. To create a SimpleCursorAdapter, you first define arrays containing the column names to map to GUI components and the resource IDs of the GUI components that will display the data from the named columns. Line 70 creates a String array indicating that only the "name" column will be displayed, and line 71 creates a parallel int array containing corresponding GUI components' resource IDs. Chapter 4 showed that you can create your own layout resources for ListView items. In this app we used a predefined Android layout resource named android.R.layout.simple_list_item_1—a layout that contains one TextView with the ID android.R.id.text1. Lines 72–73 create the SimpleCursorAdapter. Its constructor receives:

- the Context in which the ListView is running (i.e., MainActivity).
- the resource ID of the layout that's used to display each item in the ListView.

- the Cursor that provides access to the data—we supply null for this argument because we'll specify the Cursor later.
- the String array containing the column names to display.
- the int array containing the corresponding GUI resource IDs.
- the last argument is typically 0.

Line 74 uses inherited ListActivity method **setListAdapter** to bind the ListView to the CursorAdapter, so that the ListView can display the data.

viewContactListener *That Processes* ListView *Item Selection Events*

The viewContactListener (Fig. 8.28) notifies MainActivity when the user touches a contact to display. Line 84 passes the argument id—the row ID of the selected contact—to the listener's onContactSelected method (Fig. 8.17).

```
77      // responds to the user touching a contact's name in the ListView
78      OnItemClickListener viewContactListener = new OnItemClickListener()
79      {
80         @Override
81         public void onItemClick(AdapterView<?> parent, View view,
82            int position, long id)
83         {
84            listener.onContactSelected(id); // pass selection to MainActivity
85         }
86      }; // end viewContactListener
87
```

Fig. 8.28 | viewContactListener that processes ListView item selection events.

ContactListFragment *Overridden Method* onResume

Fragment lifecycle method onResume (Fig. 8.29) creates and executes an AsyncTask (line 93) of type GetContactsTask (defined in Fig. 8.30) that gets the complete list of contacts from the database and sets the contactAdapter's Cursor for populating the ContactList-Fragment's ListView. AsyncTask method **execute** performs the task in a separate thread. Method execute's argument in this case indicates that the task does not receive any arguments—this method can receive a variable number of arguments that are, in turn, passed as arguments to the task's doInBackground method. Every time line 93 executes, it creates a new GetContactsTask object—this is required because each AsyncTask can be executed *only once*.

```
88      // when fragment resumes, use a GetContactsTask to load contacts
89      @Override
90      public void onResume()
91      {
92         super.onResume();
93         new GetContactsTask().execute((Object[]) null);
94      }
95
```

Fig. 8.29 | ContactListFragment overridden method onResume.

GetContactsTask *Subclass of* AsyncTask

Nested class GetContactsTask (Fig. 8.30) extends class AsyncTask. The class defines how to interact with the DatabaseConnector (Section 8.9) to get the names of all the contacts and return the results to this Activity's GUI thread for display in the ListView. AsyncTask is a generic type that requires three type parameters:

- The variable-length parameter-list type for AsyncTask's **doInBackground** method (lines 103–108)—When you call the task's execute method, doInBackground performs the task in a separate thread. We specify Object as the type parameter and pass null as the argument to the AsyncTask's execute method, because GetContactsTask does not require additional data to perform its task.

- The variable-length parameter-list type for the AsyncTask's **onProgressUpdate** method—This method executes in the GUI thread and is used to receive *intermediate updates* of the specified type from a long-running task. We don't use this feature in this example, so we specify type Object here and ignore this type parameter.

- The type of the task's result, which is passed to the AsyncTask's **onPostExecute** method (lines 111–116)—This method executes in the GUI thread and enables the ContactListFragment to use the AsyncTask's results.

A key benefit of using an AsyncTask is that it handles the details of creating threads and executing its methods on the appropriate threads for you, so that you do not have to interact with the threading mechanism directly.

```java
96    // performs database query outside GUI thread
97    private class GetContactsTask extends AsyncTask<Object, Object, Cursor>
98    {
99       DatabaseConnector databaseConnector =
100         new DatabaseConnector(getActivity());
101
102      // open database and return Cursor for all contacts
103      @Override
104      protected Cursor doInBackground(Object... params)
105      {
106         databaseConnector.open();
107         return databaseConnector.getAllContacts();
108      }
109
110      // use the Cursor returned from the doInBackground method
111      @Override
112      protected void onPostExecute(Cursor result)
113      {
114         contactAdapter.changeCursor(result); // set the adapter's Cursor
115         databaseConnector.close();
116      }
117   } // end class GetContactsTask
118
```

Fig. 8.30 | GetContactsTask subclass of AsyncTask.

Lines 99–100 create a new object of our utility class DatabaseConnector, passing the Context (the ContactListFragment's host Activity) as an argument to the class's constructor. Method doInBackground uses databaseConnector to open the database connection and get all the contacts from the database. The Cursor returned by getAllContacts is passed to method onPostExecute, which receives the Cursor containing the results and passes it to the contactAdapter's changeCursor method. This enables the ContactList-Fragment's ListView to populate itself with the contacts' names.

ContactListFragment *Overridden Method* onStop

Fragment lifecycle method **onStop** (Fig. 8.31) is called after onPause when the Fragment is no longer visible to the user. In this case, the Cursor that allows us to populate the List-View is not needed, so line 123 calls CursorAdapter method **getCursor** to get the current Cursor from the contactAdapter. Line 124 calls CursorAdapter method **changeCursor** with the argument null to remove the Cursor from the CursorAdapter. Then line 127 calls Cursor method **close** to release resources used by the Cursor.

```
119    // when fragment stops, close Cursor and remove from contactAdapter
120    @Override
121    public void onStop()
122    {
123       Cursor cursor = contactAdapter.getCursor(); // get current Cursor
124       contactAdapter.changeCursor(null); // adapter now has no Cursor
125
126       if (cursor != null)
127          cursor.close(); // release the Cursor's resources
128
129       super.onStop();
130    }
131
```

Fig. 8.31 | ContactListFragment overridden method onStop.

ContactListFragment *Overridden Methods* onCreateOptionsMenu *and* onOptionsItemSelected

Method onCreateOptionsMenu (Fig. 8.32, lines 133–138) uses its MenuInflater argument to create the menu from fragment_contact_list_menu.xml, which contains the definition of the add (⊕) menu item. If the user touches that MenuItem, method onOptionsItemSelected (lines 141–152) calls listener's onAddContact method to notify the MainActivity that the user wants to add a new contact. MainActivity then displays the AddEditFragment (Section 8.7).

```
132    // display this fragment's menu items
133    @Override
134    public void onCreateOptionsMenu(Menu menu, MenuInflater inflater)
135    {
```

Fig. 8.32 | ContactListFragment overridden methods onCreateOptionsMenu and onOptionsItemSelected. (Part 1 of 2.)

```
136          super.onCreateOptionsMenu(menu, inflater);
137          inflater.inflate(R.menu.fragment_contact_list_menu, menu);
138      }
139
140      // handle choice from options menu
141      @Override
142      public boolean onOptionsItemSelected(MenuItem item)
143      {
144          switch (item.getItemId())
145          {
146            case R.id.action_add:
147                listener.onAddContact();
148                return true;
149          }
150
151          return super.onOptionsItemSelected(item); // call super's method
152      }
153
```

Fig. 8.32 | ContactListFragment overridden methods onCreateOptionsMenu and onOptionsItemSelected. (Part 2 of 2.)

ContactListFragment *Method* updateContactList

Method updateContactList (Fig. 8.33) creates and executes a GetContactsTask to update the contact list.

```
154      // update data set
155      public void updateContactList()
156      {
157          new GetContactsTask().execute((Object[]) null);
158      }
159  } // end class ContactListFragment
```

Fig. 8.33 | ContactListFragment method updateContactList.

8.7 AddEditFragment Class

The AddEditFragment (Figs. 8.34–8.40) provides the interface for adding new contacts or editing existing ones.

AddEditFragment package *Statement and* import *Statements*

Figure 8.34 lists the package statement and import statements for class AddEditFragment. No new classes are used in this Fragment.

```
1    // AddEditFragment.java
2    // Allows user to add a new contact or edit an existing one
3    package com.deitel.addressbook;
4
```

Fig. 8.34 | AddEditFragment package statement and import statements. (Part 1 of 2.)

```
5   import android.app.Activity;
6   import android.app.AlertDialog;
7   import android.app.Dialog;
8   import android.app.DialogFragment;
9   import android.app.Fragment;
10  import android.content.Context;
11  import android.os.AsyncTask;
12  import android.os.Bundle;
13  import android.view.LayoutInflater;
14  import android.view.View;
15  import android.view.View.OnClickListener;
16  import android.view.ViewGroup;
17  import android.view.inputmethod.InputMethodManager;
18  import android.widget.Button;
19  import android.widget.EditText;
20
21  public class AddEditFragment extends Fragment
22  {
```

Fig. 8.34 | AddEditFragment package statement and import statements. (Part 2 of 2.)

AddEditFragmentListener *Interface*

Figure 8.35 declares the nested interface AddEditFragmentListener containing the callback method onAddEditCompleted that MainActivity implements to be notified when the user saves a new contact or saves changes to an existing one.

```
23      // callback method implemented by MainActivity
24      public interface AddEditFragmentListener
25      {
26          // called after edit completed so contact can be redisplayed
27          public void onAddEditCompleted(long rowID);
28      }
29
```

Fig. 8.35 | AddEditFragmentListener interface.

AddEditFragment *Instance Variables*

Figure 8.36 lists the class's instance variables:

- Variable listener refers to the AddEditFragmentListener that's notified when the user clicks the **Save Contact** button.

- Variable rowID represents the current contact being manipulated if this Fragment was displayed to allow the user to edit an existing contact.

- Variable contactInfoBundle will be null if a new contact is being added or will refer to a Bundle of contact information if an existing contact is being edited.

- The instance variables at lines 36–42 will refer to the Fragment's EditTexts.

```
30     private AddEditFragmentListener listener;
31
32     private long rowID; // database row ID of the contact
33     private Bundle contactInfoBundle; // arguments for editing a contact
34
35     // EditTexts for contact information
36     private EditText nameEditText;
37     private EditText phoneEditText;
38     private EditText emailEditText;
39     private EditText streetEditText;
40     private EditText cityEditText;
41     private EditText stateEditText;
42     private EditText zipEditText;
43
```

Fig. 8.36 | AddEditFragment instance variables.

AddEditFragment *Overridden Methods* onAttach *and* onDetach

Class AddEditFragment overrides Fragment lifecycle methods onAttach and onDetach (Fig. 8.37) to set instance variable listener to refer to the host Activity (line 49) when the AddEditFragment is attached and to set listener to null (line 57) when the AddEdit-Fragment is detached.

```
44     // set AddEditFragmentListener when Fragment attached
45     @Override
46     public void onAttach(Activity activity)
47     {
48        super.onAttach(activity);
49        listener = (AddEditFragmentListener) activity;
50     }
51
52     // remove AddEditFragmentListener when Fragment detached
53     @Override
54     public void onDetach()
55     {
56        super.onDetach();
57        listener = null;
58     }
59
```

Fig. 8.37 | AddEditFragment overridden methods onAttach and onDetach.

AddEditFragment *Overridden Method* onCreateView

In method onCreateView (Fig. 8.38), lines 70–78 inflate the GUI and get the Fragment's EditTexts. Next, we use Fragment method getArguments to get the Bundle of arguments (if any). When we launch the AddEditFragment from the MainActivity, we don't pass a Bundle, because the user is adding a new contact's information. In this case, getArguments will return null. If it returns a Bundle (line 82), then the AddEditFragment was launched from the DetailsFragment and the user chose to edit an existing contact. Lines 84–91 read the arguments out of the Bundle by calling methods getLong (line 84) and get-

String, and the String data is displayed in the EditTexts for editing. Lines 95–97 register a listener (Fig. 8.39) for the **Save Contact** Button.

```
60      // called when Fragment's view needs to be created
61      @Override
62      public View onCreateView(LayoutInflater inflater, ViewGroup container,
63          Bundle savedInstanceState)
64      {
65          super.onCreateView(inflater, container, savedInstanceState);
66          setRetainInstance(true); // save fragment across config changes
67          setHasOptionsMenu(true); // fragment has menu items to display
68
69          // inflate GUI and get references to EditTexts
70          View view =
71              inflater.inflate(R.layout.fragment_add_edit, container, false);
72          nameEditText = (EditText) view.findViewById(R.id.nameEditText);
73          phoneEditText = (EditText) view.findViewById(R.id.phoneEditText);
74          emailEditText = (EditText) view.findViewById(R.id.emailEditText);
75          streetEditText = (EditText) view.findViewById(R.id.streetEditText);
76          cityEditText = (EditText) view.findViewById(R.id.cityEditText);
77          stateEditText = (EditText) view.findViewById(R.id.stateEditText);
78          zipEditText = (EditText) view.findViewById(R.id.zipEditText);
79
80          contactInfoBundle = getArguments(); // null if creating new contact
81
82          if (contactInfoBundle != null)
83          {
84              rowID = contactInfoBundle.getLong(MainActivity.ROW_ID);
85              nameEditText.setText(contactInfoBundle.getString("name"));
86              phoneEditText.setText(contactInfoBundle.getString("phone"));
87              emailEditText.setText(contactInfoBundle.getString("email"));
88              streetEditText.setText(contactInfoBundle.getString("street"));
89              cityEditText.setText(contactInfoBundle.getString("city"));
90              stateEditText.setText(contactInfoBundle.getString("state"));
91              zipEditText.setText(contactInfoBundle.getString("zip"));
92          }
93
94          // set Save Contact Button's event listener
95          Button saveContactButton =
96              (Button) view.findViewById(R.id.saveContactButton);
97          saveContactButton.setOnClickListener(saveContactButtonClicked);
98          return view;
99      }
100
```

Fig. 8.38 | AddEditFragment overridden method onCreateView.

OnClickListener *to Process* Save Contact Button *Events*

When the user touches the **Save Contact** Button, the saveContactButtonClicked listener (Fig. 8.39) executes. To save a contact, the user must enter at least the contact's name. Method onClick ensures that the length of the name is greater than 0 characters (line 107) and, if so, creates and executes an AsyncTask (to perform the save operation). Method doInBackground (lines 113–118) calls saveContact (Fig. 8.40) to save the contact into the database. Method onPostExecute (lines 120–131) programmatically hides the keyboard (lines 124–128), then notifies MainActivity that a contact was saved (line 130). If the nameEditText is empty, lines 139–153 display a DialogFragment telling the user that a contact name must be provided to save the contact.

```
101    // responds to event generated when user saves a contact
102    OnClickListener saveContactButtonClicked = new OnClickListener()
103    {
104       @Override
105       public void onClick(View v)
106       {
107          if (nameEditText.getText().toString().trim().length() != 0)
108          {
109             // AsyncTask to save contact, then notify listener
110             AsyncTask<Object, Object, Object> saveContactTask =
111                new AsyncTask<Object, Object, Object>()
112                {
113                   @Override
114                   protected Object doInBackground(Object... params)
115                   {
116                      saveContact(); // save contact to the database
117                      return null;
118                   }
119
120                   @Override
121                   protected void onPostExecute(Object result)
122                   {
123                      // hide soft keyboard
124                      InputMethodManager imm = (InputMethodManager)
125                         getActivity().getSystemService(
126                            Context.INPUT_METHOD_SERVICE);
127                      imm.hideSoftInputFromWindow(
128                         getView().getWindowToken(), 0);
129
130                      listener.onAddEditCompleted(rowID);
131                   }
132                }; // end AsyncTask
133
134             // save the contact to the database using a separate thread
135             saveContactTask.execute((Object[]) null);
136          }
137          else // required contact name is blank, so display error dialog
138          {
139             DialogFragment errorSaving =
140                new DialogFragment()
141                {
142                   @Override
143                   public Dialog onCreateDialog(Bundle savedInstanceState)
144                   {
145                      AlertDialog.Builder builder =
146                         new AlertDialog.Builder(getActivity());
147                      builder.setMessage(R.string.error_message);
```

Fig. 8.39 | OnClickListener to process **Save Contact** Button events. (Part 1 of 2.)

```
148                    builder.setPositiveButton(R.string.ok, null);
149                    return builder.create();
150                 }
151              };
152
153           errorSaving.show(getFragmentManager(), "error saving contact");
154        }
155     } // end method onClick
156  }; // end OnClickListener saveContactButtonClicked
157
```

Fig. 8.39 | OnClickListener to process **Save Contact** Button events. (Part 2 of 2.)

AddEditFragment Method saveContact

The saveContact method (Fig. 8.40) saves the information in this Fragment's EditTexts. First, lines 162–163 create the DatabaseConnector object, then we check whether the contactInfoBundle is null. If so, this is a new contact and lines 168–175 get the Strings from the EditTexts and pass them to the DatabaseConnector object's insertContact method to create the new contact. If the Bundle is not null, an existing contact is being updated. In this case, we get the Strings from the EditTexts and pass them to the DatabaseConnector object's updateContact method, using the existing rowID to indicate which record to update. DatabaseConnector methods insertContact and updateContact each handle opening and closing the database.

```
158  // saves contact information to the database
159  private void saveContact()
160  {
161     // get DatabaseConnector to interact with the SQLite database
162     DatabaseConnector databaseConnector =
163        new DatabaseConnector(getActivity());
164
165     if (contactInfoBundle == null)
166     {
167        // insert the contact information into the database
168        rowID = databaseConnector.insertContact(
169           nameEditText.getText().toString(),
170           phoneEditText.getText().toString(),
171           emailEditText.getText().toString(),
172           streetEditText.getText().toString(),
173           cityEditText.getText().toString(),
174           stateEditText.getText().toString(),
175           zipEditText.getText().toString());
176     }
177     else
178     {
179        databaseConnector.updateContact(rowID,
180           nameEditText.getText().toString(),
181           phoneEditText.getText().toString(),
182           emailEditText.getText().toString(),
```

Fig. 8.40 | AddEditFragment method saveContact. (Part 1 of 2.)

```
183              streetEditText.getText().toString(),
184              cityEditText.getText().toString(),
185              stateEditText.getText().toString(),
186              zipEditText.getText().toString());
187        }
188     } // end method saveContact
189  } // end class AddEditFragment
```

Fig. 8.40 | AddEditFragment method saveContact. (Part 2 of 2.)

8.8 DetailsFragment Class

The DetailsFragment (Figs. 8.41–8.50) displays one contact's information and provides menu items that enable the user to edit or delete that contact.

DetailsFragment package *Statement and* **import** *Statements*

Figure 8.41 lists the package statement, the import statements and the beginning of class ContactListFragment's declaration. There are no new classes and interfaces used in this class.

```
1   // DetailsFragment.java
2   // Displays one contact's details
3   package com.deitel.addressbook;
4
5   import android.app.Activity;
6   import android.app.AlertDialog;
7   import android.app.Dialog;
8   import android.app.DialogFragment;
9   import android.app.Fragment;
10  import android.content.DialogInterface;
11  import android.database.Cursor;
12  import android.os.AsyncTask;
13  import android.os.Bundle;
14  import android.view.LayoutInflater;
15  import android.view.Menu;
16  import android.view.MenuInflater;
17  import android.view.MenuItem;
18  import android.view.View;
19  import android.view.ViewGroup;
20  import android.widget.TextView;
21
22  public class DetailsFragment extends Fragment
23  {
```

Fig. 8.41 | DetailsFragment package statement and import statements.

DetailsFragmentListener *Interface*

Figure 8.42 declares the nested interface DetailsFragmentListener containing the callback methods that MainActivity implements to be notified when the user deletes a contact (line 28) and when the user touches the edit menu item to edit a contact (line 31).

```
24      // callback methods implemented by MainActivity
25      public interface DetailsFragmentListener
26      {
27         // called when a contact is deleted
28         public void onContactDeleted();
29
30         // called to pass Bundle of contact's info for editing
31         public void onEditContact(Bundle arguments);
32      }
33
```

Fig. 8.42 | DetailsFragmentListener interface.

DetailsFragment *Instance Variables*

Figure 8.43 shows the class's instance variables. Line 34 declares variable listener which will refer to the object (MainActivity) that implements the DetailsFragmentListener interface. Variable rowID represents the current contact's unique row ID in the database. The TextView instance variables (lines 37–43) are used to display the contact's data on the screen.

```
34      private DetailsFragmentListener listener;
35
36      private long rowID = -1; // selected contact's rowID
37      private TextView nameTextView; // displays contact's name
38      private TextView phoneTextView; // displays contact's phone
39      private TextView emailTextView; // displays contact's email
40      private TextView streetTextView; // displays contact's street
41      private TextView cityTextView; // displays contact's city
42      private TextView stateTextView; // displays contact's state
43      private TextView zipTextView; // displays contact's zip
44
```

Fig. 8.43 | DetailsFragment instance variables.

DetailsFragment *Overridden Methods* **onAttach** *and* **onDetach**

Class DetailsFragment overrides Fragment lifecycle methods onAttach and onDetach (Fig. 8.44) to set instance variable listener when the DetailsFragment is attached and detached, respectively.

```
45      // set DetailsFragmentListener when fragment attached
46      @Override
47      public void onAttach(Activity activity)
48      {
49         super.onAttach(activity);
50         listener = (DetailsFragmentListener) activity;
51      }
52
```

Fig. 8.44 | DetailsFragment overridden methods onAttach and onDetach. (Part 1 of 2.)

```
53        // remove DetailsFragmentListener when fragment detached
54        @Override
55        public void onDetach()
56        {
57            super.onDetach();
58            listener = null;
59        }
60
```

Fig. 8.44 | `DetailsFragment` overridden methods `onAttach` and `onDetach`. (Part 2 of 2.)

DetailsFragment Overridden Method onCreateView

The onCreateView method (Fig. 8.45) obtains the selected contact's row ID (lines 70–79). If the Fragment is being restored, we load the rowID from the savedInstanceState bundle; otherwise, we get it from the Fragment's Bundle of arguments. Lines 82–93 inflate the GUI and get references to the TextViews.

```
61        // called when DetailsFragmentListener's view needs to be created
62        @Override
63        public View onCreateView(LayoutInflater inflater, ViewGroup container,
64            Bundle savedInstanceState)
65        {
66            super.onCreateView(inflater, container, savedInstanceState);
67            setRetainInstance(true); // save fragment across config changes
68
69            // if DetailsFragment is being restored, get saved row ID
70            if (savedInstanceState != null)
71                rowID = savedInstanceState.getLong(MainActivity.ROW_ID);
72            else
73            {
74                // get Bundle of arguments then extract the contact's row ID
75                Bundle arguments = getArguments();
76
77                if (arguments != null)
78                    rowID = arguments.getLong(MainActivity.ROW_ID);
79            }
80
81            // inflate DetailsFragment's layout
82            View view =
83                inflater.inflate(R.layout.fragment_details, container, false);
84            setHasOptionsMenu(true); // this fragment has menu items to display
85
86            // get the EditTexts
87            nameTextView = (TextView) view.findViewById(R.id.nameTextView);
88            phoneTextView = (TextView) view.findViewById(R.id.phoneTextView);
89            emailTextView = (TextView) view.findViewById(R.id.emailTextView);
90            streetTextView = (TextView) view.findViewById(R.id.streetTextView);
91            cityTextView = (TextView) view.findViewById(R.id.cityTextView);
92            stateTextView = (TextView) view.findViewById(R.id.stateTextView);
93            zipTextView = (TextView) view.findViewById(R.id.zipTextView);
```

Fig. 8.45 | `DetailsFragment` overridden method `onCreateView`. (Part 1 of 2.)

```
94          return view;
95      }
96
```

Fig. 8.45 | DetailsFragment overridden method onCreateView. (Part 2 of 2.)

DetailsFragment Overridden Method onResume

Fragment lifecycle method onResume (Fig. 8.46) creates and executes an AsyncTask (line 102) of type LoadContactTask (defined in Fig. 8.49) that gets the specified contact from the database and displays its data. Method execute's argument in this case is the rowID of the contact to load. Every time line 102 executes, it creates a new LoadContactTask object—again, this is required because each AsyncTask can be executed *only once*.

```
97       // called when the DetailsFragment resumes
98       @Override
99       public void onResume()
100      {
101          super.onResume();
102          new LoadContactTask().execute(rowID); // load contact at rowID
103      }
104
```

Fig. 8.46 | DetailsFragment overridden method onResume.

DetailsFragment Overridden Method onSaveInstanceState

Fragment method onSaveInstanceState (Fig. 8.47) saves the selected contact's rowID when the configuration of the device changes during the app's execution—for example, when the user rotates the device or slides out a keyboard on a device with a hard keyboard. The state of the GUI components is saved for you automatically, but any other items that you wish to restore during a configuration change should be stored in the Bundle that onSaveInstanceState receives.

```
105      // save currently displayed contact's row ID
106      @Override
107      public void onSaveInstanceState(Bundle outState)
108      {
109          super.onSaveInstanceState(outState);
110          outState.putLong(MainActivity.ROW_ID, rowID);
111      }
112
```

Fig. 8.47 | DetailsFragment overridden method onSaveInstanceState.

DetailsFragment Overridden Methods onCreateOptionsMenu and onOptionsItemSelected

The DetailsFragment's menu provides options for editing the current contact and for deleting it. Method onCreateOptionsMenu (Fig. 8.48, lines 114–119) inflates the menu resource file fragment_details_menu.xml. Method onOptionsItemSelected (lines 122–

146) uses the selected `MenuItem`'s resource ID to determine which one was selected. If the user selected the menu item with ID `R.id.action_edit`, lines 129–137 create a `Bundle` containing the contact's data, then line 138 passes the `Bundle` to the `DetailsFragment-Listener` for use in the `AddEditFragment`. If the user selected the menu item with ID `R.id.action_delete`, line 141 calls method `deleteContact` (Fig. 8.50).

```
113   // display this fragment's menu items
114   @Override
115   public void onCreateOptionsMenu(Menu menu, MenuInflater inflater)
116   {
117      super.onCreateOptionsMenu(menu, inflater);
118      inflater.inflate(R.menu.fragment_details_menu, menu);
119   }
120
121   // handle menu item selections
122   @Override
123   public boolean onOptionsItemSelected(MenuItem item)
124   {
125      switch (item.getItemId())
126      {
127         case R.id.action_edit:
128            // create Bundle containing contact data to edit
129            Bundle arguments = new Bundle();
130            arguments.putLong(MainActivity.ROW_ID, rowID);
131            arguments.putCharSequence("name", nameTextView.getText());
132            arguments.putCharSequence("phone", phoneTextView.getText());
133            arguments.putCharSequence("email", emailTextView.getText());
134            arguments.putCharSequence("street", streetTextView.getText());
135            arguments.putCharSequence("city", cityTextView.getText());
136            arguments.putCharSequence("state", stateTextView.getText());
137            arguments.putCharSequence("zip", zipTextView.getText());
138            listener.onEditContact(arguments); // pass Bundle to listener
139            return true;
140         case R.id.action_delete:
141            deleteContact();
142            return true;
143      }
144
145      return super.onOptionsItemSelected(item);
146   }
147
```

Fig. 8.48 | `DetailsFragment` overridden methods `onCreateOptionsMenu` and `onOptionsItemSelected`.

LoadContactTask Subclass of AsyncTask

Nested class `LoadContactTask` (Fig. 8.49) extends class `AsyncTask` and defines how to interact with the database to get one contact's information for display. In this case the three generic type parameters are:

- `Long` for the variable-length argument list passed to `AsyncTask`'s `doInBackground` method. This will contain the row ID needed to locate one contact.

- Object for the variable-length argument list passed to AsyncTask's onProgress-Update method, which we don't use in this example.

- Cursor for the type of the task's result, which is passed to the AsyncTask's on-PostExecute method.

```
148    // performs database query outside GUI thread
149    private class LoadContactTask extends AsyncTask<Long, Object, Cursor>
150    {
151       DatabaseConnector databaseConnector =
152          new DatabaseConnector(getActivity());
153
154       // open database & get Cursor representing specified contact's data
155       @Override
156       protected Cursor doInBackground(Long... params)
157       {
158          databaseConnector.open();
159          return databaseConnector.getOneContact(params[0]);
160       }
161
162       // use the Cursor returned from the doInBackground method
163       @Override
164       protected void onPostExecute(Cursor result)
165       {
166          super.onPostExecute(result);
167          result.moveToFirst(); // move to the first item
168
169          // get the column index for each data item
170          int nameIndex = result.getColumnIndex("name");
171          int phoneIndex = result.getColumnIndex("phone");
172          int emailIndex = result.getColumnIndex("email");
173          int streetIndex = result.getColumnIndex("street");
174          int cityIndex = result.getColumnIndex("city");
175          int stateIndex = result.getColumnIndex("state");
176          int zipIndex = result.getColumnIndex("zip");
177
178          // fill TextViews with the retrieved data
179          nameTextView.setText(result.getString(nameIndex));
180          phoneTextView.setText(result.getString(phoneIndex));
181          emailTextView.setText(result.getString(emailIndex));
182          streetTextView.setText(result.getString(streetIndex));
183          cityTextView.setText(result.getString(cityIndex));
184          stateTextView.setText(result.getString(stateIndex));
185          zipTextView.setText(result.getString(zipIndex));
186
187          result.close(); // close the result cursor
188          databaseConnector.close(); // close database connection
189       } // end method onPostExecute
190    } // end class LoadContactTask
191
```

Fig. 8.49 | LoadContactTask subclass of AsyncTask.

Lines 151–152 create a new object of our `DatabaseConnector` class (Section 8.9). Method `doInBackground` (lines 155–160) opens the connection to the database and calls the `DatabaseConnector`'s `getOneContact` method, which queries the database to get the contact with the specified `rowID` that was passed as the only argument to this `AsyncTask`'s `execute` method. In `doInBackground`, the `rowID` is stored in `params[0]`.

The resulting `Cursor` is passed to method `onPostExecute` (lines 163–189). The `Cursor` is positioned *before* the first row of the result set. In this case, the result set will contain only one record, so `Cursor` method **`moveToFirst`** (line 167) can be used to move the `Cursor` to the first row in the result set. [*Note:* It's considered good practice to ensure that `Cursor` method `moveToFirst` returns `true` before attempting to get data from the `Cursor`. In this app, there will always be a row in the `Cursor`.]

We use `Cursor`'s **`getColumnIndex` method** (lines 170–176) to get the column indices for the columns in the database's `contacts` table. (We hard coded the column names in this app, but these could be implemented as `String` constants as we did for `ROW_ID` in class `MainActivity` in Fig. 8.14.) This method returns -1 if the column is not in the query result. Class `Cursor` also provides method **`getColumnIndexOrThrow`** if you prefer to get an exception when the specified column name does not exist. Lines 179–185 use `Cursor`'s **`getString` method** to retrieve the `String` values from the `Cursor`'s columns, then display these values in the corresponding `TextView`s. Lines 187–188 close the `Cursor` and the connection to the database, as they're no longer needed. It's good practice to release resources like database connections when they are not being used so that other activities can use the resources.

Method deleteContact and DialogFragment `confirmDelete`

Method `deleteContact` (Fig. 8.50, lines 193–197) displays a `DialogFragment` (lines 200–252) asking the user to confirm that the currently displayed contact should be deleted. If so, the `DialogFragment` uses an `AsyncTask` to delete the contact from the database. If the user clicks the **Delete** `Button` in the dialog, lines 222–223 create a new `Database-Connector`. Lines 226–241 create an `AsyncTask` that, when executed (line 244), passes a `Long` value representing the contact's row ID to the `doInBackground`, which then deletes the contact. Line 232 calls the `DatabaseConnector`'s `deleteContact` method to perform the actual deletion. When the `doInBackground` completes execution, line 239 calls the `listener`'s `onContactDeleted` method so that `MainActivity` can remove the `Details-Fragment` from the screen.

```
192    // delete a contact
193    private void deleteContact()
194    {
195       // use FragmentManager to display the confirmDelete DialogFragment
196       confirmDelete.show(getFragmentManager(), "confirm delete");
197    }
198
199    // DialogFragment to confirm deletion of contact
200    private DialogFragment confirmDelete =
201       new DialogFragment()
202       {
```

Fig. 8.50 | Method `deleteContact` and `DialogFragment` `confirmDelete`. (Part 1 of 2.)

```
203            // create an AlertDialog and return it
204            @Override
205            public Dialog onCreateDialog(Bundle bundle)
206            {
207               // create a new AlertDialog Builder
208               AlertDialog.Builder builder =
209                  new AlertDialog.Builder(getActivity());
210
211               builder.setTitle(R.string.confirm_title);
212               builder.setMessage(R.string.confirm_message);
213
214               // provide an OK button that simply dismisses the dialog
215               builder.setPositiveButton(R.string.button_delete,
216                  new DialogInterface.OnClickListener()
217                  {
218                     @Override
219                     public void onClick(
220                        DialogInterface dialog, int button)
221                     {
222                        final DatabaseConnector databaseConnector =
223                           new DatabaseConnector(getActivity());
224
225                        // AsyncTask deletes contact and notifies listener
226                        AsyncTask<Long, Object, Object> deleteTask =
227                           new AsyncTask<Long, Object, Object>()
228                           {
229                              @Override
230                              protected Object doInBackground(Long... params)
231                              {
232                                 databaseConnector.deleteContact(params[0]);
233                                 return null;
234                              }
235
236                              @Override
237                              protected void onPostExecute(Object result)
238                              {
239                                 listener.onContactDeleted();
240                              }
241                           }; // end new AsyncTask
242
243                        // execute the AsyncTask to delete contact at rowID
244                        deleteTask.execute(new Long[] { rowID });
245                     } // end method onClick
246                  } // end anonymous inner class
247               ); // end call to method setPositiveButton
248
249               builder.setNegativeButton(R.string.button_cancel, null);
250               return builder.create(); // return the AlertDialog
251            }
252         }; // end DialogFragment anonymous inner class
253 } // end class DetailsFragment
```

Fig. 8.50 | Method deleteContact and DialogFragment confirmDelete. (Part 2 of 2.)

8.9 DatabaseConnector Utility Class

The DatabaseConnector utility class (Figs. 8.51–8.58) manages this app's interactions with SQLite for creating and manipulating the UserContacts database, which contains one table named contacts.

package *Statement,* import *Statements and Fields*

Figure 8.51 lists class DatabaseConnector's package statement, import statements and fields. We've highlighted the import statements for the new classes and interfaces discussed in Section 8.3. The String constant DATABASE_NAME (line 16) specifies the name of the database that will be created or opened. *Database names must be unique within a specific app but need not be unique across apps.* A SQLiteDatabase object (line 18) provides read/write access to a SQLite database. The DatabaseOpenHelper (line 19) is a private nested class that extends abstract class SQLiteOpenHelper—such a class is used to manage creating, opening and upgrading databases (perhaps to modify a database's structure). We discuss SQLiteOpenHelper in more detail in Fig. 8.58.

```
1   // DatabaseConnector.java
2   // Provides easy connection and creation of UserContacts database.
3   package com.deitel.addressbook;
4
5   import android.content.ContentValues;
6   import android.content.Context;
7   import android.database.Cursor;
8   import android.database.SQLException;
9   import android.database.sqlite.SQLiteDatabase;
10  import android.database.sqlite.SQLiteOpenHelper;
11  import android.database.sqlite.SQLiteDatabase.CursorFactory;
12
13  public class DatabaseConnector
14  {
15     // database name
16     private static final String DATABASE_NAME = "UserContacts";
17
18     private SQLiteDatabase database; // for interacting with the database
19     private DatabaseOpenHelper databaseOpenHelper; // creates the database
20
```

Fig. 8.51 | DatabaseConnector class's package statement, import statements and instance variables.

DatabaseConnector *Constructor and Methods* open *and* close

DatabaseConnection's constructor (Fig. 8.52, lines 22–27) creates a new object of class DatabaseOpenHelper (Fig. 8.58), which will be used to open or create the database. We discuss the details of the DatabaseOpenHelper constructor in Fig. 8.58. The open method (lines 30–34) attempts to establish a connection to the database and throws a SQLException if the connection attempt fails. Method **getWritableDatabase** (line 33), which is inherited from SQLiteOpenHelper, returns a SQLiteDatabase object. If the database has not yet been created, this method will create it; otherwise, the method will open it. Once the database is opened successfully, it will be *cached* by the operating system to improve the performance of future database interactions. The close method (lines 37–41) closes the database connection by calling the inherited SQLiteOpenHelper method **close**.

```
21    // public constructor for DatabaseConnector
22    public DatabaseConnector(Context context)
23    {
24        // create a new DatabaseOpenHelper
25        databaseOpenHelper =
26            new DatabaseOpenHelper(context, DATABASE_NAME, null, 1);
27    }
28
29    // open the database connection
30    public void open() throws SQLException
31    {
32        // create or open a database for reading/writing
33        database = databaseOpenHelper.getWritableDatabase();
34    }
35
36    // close the database connection
37    public void close()
38    {
39        if (database != null)
40            database.close(); // close the database connection
41    }
42
```

Fig. 8.52 | DatabaseConnector constructor and methods open and close.

DatabaseConnector Method insertContact

Method insertContact (Fig. 8.53) inserts a new contact with the given information into the database. We first put each piece of contact information into a new **ContentValues** object (lines 47–54), which maintains a map of key–value pairs—the database's column names are the keys. Lines 56–58 open the database, insert the new contact and close the database. SQLiteDatabase's **insert method** (line 57) inserts the values from the given ContentValues into the table specified as the first argument—the "contacts" table in this case. The second parameter of this method, which is not used in this app, is named null-ColumnHack and is needed because *SQLite does not support inserting a completely empty row into a table*—this would be the equivalent of passing an empty ContentValues object to insert. Instead of making it illegal to pass an empty ContentValues to the method, the nullColumnHack parameter is used to identify a column that accepts NULL values.

```
43    // inserts a new contact in the database
44    public long insertContact(String name, String phone, String email,
45        String street, String city, String state, String zip)
46    {
47        ContentValues newContact = new ContentValues();
48        newContact.put("name", name);
49        newContact.put("phone", phone);
```

Fig. 8.53 | DatabaseConnector method insertContact. (Part 1 of 2.)

```
50        newContact.put("email", email);
51        newContact.put("street", street);
52        newContact.put("city", city);
53        newContact.put("state", state);
54        newContact.put("zip", zip);
55
56        open(); // open the database
57        long rowID = database.insert("contacts", null, newContact);
58        close(); // close the database
59        return rowID;
60     } // end method insertContact
61
```

Fig. 8.53 | DatabaseConnector method insertContact. (Part 2 of 2.)

DatabaseConnector *Method* updateContact

Method updateContact (Fig. 8.54) is similar to method insertContact, except that it calls SQLiteDatabase's **update method** (line 76) to update an existing contact. The update method's third argument represents a SQL WHERE clause (without the keyword WHERE) that specifies which record(s) to update. In this case, we use the record's row ID to update a specific contact.

```
62     // updates an existing contact in the database
63     public void updateContact(long id, String name, String phone,
64        String email, String street, String city, String state, String zip)
65     {
66        ContentValues editContact = new ContentValues();
67        editContact.put("name", name);
68        editContact.put("phone", phone);
69        editContact.put("email", email);
70        editContact.put("street", street);
71        editContact.put("city", city);
72        editContact.put("state", state);
73        editContact.put("zip", zip);
74
75        open(); // open the database
76        database.update("contacts", editContact, "_id=" + id, null);
77        close(); // close the database
78     }
79
```

Fig. 8.54 | DatabaseConnector method updateContact.

Method getAllContacts

Method getAllContacts (Fig. 8.55) uses SqLiteDatabase's **query method** (lines 83–84) to retrieve a Cursor that provides access to the IDs and names of all the contacts in the database. The arguments are:

- the name of the table to query.
- a String array of the column names to return (the _id and name columns here)— null returns all columns in the table, which is generally a poor programming

practice, because to conserve memory, processor time and battery power, you should obtain only the data you need.

- a SQL WHERE clause (without the keyword WHERE), or null to return all rows.

- a String array of arguments to be substituted into the WHERE clause wherever ? is used as a placeholder for an argument value, or null if there are no arguments in the WHERE clause.

- a SQL GROUP BY clause (without the keywords GROUP BY), or null if you don't want to group the results.

- a SQL HAVING clause (without the keyword HAVING) to specify which groups from the GROUP BY clause to include in the results—null is required if the GROUP BY clause is null.

- a SQL ORDER BY clause (without the keywords ORDER BY) to specify the order of the results, or null if you don't wish to specify the order.

The Cursor returned by method query contains all the table rows that match the method's arguments—the so-called *result set*. The Cursor is positioned *before* the first row of the result set—Cursor's various move methods can be used to move the Cursor through the result set for processing.

```
80      // return a Cursor with all contact names in the database
81      public Cursor getAllContacts()
82      {
83         return database.query("contacts", new String[] {"_id", "name"},
84            null, null, null, null, "name");
85      }
86
```

Fig. 8.55 | DatabaseConnector method getAllContacts.

Method getOneContact
Method getOneContact (Fig. 8.56) also uses SqLiteDatabase's query method to query the database. In this case, we retrieve all the columns in the database for the contact with the specified ID.

```
87      // return a Cursor containing specified contact's information
88      public Cursor getOneContact(long id)
89      {
90         return database.query(
91            "contacts", null, "_id=" + id, null, null, null, null);
92      }
93
```

Fig. 8.56 | DatabaseConnector method getOneContact.

Method deleteContact
Method deleteContact (Fig. 8.57) uses SqLiteDatabase's **delete** method (line 98) to delete a contact from the database. In this case, we retrieve all the columns in the database

for the contact with the specified ID. The three arguments are the database table from which to delete the record, the WHERE clause (without the keyword WHERE) and, if the WHERE clause has arguments, a String array of values to substitute into the WHERE clause (null in our case).

```
94     // delete the contact specified by the given String name
95     public void deleteContact(long id)
96     {
97         open(); // open the database
98         database.delete("contacts", "_id=" + id, null);
99         close(); // close the database
100    }
101
```

Fig. 8.57 | DatabaseConnector method deleteContact.

private Nested Class DatabaseOpenHelper *That Extends* SQLiteOpenHelper

The private nested class DatabaseOpenHelper (Fig. 8.58) extends abstract class SQLite-OpenHelper, which helps apps create databases and manage version changes. The constructor (lines 105–109) simply calls the superclass constructor, which requires four arguments:

- the Context in which the database is being created or opened,
- the database name—this can be null if you wish to use an in-memory database,
- the CursorFactory to use—null indicates that you wish to use the default SQLite CursorFactory (typically for most apps) and
- the database version number (starting from 1).

You must override this class's abstract methods onCreate and onUpgrade. If the database does not yet exist, the DatabaseOpenHelper's **onCreate method** will be called to create it. If you supply a newer version number than the database version currently stored on the device, the DatabaseOpenHelper's **onUpgrade method** will be called to upgrade the database to the new version (perhaps to add tables or to add columns to an existing table).

```
102    private class DatabaseOpenHelper extends SQLiteOpenHelper
103    {
104        // constructor
105        public DatabaseOpenHelper(Context context, String name,
106            CursorFactory factory, int version)
107        {
108            super(context, name, factory, version);
109        }
110
111        // creates the contacts table when the database is created
112        @Override
113        public void onCreate(SQLiteDatabase db)
114        {
```

Fig. 8.58 | SQLiteOpenHelper class DatabaseOpenHelper. (Part 1 of 2.)

```
115            // query to create a new table named contacts
116            String createQuery = "CREATE TABLE contacts" +
117               "(_id integer primary key autoincrement," +
118               "name TEXT, phone TEXT, email TEXT, " +
119               "street TEXT, city TEXT, state TEXT, zip TEXT);";
120
121            db.execSQL(createQuery); // execute query to create the database
122         }
123
124         @Override
125         public void onUpgrade(SQLiteDatabase db, int oldVersion,
126            int newVersion)
127         {
128         }
129      } // end class DatabaseOpenHelper
130   } // end class DatabaseConnector
```

Fig. 8.58 | SQLiteOpenHelper class DatabaseOpenHelper. (Part 2 of 2.)

The onCreate method (lines 112–122) specifies the table to create with the SQL CREATE TABLE command, which is defined as a String (lines 116–119). In this case, the contacts table contains an integer primary key field (_id) that's auto-incremented, and text fields for all the other columns. Line 121 uses SQLiteDatabase's **execSQL** method to execute the CREATE TABLE command. Since we don't need to upgrade the database, we simply override method onUpgrade with an empty body. Class SQLiteOpenHelper also provides the **onDowngrade method** that can be used to downgrade a database when the currently stored version has a higher version number than the one requested in the call to class SQLiteOpenHelper's constructor. Downgrading might be used to revert the database back to a prior version with fewer columns in a table or fewer tables in the database—perhaps to fix a bug in the app.

All the SQLiteDatabase methods we used in class DatabaseConnector have corresponding methods which perform the same operations but throw exceptions on failure, as opposed to simply returning -1 (e.g., insertOrThrow vs. insert). These methods are interchangeable, allowing you to decide how to deal with database read and write errors.

8.10 Wrap-Up

In this chapter, you created an **Address Book** app that enables users to add, view, edit and delete contact information that's stored in a SQLite database. You defined common GUI component attribute–value pairs as XML style resources, then applied the styles to all components that share those values by using the components' style attribute. You added a border to a TextView by specifying a Drawable as the value for the TextView's android:background attribute and you created a custom Drawable using an XML representation of a shape. You also used Android standard icons to enhance the visual appearance of the app's menu items.

When an Fragment's primary task is to display a scrollable list of items, you learned that you can extend class ListFragment to create a Fragment that displays a ListView in its default layout. You used this to display the contacts stored in the app's database. You bound data to the ListView via a CursorAdapter that displayed the results of a database query.

In this app's `Activity`, you used `FragmentTransactions` to add `Fragments` to and replace `Fragments` in the GUI dynamically. You also used the `Fragment` back stack to support the back button for returning to a previously displayed `Fragment` and to allow the app's `Activity` to programmatically return to previous `Fragments`.

We demonstrated how to communicate data between `Fragments` and a host `Activity` or the `Activity`'s other `Fragments` via interfaces of callback methods that are implemented by the host `Activity`. You also used `Bundles` to pass arguments to `Fragments`.

You used a subclass of `SQLiteOpenHelper` to simplify creating the database and to obtain a `SQLiteDatabase` object for manipulating a database's contents. You processed query results via a `Cursor`. You used subclasses of `AsyncTask` to perform database tasks outside the GUI thread and return results to the GUI thread. This allowed you to take advantage of Android's threading capabilities without directly creating and manipulating threads.

In Chapter 9, we discuss the business side of Android app development. You'll see how to prepare your app for submission to Google Play, including making icons. We'll discuss how to test your apps on devices and publish them on Google Play. We discuss the characteristics of great apps and the Android design guidelines to follow. We provide tips for pricing and marketing your app. We also review the benefits of offering your app for free to drive sales of other products, such as a more feature-rich version of the app or premium content. We show how to use Google Play to track app sales, payments and more.

Google Play and App Business Issues

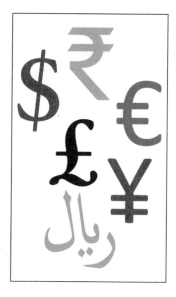

Objectives

In this chapter you'll be introduced to:

- Preparing your apps for publication.
- Pricing your apps and the benefits of free vs. paid apps.
- Monetizing your apps with in-app advertising.
- Selling virtual goods using in-app billing.
- Registering for Google Play.
- Setting up a Google Wallet merchant account.
- Uploading your apps to Google Play.
- Launching the **Play Store** from within an app.
- Other Android app marketplaces.
- Other popular mobile app platforms to which you can port your apps to broaden your market.
- Marketing your apps.

9.1 Introduction

In Chapters 2–8, we developed a variety of complete working Android apps. Once you've developed and tested your own apps, both in the emulator and on Android devices, the next step is to submit them to Google Play—and/or other app marketplaces—for distribution to a worldwide audience. In this chapter, you'll learn how to register for Google Play and set up a Google Wallet account so that you can sell your apps. You'll learn how to prepare your apps for publication and how to upload them to Google Play. In a few cases, we'll refer you to Android documentation instead of showing the steps in the book, because the steps are likely to change. We'll tell you about additional Android app marketplaces where you can distribute your apps. We'll discuss whether you should offer your apps for free or for a fee, and mention key resources for monetizing apps such as in-app advertising and selling virtual goods. We'll provide resources for marketing your apps, and mention other app platforms to which you may port your Android apps to broaden your marketplace.

9.2 Preparing Your Apps for Publication

The *Preparing for Release* section in the *Dev Guide* (http://developer.android.com/tools/publishing/preparing.html) lists items to consider before publishing your app on Google Play, including:

- *Testing* your app on Android devices
- Including an *End User License Agreement* with your app (optional)
- Adding an *icon* and label to the app's manifest
- *Versioning* your app (e.g., 1.0, 1.1, 2.0, 2.3, 3.0)
- Getting a *cryptographic key* for *digitally signing* your app
- *Compiling* your app

You should also read the *Launch Checklist* (`http://developer.android.com/distribute/googleplay/publish/preparing.html`) and the *Tablet App Quality Checklist* (`http://developer.android.com/distribute/googleplay/quality/tablet.html`) before publishing your app.

9.2.1 Testing Your App

Before submitting your app to Google Play, test it thoroughly on a variety of devices. Although the app might work perfectly using the emulator on your computer, problems could arise when running it on particular Android devices. The Google Play Developer Console now provides support for alpha and beta testing apps with groups of people through Google+. For more information, visit:

```
https://play.google.com/apps/publish/
```

9.2.2 End User License Agreement

You have the option to include an **End User License Agreement** (**EULA**) with your app. An EULA is an agreement through which you license your software to the user. It typically stipulates terms of use, limitations on redistribution and reverse engineering, product liability, compliance with applicable laws and more. You might want to consult an attorney when drafting an EULA for your app. To view a sample EULA, see

```
http://www.rocketlawyer.com/document/end-user-license-agreement.rl
```

9.2.3 Icons and Labels

Design an icon for your app and provide a text label (a name) that will appear in Google Play and on the user's device. The icon could be your company logo, an image from the app or a custom image. The Android Asset Studio provides a tool for creating app icons:

```
http://android-ui-utils.googlecode.com/hg/asset-studio/dist/
index.html
```

Create a version of your icon for each of these screen densities:

- `xx-high` (XXHDPI): 144 x 144 pixels
- `x-high` (XHDPI): 96 x 96 pixels
- `high` (HDPI): 72 x 72 pixels
- `medium` (MDPI): 48 x 48 pixels

You'll also need a high-resolution icon for use in Google Play. This icon should be:

- 512 x 512 pixels
- 32-bit PNG
- 1 MB maximum

Since the icon is the most important brand asset, having one that's high quality is important. Consider hiring an experienced graphic designer to help you create a compelling, professional icon. Figure 9.1 lists several design firms that offer free, professionally designed icons and paid custom icon design services. Once you've created the icon and label, you'll need to specify them in the app's `AndroidManifest.xml` file by setting the `android:icon` and `android:label` attributes of the application element.

Company	URL	Services
glyphlab	`http://www.glyphlab.com/icon_design/`	Custom icon design and some *free* downloadable icons.
Androidicons	`http://www.androidicons.com`	Designs custom icons, sells a set of 200 icons for a flat fee and has some *free* downloadable icons.
Iconiza	`http://www.iconiza.com`	Designs custom icons for a flat fee and sells stock icons.
Aha-Soft	`http://www.aha-soft.com/icon-design.htm`	Designs custom icons for a flat fee.
Rosetta®	`http://icondesign.rosetta.com/`	Designs custom icons for a fee.
Elance®	`http://www.elance.com`	Search for freelance icon designers.

Fig. 9.1 | Custom app icon design firms.

9.2.4 Versioning Your App

It's important to include a *version name* (shown to the users) and a *version code* (an integer version number used internally by Google Play) for your app, and to consider your strategy for numbering updates. For example, the first version name of your app might be 1.0, minor updates might be 1.1 and 1.2, and the next major update might be 2.0. The version code is an integer that typically starts at 1 and is incremented by 1 for each new version of your app that you post. For additional guidelines, see *Versioning Your Applications* at

> `http://developer.android.com/tools/publishing/versioning.html`

9.2.5 Licensing to Control Access to Paid Apps

The Google Play *licensing service* allows you to create licensing policies to control access to your paid apps. For example, you might use a licensing policy to limit how many simultaneous device installs are allowed. To learn more about the licensing service, visit

> `http://developer.android.com/google/play/licensing/index.html`

9.2.6 Obfuscating Your Code

You should "obfuscate" any apps you upload to Google Play to discourage reverse engineering of your code and further protect your apps. The free **ProGuard** tool—which runs when you build your app in *release mode*—shrinks the size of your `.apk` file (the Android app package file that contains your app for installation) and optimizes and obfuscates the code "by removing unused code and renaming classes, fields, and methods with semantically obscure names."[1] To learn how to set up and use the ProGuard tool, go to

> `http://developer.android.com/tools/help/proguard.html`

For additional information about protecting your apps from piracy using code obfuscation, visit

```
http://www.techrepublic.com/blog/app-builder/
    protect-your-android-apps-with-obfuscation/1724
```

9.2.7 Getting a Private Key for Digitally Signing Your App

Before uploading your app to a device, Google Play or other app marketplaces, you must *digitally sign* the .apk file using a **digital certificate** that identifies you as the author of the app. A digital certificate includes your name or company name, contact information, etc. It can be self-signed using a **private key** (i.e., a secure password used to *encrypt* the certificate); you do not need to purchase a certificate from a third-party certificate authority (though it's an option). Eclipse automatically digitally signs your app when you execute it in an emulator or on a device for *debugging* purposes. That digital certificate is *not* valid for use with Google Play, and it expires 365 days after it's created. For detailed instructions on digitally signing your apps, see *Signing Your Applications* at:

```
http://developer.android.com/tools/publishing/app-signing.html
```

9.2.8 Screenshots

Take *at least* two screenshots of your app (you may upload a maximum of eight screenshots each for a smartphone, a 7" tablet and a 10" tablet) that will be included with your app description in Google Play (Fig. 9.2). These provide a preview of your app, since users can't test the app before downloading it (although they may return an app for a refund within 15 minutes after purchasing and downloading it). Choose attractive screenshots that show the app's functionality.

Specification	Description
Size	Minimum dimension of 320 pixels and maximum dimension of 3840 pixels (the maximum dimension may not be more than twice the length of the minimum).
Format	24-bit PNG or JPEG format with no alpha (transparency) effects.
Image	Full bleed to the edge with no borders.

Fig. 9.2 | Screenshot specifications.

The Dalvik Debug Monitor Service (DDMS), which is installed with the ADT Plugin for Eclipse and helps you debug your apps running on actual devices, also enables you to capture screenshots on your device. To do so, perform the following steps:

1. Run the app on your device as described at the end of Section 1.9.

2. In Eclipse, select **Window > Open Perspective > DDMS**, which allows you to use the DDMS tools.

---

1. http://developer.android.com/tools/help/proguard.html#enabling.

3. In the **Devices** window (Fig. 9.3), select the device from which you'd like to obtain a screen capture.

Screen Capture button

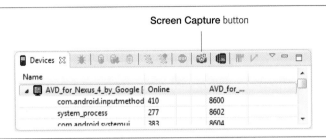

Fig. 9.3 | **Devices** window in the DDMS perspective.

4. Click the **Screen Capture** button to display the **Device Screen Capture** window (Fig. 9.4).

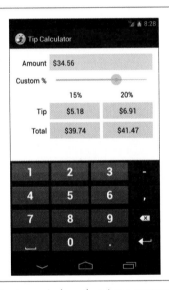

Fig. 9.4 | **Device Screen Capture** window showing a capture of the **Tip Calculator** app from Chapter 3.

5. After you've ensured that the screen is showing what you'd like to capture, click the **Save** button to save the image.

6. If you wish to change what's on your device's screen before saving the image, make the change on the device, then press the **Refresh** button in the **Device Screen Capture** window to recapture the device's screen.

9.2.9 Promotional App Video

When you upload your app to Google Play, you'll have the option to include a URL for a short promotional video on YouTube. Figure 9.5 lists several examples. Some videos show a person holding a device and interacting with the app. Other videos use screen captures. Figure 9.6 lists several video creation tools and services (some free, some paid).

App	URL
Temple Run®: Oz	http://www.youtube.com/watch?v=QM9sT1ydtjO
GT Racing: Motor Academy	http://www.youtube.com/watch?v=2Z90PICdgoA
Beach Buggy Blitz™	http://www.youtube.com/watch?v=YqDczawTsYw
Real Estate and Homes by Trulia®	http://www.youtube.com/watch?v=rLn697AszGs
Zappos.com®	http://www.youtube.com/watch?v=U-oNyK9kl_Q
Megopolis International	http://www.youtube.com/watch?v=JrqeEJ1xzCY

Fig. 9.5 | Examples of promotional videos for apps in Google Play.

Tools and services	URL
Animoto	http://animoto.com
Apptamin	http://www.apptamin.com
Movie Maker for Microsoft Windows	http://windows.microsoft.com/en-us/windows-live/movie-maker
CamStudio™	http://camstudio.org
Jing	http://www.techsmith.com/jing.html
Camtasia Studio®	http://www.techsmith.com/camtasia.html
TurboDemo™	http://www.turbodemo.com/eng/index.php

Fig. 9.6 | Tools and services for creating promotional videos.

To upload your video, create an account or sign into your existing YouTube account. Click **Upload** at the top-right of the page. Click **Select files to upload** to choose a video from your computer or simply drag and drop the video file onto the web page.

9.3 Pricing Your App: Free or Fee

You set the prices for your apps that are distributed through Google Play. Many developers offer their apps for free as a marketing, publicity and branding tool, earning revenue through increased sales of products and services, sales of more feature-rich versions of the same apps and sales of additional content through the apps using *in-app purchase* or *in-app advertising*. Figure 9.7 lists ways to monetize your apps.

Ways to monetize an app
• Sell the app in Google Play.
• Sell the app in other Android app marketplaces.

Fig. 9.7 | Ways to monetize an app. (Part 1 of 2.)

> **Ways to monetize an app**
>
> - Sell paid upgrades.
> - Sell virtual goods (Section 9.5).
> - Sell an app to a company that brands it as their own.
> - Use mobile advertising services for in-app ads (Section 9.4).
> - Sell in-app advertising space directly to your customers.
> - Use it to drive sales of a more feature-rich version of the app.

Fig. 9.7 | Ways to monetize an app. (Part 2 of 2.)

9.3.1 Paid Apps

The average price for apps varies widely by category. For example, according to the app discovery site AppBrain (`http://www.appbrain.com`), the average price for puzzle game apps is $1.54 and for business apps is $6.47.[2] Although these prices may seem low, keep in mind that successful apps could sell tens of thousands, hundreds of thousands or even millions of copies.

When setting a price for your app, start by researching your competition. How much do they charge? Do their apps have similar functionality? Is yours more feature-rich? Will offering your app at a lower price than the competition attract users? Is your goal to recoup development costs and generate additional revenue?

If you change your strategy, you can eventually offer your paid app for free permanently. However it's not currently possible to change your free apps to paid.

Financial transactions for paid apps in Google Play are handled by Google Wallet (`http://google.com/wallet`), though customers of some mobile carriers (such as AT&T, Sprint and T-Mobile) can opt to use carrier billing to charge paid apps to their wireless bill. Earnings are paid to Google Wallet merchants monthly.[3] You're responsible for paying taxes on the revenue you earn through Google Play.

9.3.2 Free Apps

Approximately 80% of apps on Google Play are free, and they comprise the vast majority of downloads.[4] Given that users are more likely to download an app if it's free, consider offering a free "lite" version of your app to encourage users to try it. For example, if your app is a game, you might offer a free lite version with just the first few levels. When the user has finished playing the free levels, the app would offer an option to buy through Google Play your more robust app with numerous game levels. Or, your app would display a message that the user can purchase additional levels from within the app for a more seamless upgrade (see Section 9.5). According to a recent study by AdMob, *upgrading from the "lite" version is the number-one reason why users purchase a paid app.*[5]

---

2. `http://www.appbrain.com/stats/android-market-app-categories`.
3. `http://support.google.com/googleplay/android-developer/answer/137997?hl=en&ref_topic=15867`.
4. `http://www.gartner.com/newsroom/id/2592315`.
5. `http://metrics.admob.com/wp-content/uploads/2009/08/AdMob-Mobile-Metrics-July-09.pdf`.

Many companies use free apps to build brand awareness and drive sales of other products and services (Fig. 9.8).

Free app	Functionality
Amazon® Mobile	Browse and purchase items on Amazon.
Bank of America	Locate ATMs and bank branches in your area, check balances and pay bills.
Best Buy®	Browse and purchase items.
CNN	Get the latest world news, receive breaking news alerts and watch live video.
Epicurious Recipe	View thousands of recipes from several Condé Nast magazines, including *Gourmet* and *Bon Appetit*.
ESPN® ScoreCenter	Set up personalized scoreboards to track your favorite college and professional sports teams.
NFL Mobile	Get the latest NFL news and updates, live programming, NFL Replay and more.
UPS® Mobile	Track shipments, find drop-off locations, get estimated shipping costs and more.
NYTimes	Read articles from the *New York Times*, free of charge.
Pocket Agent™	State Farm Insurance's app enables you contact an agent, file claims, find local repair centers, check your State Farm bank and mutual fund accounts and more.
Progressive® Insurance	Report a claim and submit photos from the scene of a car accident, find a local agent, get car safety information when you're shopping for a new car and more.
USA Today®	Read articles from *USA Today* and get the latest sports scores.
Wells Fargo® Mobile	Locate ATMs and bank branches in your area, check balances, make transfers and pay bills.
Women's Health Workouts Lite	View numerous workouts from one of the leading women's magazines.

Fig. 9.8 | Companies using free Android apps to build brand awareness.

9.4 Monetizing Apps with In-App Advertising

Many developers offer free apps monetized with **in-app advertising**—often banner ads similar to those you find on websites. Mobile advertising networks such as AdMob (`http://www.admob.com/`) and Google AdSense for Mobile (`http://www.google.com/mobileads/publisher_home.html`) aggregate advertisers for you and serve relevant ads to your app (see Section 9.13). You earn advertising revenue based on the number of click-throughs. The top 100 free apps might earn a few hundred dollars to a few thousand dollars per day. In-app advertising does not generate significant revenue for most apps, so if your goal is to recoup development costs and generate profits, you should consider charging a fee for your app.

9.5 Monetizing Apps: Using In-App Billing to Sell Virtual Goods

Google Play's **in-app billing** service (`http://developer.android.com/google/play/billing/index.html`) enables you to sell **virtual goods** (e.g., digital content) through apps on devices running Android 2.3 or higher (Fig. 9.9). According to Google, apps that use in-app billing earn profoundly more revenue than paid apps alone. Of the 24 top-grossing apps on Google Play, 23 use in-app billing.[6] The in-app billing service is available only for apps purchased through Google Play; it may *not* be used in apps sold through third-party app stores. To use in-app billing, you'll need a Google Play publisher account (see Section 9.6) and a Google Wallet merchant account (see Section 9.7). Google pays you 70% of the revenue for all in-app purchases made through your apps.

Virtual goods		
Magazine e-subscriptions	Localized guides	Avatars
Virtual apparel	Additional game levels	Game scenery
Add-on features	Ringtones	Icons
E-cards	E-gifts	Virtual currency
Wallpapers	Images	Virtual pets
Audios	Videos	E-books and more.

Fig. 9.9 | Virtual goods.

Selling virtual goods can generate higher revenue *per user* than in-app advertising.[7] A few apps that have been particularly successful selling virtual goods include Angry Birds, DragonVale, Zynga Poker, Bejeweled Blitz, NYTimes and Candy Crush Saga. Virtual goods are particularly popular in mobile games.

To implement in-app billing, follow the steps at

```
http://developer.android.com/google/play/billing/
billing_integrate.html
```

For additional information about in-app billing, including subscriptions, sample apps, security best practices, testing and more, visit `http://developer.android.com/google/play/billing/billing_overview.html`. You can also take the free *Selling In-app Products* training class at

```
http://developer.android.com/training/in-app-billing/index.html
```

In-App Purchase for Apps Sold Through Other App Marketplaces

If you choose to sell your apps through other marketplaces (see Section 9.11), several third-party mobile payment providers can enable you to build *in-app purchase* into your apps using

---

6. `http://android-developers.blogspot.com/2012/05/in-app-subscriptions-in-google-play.html`.
7. `http://www.businessinsider.com/its-morning-in-venture-capital-2012-5?utm_source=readme&utm_medium=rightrail&utm_term=&utm_content=6&utm_campaign=recirc`.

APIs from mobile payment providers (Fig. 9.10)—you cannot use Google Play's in-app billing. Start by building the additional *locked functionality* (e.g., game levels, avatars) into your app. When the user opts to make a purchase, the in-app purchasing tool handles the financial transaction and returns a message to the app verifying payment. The app then unlocks the additional functionality. Mobile carriers collect between 25% and 45% of the price.

Provider	URL	Description
PayPal Mobile Payments Library	`http://developer.paypal.com/` `webapps/developer/docs/` `classic/mobile/gs_MPL/`	Users click the **Pay with PayPal** button, log into their PayPal account, then click **Pay**.
Amazon In-App Purchasing	`http://developer.amazon.com/sdk/` `in-app-purchasing.html`	In-app purchase for apps sold through the Amazon App Store for Android.
Zong	`http://www.zong.com/android`	Provides **Buy** button for one-click payment. Payments appear on the user's phone bill.
Samsung In-App Purchase	`http://developer.samsung.com/` `android/tools-sdks/` `In-App-Purchase-Library`	In-app purchase for apps designed specifically for Samsung devices.
Boku	`http://www.boku.com`	Users click **Pay by Mobile**, enter their mobile phone number, then complete the transaction by replying to a text message sent to their phone.

Fig. 9.10 | Mobile payment providers for in-app purchase.

9.6 Registering at Google Play

To publish your apps on Google Play, you must register for an account at

`http://play.google.com/apps/publish`

There's a one-time $25 registration fee. Unlike other popular mobile platforms, *Google Play has no approval process for uploading apps.* You must, however, adhere to the *Google Play Developer Program Policies.* If your app is in violation of these policies, it can be removed at any time; serious or repeated violations may result in account termination (Fig. 9.11).

Violations of the *Google Play Content Policy for Developers*	
• Infringing on others' intellectual property rights (e.g., trademarks, patents and copyrights). • Illegal activities.	• Invading personal privacy. • Interfering with the services of other parties. • Harming the user's device or personal data. • Gambling.

Fig. 9.11 | Some violations of the *Google Play Content Policy for Developers* (`http://play.google.com/about/developer-content-policy.html#showlanguages`). (Part I of 2.)

Violations of the *Google Play Content Policy for Developers*	
• Creating a "spammy" user experience (e.g., misleading the user about the app's purpose).	• Promoting hate or violence.
• Adversely impacting a user's service charges or a wireless carrier's network.	• Providing pornographic or obscene content, or anything unsuitable for children under age 18.
• Impersonation or deception.	• Ads in system-level notifications and widgets.

Fig. 9.11 | Some violations of the *Google Play Content Policy for Developers* (`http://play.google.com/about/developer-content-policy.html#showlanguages`). (Part 2 of 2.)

9.7 Setting Up a Google Wallet Merchant Account

To sell your apps on Google Play, you'll need a **Google Wallet merchant account**, available to Google Play developers in 32 countries (Fig. 9.12).[8] Google Wallet is used as a payment service for online transactions. Once you've registered and logged into Google Play at `http://play.google.com/apps/publish/`, click the **Financial Reports** link, then click **Set up a merchant account.** You'll need to

- provide private information by which Google can contact you

- provide customer-support contact information where users can contact you

- provide financial information so that Google may perform a credit check

- agree to the Terms of Service, which describe the features of the service, permissible transactions, prohibited actions, service fees, payment terms and more.

Countries			
Argentina	Denmark	Italy	Russia
Australia	France	Mexico	Spain
Austria	Germany	Netherlands	South Korea
Belgium	Hong Kong	New Zealand	Sweden
Brazil	India	Norway	Switzerland
Canada	Ireland	Poland	Taiwan
Czech Republic	Israel	Portugal	United Kingdom
Finland	Japan	Singapore	United States

Fig. 9.12 | Countries in which Google Wallet merchant accounts are available.

Google Wallet processes payments and helps protect you from fraudulent purchases. The standard payment processing rates are waived for your Google Play sales.[9] Google pays you 70% of the app price. Once you set up a Google Wallet account, you'll be able

---

8. `http://support.google.com/googleplay/android-developer/answer/150324?hl=en&ref_topic=15867.`
9. `http://checkout.google.com/termsOfService?type=SELLER.`

to use it for more activities than just selling your apps, such as making purchases at participating stores.

9.8 Uploading Your Apps to Google Play

Once you've prepared your files and you're ready to upload your app, review the steps in the *Launch Checklist* at:

```
http://developer.android.com/distribute/googleplay/publish/
    preparing.html
```

Then log into Google Play at `http://play.google.com/apps/publish` (Section 9.6) and click the **Publish an Android App on Google Play** button to begin the upload process. You will be asked to upload the following assets:

1. *App .apk file* that includes the app's code files, assets, resources and the manifest file.

2. At least *two screenshots* of your app to be included in Google Play. You may include screenshots for an Android phone, 7" tablet and 10" tablet.

3. *High-resolution app icon* (512 x 512 pixels) to be included in Google Play.

4. *Promotional graphic* (optional) for Google Play to be used by Google if they decide to promote your app (for examples, check out some of the graphics for featured apps on Google Play). The graphic must be 180 pixels wide by 120 pixels tall in 24-bit PNG or JPEG format with *no alpha transparency effects*. It must also have a full bleed (i.e., go to the edge of the screen with no border in the graphic).

5. *Promotional video* (optional) to be included in Google Play. You may include a URL for a promotional video for your app (e.g., a YouTube link to a video that demonstrates how your app works).

In addition to app assets, you will be asked to provide the following additional listing details for Google Play:

1. **Language.** By default, your app will be listed in English. If you'd like to list it in additional languages, select them from the list provided (Fig. 9.13).

Language				
Afrikaans	Amharic	Arabic	Belarusian	Catalan
Chinese (simplified or traditional)		Croatian	Czech	Danish
Dutch	English (UK or United States)		Estonian	Filipino
Finnish	French	German	Greek	Hebrew
Hindi	Hungarian	Indonesian	Italian	Japanese
Korean	Latvian	Lithuanian	Malay	Norwegian
Persian	Polish	Portuguese (Brazil or Portugal)		Romanian
Romansh	Russian	Serbian	Slovak	Slovenian
Spanish (Latin America, Spain or United States)			Swahili	Swedish
Thai	Turkish	Ukrainian	Vietnamese	Zulu

Fig. 9.13 | Languages for listing apps in Google Play.

2. *Title.* The title of your app as it will appear in Google Play (30 characters maximum). It does *not* need to be unique among all Android apps.

3. *Description.* A description of your app and its features (4,000 characters maximum). It's recommended that you use the last portion of the description to explain why each permission is required and how it's used.

4. *Recent changes.* A walkthrough of any changes specific to the latest version of your app (500 characters maximum).

5. *Promo text.* The promotional text for marketing your app (80 characters max).

6. *App type.* Choose **Applications** or **Games**.

7. *Category.* Select the category (see Fig. 1.9) that best suits your game or app.

8. *Price.* The default setting is **Free**. To sell your app for a fee, you'll need to set up a merchant account at Google Wallet.

9. *Content rating.* You may select **High Maturity**, **Medium Maturity**, **Low Maturity** or **Everyone**. For more information, see *Rating your application content for Google Play* at `http://support.google.com/googleplay/android-developer/answer/188189`.

10. *Locations.* By default, the app will be listed in all current and future Google Play countries. If you do not want your app to be available in all these countries, you may pick and choose specific ones where you'd like your app to be listed.

11. *Website.* A **Visit Developer's Website** link will be included in your app's listing in Google Play. Provide a direct link to the page on your website where users interested in downloading your app can find more information, including marketing copy, feature listings, additional screenshots, instructions, etc.

12. *E-mail.* Your e-mail address will also be included in Google Play, so that customers can contact you with questions, report errors, etc.

13. *Phone number.* Sometimes your phone number is included in Google Play. Therefore it's recommended that you leave this field blank unless you provide phone support. You may want to provide a customer service phone number on your website.

9.9 Launching the Play Store from Within Your App

To drive additional sales of your apps, you can launch the **Play Store** app (Google Play) from within your app (typically by including a button) so that the user can download other apps you've published or purchase a related app with functionality beyond that of the previously downloaded "lite" version. You can also launch the **Play Store** app to enable users to download the latest updates.

There are two ways to launch the **Play Store** app. First, you can bring up Google Play search results for apps with a specific developer name, package name or string of characters. For example, if you want to encourage users to download other apps you've published, you could include a button in your app that, when touched, launches the **Play Store** app and initiates a search for apps containing your name or company name. The second option is to bring the user to the details page in the **Play Store** app for a specific app.

To learn about launching **Play Store** from within an app, see *Linking Your Products* at `http://developer.android.com/distribute/googleplay/promote/linking.html`.

9.10 Managing Your Apps in Google Play

The *Google Play Developer Console* allows you to manage your account and your apps, check users' star ratings for your apps (0 to 5 stars), respond to users' comments, track the overall number of installs of each app and the number of active installs (installs minus uninstalls). You can view installation trends and the distribution of app downloads across Android versions, devices, and more. Crash reports list any crash and freeze information from users. If you've made upgrades to your app, you can easily publish the new version. You can remove the app from Google Play, but users who downloaded it previously may keep it on their devices. Users who uninstalled the app will be able to reinstall it even after it's been removed (it will remain on Google's servers unless it's removed for violating the Terms of Service).

9.11 Other Android App Marketplaces

In addition to Google Play, you may choose to make your apps available through other Android app marketplaces (Fig. 9.14), or through your own website using services such as AndroidLicenser (`http://www.androidlicenser.com`). To learn more about releasing your app through a website see

```
http://developer.android.com/tools/publishing/
publishing_overview.html
```

Marketplace	URL
Amazon Appstore	`http://developer.amazon.com/welcome.html`
Opera Mobile Store	`http://apps.opera.com/en_us/index.php`
Moborobo	`http://www.moborobo.com`
Appitalism®	`http://www.appitalism.com/index.html`
Samsung Apps	`http://apps.samsung.com/mars/main/getMain.as`
GetJar	`http://www.getjar.com`
SlideMe	`http://www.slideme.org`
Handango	`http://www.handango.com`
Mplayit™	`http://www.mplayit.com`
AndroidPIT	`http://www.androidpit.com`

Fig. 9.14 | Other Android app marketplaces.

9.12 Other Popular Mobile App Platforms

According to ABI Research, 56 billion smartphone apps and 14 billion tablet apps will be downloaded in 2013.[10] By porting your Android apps to other mobile app platforms, especially to iOS (for iPhone, iPad and iPod Touch devices), you could reach an even bigger audience (Fig. 9.15). Android can be developed on Windows, Linux or Mac computers

---

10. `http://www.abiresearch.com/press/android-will-account-for-58-of-smartphone-app-down`.

with Java—one of the world's most widely used programming languages. However, iOS apps must be developed on Macs, which can be costly, and with the Objective-C programming language, which only a small percentage of developers know. Google has created the open-source J2ObjC tool to help you translate your Java app code to Objective-C for iOS apps. To learn more, see `http://code.google.com/p/j2objc/`.

Platform	URL	Worldwide app downloads market share
Android	`http://developer.android.com`	58% smartphone apps 17% tablet apps
iOS (Apple)	`http://developer.apple.com/ios`	33% smartphone apps 75% tablet apps
Windows Phone 8	`http://developer.windowsphone.com`	4% smartphone apps 2% tablet apps
BlackBerry (RIM)	`http://developer.blackberry.com`	3% smartphone apps
Amazon Kindle	`http://developer.amazon.com`	4% tablet apps

Fig. 9.15 | Popular mobile app platforms. (`http://www.abiresearch.com/press/android-will-account-for-58-of-smartphone-app-down`).

9.13 Marketing Your Apps

Once your app has been published, you'll want to market it to your audience.[11] *Viral marketing* through social media sites such as Facebook, Twitter, Google+ and YouTube can help you get your message out. These sites have tremendous visibility. According to a Pew Research Center study, 72% of adults on the Internet use social networks—and 67% of those are on Facebook.[12] Figure 9.16 lists some of the most popular social media sites. Also, e-mail and electronic newsletters are still effective and often inexpensive marketing tools.

Name	URL	Description
Facebook	`http://www.facebook.com`	Social networking
Twitter	`http://www.twitter.com`	Microblogging, social networking
Google+	`http://plus.google.com`	Social networking
Groupon	`http://www.groupon.com`	Daily deals

Fig. 9.16 | Popular social media sites. (Part I of 2.)

---

11. To learn more about marketing your Android apps, check out the book *Android Apps Marketing: Secrets to Selling Your Android App* by Jeffrey Hughes.

12. `http://pewinternet.org/Commentary/2012/March/Pew-Internet-Social-Networking-full-detail.aspx`.

Name	URL	Description
Foursquare	`http://www.foursquare.com`	Check-in
Pinterest	`http://www.pinterest.com`	Online pinboard
YouTube	`http://www.youtube.com`	Video sharing
LinkedIn	`http://www.linkedin.com`	Social networking for business
Flickr	`http://www.flickr.com`	Photo sharing

Fig. 9.16 | Popular social media sites. (Part 2 of 2.)

Facebook

Facebook, the premier social networking site, has more than one billion active users[13] and over 150 billion friend connections.[14] It's an excellent resource for *viral marketing*. Start by setting up an official Facebook page for your app or business. Use the page to post app information, news, updates, reviews, tips, videos, screenshots, high scores for games, user feedback and links to Google Play where users can download your app. For example, we post news and updates about Deitel publications on our Facebook page at `http://www.facebook.com/DeitelFan`.

Next, you need to spread the word. Encourage your co-workers and friends to "like" your Facebook page and ask their friends to do so as well. As people interact with your page, stories will appear in their friends' news feeds, building awareness to a growing audience.

Twitter

Twitter is a microblogging, social networking site with over 554 million active registered users.[15] You post tweets—messages of 140 characters or less. Twitter then distributes your tweets to all of your followers (at the time of this writing, one famous pop star had over 40 million followers). Many people use Twitter to track news and trends. Tweet about your app—include announcements about new releases, tips, facts, comments from users, etc. Also, encourage your colleagues and friends to tweet about your app. Use a *hashtag* (#) to reference your app. For example, when tweeting about *Android for Programmers, 2/e* on our `@deitel` Twitter feed, we use the hashtag `#AndroidFP2`. Others may use this hashtag as well to write comments about the book. This enables you to easily search tweets for messages related to the book.

Viral Video

Viral video—shared on video sites (e.g., YouTube, Bing Videos, Yahoo! Video), on social networking sites (e.g., Facebook, Twitter and Google+), through e-mail, etc.—is another great way to spread the word about your app. If you create a compelling video, perhaps one that's humorous or even outrageous, it may quickly rise in popularity and may be tagged by users across multiple social networks.

---

13. `http://investor.fb.com/releasedetail.cfm?ReleaseID=761090`.
14. `http://expandedramblings.com/index.php/by-the-numbers-17-amazing-facebook-stats/`.
15. `http://www.statisticbrain.com/twitter-statistics/`.

E-Mail Newsletters

If you have an e-mail newsletter, use it to promote your app. Include links to Google Play, where users can download the app. Also include links to your social networking pages, where users can stay up-to-date with the latest news about your app.

App Reviews

Contact influential bloggers and app review sites (Fig. 9.17) and tell them about your app. Provide them with a promotional code to download your app for free (see Section 9.3). Influential bloggers and reviewers receive many requests, so keep yours concise and informative without too much marketing hype. Many app reviewers post video app reviews on YouTube and other sites (Fig. 9.18).

Android app review site	URL
Android Tapp™	http://www.androidtapp.com
Appolicious™	http://www.androidapps.com
AppBrain	http://www.appbrain.com
AndroidZoom	http://www.androidzoom.com
Appstorm	http://android.appstorm.net
Best Android Apps Review	http://www.bestandroidappsreview.com
Android App Review Source	http://www.androidappreviewsource.com
Androinica	http://www.androinica.com
AndroidLib	http://www.androlib.com
Android and Me	http://www.androidandme.com
AndroidGuys	http://www.androidguys.com/category/reviews
Android Police	http://www.androidpolice.com
AndroidPIT	http://www.androidpit.com
Phandroid	http://www.phandroid.com

Fig. 9.17 | Android app review sites.

Android app review video site	URL
Daily App Show	http://dailyappshow.com
Crazy Mike's Apps	http://crazymikesapps.com
Appolicious™	http://www.appvee.com/?device_filter=android
Life of Android™	http://www.lifeofandroid.com/video/
Android Video Review	http://www.androidvideoreview.net/

Fig. 9.18 | Android app review video sites.

Internet Public Relations

The public relations industry uses media outlets to help companies get their message out to consumers. With the phenomenon known as Web 2.0, public relations practitioners are incorporating blogs, tweets, podcasts, RSS feeds and social media into their PR campaigns. Figure 9.19 lists some free and fee-based Internet public relations resources, including press-release distribution sites, press-release writing services and more.

Internet public relations resource	URL	Description
Free Services		
PRWeb®	http://www.prweb.com	Online press-release distribution service with *free* and *fee-based* services.
ClickPress™	http://www.clickpress.com	Submit news stories for approval (*free* of charge). If approved, they'll be available on the ClickPress site and to news search engines. For a *fee*, ClickPress will distribute your press releases globally to top financial newswires.
PRLog	http://www.prlog.org/pub/	*Free* press-release submission and distribution.
i-Newswire	http://www.i-newswire.com	*Free* and *fee-based* press-release submission and distribution.
openPR®	http://www.openpr.com	*Free* press-release publication.
Fee-Based Services		
PR Leap	http://www.prleap.com	Online press-release distribution service.
Marketwire	http://www.marketwire.com	Press-release distribution service allows you to target your audience by geography, industry, etc.
Mobility PR	http://www.mobilitypr.com	Public relations services for companies in the mobile industry.
Press Release Writing	http://www.press-release-writing.com	Press-release distribution and services including press-release writing, proofreading and editing. Check out the tips for writing effective press releases.

Fig. 9.19 | Internet public relations resources.

Mobile Advertising Networks

Purchasing advertising spots (e.g., in other apps, online, in newspapers and magazines or on radio and television) is another way to market your app. Mobile advertising networks (Fig. 9.20) specialize in advertising Android (and other) mobile apps on mobile platforms. Many of these networks can target audiences by location, wireless carrier, platform (e.g., Android, iOS, Windows, BlackBerry) and more. Most apps don't make much money, so be careful how much you spend on advertising.

Mobile ad networks	URL
AdMob (by Google)	http://www.admob.com/
Medialets	http://www.medialets.com
Tapjoy®	http://www.tapjoy.com
Nexage™	http://www.nexage.com
Jumptap®	http://www.jumptap.com
Smaato®	http://www.smaato.com
mMedia™	http://mmedia.com
InMobi™	http://www.inmobi.com
Flurry™	http://www.flurry.com

Fig. 9.20 | Mobile advertising networks.

You can also use mobile advertising networks to monetize your free apps by including ads (e.g., banners, videos) in your apps. The average eCPM (effective cost per 1,000 impressions) for ads in Android apps is $0.88, according to Opera's *State of Mobile Advertising* report[16] (though the average may vary by network, device, etc.). Most ads on Android pay based on *click-through rate (CTR)* of the ads rather than the number of impressions generated. According to a report by Jumptap, CTRs average 0.65% on mobile in-app ads,[17] though this varies based on the app, the device, targeting of the ads by the ad network and more. If your app has a lot of users and the CTRs of the ads in your apps are high, you may earn substantial advertising revenue. Also, your ad network may serve you higher-paying ads, thus increasing your earnings.

9.14 Wrap-Up

In this chapter, we walked through the process of registering for Google Play and setting up a Google Wallet account so you can sell your apps. We showed how to prepare apps for submission to Google Play, including testing them on the emulator and on Android devices, creating icons and labels, and editing the `AndroidManifest.xml` file. We walked through the steps for uploading your apps to Google Play. We showed you alternative Android app marketplaces where you can sell your apps. We provided tips for pricing your apps, and resources for monetizing them with in-app advertising and in-app sales of virtual goods. And we included resources for marketing your apps, once they're available through Google Play.

Staying in Contact with Deitel & Associates, Inc.

We hope you enjoyed reading *Android for Programmers, 2/e, Volume 1* as much as we enjoyed writing it. We'd appreciate your feedback. Please send your questions, comments,

---

16. http://www.insidemobileapps.com/2012/12/14/ios-leads-the-pack-in-ecpm-traffic-and-revenue-on-operas-mobile-ad-platform-ipad-average-ecpm-of-4-42/.

17. http://paidcontent.org/2012/01/05/419-jumptap-android-the-most-popular-but-ios-still-more-interactive-for-ads/.

suggestions and corrections to deitel@deitel.com. Check out our growing list of Android-related Resource Centers at http://www.deitel.com/ResourceCenters.html. To stay up to date with the latest news about Deitel publications and corporate training sign up for the free weekly *Deitel® Buzz Online* e-mail newsletter at

> http://www.deitel.com/newsletter/subscribe.html

and follow us on

- Facebook—http://www.facebook.com/DeitelFan
- Twitter—@deitel
- Google+—http://google.com/+DeitelFan
- YouTube—http://youtube.com/DeitelTV
- LinkedIn—http://linkedin.com/company/deitel-&-associates

To learn more about Deitel & Associates' worldwide on-site programming training for your company or organization, visit:

> http://www.deitel.com/training

or e-mail deitel@deitel.com.

Index

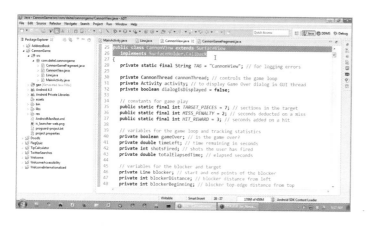

45-day FREE access to Online Edition

Your purchase of *Android™ for Programmers, Second Edition, Volume 1*, includes access to a free online edition for 45 days through the **Safari Books Online** subscription service. Nearly every Prentice Hall book is available online through **Safari Books Online**, along with thousands of books and videos from publishers such as Addison-Wesley Professional, Cisco Press, Exam Cram, IBM Press, O'Reilly Media, Que, Sams, and VMware Press.

Safari Books Online is a digital library providing searchable, on-demand access to thousands of technology, digital media, and professional development books and videos from leading publishers. With one monthly or yearly subscription price, you get unlimited access to learning tools and information on topics including mobile app and software development, tips and tricks on using your favorite gadgets, networking, project management, graphic design, and much more.

Activate your 45-day FREE access to Online Edition at informit.com/safarifree

STEP 1:   Enter the coupon code: XHTJWWA.

STEP 2:   New Safari users, complete the brief registration form.
Safari subscribers, just log in.

If you have difficulty registering on Safari or accessing the online edition,
please e-mail customer-service@safaribooksonline.com